AN INTRODUCTION TO
THE PRINCIPLES OF TRANSFORMATIONAL SYNTAX

AN INTRODUCTION TO
THE PRINCIPLES OF TRANSFORMATIONAL SYNTAX

Adrian Akmajian and Frank Heny

The MIT Press
Cambridge, Massachusetts, and London, England

Second printing, January 1976
Third printing, March 1978
Fourth printing, June 1979

This book was typed by Inge Calci,
and printed and bound by Halliday Lithograph Corporation
in the United States of America.

Library of Congress Cataloging in Publication Data

Akmajian, Adrian.
    An introduction to the principles of transformational
syntax.

    Bibliography: p.
    Includes index.
    1. English language--Grammar, Generative.
2. English language--Syntax. I. Heny, Frank, joint author.
II. Title.
PE1112.A38   425   74-30254
ISBN 0-262-01043-7

CONTENTS

ACKNOWLEDGMENTS

We are grateful to the many students who used (or suffered!) earlier drafts of this text and whose comments provided us with an invaluable guide for improving the work. In addition, we would like to thank our fellow teachers who used earlier drafts in their classrooms and who provided us with suggestions and criticisms based on their use of the book. In particular, we are grateful to Tim Austin (University of Massachusetts), Joan Bresnan (University of Massachusetts), Richard Demers (University of Massachusetts), Ray Jackendoff (Brandeis University), Tom Roeper (University of Massachusetts), and Tom Wasow (Stanford University). It is certain that these students and colleagues will not agree with every aspect of this work (for which we must assume full responsibility), but their help has been invaluable.

INTRODUCTION

AIMS OF THE BOOK

The central goal of this book is to introduce the reader to the methods of argumentation used in the construction of syntactic theory: the ways in which hypotheses are supported or shown to be inadequate. It is not so much a book <u>about</u> syntactic theory as it is an attempt to involve the reader in <u>constructing</u> syntactic theory—even at the beginning.

For this purpose it is not necessary to aim for a thorough survey of all the major constructions of English (let alone other languages, which we scarcely touch on). We have made no attempt to be exhaustive in this way. Nor have we tried to provide a survey of every theoretical principle that has been applied to the study of syntax. In fact, we have dealt with only a selected number of the clearer issues that arise in analyzing a limited set of English constructions, and we have restricted ourselves to a more or less "standard" or "classical" framework. We believe that in this way students will gain a thorough grounding in the methods of syntactic argumentation and will be well equipped to explore other areas on their own and to appreciate the significance of the many theoretical innovations that have been proposed to make up for inadequacies in the classical approach.

This text presupposes no previous knowledge of the field of syntax. It is intended for use primarily in introductory courses in linguistic theory at the undergraduate and graduate level.

In a single semester course, it is impossible to develop a feel for the methodology and philosophy that underlie linguistic theory without rather heavy concentration on a limited area, and syntactic theory provides a very sound basis for a general introduction to linguistic theory. We have found that the material contained in this book provides the basis for a demanding yet in every sense introductory course that is of interest to large numbers of undergraduates. We believe (and so, in general, do they) that they learn something useful in that course.

HOW TO USE THE BOOK

Most of the chapters have been designed to involve the reader in doing a number of in-text problems, at points designated by solid lines across the text itself. We recommend that the reader try doing these problems before proceeding further, not only because such an approach encourages active participation in the learning process, but also because many of the in-text problems

are designed to stimulate open-ended questions about the subject matter that can profitably be raised in class discussion.
Our intention is to present as many questions as answers,
since an attitude of inquiry (mixed with some skepticism!) reflects the true state of current syntactic theory much more
accurately than a dogmatic approach.

The teacher and student should also note that the exercises
at the end of each chapter have been designed in a fashion similar to the in-text problems. Whereas textbook exercises often
serve the function of simply reviewing the contents of the preceding chapter, only a few exercises in this text serve that
purpose exclusively. Most of our exercises are intended to
give the reader an opportunity to explore linguistic problems
freely and to deal with open-ended questions; hence, the exercises are really intended as topics for classroom discussion,
during which skill in argumentation can be developed. If the
student and teacher rely on the text itself to provide much of
the basic background in the subject matter, both can be freed
to use valuable classroom time to explore interesting issues
that arise from the text or the exercises.

Each chapter has been provided with a list of suggested readings. Especially in the beginning stages, the reader should not
be discouraged to find that some (or all) of the suggested readings are heavy going. We have cited journal articles dealing
with current theoretical topics, and our intention has been to
provide not only readings that students can grasp at any one
given stage but also pieces that students can return to (for term
paper topics, etc.) after mastering later chapters. Again, our
attitude has been that in the beginning stages of learning syntax,
the most important task is to try doing real problems and to
develop some feeling for the criteria used in argumentation.

AN INTRODUCTION TO
THE PRINCIPLES OF TRANSFORMATIONAL SYNTAX

Chapter 1

AN INFORMAL INTRODUCTION TO SYNTACTIC
ARGUMENTATION

1.1. TAG QUESTIONS: AN INTRODUCTION

Whenever any aspect of our environment becomes too familiar
to us, we lose our conscious awareness of it. We stop "seeing"
many familiar sights that recur in our daily routine; we become deaf to sounds we encounter day after day; when we walk
or run, we are normally completely unaware of the complex
interaction of muscles that make movement possible. There
are many such examples we could cite, but one of the most
striking would involve our normal use of language.

Linguistic activity is so much a part of being human, so
familiar to us, that we are not even conscious of language—
we just use it. So deeply ingrained in our minds is our linguistic ability that we are unaware of all but a tiny fraction of
the vast store of knowledge we have of our language. Although
we have no direct access to this knowledge, there are ways in
which we can gain indirect access to it, in that we can discover
evidence that shows that we all have a deep, unconscious grasp
of the structure of our language.

Naturally, there are many things about a language that individual speakers might not know. For example, they might
not know the meaning of a particular word, such as polyglot.
(In fact, they might not even know whether that is an English
word at all.) Then it would be necessary to look it up in the
dictionary in order to understand the following sentence:

(1.1) John is a polyglot.

In general, the existence and meaning of individual words are
somewhat isolated facts that have to be specially acquired,
and it is not at all surprising that individual speakers have
never learned many of them.

By way of contrast, however, consider the following examples:

(1.2) a. *He is a polyglot, aren't they?
      b. *Come here, isn't Bill?
      c. *Himself saw John.

d. *John saw yourself.
e. *Wash himself carefully.

The asterisk (or star) before each example indicates that it is not a possible English sentence—it is, in a special sense, "ungrammatical." The examples cited in (1.2) show that we possess a very different sort of linguistic knowledge from that which we illustrated with sentence (1.1). Any given native speaker of English may or may not know the meaning of the word polyglot; but every speaker of the language immediately recognizes that the sentences of (1.2) do not constitute possible English sentences. The reader may never have heard or read these examples before looking at this page, yet it is certainly the case that he or she could immediately judge each of these examples as ill-formed. Exactly what do we know about the examples of (1.2) that makes us reject them?

Let us start with (1.2a). It is repeated here together with a similar form that, in contrast, is a possible English sentence:

(1.2) a. *He is a polyglot, aren't they?
　　　a'. He is a polyglot, isn't he?

What makes the difference between (1.2a), with aren't they (or wasn't he, will you, has it) and (1.2a') with isn't he? To answer this, consider (1.3), (1.4), and (1.5). All of (1.4a-e) are possible sentences, while none of (1.5a-e) are.

(1.3) a. They are in town.
　　　b. It has a bell.
　　　c. She wasn't near the stream.
　　　d. We were there.
　　　e. They aren't here.

(1.4) a. They are in town, aren't they?
　　　b. It has a bell, hasn't it?
　　　c. She wasn't near the stream, was she?
　　　d. We were there, weren't we?
　　　e. They aren't here, are they?

(1.5) a. *They are in town, aren't she?

    b. *It has a bell, isn't it?
    c. *She was near the stream, was it?
    d. *We were there, wasn't we?
    e. *They aren't here, aren't they?

These examples suggest that there must be a systematic way of relating tag questions such as They are in town, aren't they? to plain statements such as They are in town. In fact, it is possible to formulate a precise rule that will begin with any plain English statement such as (1.3a) and will build another sentence that includes the appropriate tag ((1.4a) in this instance). Likewise, given (1.3b) as input, the rule would yield (1.4b) (not (1.5b)) as output—and so on, for the other examples of (1.3) and (1.4). Such a rule would be a way of representing, directly, the knowledge of English that every native speaker must possess in order to judge the examples of (1.4) to be grammatical and those of (1.5) ungrammatical.

Considering only the above examples, and temporarily ignoring any others that might complicate the issue, we could begin to formulate the Tag Rule in the following way:

Locate the verb of the sentence in question and copy it to the right of that sentence.

Given They are in town as input, this would produce They are in town are as output. Obviously the rule is incomplete. Continuing to ignore any examples other than those of (1.3)-(1.5), try to complete the rule in such a way that each of (1.4a-e) is derived from (1.3a-e).

A simple rule based on the above data alone might look something like the following:

(1.6) Tag Rule (first approximation)
    a. Locate the verb and copy it to the right of the sentence.
    b. If the original verb is negative, then make the copy of the verb in the tag question positive, and vice versa.
    c. Locate the subject of the sentence and copy it to the right of the newly copied verb (+ negative).

There are two features of rule (1.6) that need clarification.

In the first place, the first clause of the rule calls for a copy of the verb to be placed "to the right" of the sentence. In actual speech, that copy would obviously not <u>come to the right</u> of anything. In fact, it is important to realize that since we are interested in the speaker's internalized knowledge of his language we are not really concerned with <u>written</u> sentences at all, for we learn to understand and produce appropriate tagged questions long before we learn to write. Throughout this book we will use terms such as "left," "right," and so on, and will make use of written examples; but we are using these only to refer to their counterparts in the spoken language or, better still, the internalized language that is in some sense more basic.

Second, we should point out that rule (1.6) is actually very imprecise in certain respects. We have not attempted to define exactly what is meant by <u>subject</u>, <u>verb</u>, <u>negative</u>, etc. These will be discussed in later chapters. Meanwhile, the way in which these terms are being used should be clear from the context, and we will be content to leave them undefined.

Otherwise, rule (1.6) seems adequate for the data given above (as the reader should determine by applying it to each of (1.3a-e)). However, the sentences upon which it is based are all very similar, and once others are brought under consideration, it is very easy to find <u>counterexamples</u> to it: possible tags that it will not <u>generate</u> and impossible ones that it will. Such counterexamples lead to revisions in the rule, since they show that it cannot adequately represent our intuitive knowledge of the relationship between sentences and their tags. Consider the following:

(1.7) a. The boys are in town.
      b. That bicycle has a bell.
      c. Mary was near the stream.

Our rule (1.6) gives us (1.8a-c):

(1.8) a. *The boys are in town, aren't the boys?
      b. *That bicycle has a bell, hasn't that bicycle?
      c. *Mary was near the stream, wasn't Mary?

The rule has given us the wrong results because part (1.6c) tells us simply to repeat the subject of the sentence. We have

done just that in the examples of (1.8). Try to reformulate the
Tag Rule (1.6) precisely to obtain the correct tags for (1.7).

   An appropriate reformulation of the relevant part of (1.6)
might be (1.6c'):

(1.6) c'. Locate the subject and copy its corresponding
          pronoun to the right of the newly copied verb
          (+ negative).

The rule incorporating (1.6c') tells us that the pronoun corresponding to the subject of the sentence appears in the tag. For
example, the proper tag for (1.7c) is (1.8c'):

(1.8) c'. Mary was near the stream, wasn't she?

In what way does she correspond to Mary? Both forms agree
in person (third person), number (singular), and gender (fem-
inine). In each of the following examples, we have failed to
make the pronoun agree in one of the necessary ways:

(1.9) a. Person: *Mary was near the stream, wasn't I?
      b. Number: *Mary was near the stream, wasn't they?
      c. Gender: *Mary was near the stream, wasn't he?

The fact that we intuitively reject each of these as ungrammatical demonstrates very clearly that we are aware of the number,
gender, and person of the subject of (1.9a-c) (and presumably
of other similar structures). Let us restate the Tag Rule more
precisely to take these factors into account:

(1.10) Tag Rule (second approximation)
       a. Locate the verb and copy it to the right of the sentence.
       b. If the original verb is negative, then make the copy of
          the verb in the tag positive, and vice versa.
       c. Insert to the right of the newly copied verb the pro-
          noun that corresponds to the subject in person, num-
          ber, and gender.

   Notice that a rule like (1.10) shows that native speakers
must have an intuitive knowledge of a number of the structural

properties of an English sentence. Not only must they have a
systematic awareness of number, gender, and person, but
they must also possess an unconscious awareness of what constitutes the subject of a sentence. For tags are not formed
with the pronoun corresponding to just any noun phrase. A
sentence such as Mary will see him would never have the tag
*Mary will see him, won't he?; the only possible tag would be
Mary will see him, won't she? Thus, the noun phrase preceding the verb, not the one following the verb, forms the
basis for the pronoun in the tag.

Note that it is not necessarily the first noun phrase in the
sentence that is copied into the tag. Take a case in which there
are two noun phrases before the verb, such as These points,
the chairman will take up later. There is no tag for this sentence such as These points, the chairman will take up later,
won't they?, where they refers to these points. The only possible tag is These points, the chairman will take up later,
won't he?, where he refers to the chairman. Thus, we somehow know which of two noun phrases to choose to copy into the
tag, even when we cannot consciously define the structural relations of the sentence. We must be able to identify at least
one structural constituent, namely, the subject, since only
subject noun phrases are copied into tags. To say that speakers
could not recognize, in some unconscious sense, the subject of
a sentence, would be to say that they could not form tag questions that conform to the patterns we have discussed above.
And that is clearly false.

Returning now to rule (1.10), we see that it is a more ac-
curate rule than (1.6), in that it will correctly produce tags
for sentences such as (1.7). However, it is fairly easy, to
produce further data to show that even (1.10) is inadequate:

(1.11) John can leave.

Rule (1.10) states, in part, "Locate the verb and copy it to the
right of the sentence." In the case of (1.11), which word will
constitute what we call "the verb"? In traditional grammar a
distinction is often made between main verbs, such as the verb
leave in (1.11), and helping or auxiliary verbs, such as can.
For the present we can distinguish auxiliary verbs from main
verbs by a very simple test: auxiliary verbs occur first in
simple questions (such as Will John go?, Must John go?, Can

John go?, Is John going?, and so on), whereas main verbs may
never appear first in questions (for example, *Goes John?,
*Eats John?, *Reads John the book?, and so on). By this def-
inition, are, has, and was in (1.7a-c) are auxiliaries, and
those sentences contain no main verbs, since the related questions are Are the boys in town?, etc., with the verbs fronted.
Later we will have to modify this result, but it will serve for
the present.

Obviously, the verb referred to in rule (1.10) cannot always
be the main verb of the sentence—if it ever can—for rule (1.10)
would then derive (1.12) from (1.11).

(1.12) *John can leave, leaven't he?

We must reformulate rule (1.10) to take these facts into account. Notice that in the sentence John has been running there
are two auxiliaries in addition to the main verb—three verbs
in all. Since, as this shows, a sentence can contain a string
of verbs one after the other, we will have to ensure that the
rule is stated more precisely so that it copies just the right
one. On the basis of the following sentences and their appropriate tags (which we leave to the reader to form), restate rule
(1.10) appropriately:

(1.13) a. He won't leave the room.
       b. I must finish my food.
       c. Ruth has been fishing.
       d. The girls will have been studying physics.
       e. The President can't still be in China.
       f. My parents are not very happy.
       g. That dog over there is sick.
       h. Mary should see me alone.

One obvious reformulation of rule (1.10) would specify that
the first verb in a sentence is copied into the tag:

(1.14) a. John has arrived, hasn't he?
       b. John can't have been singing, can he?
       c. John is a fool, isn't he?

Notice incidentally that it is only the first verb that can be

marked as negative. Therefore, it is always that verb (i.e.,
the verb that is also copied into the tag) that determines
whether the tag should be positive or negative. To see this
clearly, construct tags for the following:

(1.15) a. John couldn't have been playing the violin.
     b. Ruth could have been playing the violin.
     c. The dog hasn't been playing the violin.
     d. My teacher isn't playing the violin.

On the basis of these observations, which suggest that it is
only the first verb that figures in the Tag Rule, it looks as
though we must restate that rule as in (1.16):

(1.16) Tag Rule (third approximation)
     a. Copy the first verb to the right of the sentence,
        making the copy negative if the original is positive,
        positive if the original is negative.
     b. Insert to the right of the newly copied verb (+ nega-
        tive) the pronoun that corresponds to the subject in
        person, number, and gender.

   Before introducing a fresh set of counterexamples (which
will lead us to rethink certain aspects of our account in a
rather radical fashion), it may be worth looking briefly at an
apparent counterexample:

(1.17) a.   The man that was playing the violin has stopped,
        hasn't he?
     b. *The man that was playing the violin has stopped,
        wasn't he?

It might seem that our rule should yield the ungrammatical
(1.17b) instead of (1.17a), for was is actually the first verb in
the original string of words preceding the tag. But was is actually part of the subject of the main sentence. Just as John is
the subject in (1.15a), so The man that was playing the violin
is the subject of (1.17). Thus the structure of (1.17a) is quite
parallel to (1.18):

(1.18) John has stopped, hasn't he?

And the auxiliary <u>was</u> is not itself properly a part of the main sentence on which we are forming a tag. We may safely assume that the Tag Rule can stand as it is and will somehow be able to recognize that <u>has</u>, not <u>was</u>, is the first relevant verbal element. We will not try to provide a more detailed account of (1.17) at this point.

1.2. THE AUXILIARY VERB <u>DO</u>

Consider now some real counterexamples to (1.16) as it stands. Construct tags for these sentences and note the <u>actual</u> tag forms as compared to what rule (1.16) <u>predicts</u> the tag forms ought to be.

(1.19) a. Mervin liked you.
      b. Bo-Peep drinks a lot.
      c. Sam and Marge love each other.
      d. Dad left over an hour ago.
      e. Shakespeare wrote <u>King Lear</u>.

Of course, all the tags contain some form of the verb <u>do</u> (<u>do</u>, <u>does</u>, <u>did</u>). But our rule (1.16) predicts something like the following:

(1.20) a. *Mervin liked you, likedn't he?
      b. *Bo-Peep drinks a lot, drinksn't she?

These ungrammatical sentences result simply because part (a) of rule (1.16) tells us to copy the first verb to the right of the sentence. In (1.20) we have done just that. It looks as though we need to change our rule so that it will not copy the first verb in the sentences of (1.19) but instead will insert the correct form of <u>do</u> in the place usually occupied by the copy—at the end of the original sentence.

The sentences of (1.19) differ from those we have examined earlier in that they contain no overt auxiliary verbs. All our previous examples contain either auxiliary verbs along with main verbs (as in (1.13)) or just <u>have</u> or <u>be</u> (as in (1.3) and (1.7)), and we have defined these as auxiliaries because they move to the front in questions. On the basis of this observation, we might reformulate rule (1.16) in part so that it states:

(1.21) If the first verb is not an auxiliary verb, insert in the
tag question an appropriate form of the verb do. Otherwise (i.e., if the first verb is an auxiliary) copy it to
the right of the sentence. . . .

This would at least distinguish between the sentences of (1.19)
and all the others. However, this restatement actually represents a great complication of our rule for forming tags.

To see this, simply consider what it means to insert an "appropriate form" of the verb do in the tag. Consider simple examples such as (1.22a-e):

(1.22) a. Mervin liked you, didn't he?
b. Bo-Peep drinks a great deal, doesn't she?
c. Sam and Marge love each other, don't they?
d. Dad left an hour ago, didn't he?
e. Shakespeare wrote King Lear, didn't he?

Our revised Tag Rule would have to contain instructions such
as (a) "Insert a past tense form of the verb do (didn't) if the
verb of the main sentence is past tense (or in an analogous way
for present tense)" and (b) "Insert a plural form (singular form)
when the verb of the main sentence is plural (singular)," and so
on. We thus reach a point where our original rule—stated simply
in terms of copying the first verb—has become grossly complex.

In fact, there is a more satisfactory treatment of tags containing do. To develop this alternative analysis, we must look
at some new data. First of all, let us examine some negative
sentences. Most positive English sentences have negative
counterparts, the negative of John will go being John will not
go. But what are the negative counterparts of (1.19a-e)?

_____

The appropriate negative forms are, of course, (1.23a-e):

(1.23) a. Mervin didn't like you.
b. Bo-Peep doesn't drink a lot.
c. Sam and Marge don't love each other.
d. Dad didn't leave over an hour ago.
e. Shakespeare didn't write King Lear.

Compare (1.23a-e) with the tags for (1.19). Notice that (1.23a)
contains <u>do</u> in exactly the same form as in the tag for (1.19a);
the facts are similar for (1.19b-e) and (1.23b-e). Moreover,
provided we regard <u>do</u> as a verb, our unmodified rule (1.16a)
will give us the correct tags for (1.23a-e):

(1.24) a. Mervin didn't like you, did he?
      b. Bo-Peep doesn't drink a lot, does she?
      c. Sam and Marge don't love each other, do they?
      d. Dad didn't leave over an hour ago, did he?
      e. Shakespeare didn't write <u>King Lear</u>, did he?

We have followed our rule and simply copied the first verb of
the sentence, while making the appropriate change of negative
to positive and vice versa.

    On the one hand then, there are positive sentences that have
no auxiliary and that seem to <u>insert do</u> in their tags in a complex fashion, playing havoc with our original Tag Rule (which
<u>copied</u> a verbal element); on the other hand, those same posi-
tive sentences have negative counterparts in which the "appropriate" form of <u>do</u> already appears and for which the copying rule works well indeed.

    Now let us suppose that the input sentence for the tagged
question <u>Mervin liked you, didn't he?</u> is not <u>Mervin liked you</u>
but instead <u>Mervin did like you</u>, and so on for the other examples of (1.22). The input sentence will now contain an appropriate auxiliary verb, and rule (1.16) will produce the correct tags:

(1.25) a. <u>Input</u>:   Mervin did like you.

             | <u>Tag Rule</u> (1.16)

     b. <u>Output</u>: Mervin did like you, didn't he?

Of course, although the tag itself is now correct, we have
ended up not with the tagged sentence <u>Mervin liked you, didn't</u>
<u>he?</u> but with (1.25b), which contains <u>did like</u> instead of <u>liked</u>.
However, it would require only a very simple change to turn
(1.25b) into the desired output and to deal in a comparable
fashion with the tagged questions corresponding to the other
examples of (1.19). We need only suppose that <u>did like</u> becomes

liked, does like becomes likes, do like becomes like, and so
on.
   To make this hypothesis a little more precise, let us postulate a rule (which we can call Do Drop), which takes the output of the Tag Rule and deletes do from its place immediately
before the main verb, presumably making that verb agree with
the subject and making it carry the tense previously borne by
do. Then the derivation of (1.22a) (i.e., Mervin liked you,
didn't he?) would not be exactly as shown in (1.25) but would
contain an extra step:

(1.26) a. Mervin did like you.

   ↓   Tag Rule (1.16)

   b. Mervin did like you, didn't he?

   ↓   Do Drop

   c. Mervin liked you, didn't he? (= (1.22a))

In this way, all the tagged sentences of (1.22) could be generated by means of a completely regular use of the Tag Rule
(1.16).
   At this point we clearly have to ask whether there is any
point in introducing this rather mysterious extra do into
English structure simply in order to retain (1.16) as the Tag
Rule (i.e., to avoid the complex reformulation set out in
(1.21)). On the basis of tags alone it would be hard to choose
in any principled way between the two analyses presented so
far; the first requires that the Tag Rule be rather complex,
while the second forces us to add an apparently ad hoc rule deleting do when it ends up next to a verb. Why then did we claim
at the outset that this second analysis was "more satisfactory"?
   To answer this we must consider negative sentences in more
detail. It was noted above that every positive sentence has a related negative counterpart:

(1.27) a. She will leave.
       b. She will not leave.

(1.28) a. John has gone.
       b. John has not gone.

(1.29) a. Mary might have gone.
      b. Mary might not have gone.

(1.30) a. They could have been going.
      b. They could not have been going.

(Each of these negatives has a <u>contracted</u> form, which we will temporarily ignore.) As these forms suggest, it is possible to set up a very general rule for forming negative sentences. Try to state such a rule. It should operate on any positive statement of English (such as the preceding (a) sentences) to produce the corresponding negative.

   One rough formulation is as follows:

(1.31) <u>Negative Rule</u>
     Given a positive sentence as input, add <u>not</u> after the first auxiliary verb.

This will generate the (b) sentences of (1.28)-(1.30). However, recall that the negative counterpart of (1.19a) was (1.23a):

(1.19) a. Mervin liked you.

(1.23) a. Mervin didn't like you.

(The negatives of (1.19b-e) were given in (1.23b-e).) Each of these negatives contains some form of <u>do</u>. Apparently, <u>not</u> is added to the appropriate form of <u>do</u>, and the Negative Rule (1.31) will have to incorporate a special statement to that effect—unless we include <u>do</u> in the input to that rule in these instances. In other words, if the "underlying" structure of <u>Mervin liked you</u> is really <u>Mervin did like you</u>, then rule (1.31) will operate perfectly regularly to produce the desired output:

(1.32) a. Mervin did like you.

        | <u>Negative Rule</u> (1.31)
        ↓

    b. Mervin did not like you. (=(1.23a))

(Notice that Do Drop will not apply to negatives such as (1.32b), because do is not to the immediate left of the verb.) Observe how the postulated do begins to seem more credible. Two distinct rules of English (Tag and Negative) would have to be complicated in quite similar ways if we failed to set up this analysis.

   In fact, there is yet more independent evidence for an underlying do. Just as there are rules for forming tags and negatives, so there are rules for generating questions. Given a statement as input, we can form a question by moving the first auxiliary to the front of the sentence:

(1.33) a. John will go.
       b. Will John go?

(1.34) a. John has been running.
       b. Has John been running?

We can roughly formulate the rule as (1.35):

(1.35) Question Rule
       To form a question from a statement, move the first
       auxiliary to the left of the subject.

Once again the operation of this rule on the sentences of (1.19) is superficially irregular:

(1.36) a. Mervin liked you.

         $\downarrow$ Question Rule (?)

       b. Did Mervin like you?

To have this effect, rule (1.35) would have to be modified by the addition of the following statement: "If there is no auxiliary verb, add an appropriate form of do at the left of the subject." However, if (1.19a) is itself derived from a form containing do, then the derivation of (1.36b) is perfectly regular:

(1.37) a. Mervin did like you.

         $\downarrow$ Question Rule (1.35)

       b. Did Mervin like you?

Again <u>Do</u> Drop will not apply. In example (1.37b) <u>do</u> is not next to a main verb, so it will not be deleted.

Note, finally, that if we assume that <u>do</u> is present in sentences such as those of (1.19), we can simplify the relation between sentences and their <u>emphatic</u> forms. If we examine pairs of sentences such as <u>John will go</u>/John will go, <u>John might have left</u>/John might have left, and so on (where the underlined element is <u>heavily</u> stressed), it is clear that emphasis is placed on the first verb (just as <u>not</u> is placed after this same element). Then, when we examine pairs such as <u>John left</u>/John did leave, we see that <u>do</u> once again appears, this time to bear the emphatic stress. If we assume that <u>do</u> was really there all the time, our rule for placement of emphasis will be kept as simple as possible. All that is necessary is to modify <u>Do</u> Drop so that it deletes only an <u>unstressed</u> <u>do</u> that ends up next to a main verb.

Thus at least four independent pieces of evidence point toward an underlying <u>do</u> in sentences such as (1.19). This evidence is drawn from tags, negatives, questions, and emphatic sentences.

We can now see that in order to construct an adequate hypothesis concerning the structure of English, we are (rather surprisingly) <u>forced</u> to posit this underlying <u>do</u> together with the rule of <u>Do</u> Drop. Otherwise four separate rules of English would have to be complicated in just the <u>same</u> way to account for <u>do</u>, and this formulation would miss a significant generalization about English—and hence misrepresent an important feature of the structure of language. Although the argument we have just given for an underlying <u>do</u> needs to be refined in detail in various ways, it is nevertheless representative of a very typical mode of argumentation in linguistics, one which we will encounter repeatedly in this book: given a set of data, we <u>construct a hypothesis</u> (i.e., a rule or set of rules) to account for the data; once formulated, the hypothesis must be <u>tested</u> against further data, <u>reformulated</u> where necessary (to account for counterexamples), and, we hope, <u>confirmed</u> by independent evidence.

1.3. THE SIGNIFICANCE OF LINGUISTIC RULES
So far we have been concentrating on some aspects of English tags, constructing a rule to describe how they are formed in as precise and general terms as possible. It may seem perverse to have begun a book on theoretical syntax with a detailed

discussion of one apparently unimportant and obscure aspect
of the structure of English. We might at least have defined
what syntax is, or better still, have started with a discussion
of the principles of syntactic theory.

However, this is not so much a book <u>about</u> syntactic theory
as it is an attempt to involve the reader as quickly as possible
in <u>doing</u> syntactic analysis. We believe that only by working on
relevant problems can we acquire a real understanding of the
nature of syntactic theory. So we have had to introduce at the
same time both our subject matter and our method of tackling
it, helping the reader to develop useful hypotheses about linguistic structures on the basis of his or her own judgments
about English sentences. And it happens that English tag questions provide a good introduction to doing syntax.

Now that we have a tentative statement of the Tag Rule, we
must pause to reflect for a while on what it is that we have discovered and how we want to proceed. The rule is an example
(albeit very roughly formulated) of the kind of analysis that we
will be doing throughout this book; what kind of a rule is it—
and what is the point of trying to discover such rules?

This much is clear: the rule is a hypothesis about the nature
of the relationships that hold among various English sentences.
It has nothing to do with good usage, is to be found in no grammar book of English, and obviously has not been handed down
by grammatical experts. So what is the real basis of this rule?

Let us consider again how we discovered it. We built it up on
the basis of our own judgments about whether or not certain
strings of words were possible English sentences; so it must
in some way reflect our own knowledge of the structure of
English.

This is clearly not just a knowledge gleaned from a careful
observation of what actually happens when people speak English.
From time to time, any of us might come out with utterances
like the following:

(1.38) a. *John and his brother went to town, didn't he?
       b. *Bill will take you, can't he?
       c. *Mary says that you've been ill, haven't you?

Yet on hearing them repeated or reflecting on what we had just
said, we would almost certainly reject every one of these forms
(possibly as "slips of the tongue" or "mistakes"). Some speak-

ers might have a tendency to make such mistakes quite frequently even though their linguistic judgment remained unaf-
fected. Our knowledge of English permits us to go beyond
what is actually said, to make certain intuitive judgments
about the sentences we use; some of these we regard as <u>pos-
sible</u> English sentences, others as <u>impossible</u> (or <u>ungram-
matical</u>).

To explain how speakers are able to make systematic judgments in this way, we must suppose that knowledge of a language consists in part of an unconscious knowledge of systematic rules such as the Tag Rule. In a real sense, to "know" a
language is to know those rules; and there is no language,
<u>English</u>, apart from the rules for English. In the same way,
there is no game of chess apart from the rules for chess. The
rules are the game, and likewise the rules are the language.
English is the total set of rules possessed by each individual
speaker of the language (i.e., the <u>grammar</u>, as it has been
called, by an extension of an old term).

There is, of course, a clear difference between chess and
English: the former consists of precisely formulated, explicit
rules to which all players agree. One learns chess by consciously learning those rules. English is learned in quite a
different way. For example, the Tag Rule is not consciously
known by native speakers of English; hence, it could not be
consciously taught to a child learning the language.

In fact, the child does not even copy what he or she hears,
but often produces entirely new patterns that can never have
been heard in the environment. For example, the authors
have observed a three-year-old girl regularly producing
sentences like the following:

(1.39) a. Is I can do that?
       b. Is you should eat the apple?
       c. Is Ben did go?
       d. Is you be here?
       e. Is the apple juice won't spill?

We can assume that the adult versions of such questions would
be (1.40a-e):

(1.40) a. Can I do that?
       b. Should you eat the apple?

    c. Did Ben go?
    d. Are you there?
    e. Will the apple juice not spill?

Many linguists have discussed the implications of such systematic deviation from adult speech patterns in the speech of children. They seem to provide very strong evidence for something like the following theory. Children learn language by constructing their own grammars (i.e., sets of internalized rules); and they do this by a process of analysis: constructing, testing, and modifying hypotheses about the sentences that they encounter. At first, these hypotheses amount to guesses about the nature of the rules that underlie the sentences of the language. The rules are incorporated into the child's own developing grammar, which in time more and more closely approximates the grammars of the adult speech community.

So the child who produced the sentences (1.39a-e) had presumably adopted a rule (i.e., formed a hypothesis) based on sentences that she had heard, like Is Daddy coming?, and had generalized it to cover all similar questions, whether the initial word should have been is or something else. Her rule for questions involved little more than inserting the word is before the corresponding statement. Had she gone on producing questions by this rule, her speech would have in the end been very different from that of her parents. However, very soon, presumably recognizing counterexamples in her parents' speech, she abandoned her hypothesis for something more adequate—just as we abandoned our earlier formulations of the Tag Rule.

One interesting result of the active role of the language learner in constructing a grammar is the variation among groups of speakers that can be observed in judgments of grammaticality. It is well known that British English varies somewhat from American English and that New Englanders have a somewhat different dialect from Southerners. What is perhaps even more interesting is the variation that seems to occur even among speakers from the same area. To take tags again, we have been dealing with a dialect (in a rather special sense of that word) in which the tagged question related to (1.41a) is (1.41b).

(1.41) a. John could have left.
        b. John could have left, couldn't he?

But there are dialects (whose speakers seem to come from
diverse places) that permit (1.41c) as well:

(1.41) c. John could have left, couldn't he have?

The speakers of this dialect appear to have a slightly different
rule for tags whereby all (?) the auxiliary verbs of the sentence are copied into the tag, only the first of them actually
preceding the subject. In some sense this rule is more general than the more widely applicable rule we have been considering.

    As a result of such minor differences in the grammar of in-
dividuals, we cannot point to any single, monolithic language
English, which is spoken identically by every speaker. However, it is obvious that while speakers of English may vary in
terms of certain rules or constructions, they nevertheless
have enough rules in common so that we can accurately say
that all of them speak the "same" language. And this brings
out a very interesting aspect of the nature of language: if the
speakers of a language all share a body of linguistic rules,
then we can rightfully say that they all share a certain conceptual mechanism. We are not merely studying individual
rules when we study the language of a given speaker, but we
are in fact studying a cognitive or mental ability that is shared
by a wide number of other humans, i.e., the ability to use and
understand sentences of their language. We have already indicated that our language and its rules cannot be taught to us
in any conscious way, and that each child must essentially reconstruct a grammar as part of the language-learning process.
Yet, despite the fact that each individual has essentially
learned a language independently, the adult community of
speakers has finally constructed a set of remarkably similar
grammars, which makes intelligible communication possible.
Thus, by studying the syntax of English, we are indeed studying a certain aspect of the conceptual framework of all English
speakers.

    For this reason, one of the principal (though distant) goals
of the linguist in analyzing language is to understand the central mechanisms of the mind. Since the individual's grammar

is the product of the language-learning process—a mental process—the linguist, even in making conscious his own internal grammar, is making discoveries about the mind. This larger goal of linguistics is summed up nicely in the words of Morris Halle (1970):

"Linguists are often asked by laymen why anyone not interested in mastering a foreign language should be interested in the study of language. The best answer to this question was, I think, provided over a century ago by the French physiologist Claude Bernard who remarked that language was the best window into man's mind. There is good reason to believe that Bernard chose language over other manifestations of man's mind because even a century ago language was understood in much greater detail and to a greater depth than any other mental phenomena of comparable complexity."

CHAPTER 1: EXERCISES

(E 1.1) We argued in this chapter that certain sentences with no overt auxiliary verb should really be viewed as having an auxiliary verb do, which is deleted under certain circumstances. We claim this analysis allows us to state the Tag Rule in the simplest possible way. Now consider imperative sentences, such as (ia-d):

(i)   a. Come here!
      b. Leave the room!
      c. Drink your milk!
      d. Wash your face!

These sentences have no explicit subject and simply begin with a main verb. In traditional grammar, it is said that imperative sentences have an "understood" subject, namely, you. Now consider the following tag questions for the sentences of (i):

(ii)   a. Come here, won't you?
      b. Leave the room, won't you?
      c. Drink your milk, won't you?
      d. Wash your face, won't you?

And notice that sentences such as the following are not possible:

(iii) a. *Come here, can't he?
     b. *Leave the room, won't they?
     c. *Drink your milk, must you?
     d. *Wash your face, may I?

A. Using the data we have listed above, try to derive the tagged forms of (ii) by applying the Tag Rule. Why do imperatives present a problem for this rule? Show explicitly what the problem is, and then use this to construct an argument demonstrating that imperative sentences must be analyzed as having a subject (even though none appears on the surface), and state what the subject must be. Keep in mind that your analysis must be such that the sentences of (iii) will be excluded as a result of the way in which the Tag Rule applies.

B. Using the same data and method, construct a similar argument showing that imperative sentences must be analyzed as having an auxiliary verb (even though none appears) and state what the auxiliary verb must be.

(E 1.2) Examine the following sentences, and formulate appropriate tag questions for each. (Note that some sentences may have more than one possible tag question.) If, as we have supposed, the pronoun in the tag refers to the subject of the sentence, what is the subject phrase of each of these sentences (based on the tag you have formed)?

(i)   a. There were three men in the park.
      b. Three men were in the park.
      c. In the park were three men.
(ii) a. That John arrived late annoyed Bill.
      b. For you to do that would be crazy.
(iii)   Flying planes can be dangerous. (Two different tags.)
(iv) a. Drowning cats always terrifies Bill.
      b. Drowning cats always terrify Bill.
(v)   I bet Mary won't leave today.
(vi) a. I expect John won't sing the songs.
      b. I don't expect John will sing the songs.
(vii) a. John is the one who robbed the bank.
      b. It was John who robbed the bank.
      c. The one who robbed the bank was John.

Once you have constructed the tags, write briefly on some of
the problems that they introduce into any attempt to provide
a systematic account of what can occur as the subject of a
sentence. This is an open-ended exercise, and there are no
absolutely right or wrong answers for a problem of this sort.
Rather, use the examples above to explore the implications
of tag question formation further, noting problems along the
way.

CHAPTER 1: SUGGESTED READINGS
Not all the following readings are directly concerned with the
material covered in this chapter; some either supplement it
or lead on to the next chapter. As background for the chapters which follow, Chomsky (1966a) and O'Neill (1969) provide
a general discussion of transformational linguistics and of
some reasons for studying it. These are fairly simple papers
and presuppose no background in linguistics on the part of the
reader. Postal (1964b) should be read after the first exercise
has been completed, Langendoen (1970) after doing the second.
    The study of child language has produced an ever growing
body of literature. McNeill (1970) reviews recent work, and
the books edited by Bar-Adon and Leopold (1971) and Smith
and Miller (1966) contain a significant number of recent papers
in the area of child language. The paper by Klima and Bellugi
(1966) discusses points directly relevant to our discussion in
this chapter and contains further citations.
    The philosophical foundations of linguistics are explored in
some detail in the first chapter of Chomsky (1965), as well as
in Chomsky (1966b), (1967), and (1969), and in the citations
given in those works.

Chapter 2

BASIC SENTENCE STRUCTURE

2.1. THE EXISTENCE OF SYNTACTIC STRUCTURE

When we looked at tag questions in the last chapter, we discovered that the tag contains a pronoun related to the subject of the original sentence; but we left the notion <u>subject</u> completely undefined. We must now define it—and we must do so without introducing any hidden structural notions.

First, let us try the hypothesis that the pronoun of the tag, in referring back to the subject, always refers to the <u>first word in the sentence</u>. This would be consistent with the claim that English sentences are not structured at all. Let us formalize this hypothesis, representing it precisely, so that it will be easy to tell whether or not a given sentence is a counterexample. One way of doing so is to number all the words in a sentence sequentially from left to right and then restate the rule for forming tag questions so that it reads, in part, ". . . insert in the tag question a pronoun corresponding to the word marked '1' in the original sentence." This would produce the correct result for the following examples:

(2.1) John saw Mary.

(2.2) a. *John saw Mary, didn't she?
     b. John saw Mary, didn't he?

(2.3) John saw Mary, didn't he?

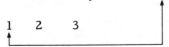

However, there are innumerable English sentences that form counterexamples to this proposal, such as (2.4a, b):

(2.4) a. Fortunately John saw Mary, didn't ___?

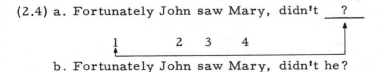

     b. Fortunately John saw Mary, didn't he?

The word marked "1" can in no way form the basis for a pro-

noun in a tag question, and indeed, the word marked "2" is the
word that forms the basis for that pronoun.

At this point we might take the following tack: let us assume
that at the very least words are categorized into parts of
speech. Let us call John a noun, fortunately an adverb, saw a
verb, and so on. Assuming, then, that we can categorize
words in this way, let us propose that the pronoun in the tag
question refers back to the first noun of the sentence, not the
first word.

But even this is inadequate. Example (2.5) shows that we
cannot simply state the tag rule in terms of the first noun.

(2.5) a. *John and Bill saw Mary, didn't he?

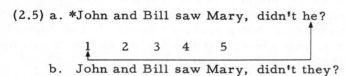

      1   2   3   4   5

    b.   John and Bill saw Mary, didn't they?

The first noun is John, yet the pronoun of the tag, which is
plural (they), must refer back to the whole group of words
John and Bill.

Clearly, then, our model of language must include some
mechanism for representing significant groups of words. The
tag pronoun can actually refer back to quite complex units,
as we see in (2.6) and (2.7):

(2.6) Those three sheep saw Mary, didn't they?

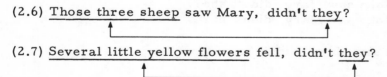

(2.7) Several little yellow flowers fell, didn't they?

On the other hand, there are groups of words that the tag pronoun cannot refer back to. Thus, as we saw earlier, he refers back to John in sentence (2.8), and fortunately forms no
part of the relevant group with John.

(2.8) Fortunately John saw Mary, didn't he?

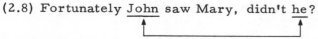

We could phrase the preceding observations in terms of the
notion of "subject" with which we started. Whereas John and
Bill or those three sheep can act as the subject of a sentence,
fortunately John cannot. Hence the subject must be a unit pos-

sessing definite structure and cannot be just any string of words preceding the verb. Such structural groupings are not relevant to this one process only (i.e., tag formation) but play a part in other grammatical processes as well. For example, consider the relation between <u>active</u> and <u>passive</u> sentences.

(2.9) a. John saw Mary. (<u>Active</u>)
     b. Mary was seen by John. (<u>Passive</u>)

We can form passive sentences from active sentences by carrying out the following sort of interchange:

(2.10) a. <u>John</u> saw <u>Mary</u>.   Active
     b. <u>Mary</u> was seen by <u>John</u>. Passive

In example (2.10), the noun that appears <u>before</u> the verb in the active sentence appears <u>after</u> the verb (after the preposition <u>by</u>) in the passive.

If we are to describe how passive sentences are formed from their active counterparts, we again need to make use of the notion "subject." It is the subject of the sentence that is moved to the end of the passive sentence. Thus, the tag of (2.10a) is <u>John saw Mary, didn't he?</u>, with <u>he</u> depending on <u>John</u>; and in the passive (i.e., (2.10b)) it is <u>John</u> that moves to the end of the sentence. From this it should begin to be clear that the subject functions in forming both tag questions and passives.

The following examples confirm that the subject is one structural grouping that figures in the active-passive relation and moreover that it is essentially a structural unit consisting sometimes of several words:

(2.11) a. <u>John and Bill</u> saw <u>Mary</u>.

     b. <u>Mary</u> was seen by <u>John and Bill</u>.

(2.12) a. Fortunately <u>those three sheep</u> didn't bite <u>the girl with the hat</u>.

     b. Fortunately <u>the girl with the hat</u> wasn't bitten by <u>those three sheep</u>.

The reader should now try to identify the subjects in the following sentences. As above, construct tag questions and passive sentence counterparts for these sentences in order to test the structure you assign:

(2.13) a. Everyone here will listen to Mary.
      b. The person who knows you will probably hire you.
      c. Reasonable people, we hope, will rule us.
      d. Oddly enough, those two ate the candy.

By now it should be clear that the subject of a sentence is an important structural element. We could provide more evidence for this, showing how it plays a crucial role in many grammatical processes. However, we will assume that to be so and will now try to define more precisely what groups of words can make up the subject. Until we do that it is pointless to claim that it is an isolable structural element. Using traditional labels (which we will not try to define precisely since that would take too long), we can say that a subject consists of

(2.14) a proper noun   e.g., John
      a pronoun   e.g., he, she, it
      an article plus a common noun e.g., a baby, the sheep
      a numeral plus a common noun e.g., three sheep
      an article, a numeral plus a
      common noun   e.g., the three sheep
      etc.

These examples include either a noun of some sort or a pronoun. Hence such a group of words has come to be called a noun phrase (NP). Sometimes a noun phrase may consist of just a single word (e.g., a pronoun or a proper noun); at other times it can be complex, as the examples of (2.14) show.

In developing a general method for specifying the structure of noun phrases, we must ensure that it is capable of representing the fact that although noun phrases may vary (within so far unspecified limits) in internal structure, nevertheless they all act alike in regard to the way tags or passives are formed. More specifically, then, (2.15a) and (2.15b) must both be analyzed as in (2.15c), despite their very different subject noun phrases:

(2.15) a. <u>John</u> saw Mary.
      b. <u>Those three sheep</u> saw Mary.
      c. <u>Noun Phrase</u> saw Mary.

At the same time, the NP in each case must be broken up in different ways:

(2.16) a.

Noun Phrase	
Proper Noun	saw Mary
John	

     b.

Noun Phrase			
Article	Numeral	Noun	saw Mary
those	three	sheep	

Any appropriate model of English must obviously permit us to represent the hierarchical relationships exhibited in the diagrams above, while excluding relationships such as we show in (2.16c):

(2.16) c.

Noun Phrase		
Adverb	Proper Noun	saw Mary
fortunately	John	

    If we found a very general way of building boxed diagrams like (2.16a) and (2.16b), while excluding (2.16c), this would begin to model the structure of English noun phrases (NPs). In fact, that is precisely what linguists have done, using a slightly different (but equivalent) notational device. Thus it has become customary to represent the structure of the noun phrase shown in (2.16a) as follows:

(2.17) a.   NP
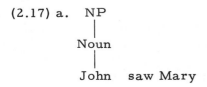

(We will use <u>Noun</u> to refer both to proper nouns and to common nouns. It will be abbreviated as "N".)
  The noun phrase in (2.16b) will be represented thus:

(2.17) b.

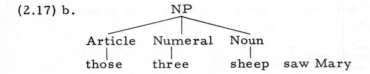

In these <u>tree diagrams</u> showing the hierarchical structure of
the two noun phrases, notice how the symbol NP (for Noun
Phrase) is used to represent the fact that from one point of
view <u>John</u> and <u>those three sheep</u> are alike. Both phrases are
<u>dominated</u> by that symbol. At the same time, notice how the
difference in the structure of these two NPs is explicitly represented by the differences in the structure and labeling of
the lower parts of the trees.
  We must now try to generalize these diagrams to account
for the structure of the rest of the sentence. Do the other two
words, <u>saw Mary</u>, fit into clearly definable positions in diagrams similar to (2.17) representing the structure of the entire sentence?
  First, it is obvious that in these two sentences, (2.16a) and
(2.16b), there must be a noun phrase after the verb as well as
before the verb, for the kinds of phrases that function as subjects can also appear immediately to the right of the verb—as
<u>objects</u>:

(2.18) a. Mary saw <u>John</u>.   (cf. <u>John</u> saw Mary.)
       b. Mary saw <u>those three sheep</u>. (cf. <u>Those three sheep</u>
                                               saw Mary.)

We should presumably analyze these sentences so as to permit
a noun phrase to occur either as a subject or as an object in a
sentence, e.g.:

(2.19)

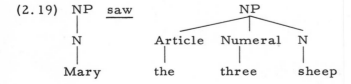

In this way, our model reflects the fact that subjects and objects are made up of the same kinds of phrases; we assign
such phrases a single label, namely, NP.

What is left now is the verb saw. Therefore, the minimal
structure that we could postulate would be represented thus:

(2.20) a.

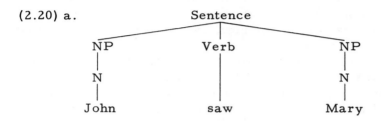

Is there any reason to add further structure, associating one
or the other NP more closely with the verb? In other words,
should we select either of the alternatives in (2.20b) and (2.20c)
instead of (2.20a)? (The term Verb Phrase (VP) is applied to
the constituent consisting of a verb (V) and a noun phrase together).

(2.20) b.

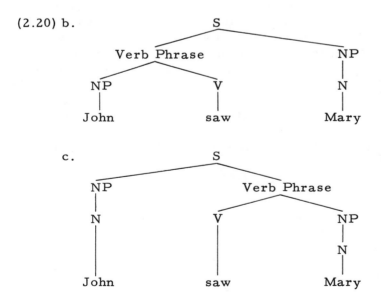

We will not pursue this question further. It turns out that
structure (2.20b) is the least likely to be correct; there are a

number of arguments against it. However, it is not easy to
choose between structures (2.20a) and (2.20c). Whether or not
there exists a constituent VP of the sort shown in (2.20c) is a
question that is still somewhat debatable, though there appears to be some evidence for adding a VP node over the verb
and its object. This evidence is too complex to discuss at this
stage of our study, but we will return to the question of a VP
constituent in chapter 7. For now, we will simply assume that
structure (2.20c) is correct.

Although we have managed to assign a structure to the sentence John saw Mary, we still have no general way of assigning
structure to noun phrases or to sentences as a whole. If trees
like those of (2.17) correctly represent certain aspects of the
structure of NPs, and if tree (2.20c) correctly represents the
structure of John saw Mary, that is of little consequence unless there is a general procedure available in our theory for
associating structures with phrases, sentences, etc.

In the next section we will introduce a formal means of generating structures for the various constituents of an English
sentence. In the course of our discussion we will present a
number of tree diagrams that the reader has not yet been exposed to, and we will provide little or no justification at this
point for the particular structures we discuss. The reason for
this is in part that the justification for sentence structure will
ultimately rest on rules and processes of a sort which we will
be able to discuss only in the chapters following this one. In
those chapters we will justify any structures that play an important role in our argumentation.

2.2. TOWARD A UNIFIED ACCOUNT OF BASIC SENTENCE STRUCTURE

Consider the trees in (2.21a)-(2.21f).

(2. 21) a.

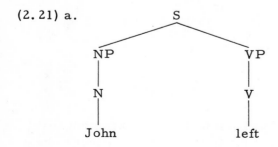

(2.21) b.

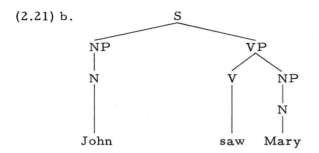

c.

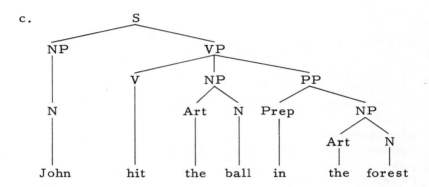

PP = Prepositional Phrase

Prep = Preposition

Art = Article

d.

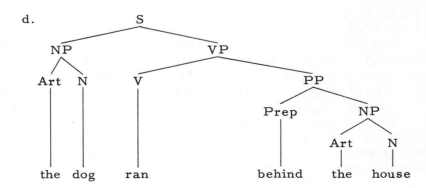

(2.21) e.

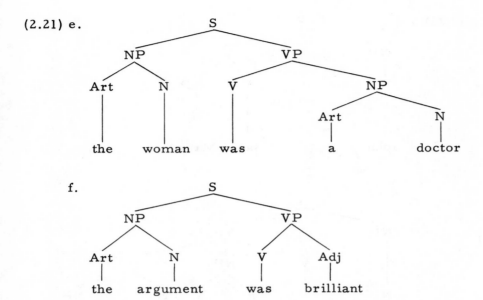

f.

It appears that all of these structures have an important component in common, namely, (2.22).

(2.22)

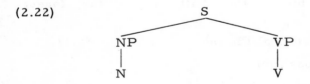

At the same time, many sentences contain structural elements
in addition to the simple structure of (2.22): for example, noun
phrases, adjectives, or prepositional phrases that follow the
main verb.

   If we wish to construct a theory of linguistic structure that
is at all adequate, then we will surely want to find some way
of representing the fact that certain structural features seem
to be part of all sentences and that others can occur optionally.
In order to do this, we could attempt to construct an abstract
device that would generate the desired structures in a precise
way and would fail to generate any impossible structure. We
would want such a device to generate the trees of (2.21) and
not to generate, for example, (2.23).

(2.23)

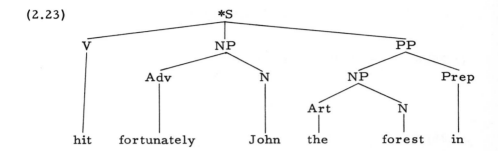

Notice that this tree does not incorporate the subtree (2.22).
If all the sentences of English incorporate this subtree (which
is not strictly true, but will do for the moment), then we can
automatically exclude (2.23) by making sure that the device for
constructing trees associated with English sentences builds
only trees that contain subtree (2.22).

The first point to notice about the basic structure of the sentences we have discussed is that it is divided into two major
constituents, NP and VP, as shown in (2.24a):

(2.24) a.

```
        S
      /   \
    NP     VP
```

We can build this part of the structure by means of the following <u>rule</u>:

(2.24) b. S → NP VP

We interpret (2.24b) as an instruction to <u>rewrite</u> (or <u>expand</u>)
the symbol on the left of the arrow (i.e., <u>S</u>) as a sequence consisting of the two symbols to the right (i.e., <u>NP</u> and <u>VP</u>). When
the symbols are used in tree diagrams to show explicitly the
hierarchical structure of the sentence, the characters to the
right of the arrow in the rule are written under S and are
joined to it by separate lines:

(2.24) c.

In a similar way, we can introduce a rule to expand VP and NP:

(2.25) a. VP → V "VP expands as V" (= "VP is made up of V")
      b. NP → N "NP expands as N" (= "NP is made up of N")

These rules will generate the subtrees (2.25c and d):

(2.25) c.   VP
                       |
                       V

       d.   NP
                       |
                       N

When we combine all three of our rules, we have a device that will build structure (2.22):

(2.26) <u>Rules</u>   <u>Tree</u>
      a. S   → NP VP   S
      b. VP → V   NP   VP
                               | |
      c. NP → N   N   V

Now all we need is a pair of rules rewriting N as <u>John</u> and V as <u>left</u>:

(2.27) a. N → John
      b. V → left

Adding these to (2.26), we obtain our original tree (2.21a):

(2.21) a.
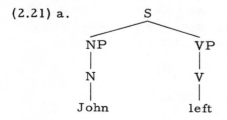

The rules apply in sequence, resulting in a pyramid of symbols (a <u>derivation</u>) with S at the top, and the tree is built up from those given in (2.28). (Repeated symbols are omitted from tree structures.)

(2.28) <u>Rules</u>   <u>Derivation</u>   <u>Tree</u>


```
                                    S                        S
a. S  → NP  VP       NP      VP      NP              VP
b. VP → V            NP      V       |               |
c. NP → N            N       V       N               V
d. N  → John         John    V       |               |
e. V  → left         John    left    John            left
```

Although our rules will now exclude the unwanted tree (2.23) and will ensure that all trees for English contain (2.22) as a subtree, they are clearly inadequate, for they will only generate a single sentence: <u>John left</u>. We must obviously modify our rules to permit the derivation of (2.21b) in addition to (2.21a). Those two structures differ only in that (i) there is an extra NP in (2.21b); (ii) the N of the NP is <u>Mary</u>, not <u>John</u>; and (iii) the V of the sentence is <u>saw</u>, not <u>left</u>.

The first change requires that we permit an NP object to appear in the VP in addition to the V that obligatorily occurs there. We need to add a second rule for the VP, in addition to the rule already given (repeated here as (2.29a)):

(2.29) a. VP → V
       b. VP → V NP

The two rules we have formulated now allow VP to be expanded as V alone, or as V followed by NP. Notice that our two rules are in part identical—both contain the symbol V as the initial element of VP, and they differ only in that one rule allows NP to follow. This duplication in the rules indicates that a generalization is being missed. We can achieve a simpler and more general description of the VP if we <u>collapse</u> the two rules by using the <u>notational device</u> of parentheses, ( ), as follows:

(2.29) c. VP → V (NP)

Whenever an item is enclosed within parentheses, as is the NP

above, then it may <u>optionally</u> be chosen within the expansion of
the rule. Items not enclosed in parentheses <u>must</u> be chosen.
Hence, rule (2.29c) is equivalent to the two rules (2.29a) and
(2.29b) taken together. We will use parentheses in this fashion throughout this book, and the reader should bear in mind
that any rule containing items in parentheses is an abbrevia-
tion for a set of rules which is collapsed in the manner described above for (2.29a) and (2.29b).

By modifying the VP rule in this way we generate either
(2.21a)—if NP is not chosen—or (2.21b). For the latter, the
NP is in fact chosen:

(2.21) b.

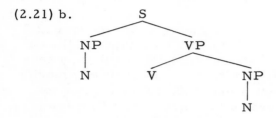

Hence we can now generate sentences with a <u>direct object</u> NP
as well as a subject NP.

Now we need only permit the rules to rewrite N and V as
<u>Mary</u> and <u>saw</u> respectively. This can be done by using a com-
ma to separate alternatives appearing on the right-hand side
of a rule:

(2.30) a. N → John, Mary
       b. V → left, saw

The derivation will now proceed roughly as shown in (2.31).

(2.31) <u>Rules Applied</u>   <u>Derivation</u>   <u>Tree</u>

		S	S
a. S → NP VP	NP	VP	NP VP
b. VP → V (NP)	NP V	NP	V NP
c. NP → N	N V	N	N N
d. N → John, Mary	John V	Mary	
e. V → left, saw	John saw Mary		John saw Mary

Observe that the rule NP → N will serve to define the structure of the object NP (inside the VP) as well as that of the subject NP. We do not need a new and separate structure rule for each NP in the sentence, just as long as we permit the same rule (NP → N) to expand all NPs in a sentence. If both subject and object NPs are expanded by the same rule, our theory captures the fact that they are made up of the same kinds of basic elements.

As we expand our rules to generate more varied structures, we must ensure that they continue to generate only English sentences. If our rules ever generate ill-formed structures (such as (2.23)), then they have ceased to provide a model of the speaker's knowledge of what constitutes a grammatical sentence in his language, the model that he uses both in analyzing sentences he hears or reads and in constructing new ones. We can think of this problem from the point of view of theory-building. Each new set of rules that we develop here through our analysis of English sentences constitutes a hypothesis about (a part of) the structure of the language. Once that hypothesis is formulated, it must be tested, just as hypotheses were tested in the first chapter. To test the consequences of a set of rules, we must find out what trees these rules permit us to construct (or generate). Every good tree generated may constitute partial confirmation of our hypothesis, but at the same time every tree ending in a string that is not an English sentence forms a counterexample to our hypothesis and forces us to change those rules.

Now notice that the few slight changes made in our original rules, changes made only in order to generate tree (2.21b), generate not just one extra tree (i.e., sentence) but a good number of them. Nothing prevents the rule N → John, Mary from inserting Mary as the subject of left. Hence, the tree shown in (2.32) can be built. (Note that we have not chosen the NP that appears in (2.32b).)

(2.32) Rules   Derivation   Tree

Rules	Derivation		Tree
	S		S
a. S → NP VP	NP	VP	NP VP
b. VP → V (NP)	NP	V	| |
c. NP → N	N	V	N V
d. N → John, Mary	Mary	V	| |
e. V → left, saw	Mary	left	Mary left

Work through the other possible derivations using the rules shown in (2.32), building all the trees before reading further.

The set of rules discussed so far should have enabled you to generate trees for the following:

(2.33) a. Mary saw John.
      b. John left Mary.
      c. Mary left John.
      d. ?Mary saw.
      e. ?John saw.

It is not clear whether the last two should be considered fully grammatical (hence the ? notation, parallel to * marking un- grammatical Ss), but we will regard them as such for the moment. That is an important assumption, since, as we have just pointed out, we must not permit our rules to generate un- grammatical sentences. However, it will do no harm to re- gard these two strings as good sentences for the time being, and we will return to them later in the chapter. (See section 2.4.)

We still have to modify our rules in order to generate the tree for the sentence (2.21c), John hit the ball in the forest. The modifications are very slight in themselves, but once made they will add to our ability to characterize the structure of English sentences. Using the devices of parentheses and commas, introduced in rules (2.29) and (2.30), the reader should modify the rules (2.32a)-(2.32e) and use the new set to construct the desired tree. (Do not worry about whether your rules also generate some sentences with strange meanings.)

The following set of rules will suffice; they will generate the trees (2.21a)-(2.21c):

(2.34) a. S   → NP VP
      b. VP   → V   (NP) (PP)
      c. PP   → Prep NP
      d. NP   → (Art) N
      e. V   → left, saw, hit
      f. N   → John, Mary, ball, forest

     g. Prep → in
     h. Art   → the

The reader should check to make sure that the tree in (2.35) is generated by the rules of (2.34).

(2.35) (= (2.21c)) S

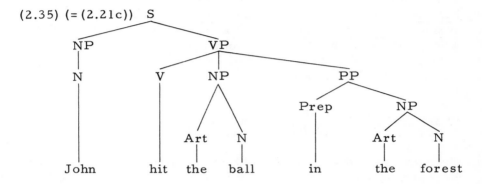

    The rules given in (2.34) generate a large number of trees— some obviously corresponding to English sentences and some less desirable. However, of the remaining trees given in (2.21), only two are generated by these rules—and then only if some other words are added to the right side of rules (2.34e)- (2.34h). What words have to be added—and which tree is still not generated?

    The rules in question have to be modified thus:

(2.34') e. V   → left, saw, hit, ran, was
       f. N   → John, Mary, ball, forest, dog, house,
                doctor, argument, woman
      g. Prep → in, behind
      h. Art   → the, a

Even when these changes are made, the rules will not generate (2.21f), since an <u>adjective</u> follows the verb in that example. Consequently, we need to include the following two rules for VP in our grammar:

(2.36) a. VP → V (NP) (PP)
      b. VP → V (Adj) (PP)

Rule (2.36a) will generate an optional NP after the verb, while
rule (2.36b) will generate an optional adjective after the verb
in that position; the effect of the two rules is to make the
choice of adjective an alternative to the choice of NP for the
given position in the rule. Note that the category PP may follow either an NP or an adjective. Hence a VP such as <u>hit the</u>
<u>ball in the forest</u> is an instance of V NP PP, while the phrase
<u>is short for a basketball player</u> is an instance of V Adj PP.
Thus, either NP or Adj may occur between V and PP.

Once again, our two rules for VP are partially identical,
and we can abbreviate the two rules using <u>braces</u>, {}, as follows:

(2.36) c. VP → V $\left(\left\{\begin{matrix} NP \\ Adj \end{matrix}\right\}\right)$ (PP)

Here we have written a complex expression ({NP/Adj}) in our
VP rule, which we interpret as follows: following the main
verb, we can have either an NP or an adjective, but not both.
This is represented by braces, which always indicate alternative choices. However, neither NP nor Adj must appear;
they are both optional. Hence parentheses surround the expression in braces. (Of course, we must also add a rule expanding Adj appropriately. For the moment, let us assume
that the rule is <u>Adj → brilliant, tall, red, etc.</u>)

The <u>abbreviatory devices</u> of parentheses and braces have
allowed us to collapse six separate VP rules into the single
VP rule (2.36c). The six separate rules are those shown in
(2.36d):

(2.36) d. (i)   VP → V
         (ii) VP → V NP
         (iii) VP → V NP PP
         (iv) VP → V Adj
         (v)   VP → V Adj PP
         (vi) VP → V PP

Since V occurs in all these rules it is not contained in parentheses in (2.36c); the constituent PP may occur with any combination of other VP elements but need not appear. Hence it is
placed in parentheses at the end of (2.36c). Between V and the
optional PP we may have either an NP or an Adj, and this al-

ternative is expressed by using braces enclosed within parentheses.

2.3. PHRASE STRUCTURE RULES FOR THE ENGLISH NOUN PHRASE

We began our discussion of English structure by attempting to
characterize units that we called noun phrases (NPs). The NP
is a major structural component of sentences, and it would be
worthwhile to explore in a little more detail the internal structure of this category, not only to discover what this structure
is, but also to note certain important principles that emerge
from our attempt to construct an NP rule.

First of all, to the left of the head noun (N) within the NP,
a variety of elements may occur. (The head noun of an NP is
represented by the symbol N in the rule NP → . . . N . . . .)
For example, we must find a way to represent the fact that
the and a are not the only words that can fill the slot in which
they appear, as is shown by the following:

(2.37) a. the book
      b. a book

(2.38) a. these books
      b. those books

(2.39) a. that book
      b. this book

(2.40) a. John's book
      b. my book

Words such as these, those, this, that (called demonstratives),
and possessive words such as my, your, and John's, occur in
the same place within the NP as the articles the and a. In order
to capture the fact that this class of words is syntactically
parallel to the articles, we assign the entire class, including
articles, to a single constituent category, which we can call
Determiner (abbreviated in trees as Det). Notice that these
groups of words may not cooccur with each other within an NP.
Hence we do not have NPs such as *the this book, *the my
books, *the your these books, and so on. These facts can be
captured by the rules given in (2.41).

(2.41) a. NP → (Det) N

b. Det → $\left\{\begin{array}{l}\text{the}\\ \text{a}\\ \text{this}\\ \text{that}\\ \text{these}\\ \text{those}\\ \text{my}\\ \text{your}\\ \text{his}\\ \text{her}\\ \text{its}\\ \text{our}\\ \text{your}\\ \text{their}\\ \text{NP}\end{array}\right\}$

In the rule for Det, we have listed the individual articles, demonstratives, and possessives within a single set of braces, without attempting to assign them to distinct subcategories. Our rule correctly predicts the fact that members of the three categories occur in the same position under NP, but it does not account for certain differences between the categories (e.g., demonstratives can occur in environments that prohibit articles, as in those of the boys who were sick, vs. *the of the boys who were sick). To account for these differences, we might need to introduce subcategories of determiners under Det.

It will be noticed that in our rule for Det we have included the constituent NP. This reflects the fact that possessive phrases can consist of entire noun phrases, as in the man's book, the car's fender, this lamb's fleece, and so on. Given the rules set out in (2.41), we assign these phrases structures such as that of (2.42), using the man's book as our example. We have not provided a means of attaching the possessive suffix 's to the NP dominated by Det, but it would be a simple matter to revise our rule so that every NP dominated by Det is automatically assigned the suffix 's (e.g., Det → NP + 's). Given the modifications we have proposed in (2.42), our rules will now generate a wide class of determiners. Determiners do not exhaust the possible elements that may appear before

(2.42)

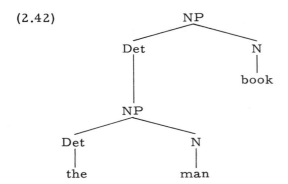

the head noun—for example, adjectives (<u>John's red book</u>) and
so-called <u>quantifiers</u> may also precede the head (<u>his many</u>
<u>books</u>). However, we will not deal with these elements at this
point.

Having examined some of the "prenominal" elements within
the NP, let us turn our attention to NP elements that can follow the head noun:

(2.43) a. the house <u>in the woods</u>
       b. the weather <u>in England</u>
       c. the prospects <u>for peace</u>
       d. the theory <u>of fluid dynamics</u>
       e. the keys <u>to the kingdom</u>
       f. the lock <u>on the door</u>

Our rule for expanding NP (i.e., <u>NP → (Det) N</u>) will not generate examples such as these, since the rule provides for no
elements following N. How should we modify that rule so that
it will generate NPs like those in (2.43)? First, try to determine what kind of category label should be assigned to phrases
such as <u>in the woods</u>, <u>in England</u>, <u>on the door</u>, etc., and then
determine how this should be built into the NP rule.

A very simple modification of the NP rule will allow us to
generate NPs such as those in (2.43), namely (2.44):

(2.44) NP → (Det) N (PP)

An optional prepositional phrase appears after the head noun, and this rule, in conjunction with the rule for expanding PP (PP → Prep NP), will now automatically generate NPs such as (2.45a).

(2.45) a.

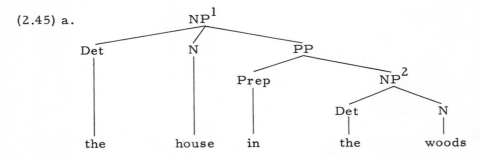

(We have numbered the NPs in (2.45a) for ease of reference below.) Furthermore, the same simple set of rules will automatically generate much more complex structures. In the NP (2.45a) we have chosen to expand NP^2 with a Det and N alone, but we might have chosen a postnominal PP in that lower NP structure, since rule (2.44) tells us that the category PP may follow N, as seen in (2.45b).

(2.45) b.

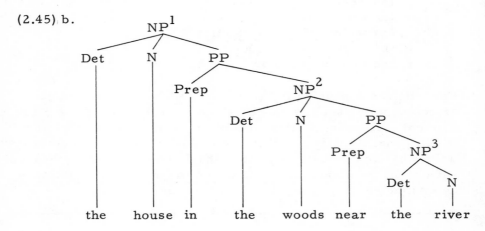

Structure (2.45b) differs from (2.45a) only in that NP^2 has a PP after the head noun. There is no limit to this process. In the structure given in (2.45b), NP^3 has only a Det and an N, but here too the NP could have a postnominal PP, as shown in (2.45c). Clearly, we could continue this process ad infinitum.

(2.45) c.

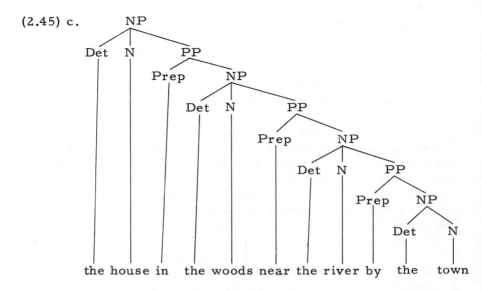

the house in the woods near the river by the town

The situation we have reached reveals an important property of our grammar—and of human language in general. We now
have a grammar that is recursive, i.e., one that will generate
an infinite set of structures. The recursive property of the
grammar derives from the way in which NP and PP interact in
the following rules:

(2.46) a. NP → (Det) N (PP)

b. PP → Prep NP

Every NP is allowed to contain a PP, which in turn contains an
NP, which in turn may contain a PP, and so on. This set of
rules predicts that there is in principle no bound on the length
of a noun phrase.

If this is true, then there is no bound on the number of possible NPs. And if it is the case that there is an unbounded (i.e.,
potentially infinite) number of NPs, then it will follow that there
is also an infinite number of sentences in our language. The
reason is simple: if for every NP of the form (2.45c) we can
construct another NP that contains an additional PP, then for
every sentence containing such an NP we can always construct
a sentence with a longer NP:

(2.47) a. I saw the house in the woods.

     b. I saw the house in the woods by the river.
     c. I saw the house in the woods by the river by the town.
     d. I saw the house in the woods by the river by the town
        near the mountain.
     e. I saw the house in the woods by the river by the town
        near the mountain over the freeway.

If we continued to make this sentence longer we would, of
course, soon reach the point where it would become difficult
to breathe or to recall what had been said in an earlier part
of the sentence; but it would be completely arbitrary to say
that the sentence was "ungrammatical" past any given length.
Hence, any adequate grammar of English—or of any other
language, for that matter—will generate an infinite number of
sentences.
   Now that we have modified our NP rule so as to allow an optional PP to follow the head noun, it is interesting to note that
we have two rules in our grammar that include PP:

(2.48) a. NP → (Det) N   (PP)

      b. VP → V   ($\left\{\begin{matrix} \text{NP} \\ \text{Adj} \end{matrix}\right\}$) (PP)

Thus, prepositional phrases may be generated at the end of
NPs as well as at the end of VPs, and this means that the
rules of (2.48) <u>predict</u> that the following structures, among
others, are all possible:

(2.49) a.

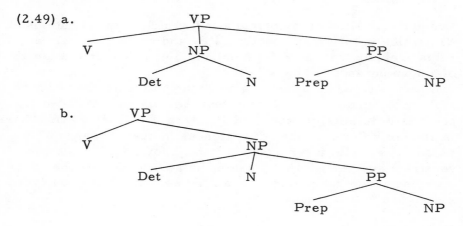

c.

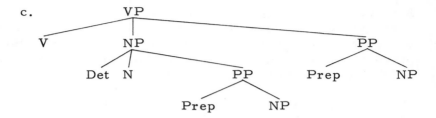

In other words, a VP may contain an NP followed by a separate PP, as in (2.49a); or an NP which includes within it a PP, as in (2.49b); or both of these possibilities, as in (2.49c). In each case, our trees make different claims about the constituent structure of the NP in relation to the PP: in (2.49a) NP and PP are separate, independent units; in (2.49b), the PP forms a single unit with the NP; and in (2.49c) the first PP forms a unit with the NP, while the second PP is independent of it. We must now ask whether these various constituent structures are ever realized in English. Try to construct actual sentences with verb phrases that exemplify each of the three structures given in (2.49), and try to find confirming evidence that the structures are correct. (Hint: Confirming evidence can be found in the formation of passive counterparts to the sentences you con-struct—see section 2.1.)

First, let us examine structure (2.49a), in which the object NP and PP are independent constituents. We might hypothesize that the sentence illustrated in (2.50) contains an instance of that structure.

(2.50)

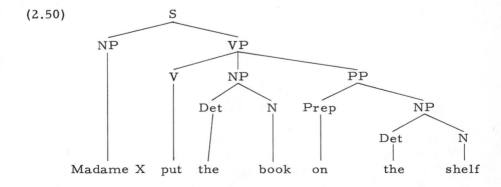

Recall that in forming the passive counterpart for an active
sentence, we must move the object NP into subject position,
while moving the subject to the end of the sentence. If this
process of passive-formation is applied to the sentence just
cited, the result is (2.51b).

(2.51) a. Madame X put the book on the shelf.

     b. The book was put on the shelf by Madame X.

The object NP, the book, has been moved to subject position,
and the PP, on the shelf, has remained in its original position.
Notice, furthermore, that if we try to form a passive sentence
in which the PP has moved with the NP, as though it formed a
unit with the NP, an ungrammatical sentence results:

(2.51) c. *The book on the shelf was put by Madame X.

This confirms that the NP and PP are structurally independent
of each other, as predicted by structure (2.50).
    Now contrast this with an example of structure (2.49b), shown
in (2.52), in which the PP is contained within the NP and hence
forms a unit with that NP.

(2.52)

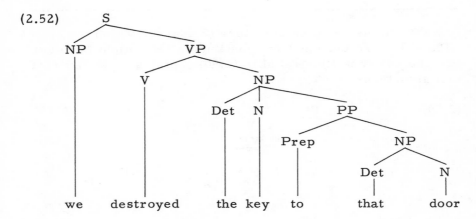

By the reasoning used above, we should not expect the NP and
PP to act independently of each other in a structure such as
(2.52), but rather we should expect that they pattern as a single
unit. With this in mind, consider the set of sentences in (2.53).

(2.53) a. We destroyed the key to that door.

   b. The key to that door was destroyed by us.
   c. *The key was destroyed to that door by us.

In forming the passive counterpart to the active sentence
(2.53a), we must move the NP and PP as a single unit. If we
try to move the NP independently of the PP, the ungrammatical sentence (2.53c) results. The contrast between the sentences of (2.51) and those of (2.53) provides good evidence that
our rules must allow an independent PP within the VP, as in
(2.50), and a "dependent" PP within the NP, as in (2.52).

   Not only are there distinct sentences that exemplify structures (2.49a) and (2.49b), but there are also single sentences
that are ambiguous between those two structures. For example, there seems to be good evidence that sentence (2.54a)
below should be associated with both structures (2.54b) and
(2.54c).

(2.54) a. Willis wrote a book about Nixon.

   b.

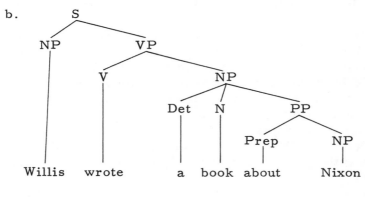

   c.

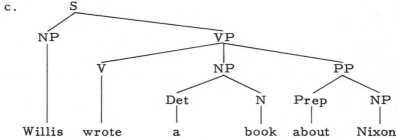

In other words, the claim is that sentence (2.54a) is structured both like sentence (2.50) and like sentence (2.52). Try
to use the passive test to confirm this claim.

(2.55) a. Willis wrote a book about Nixon.
      b. <u>A book about Nixon</u> was written by Willis.
      c. <u>A book</u> was written <u>about Nixon</u> by Willis.

The passive formation process can either move the PP along
with the object NP (consistent with structure (2.54b), where
these are a single unit), or it can move the object NP independently of the PP (consistent with structure (2.54c), where
these are independent of each other).
    If we look for further independent evidence of the structural
ambiguity of sentence (2.54a), we find that certain differences
in meaning confirm that such sentences can be associated with
either of these structures. Consider the ambiguity of the following sentence:

(2.56) Willis wrote his first book about Nixon last year.

The first meaning, where Willis is assumed to have written
a number of <u>books about Nixon,</u> claims that the first of these
was written last year. This can clearly be associated with
tree (2.54b), where the PP is part of the object NP. The second meaning, where it is claimed that Willis wrote his very
first book last year—and that in it he <u>wrote about Nixon</u>—can
be associated with tree (2.54c), in which the PP is a separate
constituent of VP. Hence this difference in meaning can be
linked with the postulated structural difference of (2.54b) and
(2.54c).
    Ambiguous sentences such as (2.56) provide good evidence
that sentences cannot be regarded as unstructured strings of
words. For if that were the case, there would be no way to
explain how it is that a single sentence, containing a set of
unambiguous words, could nevertheless have more than one
interpretation. Only if we assume that sentences possess abstract structure can we explain the ambiguity of sentences such
as (2.56), precisely by assigning the sentence more than one
abstract structure.
    We have shown that structures (2.49a) and (2.49b) are needed.

Structure (2.49c) is necessary too. It is simply a combination of structures (2.49a) and (2.49b) and can be illustrated by sentences such as (2.57).

(2.57)

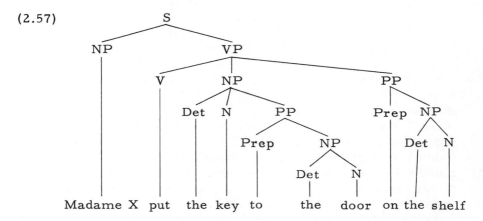

By using the passive test, the reader should be able to justify structure (2.57), and we leave this as an exercise.

In closing this section, we should stress that we have by no means exhausted the structural possibilities within the NP. For example, we have already noted that our NP rule makes no provision for adjectives or quantifiers, nor does it yet allow for postnominal modifiers other than PP (such as relative clauses of the sort found in examples like the man who I know). However, it is striking that a simple modification of the NP rule—namely, the addition of an optional PP after the head noun—not only makes our grammar recursive (as any grammar must be to account for the examples in (2.47)), but also makes a number of interesting structural predictions, illustrated in (2.49), which turn out to be confirmed.

2.4. THE LEXICON AND LEXICAL INSERTION

Our total set of rules can now be summarized as follows:

(2.58) a. S → NP VP

b. VP → V $(\begin{Bmatrix} NP \\ Adj \end{Bmatrix})$ (PP)

c. NP → (Det) N (PP)

d. PP → Prep NP

   e. Det → the, a, this, that, these, those, my, your,
        his, her, its, our, your, their, NP's
   f. Prep → in, behind, on, over, . . .
   g. N → John, ball, doctor, woman, argument,
        beauty, astrophysics, . . .
   h. V → left, saw, hit, is, conjugate, seem, . . .
   i. Adj → brilliant, tall, red, fabulous, insecure, . . .

(Note: In rules (2.58e-i) we have listed the items on the right
of the arrow in a horizontal line, with each item separated by
a comma. We have used this device merely to save space, and
these rules should be interpreted in the same way as rules
using braces, as in rule (2.41b).) Although our rules now provide us with a more adequate account of English structure than
those we developed at the beginning of section 2.2, it is nevertheless apparent that these rules contain a number of glaring
gaps.

  For one thing, it is quite obvious that our rules for expanding
N, V, Adj, etc., are much too limited. If our phrase structure
rules are to generate English sentences, then we must obviously
include all possible English vocabulary words within the rules.
However, even if our rules are modified in this way, they will
nevertheless generate a great many ungrammatical sentences.
For example, each of the following ill-formed sentences can
be generated by the rules of (2.58).

(2.59) a.

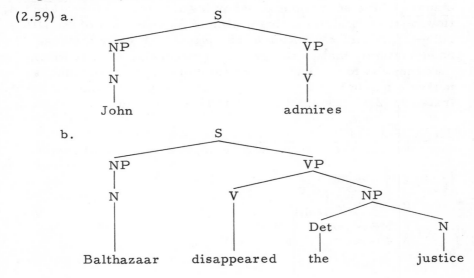

c.

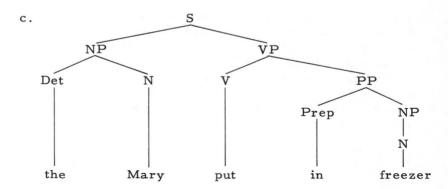

There is nothing in our model to prevent the generation of these ungrammatical sentences; we have applied our phrase structure rules in the proper way. The problem, obviously, is that our rules for N and V, which are simply unstructured lists of words, allow us to insert vocabulary items into our trees randomly, without taking into account the contextual restrictions of the words. Before going on, the reader should attempt to specify, as precisely as possible, what is wrong with each tree of (2.59): what makes each sentence ungrammatical? (Note: In (2.59b)-(2.59c) there is more than one factor contributing to ungrammaticality.)

First of all, notice that our model fails to make any distinction between <u>transitive verbs</u> (those that require objects) and <u>intransitive verbs</u> (those that may not occur with an object). For example, the verb <u>admire</u> is transitive, and hence sentences such as *<u>John admired</u> are ungrammatical, while sentences such as <u>John admired the car</u> are good. We must therefore guarantee that verbs such as this are not inserted into intransitive structures such as (2.59a). On the other hand, the verb <u>disappear</u> is intransitive, so that <u>John disappeared</u> is grammatical, while *<u>John disappeared his dog</u> is ungrammatical. In this case, we must ensure that <u>disappear</u> does not appear in transitive structures such as (2.59b). The case of the verb <u>put</u> is a bit more complex. It is not simply a transitive verb, but one that requires a prepositional phrase of location as well. Sentences such as *<u>John put the ice cream</u> or *<u>John put the freezer</u> are ungrammatical, while sentences such as <u>John put the ice cream in the freezer</u> are perfectly good. So

we must guarantee that <u>put</u>, and verbs like it, appear in structures that contain both an object NP and a following prepositional phrase, and we must somehow prevent the generation of
sentences such as (2.59c).

We have just seen cases in which given verbs must occur in
a given syntactic context, but the same can be said for nouns
as well. Thus, consider the following NPs that appear in the
structures (2.59b)-(2.59c):

(2.60) a.

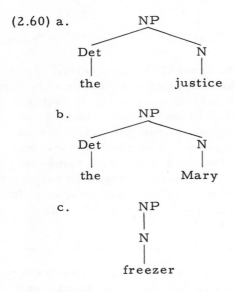

b.

c.

Our model has failed to capture the fact that <u>proper nouns</u>,
such as <u>Mary</u>, and <u>abstract mass nouns</u>, such as <u>justice</u>, generally occur with no article. (In restricted circumstances, the
definite article may appear, as in <u>the Mary that I once knew</u> or
<u>the justice that the Warren court rendered</u>. The definite article
is possible only if a modifying clause follows a proper noun or
abstract mass noun; we shall not consider such cases in formulating our argument.) On the other hand, our rules fail to capture the fact that <u>common nouns</u>, such as <u>freezer</u>, do occur
with articles and must not appear in structures such as (2.60c).
In sum, we have uncovered a defect in our syntactic model: it
does not yet account for the fact that different classes of vocabulary items can appear in different syntactic contexts.

There are various ways we can go about eliminating this defect, but we will discuss only one alternative here (see the sug-

gested readings at the end of this chapter for literature dealing with other alternatives). We will assume that our grammar
contains not only a set of rules for building trees, but also a
dictionary or lexicon. The lexicon may be thought of as somewhat like an ordinary reference dictionary (such as Webster's)
in that it is essentially a list of all the words of English (verbs,
nouns, adjectives, adverbs, etc.; i.e., all parts of speech).
Each word in the lexicon—each lexical entry—will consist of a
collection of information concerning (a) the pronunciation of the
lexical entry, (b) the semantic properties ("meaning") of the
word, and (c) certain syntactic information connected with the
word.

 We will not discuss how the pronunciation or meaning of
words is represented in the lexicon (the interested reader may
pursue this in readings given at the end of this chapter). However, it will be important to see how syntactic properties of
lexical entries are specified. First of all, each lexical entry
will be classified as a part of speech: nouns will be marked
with the syntactic feature [+N]; verbs will be marked with the
syntactic feature [+V]; adjectives with the syntactic feature
[+Adj]; and so on, as in the following sample lexical entries:

(2.61) a. BOOK
   [+N]
  b. ADMIRE
   [+V]
  c. TALL
   [+Adj]

 If our lexical entries are marked in this fashion for syntactic category, we can completely change the way in which
lexical items are inserted into trees. We will first eliminate
all rules such as (2.58f)-(2.58i), so that there are no more
rules such as N → . . . or V → . . . that introduce lexical
items. This means that our rules will simply generate tree
structures with no words in them:

(2.62)

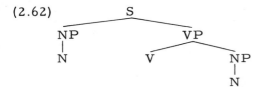

We will assume that lexical items are inserted into tress from the lexicon, by the following general convention: any lexical item marked with a feature [+ F] may be attached to any branch of a tree that ends in the label F, where F stands for the features referring to parts of speech (such as [+N], [+V], etc.). For example, any lexical item can be attached to N as long as it is marked as [+N]; any item can be attached to V as long as it is marked [+ V]; and so on. In other words, we can now insert two nouns and one verb in tree (2.62), as seen in (2.62').

(2.62')

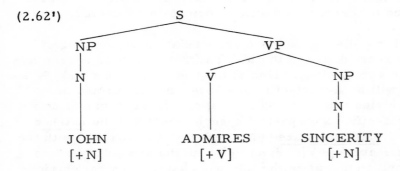

The features [+N], [+V], etc., are simply a way of guaranteeing that lexical items will be inserted at appropriate points in a tree.

Now consider the problem posed by the sentences listed in (2.59b) and (2.59c): how do we guarantee that the verb disappear is inserted only into structures containing no NP object, while the verb admire is inserted only into structures that do include an object? We can achieve this by means of contextual features or subcategorization features. Each verb in our lexicon will appear with a syntactic feature indicating the syntactic context into which it can be inserted. For example:

(2.63) a. ADMIRE

$$\begin{bmatrix} +V \\ +[\_\_NP] \end{bmatrix}$$

   b. DISAPPEAR

$$\begin{bmatrix} +V \\ +[\_\_\_\_] \end{bmatrix}$$

Both of these entries are marked as [+ V], to indicate syntactic
category. Each verb is also shown with a contextual feature:
the verb <u>admire</u> has the feature +[__ NP], which indicates that
an NP must follow it, whereas the verb <u>disappear</u> is marked
with the feature +[_____], showing that no NP object may follow it. Now consider what happens if the following two structures are generated by our rules:

(2.64) a.

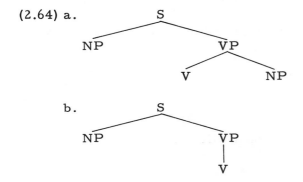

Both <u>admire</u> and <u>disappear</u> are marked [+ V], so either verb
could potentially be inserted into either tree. However, the
feature +[__ NP] on <u>admire</u> indicates that it can be inserted
under a V node only if an NP node follows. Hence, <u>admire</u> can
be inserted only into tree (2.64a) and not into (2.64b), thus preventing the generation of sentences such as (2.59a). On the
other hand, the verb <u>disappear</u> can only be inserted under a
V node in case no NP follows, since it is marked with the feature +[_____]. This means that it will be inserted only into
trees such as (2.64b), and thus our grammar will not generate
sentences such as (2.59b).

   Note that the contextual features assigned to verbs specify
the frame within the VP in which the verb can appear. Thus,
if the verb <u>disappear</u> has the feature +[_____], this does not
mean that <u>disappear</u> may be inserted into a sentence with no
noun phrases in it—our rules generate a subject NP in every
sentence, and every verb appears with a subject—but rather
that the verb appears in a VP that has no object NP. Hence
contextual features refer to the "local" structure of the VP in
which the verb appears and do not make reference to the subject NP of the sentence.

   We have presented only two possibilities for verb insertion,

but of course there are many more. For example, as mentioned above, the verb <u>put</u> not requires only a following NP
object but a prepositional phrase of location as well:

(2.65) a. *John put.
       b. *John put the tools.
       c. *John put in the shed.
       d. John put the tools in the shed.

This means that <u>put</u> can be inserted only into VPs such as the
following:

(2.66)   VP
        _____
       V   NP   PP

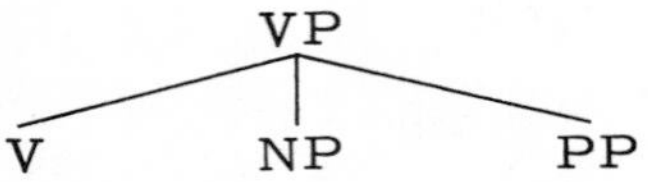

Hence, the lexical entry for <u>put</u> will have the following features:

(2.67)   PUT

       $\begin{bmatrix} +V \\ +[\_\_ \ NP \ PP] \end{bmatrix}$

There are other verbs that are <u>optionally subcategorized</u> for
certain constituents. For example, the verb <u>sell</u> must occur
with a direct object; it may optionally occur with one prepositional phrase indicating to whom something is sold and another
prepositional phrase indicating the amount of money exchanged:

(2.68) a. *John sold.
       b. John sold the car.
       c. John sold the car to Bill.
       d. John sold the car for forty dollars.
       e. John sold the car to Bill for forty dollars.

Thus, <u>sell</u> may occur in any one of the following structures:

(2.69) a.   VP
        _____
       V   NP

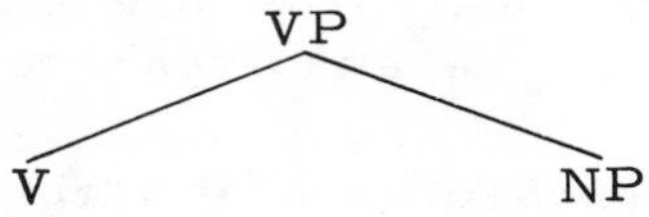

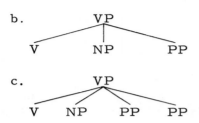

b.
```
        VP
   _____|_____
  |       |           |
  V      NP          PP
```

c.
```
        VP
   _____|_____
  |    |     |     |
  V   NP    PP    PP
```

(Note that we can easily generate a VP such as (2.69c) simply by extending our VP rule to include one more prepositional phrase: VP → V ({NP/Adj}) (PP) (PP).) Using subcategorization features, construct a lexical entry for the verb sell that will guarantee that it appears only in the structures given above in (2.69). (Since sell may optionally occur with prepositional phrases, these should be enclosed in parentheses in the lexical entry.)

The following lexical entry will guarantee that sell is inserted into the proper structures:

(2.70)   SELL

$$
\begin{bmatrix}
+ V \\
+[\underline{\quad} \ NP \ (PP) \ (PP)]
\end{bmatrix}
$$

Since the NP in the lexical entry is shown as obligatory and the PPs as optional, sell will be inserted in any of the structures of (2.69), but will never be inserted into a structure that, for example, contains only a PP after the verb. (Thus, sentences such as *Bill sold to John will not be generated.) Notice further that although the verb sell may occur with up to two PPs, it does not occur with just any random pair of PPs. Rather, the first PP must contain the preposition to, while the second must contain for:

(2.71) a. John sold the car to Bill for forty dollars.
       b. *John sold the car from Bill by forty dollars.
       c. *John sold the car at Bill near forty dollars.

We could account for this fact by elaborating the lexical entry for sell further so that the preposition of each PP is specifically mentioned:

(2.72)   SELL

$$\begin{bmatrix} +V \\ +[\underline{\quad} \text{ NP (to NP) (for NP)}] \end{bmatrix}$$

This lexical entry guarantees not only that <u>sell</u> will be inserted into trees containing up to two PPs but also that the first preposition will be <u>to</u> and the second preposition will be <u>for</u>.

Nouns, as well as verbs, could be marked with contextual features to ensure that they appear in the correct environments. We could use features to ensure that proper nouns (and abstract mass nouns) will not occur with articles, while common nouns will (recall the trees shown in (2.60)). Try to construct appropriate lexical entries for the following nouns that will allow us to prevent the generation of the ungrammatical noun phrases in (2.73b and c):

(2.73) a. the boy, the freezer, the dirt
       b. *the John, *the England, *the Fido
       c. *the sincerity, *the justice

We can represent these facts with lexical entries such as the following:

(2.74) a.   BOY

$$\begin{bmatrix} +N \\ +[\text{Det} \underline{\quad}] \end{bmatrix}$$

       b.   JOHN

$$\begin{bmatrix} +N \\ +[\underline{\qquad\quad}] \end{bmatrix}$$

       c. SINCERITY

$$\begin{bmatrix} +N \\ +[\underline{\qquad\quad}] \end{bmatrix}$$

The entry for a noun such as <u>boy</u> will indicate that it occurs with an article, while the entries for nouns like <u>John</u> and <u>sin-</u>

cerity will indicate that these items do not. Note that contextual features on nouns will refer to the internal structure of NPs
in which the nouns appear, just as such features on verbs refer
to the internal structure of the VP. (We have not tried to provide for the fact that when boy is plural it does not have to take
an article.)

Before ending our discussion, we should note that although
we have a means of preventing sentences such as those of
(2.59) from being generated, our grammar will nevertheless
yield sentences that are not completely felicitous. For example, as it now stands our grammar will generate a sentence
such as (2.75b) as easily as it will generate (2.75a):

(2.75) a. Justice frightens criminals.
       b. Criminals frighten justice.

However, we will make no attempt to exclude sentences such
as (2.75b). We will assume that such sentences are structurally
well-formed (as opposed to those of (2.59)) but somehow deviant
in meaning. At present there are no real consequences in making this assumption, and it will have little bearing on the rest
of the work in this book.

We have now constructed a syntactic model that consists of
two basic parts: (A) a set of rules that generates basic tree
structures of English, and (B) a lexicon that contains (ideally)
an exhaustive list of vocabulary items for English, in which
each entry will be specified with appropriate syntactic features.
Lexical items are inserted into basic trees in accordance with
their part of speech feature and subcategorization features. The
generative rules and lexicon together comprise the base component of our syntactic model.

2.5. PHRASE STRUCTURE GRAMMARS: TECHNICAL
SUMMARY

Even without the method of lexical insertion just described, the
rules constructed in sections 2.2 and 2.3 form a system that
begins to characterize the structure of a fragment of English;
i.e., they provide a precise definition of what it means for a
sentence of English to be grammatical. For that reason, such
a set of rules can be called a grammar for a fragment of English or, more precisely, a phrase structure grammar (PSG);
the rules themselves are generally known as phrase structure

rules or PS rules. They characterize the phrase structure of
English. We have seen that a PS grammar generates tree
structures by a series of rules that essentially indicate what
categories can make up larger categories. The rules of (2.58)
tell us, for example, that a noun phrase may be made up of a
noun or of an article followed by a noun, etc.; that a verb
phrase is made up of a verb followed by a noun, etc.; that a
verb phrase is made up of a verb followed optionally by a noun
phrase, prepositional phrase, etc.; and that a sentence is made
up of a noun phrase followed by a verb phrase. No matter how
we add or modify the basic rules (e.g., by adding a lexicon to
them), the PS rules will continue to represent such aspects of
the structure of the language.

It would be profitable at this point to introduce a certain
amount of technical background that will make it easier for us
to talk about tree diagrams and phrase structure grammars.
We will make use of this material in later chapters.

The labeled branching points in a tree are referred to as
nodes. If we can trace a path up the tree from a given node X
to a given node Y, then we say X is dominated by Y or, equivalently, Y dominates X. For example, if we begin with the
node V in tree (2.76) below we can trace a path up to the node
VP, and, hence, V is dominated by VP. We can continue trac-
ing a path upwards from VP to S, and thus V is also dominated
by S. Note that V is not dominated by the initial NP of the sentence, since there is no way to trace a path from V up to the
node NP (we can trace a path from V up to S, but then to reach
the NP node we would have to trace downward again):

(2.76)

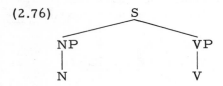

If a line can be traced up from a node X to a node Y and if
no other nodes intervene, then we say that X is directly dominated (or immediately dominated) by Y. In tree (2.76), V is
directly dominated by VP, while NP is directly dominated by
S. If any node A is directly dominated by a node X, we say that
it is a daughter node to X, and if two nodes A and B are daughters of the same node X, then they are sister nodes to each

other. For example, in (2.76), the subject NP and the VP are daughter nodes to the node S, and they are sister nodes to each other. (Despite the matriarchal implications of this terminology, the dominating node, in this case S, is not referred to as the "mother" node.)

The following restriction must be placed on PS rules: <u>one and only one symbol may be expanded by any given PS rule</u>. This restriction is necessary because, if we allowed more than one symbol to be expanded by a rule, then there would be no unique way to associate a tree with the resulting derivation. Thus, assume that we allowed a rule such as (2.77):

(2.77) AB → CDE

This rule would allow two possible trees:

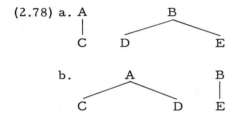

(2.78) a.

b.

If our account of structure is to be adequate, phrase structure rules must be used to build trees in an unambiguous, unique manner; thus, we must assume that they may expand only one symbol, in order to prevent the sort of ambiguity induced by rules such as (2.77). (Note: Even though we must use more than one letter to represent the symbols NP, VP, Det, etc., each one constitutes only a single symbol.)

This restriction will prevent any rule from <u>permuting</u> (transposing) elements directly; that is, rules such as the following will be excluded:

(2.79) AB → BA

If for some reason our analysis of English, or any other language, calls for rearranging constitutents from one order to another, we know that such a process will be beyond the power of a phrase structure grammar subject to the "one symbol" restriction. (There are very good technical reasons why rules such as (2.79) should be excluded. We cannot go into these here, but the interested reader is referred to the suggested readings at the end of this chapter.)

It remains only to point out a few important characteristics of the structure of natural language that are very naturally captured by phrase structure grammars. In the first place, PS rules determine the <u>linear order</u> of words in a sentence. If the rule <u>S → NP VP</u> characterizes the basic structure of an English sentence, there is absolutely no way in which a form like *Ran John can be generated; the verb must occur after the subject. Second, PS rules very effectively represent the <u>hier-archical structure</u> of sentences. At each stage in the construction of a tree, PS rules introduce nodes in such a way that the sentence is broken down into a hierarchy of ever smaller <u>con-stituents</u>. So the <u>immediate constituents</u> of S are NP and $\overline{\text{VP}}$, those of VP are V, NP, PP—or as many of these as are present in a particular tree. This hierarchical structure of con-stituents turns out to play a very important role in rules like the Tag, Negative, Question, and Passive Rules already discussed in these first two chapters (to be dealt with in much more detail later). Finally, note that phrase structure trees provide quite a precise means of defining the <u>grammatical relations</u> of a sentence. For example, the <u>subject</u> of a sentence can be defined as the NP immediately dominated by S; the <u>object</u> of a transitive verb can be defined as an NP immediately dominated by VP; and an <u>indirect object</u> (such as <u>to John</u> in the sentence <u>I gave the book to John</u>) can be defined as an NP dominated by a PP dominated by VP. Since these functional relations can be defined on a tree in this manner, we need not actually label nodes as "subject," "object," and so on.

Notice that PS rules do not merely define the grammatical sentences of a language. They define each constituent of those sentences. We noted earlier that we would want to avoid regarding <u>fortunately</u> as part of the subject NP in a sentence like (2.80):

(2.80) Fortunately John saw Mary.

Our PS rules automatically make that clear. Although we might need to modify our rule expanding S to include an optional adverb, as in (2.81),

(2.81) S → (Adv) NP VP

we do not have any reason for changing the rule for NP to include an adverb, along the following lines:

(2.82) *NP → (Adv) (Det) N . . .

Consequently, the adverb <u>fortunately</u> will never be assigned
to the subject NP of any sentence.

2.6. THE ENGLISH AUXILIARY SYSTEM: WORK SECTION

So far, in developing PS rules for English, we have made no
provision for generating sentences containing auxiliary verbs.
Our examples in this chapter have been limited to plain past
or present tense main verbs without an auxiliary (such as <u>dis-
appeared</u>, <u>fell</u>, and so on). However, English sentences often
include auxiliaries in addition to the main verb, and we must
include them in our grammar.

As we mentioned in chapter 1, auxiliaries can be distin-
guished from main verbs by their behavior in questions (as
well as in other contexts): under the right conditions, the auxiliary is placed at the front of the sentence instead of in its
normal position, but a main verb is never moved in that way.
The underlined words in the following examples are auxiliaries,
as can be shown by forming the related questions and noting the
position of these words:

(2.83) a. John <u>is</u> running down the street
   b. I <u>was</u> talking to her.
   c. They <u>are</u> writing papers.

(2.84) a. I <u>have</u> written to them.
   b. They <u>had</u> beaten the opposing team.
   c. She <u>has</u> constructed a tower.

(2.85) a. I <u>will</u> leave the room.
   b. John <u>must</u> eat the fish now.
   c. They <u>could</u> do that if they tried.
   d. Herb <u>might</u> win the contest.
   e. Mary <u>can</u> speak French.

From these and many similar examples we can establish that

the class of auxiliary verbs must include the following:

(2.86) a. Forms of the verb <u>be</u> (<u>is</u>, <u>am</u>, <u>are</u>, <u>was</u>, <u>were</u>)
     b. Forms of the verb <u>have</u> (<u>have</u>, <u>has</u>, <u>had</u>)
     c. The verbs <u>can</u>, <u>could</u>, <u>will</u>, <u>would</u>, <u>shall</u>, <u>should</u>,
       <u>may</u>, <u>might</u>, <u>must</u>, and possibly a few others. Mem-
       bers of this group are usually referred to as <u>modal</u>
       <u>auxiliaries</u>.

(In chapter 1 we suggested that <u>do</u> might be an auxiliary, but
we will postpone further discussion of this possibility, and
hence of sentences containing <u>do</u>, until chapter 4.)
   On the basis of the examples just given, we might propose
changing the first rule of the grammar to (2.87):

(2.87) S → NP Aux VP

In this way we modify our earlier rules so that a sentence can
consist of three (not just two) basic elements: a subject NP, an
auxiliary, and a verb phrase. Once the Aux node is expanded,
our grammar will generate all the sentences of (2.83)-(2.85),
assigning to (2.83a), for example, the structure shown in (2.88).

(2.88)

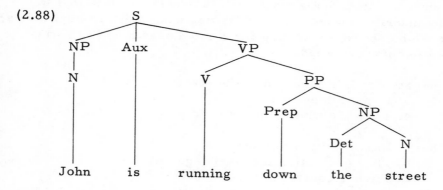

There are other conceivable ways of attaching the Aux node in
a sentence, of course. For example, we might analyze (2.83a)
as shown in (2.89). However, we will assume that (2.88) is
correct. Nothing at this stage depends on where the Aux is attached.
   Now notice that although we have dealt only with forms containing a single auxiliary, it is very easy to find examples with

(2.89)

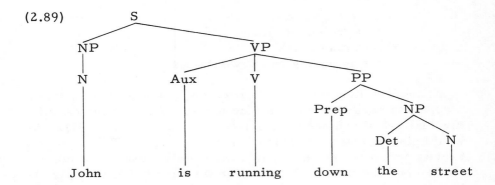

more than one:

(2.90) a. John <u>has been</u> running down the street.
     b. John <u>may be</u> running down the street.
     c. John <u>could have</u> run down the street.

(2.91) a. John <u>could have been</u> running down the street.
     b. Mary <u>will have been</u> sleeping for five hours by now.
     c. The teacher <u>might have been</u> punishing the class.

As these sentences show, it is necessary to assign <u>internal structure</u> to the auxiliary system.
    The problem, then, is to add a rule of the form (2.92) that will generate all the possible forms of the auxiliary.

(2.92) Aux → . . .

The construction of the rule is left as an exercise to finish this chapter. The reader should keep the following points in mind:

(2.93) a. <u>Optionality of auxiliary verbs</u>: A sentence may have no overt auxiliary verb, or it may have one, two, or three. Your rules must be formulated so that these optional choices will be available.
     b. <u>Order of auxiliary verbs</u>: When there is more than one auxiliary verb in a sentence, the verbs must come in a strict order; examine the sentences (2.90) and (2.91). Compare these with any of the following, all ungrammatical because of violation of this basic order:

*I have might leave.
*They are can do it.
*I will may leave.
*John is having run down the street.

A good way to approach this problem would be to construct a separate phrase structure rule (or set of rules) for each individual set of sentences (2.83)-(2.85); (2.90), and (2.91). This would give at least five rules, or sets of rules. Then, using braces or parentheses, try to collapse all these rules into one unified phrase structure rule. For the time being, simply stick to the sentences given and no others. In formulating this rule, do not try at first to take into account the variation that can occur in the form of a single verb (e.g., be, is, was, were, etc; have, has, had, etc.) but treat all such variants as though they were identical.

When you have formulated the phrase structure rule, consider how the following facts are to be handled. Notice that each auxiliary verb requires the verb immediately following it to be in a special form. For example:

(2.94) a.   John is writing.
          *John is write.
          *John is wrote.
          *John is written.
       b.   John has written.
          *John has write.
          *John has writing.
          *John has writes.
       c.   John may write (can write, will write, must write, etc.).
          *John may writing.
          *John may wrote.
          *John may written.

Consider, then, the following problem for future reference: can the phrase structure rule for the auxiliary be formulated so that the verb following any auxiliary verb will be exactly in its correct form?

CHAPTER 2: EXERCISES
(E2.1) The tree structures shown in A-C have all been left incomplete, in the sense that no words have been filled into the
structures. For each tree diagram give at least one English
sentence that exemplifies that structure, inserting each word
of the sentence under the appropriate node of the tree.

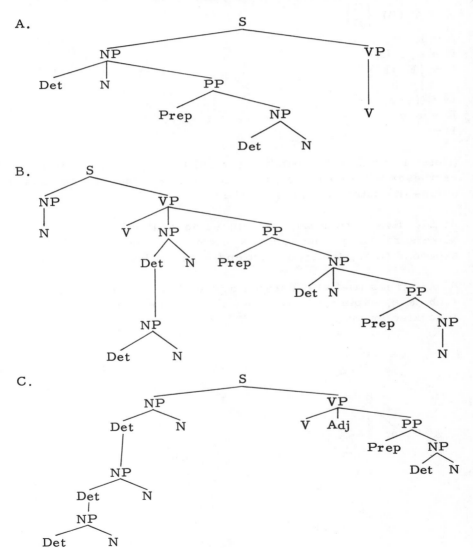

(E2.2) The following set of PS rules is made up of abstract symbols, not intended to reflect the structure of any particular language. Nevertheless, these rules are well formed and generate trees in the same way we have indicated for a grammar of English:

$$X \rightarrow A \ (B) \ \begin{Bmatrix} C \\ D \end{Bmatrix}$$

$A \rightarrow k$

$B \rightarrow e \ f \ (X)$

$$C \rightarrow \begin{Bmatrix} E \ (F) \\ g \ h \end{Bmatrix}$$

$D \rightarrow ((a \ b) \ c) \ d$

$E \rightarrow x \ y$

$F \rightarrow z$

(Note: The rule for expanding symbol D contains a set of parentheses within a larger set. The inner set may not be chosen unless the outer set has been chosen.)

A. List five distinct tree structures generated by these rules. Make sure that all the symbols of your tree have been fully expanded (i.e., the tree must end in small letter symbols).

B. Are trees (i)-(iv) generated by the above grammar? For each case, explain why the tree either is generated or is not generated by the rules.

(i)

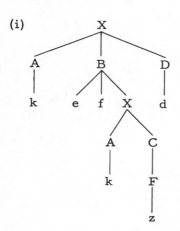

(ii)

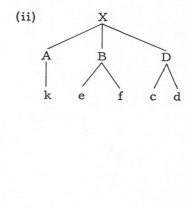

(iii)

(iv)

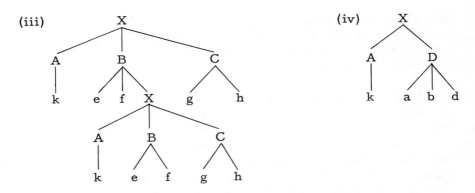

C. Is the phrase structure grammar given above recursive? If so, show why it is. If not, show why not.

(E2.3) There seems to be no bound on the possible length of possessive phrases in English, as the following noun phrases show:

(i) a. John's book
   b. John's friend's book
   c. John's friend's father's book
   d. John's friend's father's uncle's book
   e. John's friend's father's uncle's therapist's book
      etc.

Since possessive phrases are potentially infinite in length, we have another example of English structure that will call for recursive rules. Given the PS grammar cited in this chapter in (2.58), do our rules for NP and Det generate examples such as those in (i), or do we need to modify our rules for this case? If the rules do generate these examples, show how, providing trees for these examples. If they do not, show why they do not, and provide a reformulation of the rules that will work in this case.

(E2.4) Consider the following sentences, which all contain the main verb <u>trade</u>:

(i)   *I traded.
(ii)   *I traded a bicycle.
(iii)   I traded a bicycle to Bill.

(iv) *I traded to Bill.
(v)   I traded a bicycle to Bill for a scooter.
(vi)   I traded a bicycle for a scooter.
(vii) *I traded for a scooter.

A. For a large group of English speakers, the grammaticality
patterns of these sentences are as marked above. Assuming
this pattern, what subcategorization feature must be placed on
trade that will allow it to be inserted into the good sentences,
while preventing its insertion in the bad sentences? Note: In
answering this part of the exercise, assume that your subcategorization feature does not refer to specific prepositions
(cf. the discussion of sell in section 2.4).

B. The grammaticality judgments for these sentences vary
widely across dialects in English, and you may find that you
disagree with the pattern we have given. For example, some
speakers find that (iv) is grammatical while (vii) is ungrammatical, with the rest as given above. Other speakers find
that if the preposition with is substituted for to in these examples, a new pattern of grammaticality is produced. Formulate your own judgments for the sentences given above or for
a similar set containing with instead of to, and on the basis of
the facts you arrive at give a subcategorization feature for
trade that will allow it to be inserted in just the right sentences.

(E2.5) In English it is often possible to move prepositional
phrases from sentence-final position to sentence-initial position, as the following examples show:

(i)   a. He ran into the woods.
       b. Into the woods he ran.
(ii)   a. I often read books in the barn.
       b. In the barn I often read books.
(iii) a. The old man peered through the opening.
       b. Through the opening the old man peered.

Now consider the following two sentences:

(iv)   a. He ran up a big hill.
       b. He ran up a big bill.

These sentences exhibit an interesting difference when we try
to move the portion following the verb:

(v) a. <u>Up a big hill</u> he ran.
     b. *<u>Up a big bill</u> he ran.

A second difference between these sentences involves the
process of forming passive counterparts for each:

(vi) a. *A big hill was run up by him.
     b.   A big bill was run up by him.

<u>A</u>. Explain the difference between sentences (iva) and (ivb) by
assigning each sentence an explicit structure and showing, in
detail, how the difference in structure predicts the differences
in behavior illustrated in (v) and (vi). You should be able to
explain why (vb) and (via) are ungrammatical, while (va) and
(vib) are grammatical.

<u>B</u>. Explicitly list at least three additional differences between
the sentences of (iv) and show, in detail, how these differences
can be related to the structures you have assigned the two sentences. The differences between the sentences may involve:
(a) differences in the possibility for reordering the constituents of the sentences (as in the two cases cited above in (v)
and (vi)); (b) differences in meaning that can plausibly be related to your structures; or (c) differences in the behavior of
the two sentences with respect to some other criterion you may
have found.

(E2.6) There is good reason to suppose that all languages are
alike in exhibiting hierarchical structures of the sort that we
have been trying to capture by means of PS rules for English.
Very often, however, the basic constituent structure of a language seems to differ from that of English; in particular, the
basic order of the constituents may be quite different. To the
extent that this is so, we cannot use the English rules <u>S → NP
VP</u> or <u>NP → (Det) N (PP)</u>, etc., to characterize the structure of all languages, but we must use other (often very similar) rules. Consider the Japanese sentences at the end of this
paragraph. Use the translations to work out the meaning of the
various constituents, then try to formulate a set of PS rules to

generate these examples. There may be no one correct answer; nevertheless, it will be instructive to see how PS rules can be formulated to characterize structures that differ quite significantly from those of English.

(i)   John-ga kita.
         'John came.'
(ii)   Bill-ga shinda.
         'Bill died.'
(iii)   Mary-ga yonda.
         'Mary read.'
(iv)   Mary-ga hon-o yonda.
         'Mary read the book.'
(v)   Bill-ga Mary-o mita.
         'Bill saw Mary.'
(vi)   Mary-ga Bill-o mita.
         'Mary saw Bill.'
(vii)   Hon-ga akai desu.
         'The book is red.'
(viii)   Bill-ga sensei desu.
         'Bill is a teacher.'
(ix)   John-ga ookii desu.
         'John is big.'
(x)   Sono hon-ga ookii desu.
         'That book is big.'
(xi)   Sono akai hon-ga ookii desu.
         'That red book is big.'
(xii)   Bill-ga sono akai hon-o mita.
         'Bill saw that red book.'
(xiii)   Bill-ga hon-o utta.
         'Bill sold the book.'
(xiv)   Bill-ga John-ni hon-o utta.
         'Bill sold the book to John.'
(xv)   Bill-ga John-ni sono akai hon-o utta.
         'Bill sold that red book to John.'
(xvi)   Bill-ga sensei-ni hon-o ageta.
         'Bill gave the book to the teacher.'
(xvii)   Bill-ga kare-no sensei-ni sono akai hon-o ageta.
         'Bill gave that red book to his teacher.'
(xviii) Bill-ga kare-no sensei-ni kare-no hon-o ageta.
         'Bill gave his book to his teacher.'

CHAPTER 2: SUGGESTED READINGS

A concise but clear discussion of simple constituent structures can be found in chapters 2 and 3 of Cattell (1969), where a number of example structures are discussed. The tree diagrams in that work, as in many other works, are not widely accepted in detail but do give a general idea of common structural representations. Jacobs and Rosenbaum (1968, chapters 5 and 6) present some discussion of simple structures and the tests used to determine them.

More traditional, nontransformational linguists have written a good deal about constituent analysis and elementary parsing. Representative examples are the texts by Hockett (1958, chapters 17-31), Hill (1958, chapters 15 and 16), Gleason (1955), and especially Nida (1966). The works of Jespersen contain especially interesting and insightful observations about the structure of English (as well as other languages). Relevant to the discussion in this chapter are Jespersen (1965, chapters XI, XII) and (1969, chapters 34-37).

We have discussed the properties of phrase structure rules in an informal way, concentrating on how phrase structure rules express generalizations about English structure. Additional (informal) discussion of phrase structure rules can be found in Bach (1964, chapters 2 and 3), which covers further restrictions on phrase structure rules in a bit more detail. In particular, Bach provides justification for excluding permutation in a PS grammar (1964, 38). For a highly technical, mathematically precise discussion of the formal properties of phrase structure grammars, see Chomsky and Miller (1963, sections 3 and 4) and Chomsky (1963; 1964). For a thorough discussion of lexical insertion and other issues related to the lexicon, see Chomsky (1965), especially chapter 2.

A detailed discussion of the phrase structure rules for expanding the prepositional phrase (PP) can be found in Jackendoff (1973) and the references cited therein. This article formulates specific PS rules and, more importantly, can give the reader a good idea of the kinds of evidence that might be used to establish the need for particular rules.

THE NEED FOR TRANSFORMATIONS

3.1. THE ENGLISH AUXILIARY: A FIRST PASS

We will now show how the phrase structure grammar of English given in chapter 2 can be modified to accommodate those aspects of the structure of the auxiliary that were described in the final section of that chapter. (We will continue to ignore the differences among is, was, were, etc., and to treat all these forms as a single auxiliary that we will represent as BE; and we will treat HAVE in a similar way.) At the outset, we will deal with HAVE, BE, and the modals separately, and then later we will try to generate more complicated sequences.

The sentences below, which all contain the auxiliary BE, can be generated if we add to our grammar the rule shown to their right.

(3.1) a. John is hitting Bill.
     b. Mary was running away.
                            Aux → BE
     c. They are talking nonsense.
     d. You were treading on my toes.

In the same way, we could add the rule shown below to generate the sentences of (3.2).

(3.2) a. John has seen you.
     b. He had eaten the meat.   Aux → HAVE
     c. I have learned Sanskrit.

Now, since HAVE and BE may occur together in sequence in a sentence, we need another rule as shown to the right of the relevant examples below:

(3.3) a. John has been skating.
     b. Algernon has been asking about you.   Aux → HAVE BE
     c. You have been working too hard.

Notice that since HAVE and BE never occur in reverse order, as in (3.4), we do not want a rule of the form *Aux → BE HAVE.

(3.4) *John is having skated.

Now try to combine the three rules shown above next to examples (3.1), (3.2), and (3.3) into a single rule generating all these examples. Use the abbreviatory devices introduced in chapter 2.

If both HAVE and BE are enclosed in parentheses, as in (3.5), then all the above forms can be generated.

(3.5) Aux → (HAVE) (BE)

When HAVE is omitted and BE chosen, we generate the sentences of (3.1); when only HAVE is chosen, those of (3.2) are generated; if both HAVE and BE are chosen, the sentences of (3.3) are generated. (Notice that if we choose to omit both HAVE and BE, then we generate sentences without auxiliaries, such as John ran, He hit Mary, and so on. We saw in chapter 1 that it might be necessary to postulate an underlying do in such sentences to account for the tag question John ran, didn't he? and related phenomena. For the present it will be simpler to ignore such problems and to assume that there is no underlying do in John ran. In chapter 4 it will be necessary to reconsider that problem in the light of the present discussion.)

We have not accounted for all the data of section 2.6, however, since any one of the set of modals (listed there, and exemplified below) may occur instead of HAVE or BE. We may represent this fact by adding the two rules (3.6e) and (3.6f):

(3.6) a. John will hit Bill.
  b. I can see a spider.
  c. You may leave the room.
  d. Mary should arrive soon.

  e. Aux → Modal
  f. Modal → will, can, may, should, . . .

However, if we simply add these rules to the grammar in addition to rule (3.5), we fail to generate sentences such as (3.7), where a modal appears before either HAVE or BE or both:

(3.7) a. John will have left by then.

b. He <u>may be</u> singing now.
c. Mary <u>should have been</u> thinking.

To include these forms, we may modify rule (3.5), adding a modal before the other elements; if the modal is enclosed in parentheses, then it, too, will be optional:

(3.8) Aux → (Modal) (HAVE) (BE)

Rule (3.8) will generate all the good sentences we have discussed and none that are bad. The reader should verify this, using the grammar given in (2.58) of chapter 2, augmented by rule (3.8) above, to construct trees for a number of examples.

3.2. THE AUXILIARY IN YES/NO QUESTIONS

So far, we have ignored the existence of questions, in which the auxiliaries appear in slightly different positions in the sentence. For example, consider the question (3.9b), which is similar to (3.9a) but exhibits a different word order, the modal preceding the subject NP:

(3.9) a. Harold will eat liver.
      b. Will Harold eat liver?

(A question such as (3.9b) is referred to as a <u>Yes/No Question</u> since its answer will typically be a <u>yes</u> or a <u>no</u>, as opposed to questions such as <u>Who ate the liver?</u>, which instead ask for new information.) While (3.9a) is generated by our grammar, with the structure shown in (3.10a), question (3.9b), which at least at first glance seems to have the structure (3.10b), is not generated.

(3.10) a.

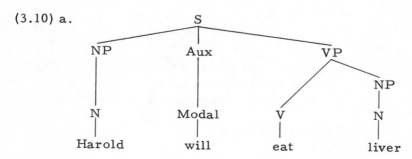

b.

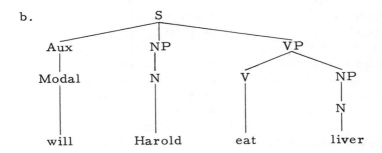

Before trying to generate such forms, let us simplify our original phrase structure grammar and work only with the following rules:

(3.11) a. S   → NP Aux VP
       b. VP → V (NP) (PP)
       c. NP → (Det) N
       d. Aux → (Modal) (HAVE) (BE)

How can this grammar be modified to generate a structure
like (3.10b)?

   For a start, we might try adding the following rule to our
grammar:

(3.12) S → Aux NP VP

Then S would be expanded in two alternative ways, either as
NP Aux VP (by the original rule (3.11a)) or as Aux NP VP
(by (3.12)). At this point—and whenever a new rule is proposed—
the reader should carefully check the consequences by using the
rule within the framework of the existing grammar. Find examples of (a) possible sentences (questions) that (3.12) cannot
generate, and (b) impossible sentences that (3.12) will wrongly
permit us to generate.
   Taking (a) first, we find that the addition of (3.12) to the
grammar will not permit us to derive (3.13a-c):

(3.13) a. Will John be coming?
       b. Could Bill have been kissing Mary?
       c. Has Mary been crying?

The underlined auxiliaries cannot be derived. For although the rule generates structures like (3.10b) where the Aux <u>precedes</u> the NP (while the original rule (3.11a) only allows us to generate ordinary statements in which the Aux <u>follows</u> the NP), we do not yet have a way of permitting some auxiliaries to precede and others to follow the NP in a single sentence.

Before trying to modify the rule so that it will generate the sentences of (3.13a-c), let us consider how it also fails by generating ungrammatical forms. The following are representative:

(3.13) d. *Will <u>have</u> John sung that song?
     e. *Would <u>have been</u> John running?
     f. *Will <u>be</u> you going to town?
     g. *Have <u>been</u> you seeing Mary?

The underlined forms should not have been permitted to appear to the left of the subject. Examples (3.13d-g) make it clear that we cannot introduce the following rule instead of (3.12), even though this proposal would allow us to obtain (3.13a-c):

(3.12') S → (Aux) NP (Aux) VP

This rule would generate (3.13a) with the following structure:

(3.13) a'.

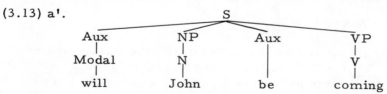

However, like rule (3.12) (i.e., S → Aux NP VP), it would also wrongly generate (3.13d), assigning it this structure:

(3.13) d'.

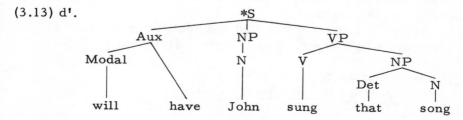

As a matter of fact, although (3.12') allows us to obtain (3.13a-c) (unlike (3.12)), it introduces the possibility of generating yet more ungrammatical forms. For example, we can use it to derive the following structure:

(3.13) h.

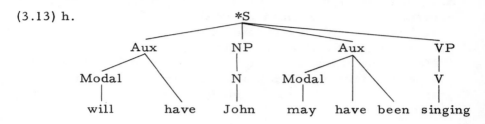

It should now be clear that questions contain one and only one auxiliary verb to the left of the subject NP. Moreover, it is always the auxiliary occupying the first position in the sequence of auxiliaries in an ordinary statement that occurs to the left of the subject in questions. Thus (3.14a) below is ungrammatical because HAVE can never occur before a modal in the first position of a statement like (3.14b). On the other hand, (3.14c) is a possible question, because will can be the first auxiliary in the statement (3.14d). Likewise, (3.15a) is unacceptable because (3.15b) is also bad: have must appear to the left of be, as in (3.15c) and (3.15d).

(3.14) a. *Has John will see her?
       b. *John has will see her.
       c. Will John have seen her?
       d. John will have seen her.

(3.15) a. *Is John having gone an hour?
       b. *John is having gone an hour.
       c. Has John been gone an hour?
       d. John has been gone an hour.

The auxiliary verb to the left of the subject is in the same order relative to the others, as if it were in its usual place. Moreover, none of the other auxiliaries change position in questions. Hence, as the reader can easily verify, there is actually no change in the relative order of the auxiliaries in questions—the first one simply appears to be placed to the left of the subject.

In the light of this observation, it should be very clear that there is no hope of introducing a new rule like (3.12) or (3.12') to derive questions. We must instead break down the structure of Aux for questions, permitting only the first of any string of auxiliaries to appear to the left of the subject. Since under appropriate circumstances any of the auxiliary verbs can appear first, we will have to introduce a number of PS rules, each one dealing with a different initial auxiliary verb.

We will begin with the simple cases and work out from sentences containing only BE in the Aux, gradually enlarging the grammar. We must generate forms of the pattern shown in (3.16):

(3.16) a. Is Hank reading?
       b. Are you eating an apple?

We cannot have the whole Aux appear to the left of the subject, for the reasons already discussed. We must generate only BE in that position. Consequently, in addition to rule (3.11a) (S → NP Aux VP), which gives us ordinary statements, we need (3.17):

(3.17) S → BE NP VP

(Check by using (3.17) to derive examples.)

Instead of BE, HAVE may occur, as in (3.18a, b):

(3.18) a. Has John left?
       b. Has John been singing?

We notice from (3.18b) that BE may optionally appear after the NP when HAVE occurs before it, so the rule for generating sentences like (3.18a) and (3.18b) must be (3.19):

(3.19) S → HAVE NP (BE) VP

Finally, modals may appear to the left of the subject, in which case HAVE and BE optionally follow it:

(3.20) a. <u>Can</u> the dog bite?
     b. <u>Will</u> John <u>have</u> left by now?
     c. <u>Should</u> you <u>have been</u> smoking?

The rule needed for such cases is (3.21):

(3.21) S → Modal NP (HAVE) (BE) VP

And the relevant parts of grammar (3.11) must now be (3.22a-e):

(3.22) a. S   → NP Aux VP
     b. S   → Modal NP (HAVE) (BE) VP
     c. S   → HAVE NP (BE) VP
     d. S   → BE NP VP
     e. Aux → (Modal) (HAVE) (BE)

Now notice that we can scarcely simplify the rules expanding S beyond factoring out the VP:

(3.23)
$$S \rightarrow \begin{Bmatrix} \text{NP Aux} \\ \text{Modal NP (HAVE) (BE)} \\ \text{HAVE NP (BE)} \\ \text{BE NP} \end{Bmatrix} \text{VP}$$

Given the conventions we have established in the last chapter, we cannot combine the subparts of (3.23) any further. This is in direct contrast with the rule for expanding Aux in ordinary positive statements, which eventually reduced to a very simple form, as in (3.22e). Yet recall that this complicated rule, (3.23), is actually representing a very simple generalization:

(3.24) In questions, the auxiliary verbs appear in the same
       relative order as in declarative sentences, but the first
       auxiliary verb occurs to the left of the subject.

In the absence of evidence to the contrary, we must assume that this generalization really captures a significant aspect of the structure of English and hence should be represented in any grammar of English.

3.3. THREE CRITERIA OF ADEQUACY

At this point, it is worth making explicit some underlying principles that have guided our discussion. A grammar for a language must:

(A) Generate <u>all the sentences</u> of that language,
(B) Generate <u>no ill-formed strings</u>, and
(C) Express the <u>linguistically significant generalizations</u> about the language.

These criteria can be illustrated by reference to the discussion of auxiliaries in this chapter.

The first two criteria are straightforward and simply ensure that the grammar generates precisely the language in question. We began the chapter by observing that our grammar would not generate sentences with auxiliaries. Hence it failed to meet the first requirement. We added rule (3.8), repeated here as (3.25):

(3.25) Aux → (Modal) (HAVE) (BE)

This enabled us to meet requirement (A) (at least for the auxiliary structure of simple statements). Our rule generated no ungrammatical forms and thus met requirement (B). Moreover, rule (3.8) seemed to express a correct generalization about the auxiliary system: auxiliary verbs are generated optionally, in a fixed order. Hence, rule (3.8) met the third requirement, but only with respect to the particular data we had examined.

However, since the rule still did not generate auxiliary verbs in questions, it really did not permit us to generate all the required forms after all. From a wider perspective, then, our grammar really failed to meet the first criterion of adequacy. Our first attempt at a more adequate PS treatment of the auxiliary system in questions was (3.12):

(3.12) S → Aux NP VP

But this rule did not allow us to derive sentences like those in (3.18) and (3.20), where parts of the auxiliary remain to the right of the subject:

(3.18) b. Has John <u>been</u> singing?
      c. Should you <u>have been</u> smoking?

Hence rule (3.12), too, failed to meet requirement (A), that a
grammar generate all the sentences of a language. In addition,
this rule generated the unacceptable forms of (3.13d-g):

(3.13) d. *Will have John sung that song?
      e. *Would have been John running?
      f. *Will be you going to town?
      g. *Have been you seeing Mary?

Hence, it also failed to meet requirement (B), that no ill-
formed sentences be generated. We then substituted rule (3.12')
for (3.12):

(3.12') S → (Aux) NP (Aux) VP

This rule, unlike (3.12), could generate grammatical sentences such as (3.18b) and (3.20c) above. Unfortunately, (3.12')
not only generated good sentences but also generated bad ones
such as (3.13h):

(3.13) h. *Will have John may have been singing?

Thus the rule failed again.
    Finally, we built up rule (3.23):

(3.23)
$$S \rightarrow \left\{ \begin{array}{lll} \text{NP} & \text{Aux} & \\ \text{Modal} & \text{NP} & \text{(HAVE) (BE)} \\ \text{HAVE} & \text{NP} & \text{(BE)} \\ \text{BE} & \text{NP} & \end{array} \right\} \text{VP}$$

Rule (3.23) allows our grammar to meet both requirements (A)
and (B) (at least for the range of data under consideration).
    However, rule (3.23) clearly fails to meet our third require-
ment, namely, that the grammar express the linguistically
significant generalizations about the language. For although it
describes which sentences can occur in English, it is only able
to guarantee the correct relative order of HAVE and BE by including <u>three</u> completely separate subrules introducing those

elements in the correct order in different contexts. The mere
fact that three rules are required to state the distribution of
auxiliary verbs is not necessarily bad in itself. But we already
have a rule for expanding Aux in our grammar, which we need
independently for simple declarative sentences (i.e., Aux →
(Modal) (HAVE) (BE)). If we now need to include the following
subparts in rule (3.23),

(3.23') Modal NP (HAVE) (BE)
        HAVE NP (BE)

we are, in effect, restating the PS rule for Aux, in that we
must mention the elements Modal, HAVE, and BE, in their
correct order, twice more in (3.23). The real objection to
rule (3.23) is that it forces us to make three separate statements to capture what seems to be a single, unified generalization about the auxiliary system. Even if rule (3.23) meets
the first two criteria of adequacy, it fails to meet the third.
Since there seems to be no way of using such PS rules to represent an obviously significant generalization about one language, namely, English, we can be sure that phrase structure
grammars cannot possibly represent all the significant aspects
of language structure. We must introduce a new kind of rule
that will permit us to do so.

3.4. THE QUESTION TRANSFORMATION
In chapter 1 we referred briefly to yes/no questions. At that
stage we did not try to define the structure of a question directly but showed how a rule could be stated that would take
any declarative sentence (statement) as input and would generate the related question as output. The rule was stated
roughly as in (3.26):

(3.26) Yes/No Question
        To form a yes/no question, take a declarative sentence
        (statement) and move the first auxiliary to the left of
        the subject NP.

When we formulated that rule we had no way of defining precisely what could constitute a declarative sentence in English.
More important, we had no way of defining the subject of a
sentence. The PS rules developed in chapter 2 generate Eng-

lish statements along with appropriate structures in such a
way that notions such as subject can now be rigorously defined: the subject is the NP directly dominated by S.

  As we have seen, however, PS rules cannot be extended to
generate English questions in any natural way. Let us therefore add to our present model (which uses PS rules alone)
transformational rules like (3.26) that operate on trees originally built by PS rules to generate new trees. (This expanded
model constitutes a more explicit version of the model we were
tacitly assuming in the first chapter.) Thus a precise statement of rule (3.26) will have to be phrased in such a way that
it will take as input a tree such as (3.27)—which is generated
directly by our PS rules—and will yield as its output tree
(3.28)—which is not directly generated by the PS rules.

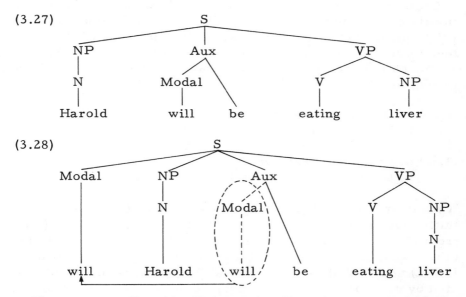

(3.27)

(3.28)

The sentence Harold will be eating liver is generated by the
PS rules and lexical insertion alone and hence is simply one of
the many possible outputs of the base component. On the other
hand, the generation of the sentence Will Harold be eating
liver? involves not only PS rules and lexical insertion but also
the use of the Yes/No Question Transformation. The only difference between (3.27) and (3.28) is the use of that transformation operating on (3.27) to produce (3.28).

  Such a rule will provide a direct representation of the syn-

tactic generalization discussed earlier. Because rule (3.26)
derives questions from statements, it guarantees that the relative order of auxiliary verbs in questions remains the same as
in statements. An ungrammatical question such as *Has he will
be eating liver? could never be generated by the rule, since the
presumed input to the transformation would have to be the ungrammatical statement *He has will be eating liver, which
would never be generated by the PS rules. The Yes/No Question Transformation permits us to derive all auxiliaries from
the common node Aux instead of forcing us to generate each
one separately in questions; hence, it allows us to avoid the ad
hoc repetitions of rule (3.23)—which were introduced solely because we were trying to use PS rules to state generalizations
that such rules cannot express in a straightforward manner.

Let us now consider one further way in which the transformational account appears to be superior: it alone reflects certain
relationships between sentences. Native speakers of English
tend to judge that statement/question pairs such as (3.29a, b)
are much more closely related to each other than, for example,
(3.30a, b):

(3.29) a. Harold will eat liver.
       b. Will Harold eat liver?

(3.30) a. Harold will eat liver.
       b. Does it often rain outside the Lake District?

A transformational treatment of questions reflects these intuitive judgments: transformation (3.26) actually derives (3.29b)
from (3.29a), but no rule derives (3.30b) from (3.30a). On the
other hand, the phrase structure account of questions treats
(3.29a) and (3.29b) as unrelated: while (3.29a) would be generated by using rule (3.11a), (3.29b) would involve rule (3.23). It
is very important to notice that we cannot appeal to raw intuition in support of an analysis. Our theory is constructed on the
basis of systematic, independent evidence. But the theory is
further confirmed insofar as it illuminates and explains the
basis for the native speaker's judgments.

3.5. THE PASSIVE TRANSFORMATION
We have seen that at least one syntactic construction of English—the yes/no question—cannot be generated by PS rules

alone but must also involve a transformational rule. In discussing the Question Transformation, we have only begun to provide justification for including such rules in our theory. There are numerous constructions in English (and other languages) that demonstrate the need for transformational rules; it is only when we have motivated a number of rules and observed their interaction that we see the strength of the evidence for including them in our theory. We will briefly consider some of the ways in which the passive construction provides further evidence that transformations must be used to state significant generalizations of English syntax.

Consider the following pairs of sentences:

(3.31) a. The Colts beat the Jets.
       b. The Jets were beaten by the Colts.

(3.32) a. The dog ate the food.
       b. The food was eaten by the dog.

(3.33) a. The police have watched John for two days.
       b. John has been watched by the police for two days.

(3.34) a. The Colts could have beaten the Jets.
       b. The Jets could have been beaten by the Colts.

(3.35) a. Herb is bothering Mary.
       b. Mary is being bothered by Herb.

Without trying to relate the active/passive pairs (and continuing to ignore the details of verb inflection), formulate changes in our phrase structure rules (i.e., grammar (3.11)) so that they generate the above passive sentences.

The passive sentences exhibit certain constant characteristics that do not need any special changes in the phrase structure rules. They all contain a phrase (after the main verb) headed by the preposition by. The noun phrase in that prepositional phrase is the same as the subject of the corresponding active sentence, while the subject of the passive sentence is the same as the object of the related active sentence. However, these facts introduce nothing that is structurally new, and a plausible structure for (3.31b) is (3.36).

(3.36)

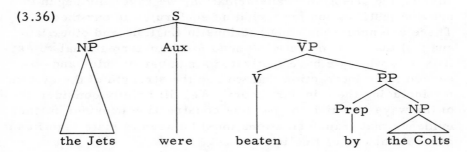

This is superficially parallel to (3.37), which is a structure already generated by the rules we formulated in grammar (3.11).

(3.37)

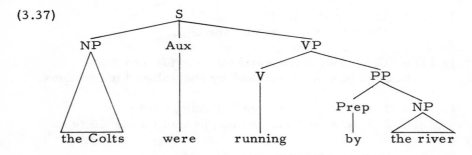

Notice that the sentence represented by structure (3.37) is not a passive sentence. The simplest way to test this at the present stage is to note that (3.37) has no sentence paired with it in the manner of the pairs (3.31)-(3.35): there is no sentence corresponding to (3.37) roughly of the form *The river ran the Colts. However, the sentence represented by (3.36) is indeed a passive sentence and is paired with an active counterpart, namely, The Colts beat the Jets. Since our phrase structure grammar already generates (nonpassive) sentences with structures that are parallel to the structure of passive sentences, it could presumably generate sentence (3.36) too.

However, there is a further characteristic of passive sentences, which, although it appears at first sight to be taken care of by our grammar, nevertheless forces changes in the system. This is the verb be, which in some form or other is present in all the (b) sentences of (3.31)-(3.35). Of course,

there is already a verb be that appears at the end of the auxiliary, introduced by the rule Aux → (Modal) (HAVE) (BE).
However, we can show that this is not the same be as that
found in the passive. Examine sentence (3.38), which has two
occurrences of be in the auxiliary:

(3.38) Mary is being bothered by Herb.

In fact, sentences like the following one appear to be perfectly
good (though hardly common in colloquial speech):

(3.39) At three o'clock that patient should have been being
       examined by the doctor.

A modal, HAVE, and two verbs be appear in (3.39). Thus, we
must at least introduce an additional be as the last element of
the auxiliary:

(3.40) Aux → (Modal) (HAVE) (BE) (be)

   There are now two verbs at the end of the auxiliary that are,
in a sense, the same verb, which we represent as BE and be.
The first of these, BE, is the so-called progressive auxiliary,
and the last, be, is the passive auxiliary. The reasons for
distinguishing between the two verbs will be discussed in chapter 4. For the moment, suffice it to say that the passive be
causes the verb following it to appear in a different form (e.g.,
broken, watched, sung) from the form of verbs immediately
following the ordinary BE discussed earlier (breaking, watching,
singing). Continuing to ignore these differences, notice that a
rule such as (3.40) will generate the basic auxiliary sequence
found in (3.38) and (3.39) and will exclude improper sequences,
such as those in (3.41), since our rule permits neither be to
occur before any other auxiliary:

(3.41) a. *John is had watched by the police.
       b. *The Jets could be have beaten by the Colts.

   Phrase structure rule (3.40) makes certain empirical predictions about the passive auxiliary be. It represents be in
exactly the same manner in which it represents the other auxiliary verbs—as a parenthesized optional element—and thus it

predicts that be will behave like any other auxiliary verb. Certainly there is nothing in the rule that would lead us to expect differences between be and the other auxiliary verbs, and indeed be does behave like other auxiliaries in certain ways. For example, it can be fronted by the Question Rule. Compare the questions corresponding to the passive sentence (3.36) and the nonpassive (3.37):

(3.42) a. Were the Colts beaten by the Jets?
       b. Were the Colts running by the river?

In both cases, be precedes the subject NP. But it turns out that rule (3.40) will create serious complications in our description of English auxiliary verbs. The prediction that the passive auxiliary functions like any other auxiliary turns out to be wrong in certain important ways.

   First, notice that since rule (3.40) makes be an optional element, it embodies the claim that we are free to choose or not to choose be in applying the rule. But examine sentences (3.31)-(3.35) again. It is possible to choose the passive be only if the main verb of the sentence is transitive. If the main verb is intransitive (i.e., if it cannot be followed by an NP in an active sentence), then be cannot occur:

(3.43)   The food was eaten (by the dog). (ate is transitive)

(3.44) *The dog was died (by the man). (die is intransitive)

No other auxiliary verb is restricted in this way; we are free to choose other auxiliaries regardless of whether the main verb is transitive or intransitive:

(3.45) a. The dog may die. (may eat the food)
       b. The dog has died. (has eaten the food)
       c. The dog may have been dying for a month. (may have
          been eating the food)

   Second, the passive be cannot be chosen if the main verb of the sentence is directly followed by a simple NP (whether or not a prepositional phrase follows that NP):

(3.46) *The food was eaten the dog (by the river).

But it must be chosen if the main verb is transitive and is followed directly by a constituent consisting of <u>by</u> and NP:

(3.47) a. *The dog has beaten by the man.
       b. The dog has <u>been</u> beaten by the man.

No other auxiliary verb is restricted in this way; the presence
or absence of an NP after the main verb does not restrict the
occurrence of any other auxiliary verb.

   Even if we could place appropriate restrictions on the occurrence of <u>be</u>, note that any phrase structure treatment of
passive sentences will be quite unable to account naturally for
the following fact: in a related active-passive pair, it is the
subject of the active sequence that appears in the <u>by phrase</u> of
the passive, while the object of the active is the <u>subject</u> of the
passive:

(3.31) a. <u>The Colts beat the Jets</u>.

       b. <u>The Jets were beaten by the Colts</u>.

Keeping this observation in mind, consider the following sentences:

(3.48) a. John admires sincerity.
       b. *Sincerity admires John.

(3.49) a. *John frightens sincerity.
       b. Sincerity frightens John.

As (3.48) shows, active sentences with the main verb <u>admire</u>
make sense only if their subjects refer to animate (better still,
human) beings. On the other hand, <u>frighten</u> requires instead
that the <u>object</u> refer to animate beings, as (3.49) shows.

   In passive sentences, these facts are exactly reversed:

(3.48') a. Sincerity is admired by John.
        b. *John is admired by sincerity.

(3.49') a. *Sincerity is frightened by John.
        b. John is frightened by sincerity.

Precisely how the facts exhibited by (3.48) and (3.49) are to be represented is not crucial here. The important point is simply this: if active-passive pairs such as (3.48a) and (3.48'a) are to be generated by separate phrase structure rules and not related in some way, then we will be forced to make statements such as (3.50):

(3.48) a. John admires sincerity.

(3.48') a. Sincerity is admired by John.

(3.50) The verb admire must have (a) an animate subject in an active sentence but (b) an animate NP in the by phrase in a passive sentence.

Yet these two statements express what is essentially a single fact about the verb admire. An analogous argument can be made for frighten, using (3.49) and (3.49').

To summarize, a phrase structure treatment of passive sentences based on rule (3.40) will fail to capture the fact that various restrictions apply to the passive be but not to other auxiliaries: (1) be occurs only with transitive verbs; (2) it cannot occur even then if the main verb is followed directly by just a simple NP; (3) it must occur if the main verb is followed directly by a PP with by and NP; and (4) when be occurs, any NP that is appropriate as the subject of the active sentence is now appropriate in the by phrase (as shown in (3.48)/(3.48') and (3.49)/(3.49')).

Since PS rules of the type discussed in chapter 2 and earlier in this chapter cannot be formulated to restrict be in this way, some other method of generating sentences seems to be required. A very natural way to proceed is to try to state a transformation for forming a passive sentence from an active sentence (just as questions were formed from declarative sentences):

(3.51) Passive Transformation
    Given an active sentence,
    a. "Interchange" the subject and object NPs of the active sentence;
    b. Insert by before the new "object"; and
    c. Insert be after all (other) members of the auxiliary.

This rule is illustrated in the following example:

(3.31) a. The Colts beat the Jets.

     b. The Jets were beaten by the Colts.

If we postulate a Passive Transformation along these lines, we can avoid the problems discussed above:

(i)   Since the Passive Transformation requires both a subject and an object to be present, it will automatically insert passive be only in transitive sentences. Hence, our original phrase structure rule for the auxiliary, Aux → (Modal) (HAVE) (BE), can be left in this general form. We do not need to have a rule Aux → (Modal) (HAVE) (BE) (be), which would introduce the problem of stating special restrictions limiting be to transitive sentences containing by.

(ii)   Sentences such as *John has beaten by Mary will not be generated, because if by is inserted before Mary, then be will be inserted by the same rule before beaten, yielding John has been beaten by Mary.

(iii) Since passive sentences are derived by interchanging the subject and object of active sentences (cf. (3.51a)), then a deviant passive sentence such as *John is admired by sincerity can be derived only from a similarly deviant sentence *Sincerity admires John. The deviant passive sentence will automatically be excluded if we exclude its active counterpart.

3.6. THE INTERACTION OF THE PASSIVE AND QUESTION RULES

We have now seen that there are sentences of English that cannot be generated by a phrase structure grammar without losing significant generalizations. Such sentences lead us to suppose that the structure of English can be adequately described only if at least two transformations are used in addition to the phrase structure rules: a Passive Transformation and a Question Transformation.

(3.52) The fly has been eaten by the mosquito.   Passive

(3.53) Has the mosquito eaten the fly?   <u>Question</u>

In each case, if we follow the arguments of the previous sections, the relevant transformation has to be applied to a tree
roughly represented by (3.54)—which was itself built by phrase
structure rules:

(3.54)

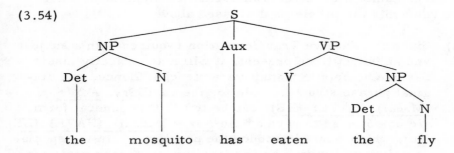

Only one transformation, Passive, is applied to (3.54) to
change it into (3.52'), the tree corresponding to example (3.52).

(3.52')

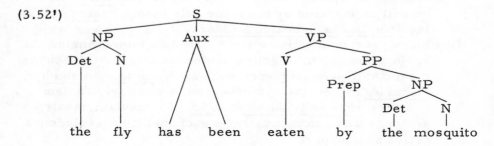

Likewise, only the Question Transformation is applied to (3.54)
to change it into (3.53'), the tree corresponding to (3.53).

(3.53')

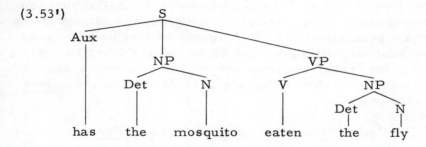

Thus, the basic sentence The mosquito has eaten the fly is derived by PS rules and lexical insertion alone and is assigned structure (3.54). The question and passive forms of that sentence are derived by using that structure as the input to two separate transformations, deriving new structures as output. The two transformations seem thus far to be entirely independent of each other. It is conceivable that in the derivation of a sentence at most one transformation applies to a basic tree built by phrase structure rules. Then we would find sentences to which either the Passive or the Question Rule had applied, or neither—but never both.

However, it turns out that there is no such limit to the number of transformations that can apply to a tree. Consider the following sentence:

(3.55) Has the fly been eaten by the mosquito?

What transformation(s) have applied in the derivation of (3.55)?

This sentence is both a passive and a question. The most obvious way of deriving it is to start with the same basic tree we proposed for (3.52) and (3.53) and then to apply both the Passive and the Question Rules, as shown in (3.56a)-(3.56c). The second of these trees, resulting from the application of the Passive to our original tree, (3.54), is, of course, just the same as (3.52'). The output of a transformation is a new structure, which in turn may become the input to another transformation. Hence, we apply the Question Transformation to the output of the Passive Transformation and produce an entirely new tree, corresponding to the passive question (3.55).

One might suppose, instead, that there is a single Passive-Question Transformation to turn (3.56a) directly into (3.56c), without the intermediate step (3.56b). The reader is invited to try formulating such a transformation, along the lines of the separate Question Rule, (3.26), and Passive Rule, (3.51). What is wrong with such an approach to the derivation of passive questions?

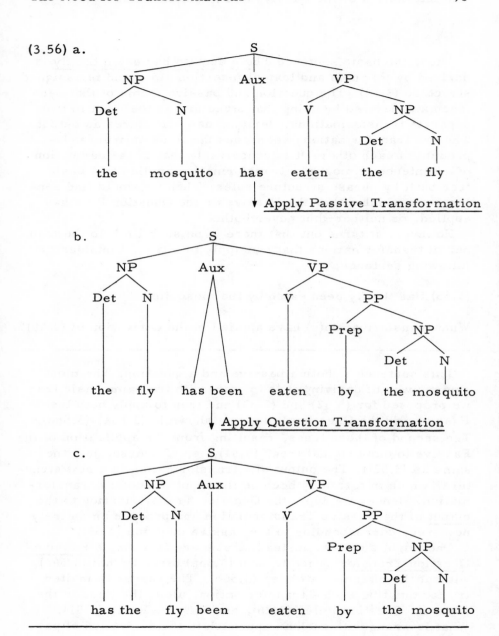

The simplest formulation of a single Passive-Question Rule seems to be no more than a juxtaposition of the already needed Passive and Question Rules:

(3.57) <u>Passive-Question Rule</u>
  a. "Interchange" the subject and object
     NPs of the active sentence;
  b. Insert <u>by</u> before the new "object";   = Passive
  c. Insert <u>be</u> after all (other) mem-   Rule (3.51)
     bers of the auxiliary; and
  d. Move the first auxiliary verb to the   = Yes/No Ques-
     left of the subject NP.   tion Rule (3.26)

Clearly there is no point in including such a rule in our
grammar when the rules that are already needed for other
purposes will do the same work if they are applied in order.
We can conclude, therefore, that (3.55) must be derived by
permitting both the Passive Rule and the Question Rule to
apply to (3.54) and therefore that more than one transformation may apply in the derivation of a single sentence.

If it is the case that certain sentences must be derived by
applying a number of transformations in sequence, then the
following possibility arises: if two transformations, A and B,
must both apply in the derivation of a sentence, then the rules
must be applied in a specific fixed order, say in the order A
first and then B, but not in the opposite order. Moreover, it
may be possible to make an even stronger claim: that there is
a single order in which those two rules are applied, so that if
they are ever applied in the order A/B, then they must always
be applied in that order.

In discussing the Passive and Question Rules, we gave derivation (3.56a)-(3.56c), in which the Passive Transformation
operated first, followed by the Question Transformation. We
did not prove that our particular ordering of rules was <u>neces-
sary</u>—only that it was <u>possible</u> in the derivation of the particular sentence under consideration. It is still quite conceivable
that we could apply the rules in either of the following orders—
or that they could sometimes apply in one order, sometimes
in the other:

(3.58) a. Passive Transformation <u>first</u>
       b. Question Transformation <u>second</u>

(3.59) a. Question Transformation <u>first</u>
       b. Passive Transformation <u>second</u>

At a rather superficial level it is easy to see that we could not derive (3.60),

(3.60) Was the fly eaten by the mosquito?

unless the rules were applied in the following order:

    1. Passive
    2. Question

To see why, consider the following derivation:

(3.61) a. The mosquito ate the fly,
       | Passive
   b. The fly was eaten by the mosquito.
       | Question
   c. Was the fly eaten by the mosquito?

The Question Transformation has to operate on the passive (3.61b) to form the passive question (3.61c). It fronts the passive be; but, of course, that be is not even present in the structure until the Passive Rule has operated. Hence there seems to be no way in which the Question Rule could yield (3.61c) (=(3.60)) unless the rules were applied in the order:

    1. Passive
    2. Question

Therefore, in the absence of counterexamples, we seem justified in assuming that these two rules are always applied in this order.

We have just seen the first of many cases in which transformational rules interact with each other. Of particular interest here is the fact that the interaction of the Passive and Question Rules provides us with evidence in favor of these transformations that goes far beyond the evidence for each rule in itself. Once we have justified independently a Question Transformation and Passive Transformation, then these rules will interact with each other in a completely automatic way to generate passive questions; if our grammar contained PS rules alone, we would need rules of incredible complexity by this

point. Not only would we need separate PS rules to generate
simple active declarative sentences, questions, and passive
sentences, as we have seen above; but also we would now need
to include yet further PS rules so that passive questions could
be generated as well. Whereas the Passive and Question Transformations automatically interact to yield passive questions,
the separate PS rules for passives and questions would not.
Instead of demonstrating this in detail, we will leave it as an
exercise for the reader and will introduce evidence for yet
another transformation that interacts with both Passive and
Question, further strengthening the evidence for a transformational account of both those constructions.

Let us examine some data that provide evidence for a rule
of Negative Insertion. Given the following sentences, try to
formulate a rule that will transform each of the positive (a)
sentences into the corresponding negative (b) sentences:

(3.62) a. The Spanish moss is growing well.
       b. The Spanish moss is not growing well.

(3.63) a. Bill has left his home.
       b. Bill has not left his home.

(3.64) a. Herb may have been canoeing down the Colorado.
       b. Herb may not have been canoeing down the Colorado.

(3.65) a. Sheila has been eating ground grasshoppers.
       b. Sheila has not been eating ground grasshoppers.

As we saw in chapter 1, the formation of negative sentences
from positive sentences is based on a very simple generalization: the negative word not is placed immediately after the first
auxiliary verb. Thus, it is quite simple to state a transformation such as the following:

(3.66) Negative Insertion (optional)
       Given a positive declarative sentence, insert the word
       not immediately after the first auxiliary verb.

To see how rule (3.66) works, consider the following pair of sentences:

(3.67) a. John will be singing.
       b. John will not be singing.

The sentence <u>John will be singing</u> derives from a structure such as (3.68a):

(3.68) a.

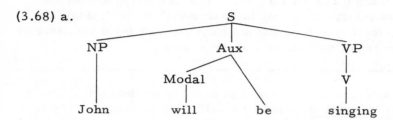

The Negative Insertion Transformation stated above will operate on a tree such as this to produce the following new tree:

(3.68) b.

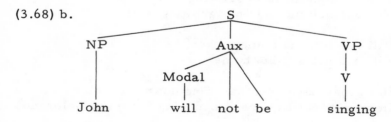

In this way, then, we are able to generate negative sentences in a relatively uncomplicated manner.

Notice that the Negative Insertion Transformation is similar to the Question Transformation in an important respect: both rules make crucial reference to the <u>first</u> auxiliary verb, whatever that verb may be. The Question Rule fronts the first aux-
iliary, placing it to the left of the subject; the Negative Inser-
tion Rule places <u>not</u> after the first auxiliary. If we attempt to generate negative sentences by means of a PS rule, we can no longer make reference to "the first auxiliary verb." A PS rule for negatives, like our PS rule for questions, must therefore list all of the different possible contexts where <u>not</u> occurs within the Aux:

(3.69)

$$\text{Aux} \rightarrow \begin{cases} \text{Modal (not) (HAVE) (BE)} \\ \text{HAVE (not) (BE)} \\ \text{BE (not)} \end{cases}$$

Once again, the transformation (3.66) seems to state a significant generalization, while this phrase structure treatment amounts to nothing more than an unilluminating list of facts. As before, we have initial evidence in favor of the transformational treatment.

However, when we look at the interaction of Negative Insertion and the other constructions we have discussed, we find much stronger evidence for a transformational treatment of negative sentences. Let us once again assume that our theory will make use of PS rules alone. As we saw earlier, this would require that we include the following rule to generate both questions and statements directly:

(3.70) a.

$$S \rightarrow \begin{cases} \text{NP Aux} \\ \text{Modal NP (HAVE) (BE)} \\ \text{HAVE NP (BE)} \\ \text{BE NP} \end{cases} \text{VP}$$

   b. Aux → (Modal) (HAVE) (BE)

Now notice that in addition to positive questions, there are negative questions:

(3.71) a. Can't John sing?
       b. Hasn't the soup spilled?
       c. Isn't Mary driving?

These sentences cannot be generated by PS rule (3.70). Assuming for the moment that can't is just the same as can + not, we could modify the rules of (3.70) to generate these new examples by introducing not into the rule, as shown below:

(3.72) a.

$$S \rightarrow \begin{cases} \text{NP Aux} \\ \text{Modal (not) NP (HAVE) (BE)} \\ \text{HAVE (not) NP (BE)} \\ \text{BE (not) NP} \end{cases} \text{VP}$$

   b.

$$\text{Aux} \rightarrow \begin{cases} \text{(Modal (not)) (HAVE) (BE)} \\ \text{(HAVE (not)) (BE)} \\ \text{(BE (not))} \end{cases}$$

By now the degree of redundancy in the PS rules is very striking—HAVE and BE occur in that order <u>four</u> times in (3.72). If
we try, in addition, to generate passives by PS rules, then we
need to add at least one more line to each of parts (a) and (b)
of (3.72) in order to generate the following, for example:

(3.73) a. Donkeys aren't eaten by many people.
       b. Wasn't that watch stolen by the burglar?

   It should be clear that the discussion in the earlier sections
of this chapter brought to light only a small number of the
ways in which the overall grammar is simplified by introducing
transformations. Notice that it is not so much that the Negative Insertion Transformation provides direct evidence for the
Question Transformation, or vice versa, for neither would be
very greatly complicated if we failed to include the other in
our theory. The rules of (3.72) show rather that, if there were
no transformations, the <u>overall grammar</u> would be very greatly
complicated, and once we include one rule of this general type,
then the way is open to include many. As we proceed in our
work we shall encounter numerous additional cases of rule interaction of the sort we have described here.

CHAPTER 3: EXERCISES
(E3.1) One form that <u>negative questions</u> can take is illustrated
in (i)-(iii):

(i)   <u>Is</u> John <u>not</u> running?
(ii)   <u>Has</u> John <u>not</u> been running?
(iii)   <u>Will</u> John <u>not</u> have been running?

In contrast, the following are ungrammatical:

(i')   *<u>Is not</u> John running?
(ii')   *<u>Has not</u> John been running?
(iii') *<u>Will not</u> John have been running?

Many speakers prefer contracted negative questions of the form
<u>Isn't John running</u>? to those of (i)-(iii), but for the purpose of
this exercise such forms should be entirely ignored. It is clear
that even speakers who find (i)-(iii) less than fully acceptable
consider them very much better than the totally unacceptable

(i')-(iii'), and for the purposes of this exercise we will treat sentences like (i)-(iii) as the only fully grammatical examples of negative questions.

Basing your answer solely on the contrast between (i)-(iii) and (i')-(iii')—and similar pairs—determine the <u>order</u> in which the Question and Negative Transformations must be applied to a declarative sentence. In answering this question, construct an explicit argument, showing in detail how the correct order allows the rules to be more simply stated than the incorrect order.

(E3.2) After doing question (E3.1), add contracted sentences to your data base:

<u>A</u>. First consider the fact that negative declarative sentences may occur in two forms:

(i)   Jane <u>is not</u> here.
(ii) Jane <u>isn't</u> here.

A transformational rule might be proposed to turn (i) into (ii), and similarly for other input-output pairs. Formulate a suitable rule, taking into account only declarative pairs such as (i) and (ii) and others like them that contain additional auxiliary verbs.

<u>B</u>. Now consider the following examples:

(iii) a.   Is John <u>not</u> here?
       b.   <u>Isn't</u> John here?
(iv) a. *<u>Is not</u> John here?
       b. *<u>Is</u> John <u>n't</u> here?

(Again assume that sentences of the form (iiia) are grammatical, even if, in your own mind, they sound too formal.)

How should the previously formulated <u>Question</u>, <u>Negative</u>, and <u>Contraction Transformations</u> be ordered so as to generate the grammatical examples (i), (ii), and (iii), while excluding the ungrammatical examples (iva) and (ivb)? Again show in detail why the ordering is necessary.

<u>C</u>. A (rather complex) set of phrase structure rules could be

formulated to generate contracted and uncontracted positive and negative statements and questions—i.e., sentences of the form (i), (ii), and (iii)—while excluding (iva) and (ivb). Try to formulate an appropriate set of rules.

<u>D</u>. Finally, show precisely where it is that these phrase structure rules are redundant and hence fail to capture important generalizations in the data that are captured very naturally by the transformational treatment using the rules of <u>Question</u>, <u>Negative Insertion</u>, and <u>Contraction</u> operating on routine declarative sentences.

Readers whose judgments of examples (i)-(iv) differ markedly from those assumed for the purposes of this exercise may find it instructive to try to provide sets of rules that account more adequately for their own dialects—and to discuss the ways in which their grammars appear to vary from that which we have assumed.

(E3.3) A. On pages 104-107 we have seen some evidence for using a transformation to generate negative sentences. Additional evidence for a transformational account of negation is provided by certain passive sentences. Assume that there is a passive transformation that operates in the way set out in the text of this chapter. Given that assumption, how do sentences like (i) provide independent evidence that there is a Negative Transformation?

(i) John was not eaten by the centipede.

In your answer you should make precise, specific reference to complexities and/or redundancies in the rules needed to generate negative and passive sentences, which are avoided if there is a negative transformation along the lines discussed in the text.

<u>B</u>. Making the same assumption (i.e., that there is a passive transformation), show how sentence (ii) provides evidence for a Question Transformation:

(ii) Was that watch stolen by the burglar?

Once again, show precisely what complications are avoided by postulating the Question Transformation.

(E3.4) In the present chapter, we have shown that although PS rules capture certain aspects of the structure of English, they must be supplemented by transformational rules. One of the constructions discussed in chapter 1 (before we had formulated either PS rules or transformations) was tag questions.

<u>A</u>. Review the discussion of chapter 1; did we assume there that tag questions were generated directly by PS rules—or that they were generated by a transformation that operated on existing trees? Justify your answer.

<u>B</u>. Is it possible to demonstrate that the simplest treatment of tag questions involves a transformation? (Consider using essentially the same method of argument as that developed in the text for the Question and Passive Transformations.) In answering this question, refer specifically to examples such as the following:

(i) a.   Mary was at home, wasn't she?
    b. *Mary was at home, aren't they?
    c. *Mary was at home, wasn't he?

Any account of tags must ensure that sentences such as (ib) and (ic) are not generated. Can this be better achieved by PS rules or by a transformation? Justify your answer in detail.

<u>C</u>. Assuming that a Tag Transformation were introduced into the grammar, how would that rule be ordered with respect to the following transformations:

(a) Passive
(b) Negative Insertion

Given the way we stated the Tag Rule in chapter 1, there is only one ordering of that rule with respect to Passive and Negative Insertion that will make the facts work out correctly. In establishing the ordering, use specific example sentences.

(E3.5) For further thinking, consider how yes/no questions and negatives are formed in some other language(s). Is there any evidence that these should be formed by transformation rather than being directly generated by phrase structure rules? In-

clude in your answer an outline phrase structure grammar of
the language(s) and roughly formulated transformations, if
any. Always provide suitable examples to motivate the rules
that you consider necessary. (N.B. You may well find that
there is no advantage in a transformational account of these
particular constructions in the language you select. What implications, if any, does this have for the idea that questions
and declaratives form related pairs in English?)

CHAPTER 3: SUGGESTED READINGS
In this chapter we have argued that certain linguistically significant generalizations cannot be expressed by a theory that
includes phrase structure rules alone and that transformations
must be postulated in addition. The classic presentation of arguments of this sort is in Chomsky (1957) (especially chapter 5).
The discussion of transformations in that work is more formal
than our discussion in this chapter, but by the end of chapter 4
it should present few problems for the reader. Chomsky (1958)
also argues for a transformational theory and, again, does so
from a more formal standpoint. Chomsky (1957) also presents
a number of arguments showing that certain sentences in natural languages cannot be generated by a phrase structure
grammar; their structure is, in principle, of a sort that lies
beyond the generative power of phrase structure grammars.
Postal (1964a) presents the same sort of argument.

The analysis of passive sentences presented in this chapter
is based on arguments first presented by Chomsky (1957). By
this stage the reader should be able to follow the general
points of the discussion of the passive transformation presented
in section 5.4 of that work. In later work, Chomsky (1965, 103-
105) presents quite a different analysis of the passive. (This
second reading is best postponed until after chapter 4.) The
reader may also wish to note for future reference other analyses of passive sentences. Hasegawa (1968) presents a much
more abstract analysis of passive sentences than that considered here, and Lakoff (1971) presents a critical review of
his analysis (as well as Chomsky's) along with further pro-
posals and problems connected with the passive.

THE STRUCTURE OF THE ENGLISH AUXILIARY

4.1. THE PROBLEM OF AUXILIARY DO

We saw in the last chapter that the Passive and Question Transformations interact to produce passive questions in derivations
such as the following:

(4.1) The mosquito ate the fly.

     ↓   Passive Transformation

(4.2) The fly was eaten by the mosquito.

     ↓   Question Transformation

(4.3) Was the fly eaten by the mosquito?

We argued that the Passive must apply before the Question
Transformation because, in producing a question such as
(4.3), the Question Rule fronts the passive auxiliary be, which
is not even present in the structure until Passive has applied.
    This rule ordering is correct, as we shall see from further
data given in the final section of this chapter. Nevertheless,
we do not have to look far to discover that there are rather
serious problems in our analysis, even if the rules apply in
their correct order. We have been ignoring the fact that the
active sentence (4.1), The mosquito ate the fly, has a related
question, namely, (4.4):

(4.4) Did the mosquito eat the fly?

In (4.4), the auxiliary do appears—a point we have been ignoring since chapter 1. There we argued that questions with do
suggest that even a sentence such as (4.1) contains a do that is
deleted under appropriate circumstances.
    If we tried to formalize that suggestion, we would have to
assume that (4.1) is actually derived from a structure like
(4.5). (We would have to modify our rule expanding Aux in some
way, since no do is introduced by the present rule Aux → (Modal)
(HAVE) (BE).)
    The Question Rule could then apply in a perfectly regular
way to (4.5), to yield the question Did the mosquito eat the fly?

(4.5)

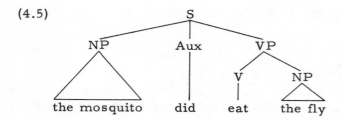

This is exactly what was suggested in the first chapter. To complete the formalization of that account, we would, of course, need a rule ordered after the Question Rule to delete the underlying do of tree (4.5), just in case the Question Rule is not applied. As long as we said that do deletes when a verb immediately follows it, our rule would allow do to remain in questions (where do is followed by an NP, not a verb) but would cause it to be deleted in statements. This would yield the related active statement (4.1), The mosquito ate the fly.

But now our simple analysis of passives and questions is thrown into doubt. For if tree (4.5) is really the underlying tree for sentence (4.1), then the Passive Rule is applied to that tree and not to the simple sentence The mosquito ate the fly. The Passive Rule (as currently stated) adds be at the end of the Aux. Hence the effect of applying the Passive to tree (4.5) is the following:

(4.6)

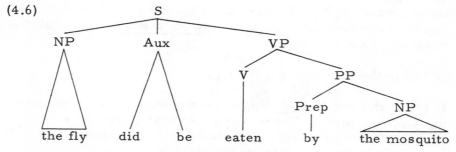

*The fly did be eaten by the mosquito.

How can we avoid this obviously ungrammatical sentence? Perhaps the rule that deletes do from statements such as The mosquito ate the fly will also delete do here, yielding sentence (4.2), The fly was eaten by the mosquito. But recall that the Question Rule must have a chance to apply to a tree before the rule deleting <u>do</u>. This is the only order that will generate questions like <u>Did the mosquito eat the fly?</u> For if the rule deleting <u>do</u> applied to tree (4.5) before the Question Rule, then there would never be a <u>do</u> left to be moved to the front of the sentence. Yet if the Question Rule preceded the rule deleting <u>do</u>, there would be nothing to prevent the former rule from operating on tree (4.6) (produced by the Passive) to yield the ungrammatical sentence (4.7):

(4.7) *Did the fly be eaten by the mosquito?

We have arrived at a syntactic paradox of sorts. On the one hand, it seems necessary to assume that auxiliary <u>do</u> is "inherent" in the structure of the sentence <u>The mosquito ate the fly</u>, for if we make that assumption, then we can generate questions such as <u>Did the mosquito eat the fly?</u> in a regular way. On the other hand, if we assume that <u>do</u> is in the underlying structure of such sentences as <u>The mosquito ate the fly</u>, then the Passive and Question Rules interact to produce ungrammatical sentences such as (4.7). All this strongly suggests that we must examine auxiliary <u>do</u> much more carefully, for until we provide a precise account of how <u>do</u> works, we cannot determine whether or not the Passive and Question Rules can interact in such a way as to generate only grammatical sentences.

4.2. THE INTERNAL STRUCTURE OF THE AUXILIARY

Before we are able to talk meaningfully about how <u>do</u> works, we must examine certain aspects of the auxiliary system that we have already attempted to account for in our rule Aux → (Modal) (HAVE) (BE). The reader may well have noticed by now a pervasive problem in our account of English sentences. We have been quite arbitrarily citing each auxiliary or main verb in its correct inflectional form, yet our grammar contains at present no explicit rules to determine that form. As is quite obvious from the following examples, the use of the wrong form of a verb produces completely ungrammatical strings:

(4.8) a. John is writing.
      b. *John is write.

            c. *John is wrote.
            d. *John is written.

(4.9)   a.   John has written.
        b. *John has writing.
        c. *John has write.
        d. *John has wrote.

(4.10) a.   John may write (can write, will write, etc.).
        b. *John may writing.
        c. *John may wrote.
        d. *John may written.

We have been assuming that the PS rules would somehow generate the following trees, in which each verb is in its correct form:

(4.11)

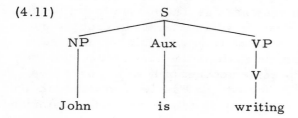

(4.12)

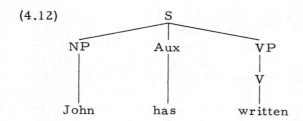

(4.13)

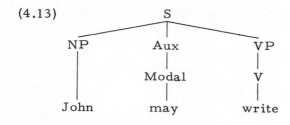

Concentrating for the moment only on the main verb, we notice
that this appears in three different forms (writing, written,
write). Yet the main verb is always dominated by the same
node V, and we can recognize the three forms as in some
sense representing the same single verb, namely, write. It
would thus appear more appropriate to represent our main
verb as a single basic form:

(4.14)

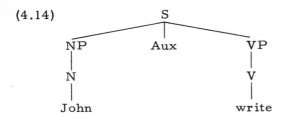

But now how do we derive the three forms shown in (4.11)-
(4.13)? Where do the suffixes -en and -ing come from?

In chapter 2, such examples were given as an exercise. The
problem was to formulate phrase structure rules and lexical
entries that would generate writing, written, write, and so
forth in their correct environments. It should have been clear
from the attempt to use phrase structure rules that they were
totally unsuited to the purpose. Only an extremely complicated
phrase structure grammar could deal with (4.8)-(4.10) in precise detail. Ignoring possible phrase structure rules, we will
simply try to provide a transformational account of the verb
forms.

The first essential is to ascertain how each auxiliary verb
affects the form of the verb immediately following it. Before
proceeding, the reader should review the problem and find
other examples that will show what specific verb form each
auxiliary causes the immediately following verb to assume.

Any verb appearing after the progressive auxiliary be must
have the suffix -ing:

(4.15) a. John is writing.
    b. John has been running.
    c. John will be drinking rum.
    d. John may have been driving the car.

The form of the verb following a modal is equally easy to determine. It is always in its basic <u>infinitive</u> form, without any suffix at all:

(4.16) a. John can be nice. (cf. <u>to be</u>)
     b. John may have seen Mary. (cf. <u>to have</u>)
     c. John should run faster. (cf. <u>to run</u>)
     d. John will have been talking. (cf. <u>to have</u>)

When we look at what happens to the right of <u>have</u>, the situation is a bit more complex:

(4.17) a. John has eaten the Christmas tree.
     b. John has been drawing on the window pane.
     c. John may have broken his toe.

(4.18) a. Mary has passed the test.
     b. Mary has dropped her violin.
     c. Mary has gulped down a gnat.

(4.19) a. The monster has run away.
     b. The monster has drunk my tea.
     c. The monster has flung peanut butter at me.

The verb form selected after the auxiliary <u>have</u> depends in part on the verb that follows <u>have</u>. One group of verbs (i.e., (4.17a-c)), including <u>be</u>, adds -en; another group (i.e., (4.18a-c)) changes into a form indistinguishable from the past tense. Finally, verbs that form their past tense by a change of vowel (cf. (4.19a-c)) appear in a distinctive form that neither has -en nor is equivalent to the standard past tense (cf. <u>The monster</u> {<u>ran</u>/*<u>run</u>} <u>away</u>). Despite these differences, all these forms have been traditionally thought of as the <u>past participle</u> or <u>perfective</u> form of the verb in question.
    It is now possible to combine the accounts of how each auxiliary affects what follows it, thus:

(4.20) a. The flea will have been drinking tea.
     b. The tea may have been standing for an hour.

    c. The flea <u>will be</u> swimm<u>ing</u> soon.
    d. The tea <u>might have</u> gon<u>e</u> cold.

After a modal comes an infinitive; after <u>have</u> comes the past
participle (i.e., a verb with an ending that we will represent
as -en, the suffix of the most distinctive form (exhibited by
(4.20a)-(4.20c)); and after <u>be</u> comes a verb with -<u>ing</u>.

    To account for these facts, the phrase structure rule that
expands Aux must be modified to include the <u>affixes</u> -en and
-<u>ing</u>, as shown:

(4.21) Aux → (Modal) (have en) (be ing)

(We shall henceforth represent these affixes as <u>en</u> and <u>ing</u>,
rather than -<u>en</u> and -<u>ing</u>.) To ensure that <u>en</u> is chosen only—
and always—when <u>have</u> is chosen, we enclose it in the parentheses along with <u>have</u>; likewise for <u>be</u> and <u>ing</u>. There is no
affix generated with the Modal. The phrase structure tree associated with sentence (4.20a) will now be (4.22):

(4.22)

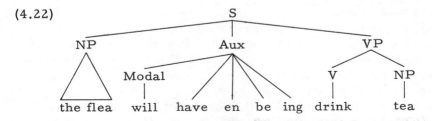

We must now add the following transformation to attach the affixes to the appropriate verbs:

(4.23) <u>Affix Hopping</u> (Obligatory)
    Every affix that is immediately followed by a verb must
    be placed on that verb, becoming part of it.

Unlike the Passive and Question Transformations, which are
<u>optional</u> in the sense that they may apply to any appropriate
tree (but do not have to do so), the rule of Affix Hopping is <u>ob-
ligatory</u>. In other words, every affix must be attached to the
verb immediately to its right, if there is a verb there.

    If Affix Hopping is applied obligatorily to (4.22), it will have
the effect shown in (4.24), where the arrows indicate the direc-

tion in which the affixes have been moved. Notice that since no affix was generated with the modal will, have appears in its infinitive form: have.

(4.24)

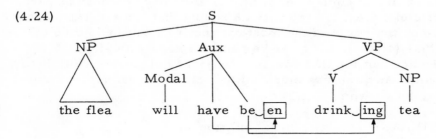

(In this chapter and the next, we will use the ligature mark, ‿, to represent the attachment of affixes to verbs. In chapter 6 we will suggest a more formally precise mode of attachment.)

As a result of Affix Hopping, the suffixes en and ing have been attached to verbs, and we are left with verbal forms represented as be‿en and drink‿ing. This is a somewhat abstract way to represent the fact that be is in its perfective form and drink is in its progressive form. (In some cases, such as the perfective run or drunk, it will be necessary to assume the existence of a set of Spell-Out Rules in our grammar, which essentially tell us how a given verb in a given tense form is actually pronounced in the language.)

So far, we have seen that the form of a verb depends on which auxiliary appears to its left in the sentence. However, what about the leftmost verb in a series consisting of auxiliaries (if any) and a main verb? Apparently nothing appears to its left. How is its form determined? Consider the following examples:

(4.25) John $\begin{Bmatrix} \text{likes} \\ \text{liked} \end{Bmatrix}$ Mary.

(4.26) John $\begin{Bmatrix} \text{is} \\ \text{was} \end{Bmatrix}$ watching Mary.

(4.27) John $\begin{Bmatrix} \text{has} \\ \text{had} \end{Bmatrix}$ been helping Mary.

(4.28) John $\begin{Bmatrix} \text{will} \\ \text{would} \end{Bmatrix}$ have been looking for Mary.

The data of (4.25)-(4.28) show that the first of any sequence of verbs in a sentence has a tense, i.e., is in present or past form.

Before going on, it would be wise to clarify what we mean by tense. In each of the above examples, the first verb of the pair is in the present tense, while the second verb is in the past tense. (Note that the modals also show tense marking: the alternation between will/would, shall/should, can/could, and may/might involves the difference between present and past. As (4.28) shows, a modal prevents the verb to its right from acquiring a tense.) We must be careful to make the distinction between the tense form of the verb and its time reference. In each of the following sentences, give the tense form of the underlined verb (i.e., is the verb in the present or past tense?), and, in addition, note the time reference of the sentence:

(4.29) a. Yesterday Dr. Scrak baked a cake.
       b. I feel sick right now.
       c. Tomorrow I go to Boston for a checkup.
       d. If you ate that you would be sick.
       e. Intelligent people write books.
       f. Did you hear what happened to me yesterday? This guy walks up to me and tells me I stole his watch.

It should be clear from the examples in (4.29) that a verb in a particular tense form can have different time references, depending on the context in which it is used. In (4.29a) baked is in the past tense, and the sentence also refers to past time. Similarly, the verb feel in (4.29b) is in the present tense, and the sentence refers to present time. However, in (4.29c) the verb go is in the present tense (as opposed to went, which is past), yet the time reference of the sentence is future time (note the presence of the adverb tomorrow). Now consider sentence (4.29d). The verb ate is in the past tense (as opposed to present tense eat), yet the sentence does not refer to past time. In a sentence such as (4.29e), the present tense verb write does not refer to present time; rather, the sentence seems to be "timeless," i.e., it seems to state a gen-

eral truth. Finally, note the sequence of sentences in (4.29f)
(this fragment of discourse is, of course, quite idiomatic, almost bordering on slang). The present tense verbs walks and
tells are used here in a sentence having past time reference.
  We will ignore time reference from now on, turning our attention to the distribution of past or present tense forms of
verbs. Most commonly tense is shown by suffix. The past
tense is typically -ed (as in walked), but it may involve a vowel
change (as in the case of ran). The actual shape of the present
tense depends on the subject of the sentence. If that is third
person singular, the suffix is -s; otherwise, no overt suffix
appears: He runs vs. They run. (The verb be is a little more
complex, as the reader can easily discover.) A very natural
modification of rule (4.21) will permit us to ensure that the
first verb always bears a tense:

(4.30) a. Aux → Tense (Modal) (have en) (be ing)

 b. Tense → $\begin{Bmatrix} \text{pres} \\ \text{past} \end{Bmatrix}$

By means of rule (4.30), we now introduce either past or pres
as the first, obligatory, member of Aux. As long as we consider Tense to be an affix, Affix Hopping will attach pres or
past (whichever occurs in a particular sentence) to whatever
verb is generated immediately to its right—the first overt verb
in the string. The following derivation illustrates the way in
which Affix Hopping must operate on the affixes generated by
rule (4.30):

(4.31)

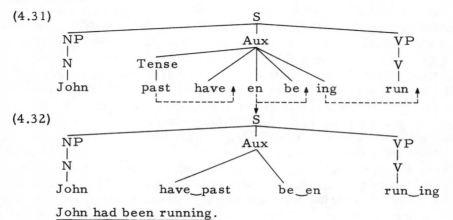

(4.32)

John had been running.

(We will assume that the late Spell-Out Rules mentioned earlier will spell out have past as had, and so on.) By considering the tenses to be affixes like en or ing, we are able to make maximum use of a rule already needed—Affix Hopping—thereby providing a satisfactory account of the distribution of tense marking in English.

Our new PS rule for the auxiliary (Aux → Tense (Modal) (have en) (be ing)), along with the Affix Hopping Transformation, will guarantee (a) that the first verb in any series of verbs will have pres or past attached to it; (b) that the verb following a modal will have no affix; and (c) that the verb following have will have en (i.e., the perfective ending) and that the verb following be will have ing. In order to make sure that the operation of the Affix Hopping Rule is clear, show how the following tree would be transformed by that rule. What does the output tree look like?

(4.33)

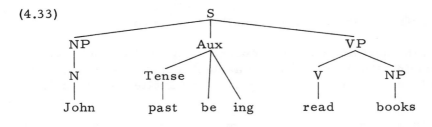

Just as with tree (4.32), Affix Hopping takes each verbal affix, including Tense, and attaches it to the verb immediately on its right:

(4.34)

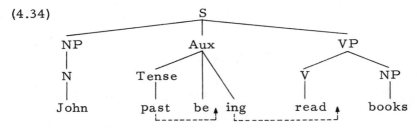

Hence, the output tree would be (4.35). (When past is attached to be, the now empty Tense node will delete by general convention.)

(4.35)

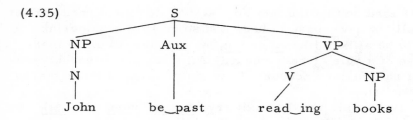

4.3. DO SUPPORT

Now that we have seen how auxiliary affixes are to be analyzed, it is possible to consider the auxiliary do. Since do appears typically in questions, let us first determine whether our detailed analysis of the Aux forces us to make any changes in our analysis of questions such as (4.37):

(4.36) Mildred's cat has broken the Ming vase.

(4.37) Has Mildred's cat broken the Ming vase?

Given the sort of analysis proposed in the last section, what underlying structure would we assign to sentence (4.36), and what transformations must we say have applied in its derivation?

Example (4.36) would be assigned the following underlying form:

(4.38) a.

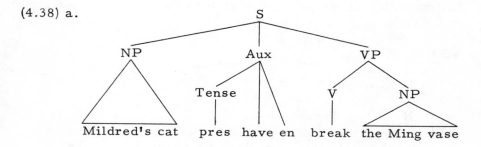

The only transformation that would apply in the derivation of sentence (4.36) is Affix Hopping, which will produce (4.38b) from (4.38a):

(4.38) b.

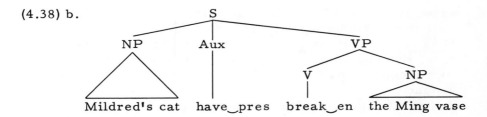

Once the affixes have been attached to the relevant verbs, the derivation of this sentence ends.

The simplest derivation for (4.37) seems to be just like that of sentence (4.36), except that the Question Transformation has operated. Thus, the underlying form of sentence (4.37), like that of sentence (4.36), is tree (4.38a). Both Affix Hopping and the Question Transformation must apply. In which order?

One might suppose that Affix Hopping could apply first, producing a tree like (4.38b), with the Question Transformation then applying to (4.38b) to produce the final output:

(4.39)

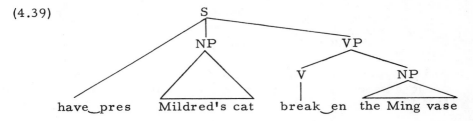

(The Aux node, which has been vacated by the operation of the Question Rule, disappears by the general convention that "empty" nodes are deleted.) The derivation of questions like (4.37) could apparently be produced by applying the following rules in the order listed:

(4.40) 1. Affix Hopping (Obligatory)
        2. Question   (Optional)

There is one modification in our rules that we are already forced to make under this analysis, though that may not be obvious. Our Question Transformation has hitherto made reference only to the first auxiliary verb. But we have now intro-

duced separable affixes into our system, and if the Question
Rule is to transform Mildred's cat have‿pres break‿en the
Ming vase into Have‿pres Mildred's cat break‿en the Ming
vase, then we must restate it so that it carries the Tense affix attached to the first auxiliary, fronting have‿pres in this
instance.

Now let us turn to another example (one in which we might
expect do to turn up) to see whether the ordering just proposed
((1) Affix Hopping, (2) Question) will work. Let us consider the
derivation of the pair Mildred's cat broke the Ming vase and
its related question Did Mildred's cat break the Ming vase?
Our present PS rules will almost generate the active statement directly, for they will generate structures in which the
Aux dominates only Tense. (Recall that rule (4.30a) makes
Tense obligatory, so every sentence must at least contain
Tense in the Aux.) Hence the PS rules will yield (4.41a):

(4.41) a.

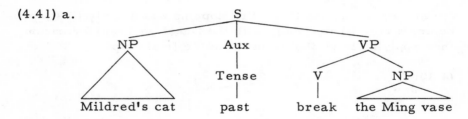

Affix Hopping must apply first to this tree (by the ordering
proposed above), and it is obligatory. This process will yield
(4.41b):

(4.41) b.

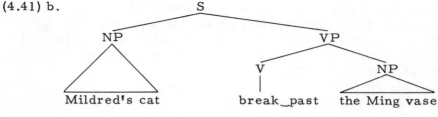

Mildred's cat broke the Ming vase.

This is the statement that we wanted to generate. Since the
Question Rule is optional, we do not need to apply it, and our
derivation is perfectly satisfactory.

But what if we now try to apply the Question Rule? By the ordering postulated in (4.40), we want the rule to generate Did Mildred's cat break the Ming vase? from structure (4.41b). We have just informally restated the Question Rule so that it fronts the first auxiliary verb plus its tense marker. What will this rule yield when applied to the above tree?

The answer is, of course, that it simply will not apply to (4.41b). The Tense affix is attached to break, which is not an auxiliary verb. Would it help if we changed the Question Rule so that it fronted any verb, along with Tense?

The output would then be *Broke Mildred's cat the Ming vase? This is no better. Since we have not provided a means of generating do in the Aux, there is no obvious way of rephrasing the rules so as to produce the desired Did Mildred's cat break the Ming vase?

However, let us take a closer look at the precise verbal forms found in the statement and in the corresponding question. In the statement we find just broke (i.e., break past), the past tense form of the verb: Mildred's cat broke the Ming vase. In the question, on the other hand, we find did and break: Did Mildred's cat break the Ming vase? The main verb has lost its past tense affix and appears in the infinitive form—the form without an affix. It is the mysterious do that now appears in the past tense form (i.e., do past = did).

This suggests that in do questions, the Question Rule must front the Tense element but not the main verb. Is there some way of guaranteeing that Tense alone is moved to the front of the sentence when there is only a Tense in the Aux? If we could modify our rules so that they had that effect, then we would have accounted for the fact that, in the question, break loses its past tense form, while the affix past occurs at the beginning of the sentence on do. It would then be necessary to account only for how do appears with that past tense affix.

Let us try to restate the Question Rule so that it moves Tense even when no auxiliary verb is present. Then let us have that rule apply to (4.41a) before Affix Hopping has applied (contrary to our previous ordering in (4.40)). This would have the desired effect of moving Tense to the initial position in the sen-

tence, preventing it from being placed by Affix Hopping on the
main verb break. An appropriate restatement of the Question
Rule might be (4.42):

(4.42) Question Transformation (Optional)
    Place Tense and the first auxiliary verb immediately on
    its right, if there is one, to the left of the subject NP.

This rule will operate on (4.41a), repeated here, to produce
(4.41c):

(4.41) a.

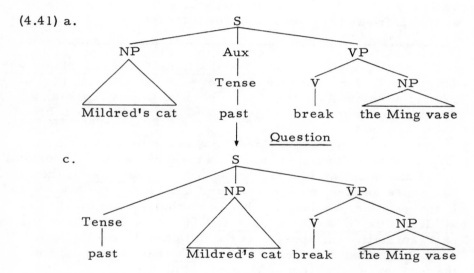

The result of our modified Question Rule, then, is to bring the
lone tense marker to the front of the sentence.
    Since we have now assumed that Affix Hopping applies after
the Question Rule, we must try to apply it at this point in the
derivation, i.e., to tree (4.41c). However, the rule of Affix
Hopping will not apply to this tree; the Affix Hopping Rule attaches the various affixes only to verbs immediately to the
right of the affixes. In (4.41c), the affix past is not followed by
a verb but rather by a noun phrase. Hence, the affix cannot be
attached to the main verb break, since that is not immediately
to its right. We are left with a sentence with a "stranded"
Tense in front, and without further modification (4.41c) is not
a possible sentence of English.
    Now we can tackle the problem of do directly. All that we

need in order to produce a perfectly good sentence from the
last tree is to insert a do to the left of past. The Spell-Out
Rules would then automatically spell out do‿past as did (just
as they spell out be‿past as was), giving the desired question
Did Mildred's cat break the Ming vase? Under what circumstances do we need to insert do? Just in those cases in which
the Tense affix is "stranded," e.g., when the new Question
Rule (4.42) moves a Tense alone to the front of the sentence,
preventing Affix Hopping from attaching that Tense to a verb.
Therefore, we could propose a transformation (which we can
call Do Support) which has the effect of inserting do in precisely those cases where the Tense has become stranded and
Affix Hopping has failed to apply. Obviously, this rule (stated
in (4.43)) must be ordered after Affix Hopping:

(4.43) Do Support (Obligatory)
       Attach the verb do immediately to the left of any Tense
       marker that is not attached to a verb.

This rule will have the effect of inserting the verb do in trees
such as (4.41c), to yield the following type of structure:

(4.41) d.

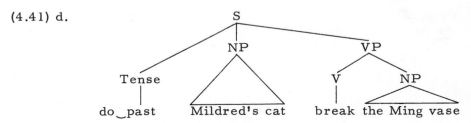

Did Mildred's cat break the Ming vase?

Hence, we can derive (4.41d) from (4.41a), as long as we have
the following rule order:

(4.44) 1. Question   (Optional)
       2. Affix Hopping (Obligatory)
       3. Do Support   (Obligatory)

All that remains, at this point, is to show that the derivation of our earlier example, Has Mildred's cat broken the
Ming vase?, can still work with the rule order we have just

argued for. Let us begin with the following underlying structure (= (4.38a)):

(4.45) a.

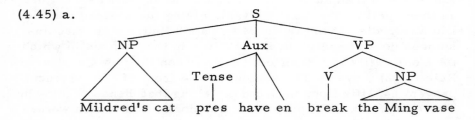

The Question Transformation can apply first. The following
structure will result (see rule (4.42)):

(4.45) b.

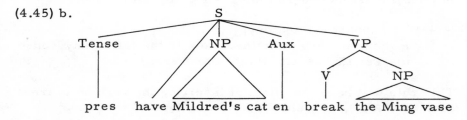

Now Affix Hopping can attach the affix pres to have and en to
break, thus deriving (4.45c):

(4.45) c.

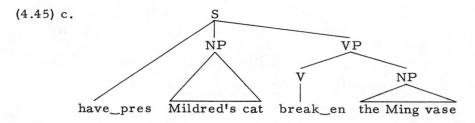

This is our desired output, and hence we see that rule ordering
(4.44) not only allows us to generate questions with do but allows us to generate questions with the other auxiliary verbs
as well.

It has turned out that our analysis of the auxiliary accounts
for the auxiliary system in questions, as long as we add a rule
of Do Support to our grammar. This rule must be ordered after
the Question Transformation and after Affix Hopping: when the
Question Rule fronts a lone tense, as above, then Affix Hopping

cannot operate; and it is precisely when Affix Hopping cannot operate that a tense marker will be stranded and <u>Do</u> Support will operate.

   To ensure that there is no confusion, we should point out that whereas in chapter 1 we argued for a <u>do</u> in the underlying form of sentences such as <u>Mildred's cat broke the Ming vase</u>, we have not actually followed up that suggestion here. Instead, we have shown how a special transformation can be added that, instead of <u>deleting</u> an underlying <u>do</u>, <u>inserts do</u> where necessary. Notice that it would have made no sense to propose such a rule until we had isolated the Tense affix, for until we had introduced that element into our analysis, as a separate element, there was no plausible way of generating <u>do</u> questions without making the assumption that <u>do</u> itself appeared in the Aux. It is worth pointing out that the notion that there is an underlying <u>do</u> has not been shown to be wrong. In section 4.5, in fact, we will sketch an analysis using an underlying <u>do</u>, which the reader will then be able to compare with the account given here.

4.4. THE ORDERING OF THE PASSIVE AND QUESTION TRANSFORMATIONS

Now that we have analyzed the auxiliary system of English in more detail, we can return to the problem that originally motivated our investigation: the interaction of the Passive and Question Rules. It will now be easy to show that they apply in the following order, producing no ungrammatical sentences involving <u>do</u>:

(4.46) 1. Passive   (Optional)
       2. Question   (Optional)
       3. Affix Hopping (Obligatory)
       4. <u>Do</u> Support   (Obligatory)

   First, let us reconsider sentence (4.47), discussed earlier in this chapter as (4.2):

(4.47) The fly was eaten by the mosquito.

We know that the Passive Transformation has applied in the derivation of this sentence. The active counterpart of (4.47) is (4.48):

(4.48) The mosquito ate the fly.

Now that we have analyzed the auxiliary in detail, we are able
to give a precise analysis for sentence (4.48), beginning with
the underlying structure (4.49a):

(4.49) a.

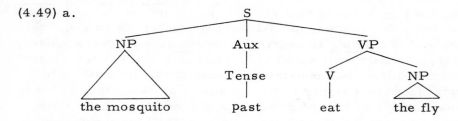

If the Passive Rule operates on this tree, it must, as always, insert be as the rightmost member of the Aux; Affix
Hopping will later attach past to be (correctly yielding was in
(4.47)). But now the main verb, eaten, is in perfective form
(i.e., the same form it would have with auxiliary have). The
reader can easily check that this is true of all passive sentences: the main verb will always be in perfective form. With
auxiliary have we were able to account for this fact by generating en along with it (cf. rule (4.30a)). We can account for
the form of passive verbs by assuming that the Passive Rule
adds not only the auxiliary be to the Aux but also en along with
be. Thus, when the Passive Rule operates on tree (4.49a), it
will add be en as the last members of Aux:

(4.49) b.

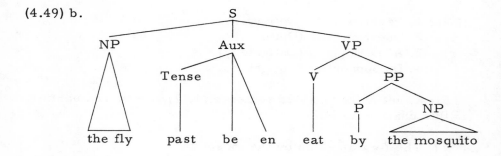

If no other rules, such as the Question Rule, are applied to this
tree, then Affix Hopping will apply, attaching past to be and en
to eat, deriving the sentence (4.49c):

(4.49) c.

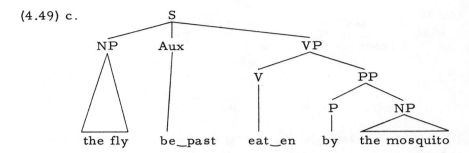

If our goal is to generate the passive question Was the fly eaten by the mosquito?, then the only rule ordering that can work is (1) Passive/(2) Question, since it is necessary to apply the Passive Rule first to produce (4.49b) before the Question Transformation may be applied to that tree to move be to the front and form (4.49d):

(4.49) d.

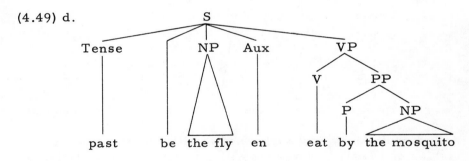

The Passive Rule has inserted the auxiliary verb be, and then the Question Rule has fronted it. We argued above that Affix Hopping must follow the Question Transformation, and thus it may now apply to tree (4.49d). Its effect, of course, will be to attach past to be and en to eat.

If we attempt to apply the rules Passive and Question in the opposite order, still taking (4.49a) as our base form, what tree will be derived by the operation of the Question Rule alone? And what ungrammatical sentence will be generated if the Passive Rule is also applied?

If tree (4.49a) is our base form, the Question Transformation will produce the following tree, if it applies first:

(4.49) e.

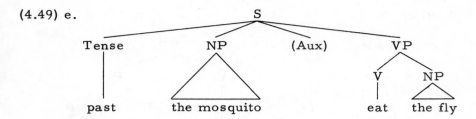

If no further rules apply to this tree, <u>Do</u> Support will apply, and we will have correctly generated the sentence <u>Did the mosquito eat the fly?</u> However, what if Passive is applied as well? It is not clear that it can apply to a tree that is in "question form" but let us assume for the sake of argument that it can. It would probably produce the following output:

(4.49) f.

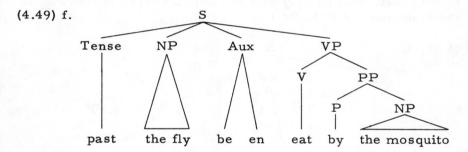

Affix Hopping may now apply, and it will have the effect of attaching <u>en</u> to <u>eat</u>; however, it will not be able to attach the marker <u>past</u> to any verb, since it has an NP following it. The output of that rule would therefore be (4.49g):

(4.49) g.

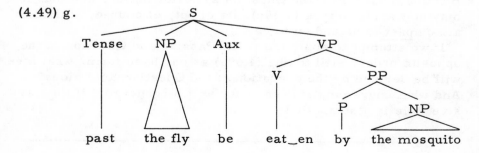

But now <u>Do</u> Support will apply to insert <u>do</u> before the Tense, since the Tense has not been placed on a verb:

(4.49) h.

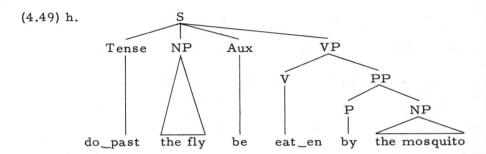

do_past   the fly   be   eat_en   by   the mosquito

In other words, we have in the end generated the ungrammatical sentence *<u>Did the fly be eaten by the mosquito</u>? Since
the ordering (1) Passive/(2) Question will generate our desired
output, while the opposite order leads to ungrammatical sentences (or simply fails to generate desired forms, if Passive
will not apply to sentences in question form), we must adopt
the first order. We have already argued that Affix Hopping and
<u>Do</u> Support follow the Question Rule, and thus we have arrived
at the following list of ordered rules:

(4.50) 1. Passive   (Optional)
       2. Question   (Optional)
       3. Affix Hopping (Obligatory)
       4. <u>Do</u> Support   (Obligatory)

4.5. AN ALTERNATIVE ACCOUNT OF AUXILIARY DO (OPTIONAL SECTION)

It is often the case that we can find alternative treatments for
a problem, at which point our task becomes to determine
whether those different treatments have different empirical
consequences and, if so, to find evidence indicating that one
alternative is better than the others. In this section, we shall
present an alternative hypothesis about the auxiliary <u>do</u>, one
in which <u>do</u> is not inserted by transformation but rather is generated by the PS rules themselves and then deleted by a transformation in just the right places. This is in fact a more direct
formalization than <u>Do</u> Support of the underlying <u>do</u> theory presented roughly in the first chapter. There are certain problems
with this analysis (as there are with the analysis presented
earlier in this chapter), and we will allude to some of these
problems in the exercises.

Suppose that in the <u>Do Deletion Hypothesis</u>, <u>do</u> is generated as an obligatory member of the Aux, as follows:

(4.51) Aux → Tense (Modal) (have en) (be ing) do

Thus, do is always the final member of the auxiliary. (In fact, there are alternative ways of generating do in the Aux—e.g., allowing do to be a modal verb—and the reader may wish to explore some of these.) If we choose only the obligatory members of the Aux, we can generate trees such as the following:

(4.52) a.

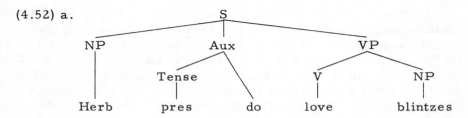

If the Question Transformation applies to a tree such as this, we can generate questions with do:

(4.52) b.

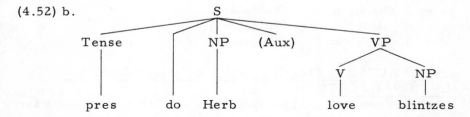

Application of Affix Hopping will result in the structure for the sentence Does Herb love blintzes?

We know that the Question Rule is optional, and thus it might not apply to a tree such as (4.52a). Since we must not be forced to generate every statement with auxiliary do in it, we will thus propose a rule of Do Deletion, which will apply after Question and before Affix Hopping.

(4.53) Do Deletion (Obligatory)
        Delete the verb do when it immediately precedes a verb.

Try to answer the following questions about this rule before going on:

(4.54) a. Why does <u>Do</u> Deletion apply between Question and
　　　　　 Affix Hopping, i.e., why are alternative orderings
　　　　　 wrong?
　　　 b. What rule ordering differences are there, so far,
　　　　　 between the <u>Do</u> Deletion theory and the <u>Do</u> Support
　　　　　 theory?

Now let us examine a case in which we have chosen to expand the auxiliary with some optional members as well as
<u>Tense</u> and <u>do</u>. For example, consider a tree such as the fol-
lowing:

(4.55)

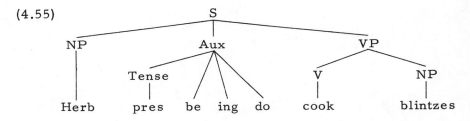

The rule ordering that the reader was asked to confirm in answering the questions of (4.54) should now be applied to tree
(4.55). It should be clear that our rules allow the following sentences to be derived from (4.55):

(4.56) a. Herb is cooking blintzes.
　　　 b. Is Herb cooking blintzes?

Make sure that you see how the proposed ordering of <u>Do</u> Deletion and Affix Hopping prevents the rules from generating *<u>Herb
is doing cook blintzes</u> and *<u>Is Herb doing cook blintzes?</u> Check
the derivation of these sentences before going on.

Let us see what happens when we attempt to apply Passive in
this <u>Do</u> Deletion system. If the Passive Transformation adds
<u>be　en</u> as the final member of the Aux, as described in earlier
sections of this chapter, it will derive the following tree when
it operates on (4.52a):

(4.52) c.

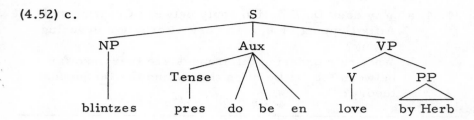

If <u>Do</u> Deletion and Affix Hopping apply, we can derive the sentence <u>Blintzes are loved by Herb</u>. On the other hand, after
Question and before <u>Do</u> Deletion we derive the following structure:

(4.52) d.

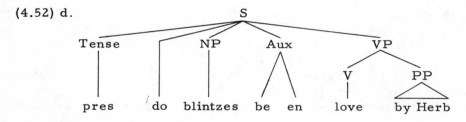

This derivation will ultimately lead to the ungrammatical sentence *<u>Do</u> blintzes be loved by Herb? The unwanted <u>do</u> in this
sentence will not be eliminated by <u>Do</u> Deletion, because it is
at the beginning of the sentence and hence not located immediately to the left of a verb. Moreover, the Passive <u>be</u> has not
been fronted as it should have been.

It thus appears as if the <u>Do</u> Deletion theory suffers from a
defect not found in the <u>Do</u> Support theory. However, there are
at least two ways of avoiding the problem of sentences such as
(4.52d):

A. Formulate a <u>special</u> <u>Do</u> Deletion Rule, which applies immediately after Passive but before Question and which deletes <u>do</u> when it precedes <u>be</u>. Thus, we would have the ordering (1) Passive/(2) Special <u>Do</u> Deletion (only before <u>be</u>)/
   (3) Question/(4) General <u>Do</u> Deletion (before verbs in general)/(5) Affix Hopping; or

B. Formulate the Passive Rule in such a way that <u>be</u> <u>en</u> is
   substituted for <u>do</u> in the auxiliary; thus <u>do</u> will always be
   automatically "deleted" by the Passive Rule.

Although both of these alternatives will get around the special problem posed by (4.52d), each seems to involve some complication in our system. Alternative (A) requires an extra, ad hoc rule in our grammar, and alternative (B), while it works nicely for passive sentences, will not get around problems posed by main verb be (see exercise 5 of this chapter). It is possible that the Do Deletion analysis could be further modified so that all complications were avoided. However, we will make use of Do Support throughout the rest of this book, mainly for convenience, since it has been more widely adopted.

CHAPTER 4: EXERCISES

(E4.1) Provide a derivation for the following sentences (i)-(iv). In each case, begin the derivation by providing a tree representing the base form, and then show in detail how the basic tree is transformed by the rules that operate on it, giving each new output tree. (See (4.45) for a sample derivation. It may be useful to review the rule of Affix Hopping and the ordering of the relevant transformations.)

(i)   The man with the mole could not have been examined by his doctor.
(ii)   Has she been teaching this class for a long time?
(iii) Herb will have finished the publisher's order by now.
(iv)   Did Henry VIII have eight wives?

Note: We will assume that modal verbs can have present and past tense forms, as follows:

will + present = will   may + present = may
will + past = would   may + past = might
can + present = can   shall + present = shall
can + past = could   shall + past = should

(E4.2) Consider the following base form:

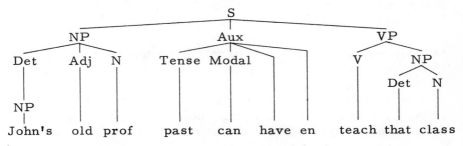

In a step-by-step fashion, show how the following sentences are derived from this base form. In each case, take particular care to apply the transformations in their proper order:

(i)   That class could have been taught by John's old prof.
(ii) That class could not have been taught by John's old prof.
(iii) Could John's old prof have taught that class?
(iv) Could that class have been taught by John's old prof?

(E4.3) In this chapter we provided arguments that the Question Transformation must precede Affix Hopping. Is it possible to construct an argument for the ordering of these two rules by using any of the following examples:

(i) a. Has Mary proved the theorem?
    b. Will Herb have been taking a shower?
    c. Must you whistle Dixie?

In answering this question, you must show either (A) how these sentences can be used to establish an order between Question and Affix Hopping, or (B) why they are irrelevant to the ordering. Go on to show what sentences would be crucial to the ordering argument.

(E4.4) In this chapter we modified our statement of the Question Transformation to take into account our new analysis of the auxiliary system. In particular, we modified the Question Rule so as to allow it to front Tense alone (when no other members of Aux follow it) or to front Tense plus the first following auxiliary element. Now consider the Negative Insertion Transformation discussed in the last chapter:

Negative Insertion
Insert the negative word not immediately after the first auxiliary verb.

Of course, we stated that rule before we had analyzed the auxiliary system to account for do.

A. Given our new analysis of the auxiliary system, in which affixes are introduced explicitly, how (if at all) must the Negative Insertion Transformation be modified so that it will generate examples such as the following:

(i)   John will <u>not</u> modify his political views.
(ii) Harry had <u>not</u> been studying <u>Das Kapital</u>.
(iii) Mary can <u>not</u> tolerate such rude insults.

<u>B</u>. Do the following examples force us to modify any of our
rules? In answering this, show explicitly how these are derived, or show why they cannot be derived:

(iv) Harry did <u>not</u> foresee this sort of trouble.
(v) The sun does <u>not</u> revolve around the earth.

State any modifications you feel are necessary in the rules we
have discussed, and show in what order the rules apply. Give
<u>explicit</u> arguments for the correct rule ordering in your an-
swer.

(E4.5) In discussing the verb <u>be</u>, we have so far come across
two of its auxiliary uses, namely, progressive <u>be</u> (associated
with <u>ing</u>) and passive <u>be</u> (associated with <u>en</u>). Notice, however,
that <u>be</u> also functions as a <u>main verb</u> in English, in sentences
such as (i):

(i)   He is noisy.

If we analyze <u>be</u> in (i) as a main verb, then, like other main
verbs, it should be able to appear with any of the auxiliary
verbs. This indeed turns out to be the case:

(ii) He <u>is</u> being noisy.
(iii) He <u>could have been</u> being noisy.

In (ii) we see that the first occurrence of <u>be</u> is the progressive
auxiliary, which causes the second occurrence of <u>be</u> to have
the affix <u>ing</u>. We can account for this by analyzing the second
<u>be</u> as a main verb, as follows:

(iv)

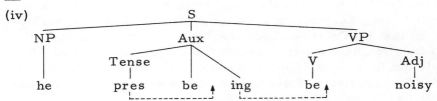

In section 4.6 we analyzed do as an obligatory member of Aux.
Given that all the other members of the auxiliary (except
Tense) are optional in that proposal, it is possible to gener-
ate base forms such as (v):

(v)
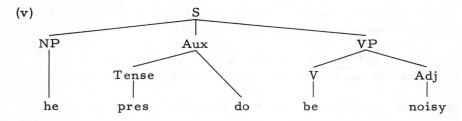

Since (v) is a possible base form, the Do Deletion grammar
introduced in section 4.6 will generate the following ungrammatical sentence:

(vi) *Does he be noisy?

Clearly, the Do Deletion theory is making incorrect predictions. Now consider the following questions:

A. Assume that the Do Deletion theory has only one rule deleting do. Show why the theory will generate the ungrammatical sentence (vi) (i.e., show why do is not deleted).

B. Is it possible to order the transformations in such a way as
to prevent the generation of (vi)? If so, will this ordering produce the wrong results in other cases? Be specific and provide
examples. (To anwer this you may wish to note that the problem illustrated by (vi) is similar to problems we encountered
in generating the passive sentence (4.49h).)

C. In order to solve the problems connected with the sentence
(4.52d) in section 4.6, we proposed two alternatives: (a) that
in the Do Deletion analysis the passive auxiliary could be inserted into a sentence in such a way as to replace the verb do;
or (b) that Do Deletion should really be two rules, a special
Do Deletion Rule ordered before Question and a general Do
Deletion Rule ordered after Question. Can either of these op-
tions be modified to solve the problems arising with the main
verb be? Be explicit in answering this.

CHAPTER 4: SUGGESTED READINGS

At this particular stage of development, it is important for the reader to get as much practice as possible in deriving sentences with the rules we have discussed and to review carefully the arguments we have used to establish our analyses. Hence, it would be valuable for the reader to concentrate more on working on the exercises in this chapter than on attempting to delve into outside readings. However, for those who wish to explore the basis for our analysis of the auxiliary system, we recommend Chomsky (1957). Of special interest is chapter 7 of that work, in which Chomsky discusses the transformations we have presented here. His analysis of the auxiliary system is adopted in this chapter (except in section 4.6).

Chapter 5

FORMALIZING TRANSFORMATIONAL RULES

5.1. THE PASSIVE TRANSFORMATION

In this chapter we will provide a rough formalization for several transformational rules we have already discussed, and
we will provide the reader with an opportunity to formalize
several others. As we will see, the formalization of transformations is not as simple a matter as is the construction of
a phrase structure grammar. The formal characteristics of
transformations are not as clearly understood, and there remain many unsolved problems in rendering this important part
of the theory precise. The recognition of this fact, established
through a careful attempt to formalize rules, constitutes a
very important stage in the understanding of current work in
linguistics. Just as the precise formulation of PS rules enabled us to see exactly to what extent such rules provided an
adequate model of natural language—and where it was that they
were inadequate—so a precise formulation of the transformational component is an essential step toward the development
of a yet more appropriate model.

The statement of a transformation consists of (a) the structural description (SD) and (b) the structural change (SC). The
structural description specifies which trees are to be affected
by the rule (the input trees), while the structural change asso-
ciates each input tree with an output tree—i.e., a tree that has
undergone the changes the rule specifies.

It should be fairly obvious by now that the Passive Transformation operates on transitive sentences, i.e., those consisting of a subject, an Aux, a main verb, and an object. Thus,
the following is a typical input for the Passive Transformation:

(5.1) a.

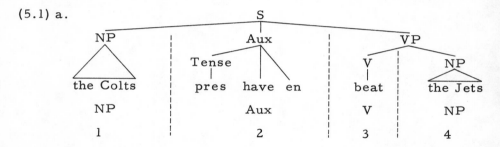

As indicated by the dotted lines, the tree can be analyzed as
a sequence of four constituents: NP - Aux - V - NP. A reasonable hypothesis is that the Passive Rule operates only on
structures that can be analyzed in that way. We can represent
this hypothesis by a Passive Rule stated as follows:

(5.2) Passive (Optional)
      SD: NP -   Aux   - V - NP
          1   2   3   4
      SC: 4   2 be   en   3   by 1

On its own, this collection of symbols is meaningless (though
no more so than S → NP Aux VP), and we need to define precisely how it is to be understood. This is quite straightforward.

The SD of (5.2) is a sequence of four constituents, numbered
so that we can keep track of them. Any tree that can be analyzed in such a way that these particular four constituents occur in the exact order given is a tree that satisfies or meets
the SD of (5.2); such a tree can undergo the change defined by
its SC. Since tree (5.1) meets the SD of Passive, it may undergo that rule. The SC of (5.2) specifies the changes that are
made in the SD sequence as a result of the operation of the
rule:

(5.1) b. NP -   Aux   - V - NP
         1   2   3   4

         4   2 be en   3 by 1

The resulting string is (5.1c):

(5.1) c. The Jets pres have en beat the Colts.
         1   2   3   4

         The Colts pres have en be en beat by the Jets.
         4   2   3   1

         The Colts have been beaten by the Jets.

Let us examine in more detail the structure of the input trees specified by the SD of the <u>Passive Transformation</u>. Determine whether or not the following trees meet the SD of (5.2):

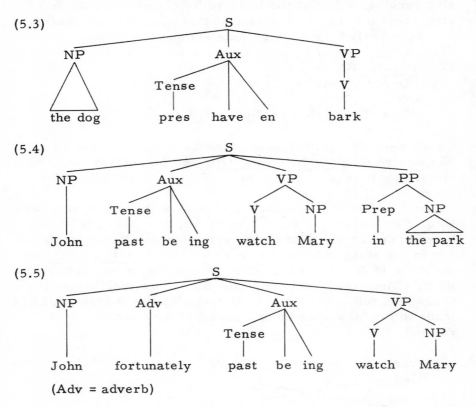

(5.3)

(5.4)

(5.5)

(Adv = adverb)

The first of these trees does not meet the SD of (5.2), although it can be analyzed in a number of ways, such as <u>NP - Tense - have - en - V</u>, NP - Aux - VP, or <u>NP - Aux - V</u>. The last analysis given approaches the requirement of the SD of Passive but lacks the necessary object NP. Thus, there is obviously no way of including (5.3) among the input trees that satisfy the SD of (5.2) and, consequently, the Passive Rule cannot operate on it. This is the correct result, since intransitive sentences do not have passive forms in English.

On the other hand, tree (5.4) does satisfy the SD of (5.2), thus:

(5.6)

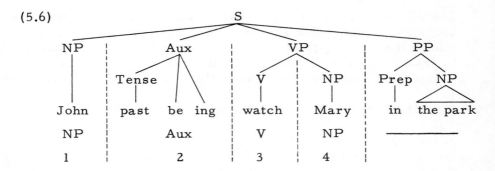

The fact that we have a PP at the end of the sentence makes no difference; there is still a unique analysis of this tree, of the form NP - Aux - V - NP, to which the rule can apply as before:

(5.7) NP -   Aux -   V - NP -   PP
       John past be ing   watch Mary   in the park
       1 ────── 2 ─────   3 ─── 4 ─────   ─────────

       4 ◄──   2   3 ───► 1
       Mary past be ing be en watch by John in the park
                              ↑   ↑

After Affix Hopping this will become (5.8):

(5.8) Mary was being watched by John in the park.

The "extra" PP is simply left, unchanged, at the end of the passive sentence, and rule (5.2) correctly yields a passive for (5.4).

When we turn to (5.5), however, there is a problem. This tree does not satisfy the SD of (5.2), because we cannot isolate the exact sequence NP - Aux - V - NP anywhere in the tree, no matter how we analyze it. The closest we can come is the sequence NP - Adv - Aux - V - NP, with Adv intervening between NP and Aux:

(5.5')

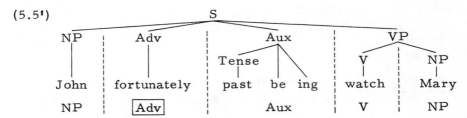

The SD of (5.2) calls for four particular terms in a strict, un-
broken sequence. This sequence does not occur in (5.5), although it did in (5.4), and hence the SD of (5.2) is not satisfied
by tree (5.5). This seems to predict that (5.5) has no passive
counterpart, and we have apparently no way of generating (5.9):

(5.9) Mary, fortunately, was being watched by John.

In the circumstances, (5.9) constitutes a prima facie problem
for our formulation of Passive; that is to say, unless we can
find some other way of generating (5.9), we must change the
SD of (5.2).

   In fact, there is a very easy way of restating the Passive
Rule, using parenthetical notation, so as to allow an optional
Adv to intervene between the subject and the Aux: NP - (Adv) -
Aux - V - NP. More generally, we could make use of a vari-
able, as in (5.2'):

(5.2') Passive (Modified Version)
       SD: NP - X - Aux - V - NP
            1   2   3   4   5
       SC: 5   2 3 be en   4 by 1

Here, the variable X simply means that the Passive Rule can
ignore any material found between the subject and the Aux. Its
SD will be satisfied no matter what occurs there—even when X
is null, that is, when nothing intervenes between NP and Aux.

   Although it is very easy to make these changes in the Passive Rule, it seems unlikely that we need to do so, for there
is another way open to us. We might try to show that the adverb fortunately (and any other material that can appear between the subject and Aux) starts out in some other part of the
structure and is moved into the position between the subject
and Aux only after the application of Passive. Thus, at the
stage when Passive applies, (5.5) and (5.9) might be something like Fortunately, John was watching Mary and Fortunately, Mary was being watched by John. Whether or not Passive
should be changed to (5.2') is best left as an open question at
this point.

5.2. THE PROBLEM OF DERIVED STRUCTURE

Let us now turn to the problem of determining the derived

structure (i.e., the form of the output trees) yielded by the
Passive Rule. So far we have discussed the effect of that rule
only in terms of strings, but, as should be clear by this point,
the output of Passive (and presumably all rules) consists of a
set of hierarchically structured trees. It is natural to interpret rule (5.2) in such a way that the SC, like the SD, defines
tree structures rather than strings. For example, in the SC
of (5.2) (i.e., 4 2 be en 3 by 1), the number "4" refers to
the fourth term of the SD—which is an NP, i.e., a structural
unit. The other terms mentioned in the SD behave similarly:
either they have changed position, or they remain right where
they were to start with. In other words, the simplest interpretation of (5.2) automatically includes the structures NP, Aux,
V, and NP in its output. All we need to do is specify how they
fit together in larger units. The Aux and V remain where they
were (with be en between them); so the output tree produced
by the Passive Rule from tree (5.1a) must have a partial structure like the following (i.e., a tree that is exactly the same as
the relevant part of the input tree, with the addition of be en
at some point):

(5.10)

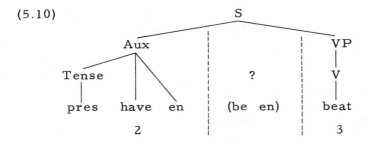

Ignoring the placement of be en, let us see how much of the
output tree is automatically given to us in a similar way. Since
the object NP of the input tree (i.e., the fourth term of the SD)
becomes the subject of the passive sentence, we can add that
NP to the tree in only one possible way, joining it directly to S:

(5.11)

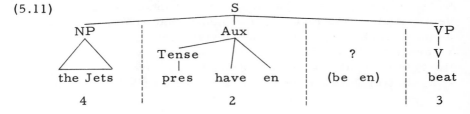

After this point we begin to encounter possible ambiguities. The final NP of the SC (i.e., term 1, <u>the Colts</u>) has to be attached to the right of V. But is it attached to VP or directly to S? Nothing in the existing tree or in the SC tells us which of the following is the output tree:

(5.12)

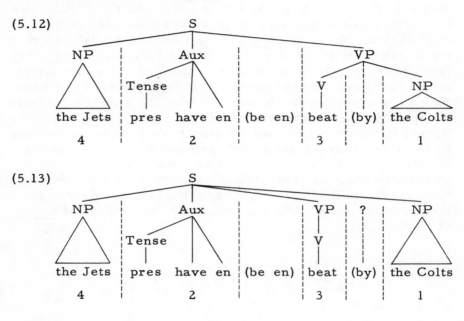

(5.13)

There are two quite distinct problems:

(a) We must provide clear motivation for choosing between (5.12) or (5.13) as the derived structure of a passive sentence; and

(b) We must provide an interpretation of the SC of rule (5.2) (or any variation of that SC) that will automatically yield one or the other of these structures.

The prior problem is, of course, that of motivating a choice. Once we had done this, we could either introduce general conventions about the placement of nodes that are moved, or we could formulate special ad hoc instructions for attaching the relevant NP to VP or S. In either way, we would ensure that the rule generated a unique derived structure.

In chapter 7, when we discuss the rule of <u>VP Deletion</u>, we

shall see that there is some motivation for preferring structures like (5.12) to those like (5.13) for passive sentences:
phrases such as beaten by the Colts in passive sentences seem
to function as single constituents, i.e., like derived VPs. Assuming, then, that we will be able to provide some evidence
for adopting (5.12) as the derived structure corresponding to
(5.11), we need to write the SC of the Passive Rule so that it
will unambiguously place term 1 (in this case, the Colts) under
the VP. Notice that in (5.12) the NP the Colts is a sister constituent to the node V; hence, we wish to formulate the Passive
Rule so that it will sister-adjoin that NP to the right of the node
V. Representing sister adjunction with the symbol +, we can
now formalize the SC of the Passive Rule as follows:

(5.14) 4 2 be en 3 + by + 1

This SC indicates that both by and term 1 are adjoined as right
sisters to V (that is, they are sister-adjoined to the right of
V); hence, both by and the NP the Colts will be dominated by
VP as in structure (5.12). Thus, the Passive Rule applied to
tree (5.1) (i.e., the tree for The Colts have beaten the Jets)
will yield, in part (5.15a):

(5.15) a.

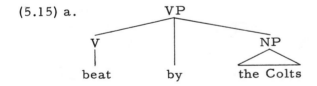

Should by be attached in this way to subtree (5.15a), or should
it be grouped with the NP the Colts? If by is grouped with the
NP, then the structure will presumably be that of a prepositional phrase:

(5.15) b.

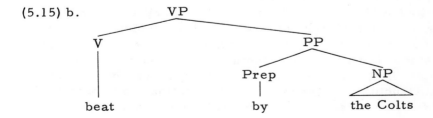

Is there any evidence that structure (5.15b) is correct for the output of the Passive?

There is. The phrase <u>by the Colts</u> patterns like an ordinary prepositional phrase. For example, that whole phrase can sometimes be moved to the front of a sentence, just as other PPs can:

(5.16) a. <u>By which river</u> are the Jets training?
       b. <u>By which team</u> were the Jets beaten?

(5.17) a. <u>By the river</u>, the Jets trained hard.
       b. <u>By the Colts</u>, the Jets were beaten soundly.

Thus, we seem to have fairly good evidence for needing a particular derived structure for the passive <u>by</u> phrase, namely, the PP structure of (5.15b). But recall the input to the Passive Rule, which we have been discussing in this section, i.e., tree (5.1):

(5.1)

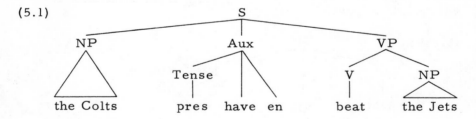

This structure contains no prepositional phrase within the VP; yet we have proposed that in the output of the Passive Rule there is a PP structure within the VP. In other words, we have implied that the Passive Transformation may <u>build structure</u>: not only would it <u>modify</u> the existing structure of its input tree, but also it would <u>add</u> new structure to it.

    However, it is not clear that we should permit transformations to build structure in this way. The problem is not merely that the present theory lacks the apparatus needed to permit transformations to build structure. That could be added. The problem is that it seems that transformations should <u>never</u> build structure. In general, transformations have been limited to modifying existing structures (which are originally built by the PS rules), and if, for example, we permitted Passive to create a PP ex nihilo, we would fail to account for the fact that the PP introduced by the transformation is exactly the same in form as any basic PP created by the PS rule PP → Prep NP.

However, there is one highly restricted structure-building operation that seems to be well motivated: namely, a transformational operation that has come to be known as Chomsky adjunction. We can illustrate this operation as follows. If by is Chomsky-adjoined to the left of the relevant NP within a passive structure, a copy of the NP node is made above the original NP, and this new NP node dominates both by and the original NP:

(5.18)

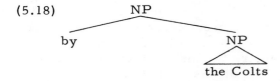

We can represent Chomsky adjunction in the SC of the Passive Rule with the symbol #, as follows:

(5.19) 4 2 be en 3 + by # 1

In this way, by is Chomsky-adjoined to the left of term 1, and the resulting new NP is sister-adjoined to the V:

(5.20)

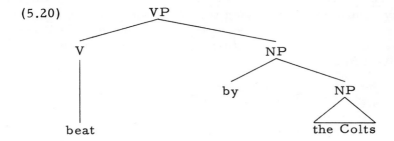

Elements can also be Chomsky-adjoined to the right of given nodes. If we Chomsky-adjoined an element a to the right of some node A, the following structure would result:

(5.21)

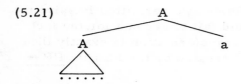

Although the derived structure of the VP given above in (5.20) is not exactly what we proposed in (5.15b), it is close to that structure. In particular, the phrase by the Colts is dominated by a single node (NP) in (5.20), whereas in tree (5.15a) by and the Colts were separate sister nodes under VP. It is not absolutely clear that Chomsky adjunction is the correct device to employ in the Passive Rule, but we will continue to assume that that is the case. As long as the Passive works in the general manner suggested here, Chomky adjunction provides the nearest approximation to the correct derived structure without making use of radical structure building. (For analyses of the Passive that do not require Chomsky adjunction, see the suggested readings at the end of this chapter.)

5.3. FURTHER PROBLEMS OF DERIVED STRUCTURE: THE PLACEMENT OF THE PASSIVE AUXILIARY BE

We have been ignoring the attachment of be en to the tree. If we assume that the two items be and en are attached to the same node, we can easily see that our statement of the SC of (5.2) automatically permits be en to be attached in at least two ways. Given that statement of the SC and taking into account the above discussion of problems relating to derived structure, show how be en may be attached to the output trees of passives in two ways while still satisfying the SC of the Passive Rule.

As Passive is stated now, either of the following trees could count as its output:

(5.22) a.

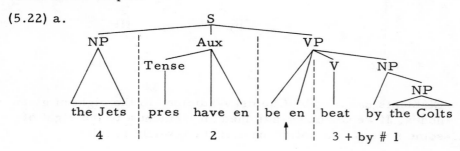

(5.22) b.

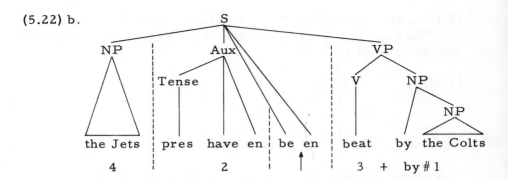

Since the SC of (5.2) inserts be en between the second and third constituents of the SC, these are the only two possible derived structures.

Now recall that when we stated the Passive Rule in words (in chapter 3), we inserted be en as the last member of the Aux, thus:

(5.22) c.

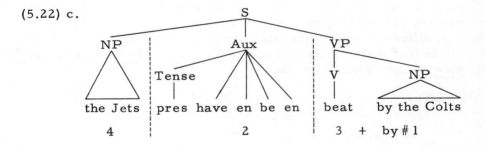

As can easily be seen from the numbering in (5.22c), this particular tree is not even a possible interpretation of the SC specified by rule (5.2), since be en is inserted as a part of term 2. There are mechanisms available that, if introduced into the SC of (5.2), will force the derived structure to be any one of (5.22a), (5.22b), or (5.22c). It is worth looking at these briefly, since they are formal devices that may be needed for other rules.

To yield (5.22a), we could modify the SC of (5.2) to read thus:

(5.23) 4 2 be + en + 3 + by # 1

Since the plus sign (+) is an instruction to sister-adjoin nodes,

(5.23) makes en a sister to term 3 (i.e., V) and be a sister to
en. The resulting derived subtree is (5.24), which is the relevant subtree of (5.22a).

(5.24)

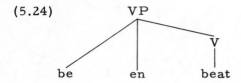

The reader should now work out how to modify (5.2) to yield
(5.22b).

To yield (5.22b) we could modify the SC of (5.2) to read:

(5.25) 4   2 + be + en   3 + by # 1

This would make be and en right sisters of the Aux, which is
just the structure given in (5.22b).

   A different formal operation would be needed to yield (5.22c),
for in that instance be and en are daughter-adjoined as the rightmost daughters of Aux, thus:

(5.26)

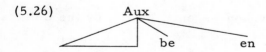

The notation ">" can be used for rightmost daughter adjunc-
tion, while "<" can be used for leftmost daughter adjunction.
To adjoin be en in the manner indicated in (5.22b), the SC of
Passive should be (5.27):

(5.27) 4   2 >   be + en   3 + by # 1

Although it is not clear whether we need to make use of daughter adjunction in stating transformations, we introduce the device because it may be required and is, in fact, the only way
of obtaining the derived structure of the Aux set out in our original description of Passive (which is a very common form of
that rule). We have now arrived at the following statement of
Passive:

(5.28) <u>Passive</u> (Optional)
    SD: NP – Aux – V – NP
        1   2   3   4
    SC: 4   2 > be + en 3 + by # 1

This rule is much more precise than the original rule (5.2) and will operate on trees such as (5.1) (reproduced here as (5.29a)), to generate structures such as (5.29b).

(5.29) a.

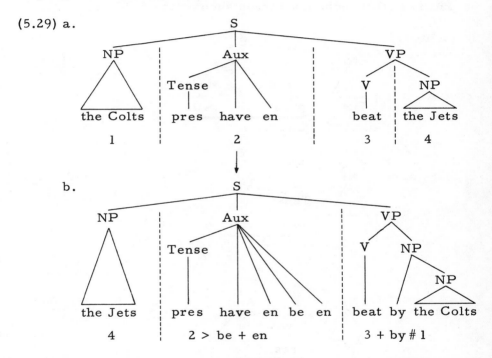

b.

By using daughter adjunction, sister adjunction, and Chomsky adjunction, we have managed to state the SC of Passive so that it will produce trees such as (5.29b) in an unambiguous manner. Although it is unlikely that all three operations are required in the statement of the Passive Rule (see the suggested readings for this chapter), these operations are fairly well motivated for a number of other rules (with the possible exception of daughter adjunction) and serve to illustrate what sorts of adjunction operations are necessary in the grammar.

5.4. THE QUESTION TRANSFORMATION STATED FORMALLY

We have described the operation of the Question Transformation informally as follows: Place Tense and the first auxiliary
verb immediately on its right, if there is one, to the left of
the subject NP. As we did for Passive, we must now specify,
precisely, the input trees for the Question Rule. It should be
clear by now that the Question Transformation operates on input trees that include subtrees such as the following:

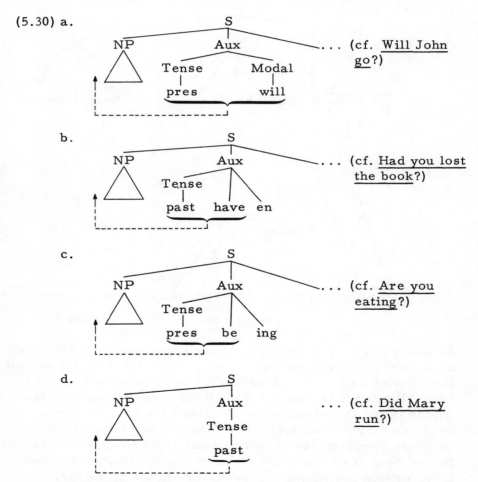

(5.30) a.   ... (cf. Will John go?)

b.   ... (cf. Had you lost the book?)

c.   ... (cf. Are you eating?)

d.   ... (cf. Did Mary run?)

(Note: Do Support will apply later to structure (5.30d).) At this
point, try to formalize the Question Transformation. Use the

same general conventions that were needed in formalizing the
Passive Transformation. Keep in mind that the SD of your
rule must be stated precisely enough to cover cases (5.30a)-
(5.30d) above. Where necessary invent your own symbolism,
but be sure to define it. As far as possible, follow the format
of the Passive Rule (5.28).

One way of formalizing the Question Rule may be stated
roughly as follows:

(5.31) <u>Yes/No Question</u> (Optional)

$$\text{SD: NP} \quad - \quad \text{Tense} \quad \left(\left\{ \begin{array}{l} \text{Modal} \\ \text{have} \\ \text{be} \end{array} \right\} \right)$$

$$\qquad\qquad 1 \qquad\qquad\qquad 2$$
$$\text{SC: } 2 \qquad\qquad\qquad 1$$

In stating the SD of the Question Rule (5.31), we have made
use of two notational devices: parentheses ( ) and braces (or
curly brackets) { }. The interpretation of these symbols is
straightforward. As we can see from the trees in (5.30), Tense
can be immediately followed by any one of three elements: a
modal verb, <u>have</u>, or <u>be</u>, depending on how the PS rule for
Aux has been expanded. We must represent these three alternatives by using curly brackets:

(5.32) a.

$$\text{Tense} \left\{ \begin{array}{l} \text{Modal} \\ \text{have} \\ \text{be} \end{array} \right\}$$

The three items in curly brackets are precisely those that
must be fronted along with Tense, if they have been generated;
if not, Tense will ultimately have the verb <u>do</u> attached to it by
Do Support. Therefore, we must state the Question Rule in
such a way that it will always front an auxiliary verb when
there is one following Tense, but so that it will also front Tense
alone if no auxiliary verb happens to have been generated along
with it. We can symbolize precisely this set of conditions by
enclosing the curly brackets expression in parentheses:

(5.32) b.

$$\text{Tense } \left\langle \left\{ \begin{array}{l} \text{Modal} \\ \text{have} \\ \text{be} \end{array} \right\} \right\rangle$$

By using parentheses in this manner, we essentially allow the
SD of the Question Rule to be satisfied under two circumstances:
A. When a modal verb, <u>have</u>, or <u>be</u> immediately follows Tense,
in which case it must be fronted by the rule; or
B. When Tense occurs alone, in which case Tense alone will
be fronted.
In order to illustrate how this rule operates, let us see in
detail how it analyzes and changes the structure shown in
(5.33a-b).

(5.33) a.

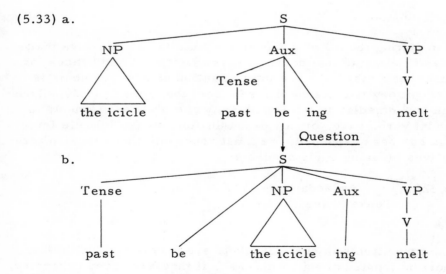

Affix Hopping will then apply, as illustrated in (5.33c).

(5.33) c.

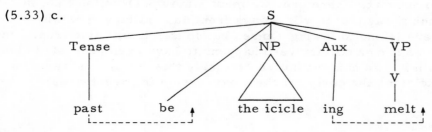

The output will then be be past the icicle melt_ing or Was the
icicle melting? One important point to notice is that rule (5.31)
only inverts Modal, have, or be along with Tense and does not
move the affix, if any, originally generated with the moved
element. So ing is left behind by the Question Rule, and consequently it can be attached to the verb following it when Affix
Hopping applies to (5.33c). Of course, this is precisely the effect we permitted the Question Rule to have when we stated it
in words in chapter 4.

There is a certain respect in which the formalized Question
Rule seems less natural than our previous informal version.
When stating the transformation in words, we were able to say,
in effect, that the subject inverts with the Tense and the first
auxiliary verb after it. But now we have no natural way of formalizing the notion "first auxiliary verb after Tense" aside
from listing all those items which can occur after Tense.

Since any of the elements Modal, have, and be appear in sequence under the Aux node, the only way we can be sure that
the first of these immediately following Tense moves with it is
to specifically mention each of the possibilities in the SD of our
rule. It may appear that our earlier Question Rule, stated in
ordinary English, was a much better representation of the facts,
since it seemed to capture a generalization that rule (5.31) does
not; the informal rule simply refers to "the first auxiliary verb"
after Tense and does not list all the possibilities separately, as
rule (5.31) does.

However, it turns out that rule (5.31), as complex as it may
appear, has further empirical consequences in English grammar that may be desirable. Since the rule simply lists be and
does not distinguish among the different occurrences of this
verb in the language, it predicts that even when be is a main
verb, and not an auxiliary verb, it will be fronted in a question.
Consider now structures such as the following:

(5.34)

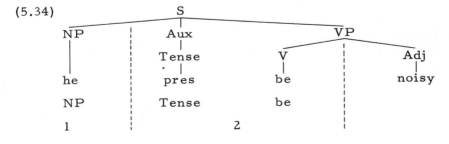

The formalized rule (5.31)—but not the Question Rule stated in words—will generalize to the case in which be is a main verb, since, as we see from tree (5.34), we can isolate the sequence NP - Tense be. Regardless of the node dominating the verb be, rule (5.31) will always front it, hence predicting that main verb be will act like an auxiliary verb and move to the front in questions. This is precisely what occurs. Whereas an ordinary main verb does not front, main verb be does:

(5.35) a. Is John a doctor?
      b. *Saw John a doctor?

Notice now that our ordinary language Question Rule (stated above), which seemed simple enough, would have to be complicated quite a bit to accommodate these new facts. That is, the rule would have to be stated something like this: Place Tense plus the first auxiliary verb after Tense (if any), to the left of the subject NP. Exception: If the main verb is be and no auxiliary verb precedes it, then front main verb be along with Tense. Yet the formalized rule (5.31) automatically generalizes to cases in which be is a main verb.

The reader may have noticed that rule (5.31) will also generalize to cases in which have is a main verb. Compare, for example, the following trees:

(5.36) a.

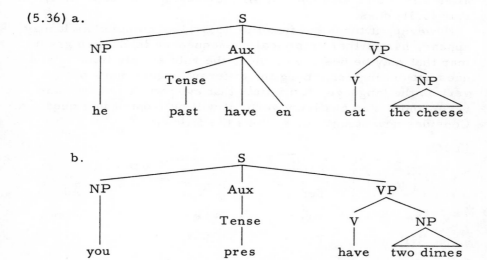

Rule (5.31) will generate <u>Has he eaten the cheese</u>? from (5.36a), where <u>have</u> is in the Aux, and <u>Have you two dimes</u>?, where <u>have</u> functions as a main verb. (It should be noted that sentences with main verb <u>have</u> also have question forms with auxiliary <u>do</u>, as in <u>Do you have two dimes</u>? Our theory as it stands will not generate these forms, because rule (5.31) will always front <u>have</u> if it occurs immediately after <u>Tense</u>, so that <u>Do</u> Support will never apply in sentences with <u>have</u>. This problem can be solved in various ways; see the suggested readings for this chapter.)

Thus, we see that our formalization of the Question Rule, (5.31), leads to certain correct predictions about the verb <u>be</u> in English, predictions that our informal rule could not make. Indeed, as we shall see in the last section of this chapter (section 5.6) and in later chapters, the similarities between auxiliary and main verb <u>be</u> will play a crucial role in a number of rules of English, and our formalism will be justified to the extent that it captures these similarities.

5.5. FORMALIZING RULES UTILIZING FEATURES: REFLEXIVIZATION

The Passive and Question Rules have the effect of restructuring trees: both reorder portions of their input trees, and, in addition, the Passive Rule adds the structural elements <u>by</u> and <u>be en</u>. Most well-motivated transformations have such an effect on the trees to which they are applied. However, it seems likely that there is another class of syntactic rules that has a rather different effect. Instead of reordering the tree structure (in the sense of changing the position and/or domination of nodes in a tree), such rules appear to change the internal composition of single elements in the tree. It has been proposed that the system of syntactic features (discussed briefly in chapter 2) should play a role in the statement of certain rules, that is, that transformations should be permitted to introduce or change syntactic features.

The rules that are most likely to make use of syntactic features tend to involve <u>agreement</u> between elements. One such rule in English is <u>Reflexivization</u>, a phenomenon that may be summarized as follows. In English there is a set of words referred to as reflexive pronouns:

(5.37) myself   ourselves
       yourself   yourselves

$$\begin{Bmatrix} \text{himself} \\ \text{herself} \\ \text{itself} \end{Bmatrix} \quad \text{themselves}$$

Each may be thought of as composed of the noun stem <u>self</u>, with
a possessive pronoun (such as <u>my</u>, <u>your</u>, <u>her</u>) attached to it.
(Exceptionally, we find <u>himself</u> and <u>themselves</u> in place of the
forms *<u>hisself</u> and *<u>theirselves</u>. We can nevertheless assume
that <u>himself</u> and <u>themselves</u> are derived from reflexive forms
that include the possessive pronouns. This will not materially
affect our account of the facts.)

Reflexive pronouns have a rather limited distribution. First,
a reflexive can never function as the subject of a sentence:

(5.38) a. *Myself is very angry today.
    b. *Yourself hurt John yesterday.
    c. *Herself finds Mary boring.

Second, even in nonsubject position the distribution of reflexives
is restricted. For example, sentences such as the following are
impossible:

(5.39) a. *I hurt yourself yesterday.
     (Cf. I hurt you yesterday.)
    b. *They will hire himself.
     (Cf. They will hire him.)
    c. *John and Mary are smarter than ourselves.
     (Cf. John and Mary are smarter than us.)

The reflexive must <u>agree</u> with the subject of the sentence, in
the sense that the possessive pronoun preceding the stem <u>self</u>
must be the same in <u>person</u>, <u>number</u>, and <u>gender</u> as the subject:

(5.40) a. <u>I</u> hurt <u>my</u>self.
    b. <u>You</u> hurt <u>your</u>self.
    c. <u>He</u> hurt <u>him</u>self; <u>John</u> hurt <u>him</u>self.
    d. <u>She</u> hurt <u>her</u>self; <u>Mary</u> hurt <u>her</u>self.
    e. <u>We</u> hurt <u>our</u>selves.
    f. <u>They</u> hurt <u>them</u>selves.

Finally, in those situations in which a reflexive can occur be-

cause the subject and object are in agreement, an ordinary
first person or second person pronoun cannot occur:

(5.41) a. I hurt myself.
       *I hurt me.   (Cf. He hurt me.)
    b. You hurt yourself.
       *You hurt you.   (Cf. He hurt you.)
    c. We hurt ourselves.
       *We hurt us.   (Cf. He hurt us.)

In order to explain these three peculiarities in the distribution of reflexive pronouns, an obligatory rule of Reflexivization has been proposed. This rule will operate on structures
such as the following:

(5.42) a.

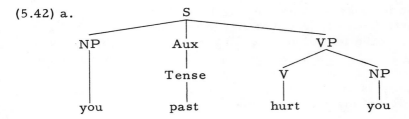

Whenever the subject of the sentence is identical with some
other NP within the sentence (as in (5.42a)), then the rightmost of the two NPs must be converted into a reflexive form.
Thus, (5.42a) must be transformed into (5.42b):

(5.42) b.

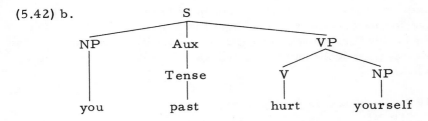

A rule having this effect would go some way toward explaining
the three distributional peculiarities set out in examples (5.38)-
(5.41): if reflexive pronouns were only introduced by that rule,
they could not occur in subject position (cf. (5.38)) and they
would agree with their subjects (cf. (5.39) or (5.40)); and as
long as the rule were obligatory, the ordinary pronouns could
not occur (cf. (5.41)).

How can we formalize such a rule? In particular, how can
we ensure that the reflexive produced by the rule agrees with
the subject in all relevant respects? After all, the crucial
change brought about by the putative rule is just the substitution of an appropriately agreeing reflexive pronoun for an NP
that is identical to the subject. To formalize the rule, we need
to be able to capture the essentials of that relationship.

Recall that in section 2.4 lexical items were eventually set
up as complex units that incorporated features like [+N], [+V],
[+[Det ___]], [+ [___ NP]], and so on. It is natural to suppose
that other syntactic features of a word are characterized in the
lexicon. So the word I must be, say, [1 person], while you is
[2 person]. In addition I is [- plural], while we is [+ plural].
All ordinary nouns are [3 person]. These characteristics of
the words will not be used only in Reflexivization but will figure also in rules such as the Tag Rule or Number Agreement
(see section 6.1.5). (Number Agreement is the rule that guarantees that the tensed verb will agree with its subject, thus
yielding I am, you are, he is, etc., while preventing *he am,
etc.).

Using syntactic features, we can represent the difference
between I and myself as follows:

(5.43)

$$
\begin{matrix}
I \\
\begin{bmatrix} 1 \text{ PERSON} \\ - \text{ PLURAL} \\ - \text{ REFLEXIVE} \end{bmatrix}
\end{matrix}
\qquad
\begin{matrix}
myself \\
\begin{bmatrix} 1 \text{ PERSON} \\ - \text{ PLURAL} \\ + \text{ REFLEXIVE} \end{bmatrix}
\end{matrix}
$$

We can make the same feature distinction between all other reflexive forms and their corresponding personal pronoun forms.
If this is the correct way to represent this distinction, then the
Reflexivization Rule can be stated as a feature-changing rule,
as follows:

(5.44) Reflexivization (Obligatory)
SD: NP - Aux - V - X - NP
       1   2   3   4   5
SC: 1 2 3 4   5
              [+ REFLEXIVE]
Condition: Term 1 must be identical with term 5.

Since the two NPs of (5.42a) are identical, rule (5.44) must apply to that tree, producing the following output:

(5.42) c.

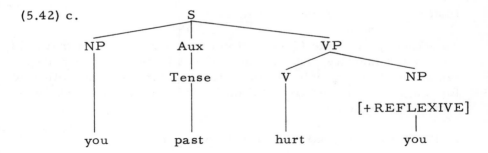

The Reflexivization Rule has the effect of placing the feature [+REFLEXIVE] on the NP node; we shall assume that by general convention this feature is then assigned to the head N of the NP, so that the object <u>you</u> in this case will automatically be marked with that feature:

(5.45)   NP

[+REFLEXIVE]
|
you

$$\begin{bmatrix} 2\ \text{PERSON} \\ -\ \text{PLURAL} \\ +\ \text{REFLEXIVE} \end{bmatrix}$$

Recall that in our discussion of Affix Hopping in chapter 4, we assumed the existence of certain Spell-Out rules (i.e., word formation, or <u>morphological</u> rules) that would indicate how certain verb + affix combinations would actually be realized in the spoken language. Here, too, we will assume the existence of morphological rules that will substitute the appropriate reflexive form for any pronoun having the feature [+REFLEXIVE]. Thus, by adding the feature [+REFLEXIVE] to the object NP in (5.42c), we can formally represent the fact that the second <u>you</u> in that structure must be in reflexive form.

Note that in the formal statement of the rule of Reflexivization, we have included a variable, <u>X</u>, between the verb and the following NP. This is because the reflexive need not immediately follow the verb. For example, in (5.46) a prepositional phrase intervenes between the main verb and the reflexive:

(5.46) I̲ talked to Mary about myself̲.

Note finally that rule (5.44) is too narrowly stated, in that it is not always identity with the subject that is required in reflex-ivization. For example, in the following sentence the reflexive form agrees with the first NP on its left and not with the sub-ject of the sentence:

(5.47) Herb will talk to you̲ about yourself̲.

However, we will not attempt to refine our formulation of the rule at this point.

5.6. WORK SECTION: THERE INSERTION

In this chapter we have explored some of the ways in which transformational rules can be stated formally, and we have also noted some of the problems we find in attempting to state rules precisely. Readers encountering this sort of enterprise for the first time will find it easier to grasp the fundamentals of rule formalization if they try to put those principles into practice. The purpose of this section is to provide this sort of practice with some guidance. After completing the section, it is strongly recommended that the reader work through the exercises at the end of this chapter, to become exposed to new rules of English that will figure in later chapters of this book.

A number of linguists have proposed that the (b) sentences of (5.48)-(5.51) are derived from the structures represented by the (a) sentences, by a transformation that has been called There Insertion:

(5.48) a. A boy was on the dock.
            ↓
       b. There was a boy on the dock.

(5.49) a. Some students are in the ballroom.
            ↓
       b. There are some students in the ballroom.

(5.50) a. Human beings might have been on that continent at
            one time.
            ↓
       b. There might have been human beings on that continent
          at one time.

(5.51) a. Only three marbles will be in that box tomorrow.

   b. There will be only three marbles in that box tomor-
      row.

We need not be concerned at this point with the motivation for
proposing a transformation to link the (b) sentences to the (a)
sentences. Some brief remarks on the justification for doing
so will be interjected where appropriate, but we are interested
mainly in problems of formalization in this section.

   Before we discuss the transformation of <u>There</u> Insertion
further, though, we must distinguish the <u>existential</u> <u>there</u>,
found in the examples above, from the <u>locative</u> <u>there</u>, which
occurs in the following sentences:

(5.52) a. <u>There</u>'s John!
   b. <u>There</u>'s the man we've been looking for, on the dock!

There are several important differences between the two uses
of <u>there</u>. First of all, sentences with existential <u>there</u> and
those with locative <u>there</u> answer different kinds of questions.
For example:

(5.53) Existential <u>there</u>
   a. Q: What do you see on the dock?
      (or: Is there anything on the dock?)

   b. A: There's a boy on the dock.

(5.54) Locative <u>there</u>
   a. Q: Do you see a boy anywhere?
      (or: Where do you see a boy?)

   b. A: Yes, <u>there</u>'s a boy, over on the dock.

Notice that locative <u>there</u>, as in (5.54b), is always somewhat
stressed (emphasized) in speech, as indicated by the underlining in the example. Existential <u>there</u> is always unstressed.
The fact that locative <u>there</u> is stressed in (5.54b) may very
well be related to the fact that it is this word that really answers the question posed in (5.54a), by indicating a direction
or location. Likewise, the lack of stress on existential <u>there</u>
may well be related to the fact that it carries little or no mean-

ing. Thus, in (5.53b), the words a boy are what really answer
the question (5.53a), while there seems quite empty of meaning.

We should emphasize that these remarks are not meant to
be taken as a precise characterization of the two uses of there
but should be regarded as pointers to be followed in attempting to recognize the existential there found in examples (5.48)-
(5.51). Before we can write a rule linking such pairs, we must
have some idea of the range of distribution of the there that occurs in the second member of each pair. Let us turn now to
that problem: where does existential there occur?

First, notice that existential there—as in all the (b) sentences of (5.48)-(5.51)—functions as an NP, more specifically,
as the subject of the sentence. We can test this by noting that
existential there can be copied into tags, as other NP subjects
can, and will invert with auxiliary verbs in questions, as other
NP subjects do:

(5.55) a. There's a boy on the dock, isn't there?
       b. Is there a boy on the dock?

This suggests that existential there should be dominated by the
node NP, in subject position. Notice, incidentally, that locative there never acts like an NP subject:

(5.56) a. There's John, by the tree.
       b. *There's John, by the tree, isn't there?

(5.57) a. There's John, by the tree.
       b. *Is there John, by the tree?

It appears that existential there cannot appear in nonsubject
position in a sentence. There are many sentences containing
there in other positions, e.g.:

(5.58) a. John is over there.
       b. The ball is there, under the tree.
       c. There he goes.

However, on the basis of what we have said so far, it seems
fairly clear that in such sentences it is the locative there that
occurs. (It is stressed, is fully meaningful, and is used to

"point" in answer to questions about direction, place, etc.)
Summarizing both aspects of this observation, then, we may
say that (existential) <u>there</u> occurs <u>only</u> as the subject of a sentence.

Second, however, existential <u>there</u> cannot occur as the subject of just any sentence. It occurs only with the verb <u>be</u> (and
perhaps a tiny number of additional verbs such as <u>occur</u> and
<u>arise</u>, as in <u>There arose a great cry from the crowd</u>—but we
will ignore these). Thus (5.59b)-(5.59c) are not grammatical:

(5.59) a.   There were two men in the room.
       b. *There laughed two men in the room.
       c. *There died two men in the room.

Finally, notice that the NP following <u>be</u> is somewhat restricted:

(5.60) a.   There were <u>some students</u> in the ballroom.
       b. *There were <u>they/them</u> in the ballroom.

(5.61) a.   There wasn't <u>a bear</u> in sight.
       b. *There wasn't <u>the bear</u> in sight.

(5.62) a.   There wasn't <u>anyone</u> near you.
       b. *There wasn't <u>John</u> near you.

In a sentence containing existential <u>there</u>, the NP following <u>be</u>
(underlined in (5.60)-(5.62)) may not be a proper noun or pronoun and must not begin with the definite article, <u>the</u>. More
generally, the NP after <u>be</u> must not refer to a specific, unique
individual. Such NPs are called <u>indefinite</u>, and we may state
the following condition: existential <u>there</u> may occur only if
there is an <u>indefinite</u> NP (e.g., <u>a boy</u>, <u>any students</u>, <u>many
people</u>) immediately to the right of <u>be</u> in the sentence.

Given our discussion so far, we can isolate three important
properties of existential <u>there</u> that our grammar will have to
account for: (a) existential <u>there</u> may occur only in subject position; (b) it may occur only with the verb <u>be</u>; and (c) in sentences containing existential <u>there</u>, an indefinite NP must occur after the verb <u>be</u>.

In order to formulate the rule of <u>There</u> Insertion, we need
to know what the input structures will be. We are assuming

that our rule will convert (5.48a) to (5.48b), and likewise for
(5.49)-(5.51). The (a) sentences of (5.48)-(5.51) can be assigned underlying structures such as the following (using
(5.48a) as our example):

(5.63)

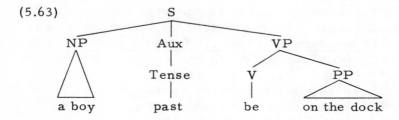

Let us now assume that the rule of There Insertion will operate on structures such as (5.63). Given only the sentence
pairs (5.48)-(5.51), try to state formally a rule of There Insertion that will transform the (a) sentences into the (b) sentences. How will a structure such as (5.63) be transformed by
the rule, and what will the output structure be?

A reasonable hypothesis is that There Insertion is stated
somewhat along the following lines:

(5.64) There Insertion (Preliminary Version) (Optional)
        SD: NP - Aux - be
             1   2   3
        SC: there   2   3 + 1

Structure (5.63) satisfies the SD of this rule:

(5.63')

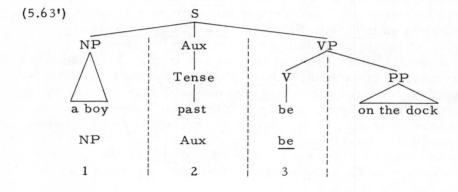

What output structure does rule (5.64) produce from this tree?

   The SC of rule (5.64) indicates that <u>there</u> has been inserted
in the position formerly occupied by term 1 (the subject NP)
and, in addition, that term 1 has been sister-adjoined to the
right of term 3 (i.e., <u>be</u>). Consequently (5.63') is converted
to (5.63") by this rule:

(5.63")

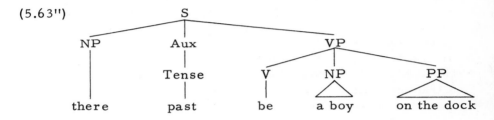

The reader should now check whether rule (5.64) generates the
rest of the (b) examples of (5.48)-(5.51).

   Although rule (5.64) will produce correct results when operating on a structure such as (5.63'), we nevertheless must
formulate the rule so that it will apply only to sentences with
indefinite subjects. If (5.63') were generated with a definite NP
in subject position (i.e., <u>The boy - past - be - on the dock</u>),
then rule (5.64) would have to be prevented from operating on
it so as to block sentences such as *<u>There was the boy on the
dock</u>. At present this condition on <u>There</u> Insertion can simply
be represented by marking term 1 as [- Definite]:

(5.65) <u>There Insertion</u> (Revision 1)

     SD: NP - Aux - <u>be</u>
         [- Def]
          1   2   3
     SC: <u>there</u>   2   3 + 1

Ideally, the definiteness restriction on <u>There</u> Insertion should
follow from some more general fact about English, but we have
no interesting alternative to suggest at this time.
   With the formulation of rule (5.65), we have in some measure

accounted for all three peculiarities that we noted in the distribution of there. Provided the existential there can appear
in sentences only as a result of the operation of this transformation, we have guaranteed (a) that existential there will occur only with indefinite NPs; (b) that there will occur only in
subject position (since it is inserted only in subject position);
and (c) that there will occur only in sentences with be (since
the SD of the rule specifically mentions be). Hence, we can
consider (5.65) as an adequate description of the facts presented so far about the distribution of existential there. (It
might be worth remarking that if there sentences were directly
generated by PS rules, the PS grammar would have to be considerably complicated in order to capture these three distributional facts. This constitutes part of the motivation for positing
a transformation of There Insertion; other relevant considerations will be mentioned later.)

Now we come to some serious counterexamples to rule (5.65).
As the rule is stated, the SD mentions the constituent Aux followed by main verb be. However, what happens in sentences
containing instances of auxiliary be? Can There Insertion apply when auxiliary be is present? At this point, try to construct
a number of sentences that contain instances of auxiliary be
and that have also undergone the rule of There Insertion. Having
constructed such sentences, try to show how they form counterexamples to rule (5.65).

Of the numerous examples one could construct, those like
(5.66) are among the most interesting:

(5.66) There were twenty men fired by the company last year.

This sentence is in passive form—i.e., the rule of There Insertion has operated on a passive structure. (Incidentally,
this shows quite conclusively that sentences with existential
there cannot be generated by PS rules alone. Why?) We know
that passive sentences contain the verb be and moreover that
the passive be is an auxiliary verb, not a main verb. The
structure underlying (5.66) at a stage immediately before
There Insertion operates is as follows:

(5.66')

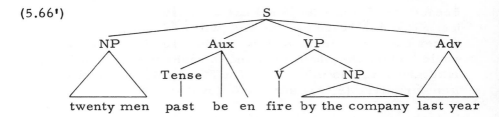

(Of course, this tree would derive, in turn, from an active
structure, i.e., <u>The company - past - fire - twenty men - last
year</u>.)
   The problem is that structure (5.66') does not satisfy the SD
of rule (5.65): that rule requires us to find the sequence <u>NP -
Aux - be</u>, and no such sequence can be found in (5.66'). Since
<u>be</u> is <u>part of</u> the Aux in that structure, we cannot isolate a se-
quence in which <u>be</u> occurs <u>after</u> Aux in linear order. Now can
we modify rule (5.65) so that it will apply to (5.66')? In particular, try to use a variable in the new version of the rule.

   The following modification would allow the rule to apply to
(5.66'), as well as to the other input trees discussed so far:

(5.67) <u>There Insertion</u> (Revision 2)

        SD: NP   -   X   -   <u>be</u>
             [- Def]
               1   2   3
        SC: <u>there</u>   2   3 + 1

Tree (5.66') meets the SD as follows:

(5.68) a.

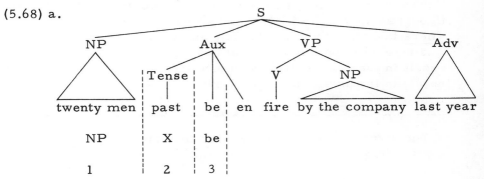

Because the SD of rule (5.67) has a variable between the subject NP and the verb be, the rule will now apply both to sentences containing main verb be (as in tree (5.63'), where X
would include the whole Aux) and to cases in which be is an
auxiliary verb, as in (5.68a). The SC of rule (5.67) will then
transform tree (5.68a) into the following:

(5.68) b.

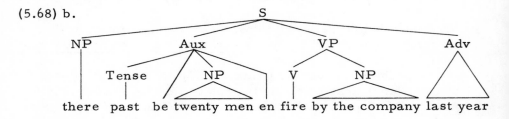

(We will discuss in a moment the derived structure of the Aux
in such examples.)

Although our latest version of There Insertion is more adequate than the earlier ones, we must modify it still further. To
see why, consider the following sentences:

(5.69) a. There were twenty patients being examined by the
           doctors.
       b. *There were being twenty patients examined by the
           doctors.

In sentence (5.69a), there are two occurrences of the verb be
(namely, were and being), and, as sentence (5.69b) shows, the
NP following there may be inserted only after the first verb be
and may not be inserted after the second occurrence of be.
However, rule (5.67) allows us to generate sentences such as
(5.69b) as well as (5.69a). To see why, first construct the pre-
There Insertion tree for (5.69a), and then apply the rule to it.
The rule will apply in either of two ways—one application would
result in the grammatical sentence (5.69a), and the other would
result in the ungrammatical (5.69b).

The structure of (5.69a) prior to the application of There Insertion is given in (5.70) below. Notice how the variable X of

the rule can be interpreted in two ways, as shown in (5.70a)
and (5.70b):

(5.70) a.

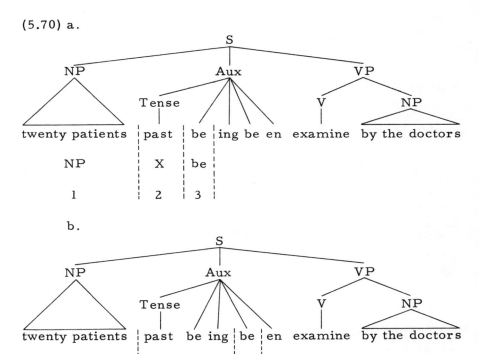

Since the variable <u>X</u> of the rule can, in this case, stand for
either <u>Tense</u> alone or for <u>Tense</u> – be – ing (depending on
which <u>be</u> is regarded as term 3 of the SD), it follows that our
rule will be able to insert the subject NP either after the first
occurrence of <u>be</u> (as (5.70a) would allow) or after the second
occurrence of <u>be</u> (as (5.70b) would allow). But that NP must be
inserted only after the <u>first</u> occurrence of <u>be</u>. How must we
restrict rule (5.67)? (Hint: What actual elements within Aux
will the first <u>be</u> follow?)

_____

It seems that the following formulation of <u>There</u> Insertion
will overcome the defects of rule (5.67):

(5.71) <u>There Insertion</u> (Revision 3)

SD: NP - Tense - (Modal) - (have en) - be
    [- Def]
      1   2   3   4   5
SC: <u>there</u>   2   3   4 5 + 1

Rule (5.71) can analyze a tree such as (5.72) in only one way:

(5.72)

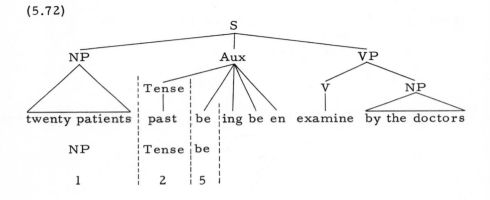

Thus, the <u>be</u> in the SD of this latest revision always refers to the first <u>be</u> following Tense (<u>Modal</u> and <u>have</u> are listed as op-tional in the SD; i.e., they need not be present in order for the rule to operate, as is the case above). Given that, the rule will move the subject NP, <u>twenty patients</u>, to the position immedi-ately following the <u>first be</u>, thus allowing sentences like (5.69a) to be generated while excluding (5.69b). The reader should check that rule (5.71) actually generates all the well-formed <u>there</u> sentences that we have discussed so far, as well as forms such as <u>There were some boys running down the road.</u>

We must make a brief note of one potential problem with the output structures of the rule, as it now stands. Whenever <u>There</u> Insertion operates on sentences containing occurrences of auxiliary <u>be</u>, it will have the effect of inserting the subject NP into Aux, in between <u>be</u> and its affix. For example, <u>There</u> Insertion operating on (5.73a) will produce (5.73b):

(5.73) a.

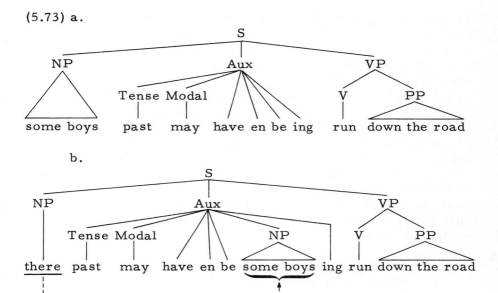

Such a derived structure seems intuitively "unnatural"; in the sentence There might have been some boys running down the road, we hardly expect the NP some boys to be part of the Aux. However, given the way we have stated There Insertion and the way Affix Hopping works, the derived structure (5.73b) is the only possible one.

First of all, the SC of There Insertion instructs us to sister-adjoin term 1 to the right of be; this has been done in tree (5.73b). Second, if term 1 (= subject NP) were to be adjoined in a more "natural" place—for example, outside Aux preceding VP—then Affix Hopping could not work. For example, consider adjoining the subject NP of (5.73a) as follows:

(5.74)

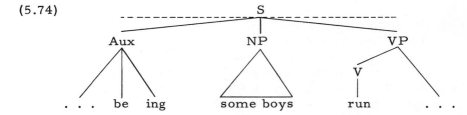

If this were done, the affix ing would no longer be adjacent to the verb run, and the rule of Affix Hopping would not be able to place it on the verb; the intervening NP <u>some boys</u> would block the application of the rule. We cannot simply reject the analysis embodied in rule (5.71) on "intuitive" grounds, though it would be good to find an alternative that avoided derived structures like (5.73b).

We have by no means said the final word on <u>There</u> Insertion. As will be clear from the suggested readings at the end of the chapter, there are other possible analyses markedly different from the one offered here. Any more detailed exploration of the area will turn up numerous other problems for our formulation, and the reader should treat rule (5.71) as only a tentative hypothesis for further study. Among the problems that could be raised, the following might be worth exploring. Will rule (5.71) generate (5.75a and b), and, if so, how could we exclude them?

(5.75) a. *There is a man a doctor.
       b. *There is a man sick.

CHAPTER 5: EXERCISES
(E5.1) Examine the following pair of sentences:

(i)   He ran up a big bill.
(ii)   He ran up a big hill.

Notice that in sentence (i), as opposed to (ii), <u>up</u> may be moved to the end of the sentence:

(iii) He ran a big bill up. (cf. *He ran a big hill up.)

There are many other pairs of sentences parallel to (i) and (iii):

(iv)   He looked <u>up</u> the number.
       He looked the number <u>up</u>.
(v)   She may send <u>out</u> the package.
       She may send the package <u>out</u>.
(vi)   Mr. X brings <u>in</u> the milk for his mother.
       Mr. X brings the milk <u>in</u> for his mother.
(vii) The President called <u>up</u> China last year.
       The President called China <u>up</u> last year.

(viii) Will you cut <u>out</u> the racket, please?
      Will you cut the racket <u>out</u>, please?
(ix)   Mary will push <u>over</u> the armchair as we watch.
      Mary will push the armchair <u>over</u> as we watch.

It appears, then, that there are a number of verbal expressions in English that consist of a verb + preposition (such as <u>in</u>, <u>up</u>, <u>out</u>, <u>over</u>), in which the preposition may be separated from the verb. These shiftable prepositions have been called <u>particles</u> and the expressions themselves <u>verb-particle expressions</u>.

    Now assume that there is a rule in English that transforms the first of each of the pairs (iv)-(ix) into the second:

(iv) He looked <u>up</u> the number. $\Rightarrow$ He looked the number <u>up</u>.

Hence, in the base form, the particle is located immediately after the verb, and the transformation separates it from the verb in the appropriate ways. Consider the following questions:

<u>A</u>. How would you state this <u>Particle Movement Transformation</u> in words? Is it an optional rule or an obligatory rule? Would it be accurate to say that the particle moves to the end of the sentence? If so, what is the evidence? If not, or if other evidence suggests otherwise, then where, exactly, does the particle move? List both grammatical and ungrammatical sentences in order to show where the particle moves.

<u>B</u>. Once you have stated the Particle Movement Transformation in words, formalize the rule as accurately as possible. (The prepositional particles can be represented as PPs or by the symbol <u>Prt</u>.) What constituents of the input sentences need to be specifically referred to in the SD of the rule? What constituents of the input sentences need not be mentioned in the SD; i.e., what constituents are irrelevant to the rule?

(E5.2) Once you have formalized the Particle Movement Rule and you are satisfied that it represents the facts of (iv)-(ix) of question (E5.1) correctly, then consider the following sentences:

(i)   *John looked up it.
       John looked it up.
(ii)   *Mary may send out it.
       Mary may send it out.
(iii) *Mr. X brought in it for his mother.
       Mr. X brought it in for his mother.
(iv)   *Will you cut out it, please?
       Will you cut it out, please?

These sentences indicate that a special condition must be placed
on the Particle Movement Rule in order to prevent the ungrammatical sentences from being generated. What is that condition? In working on this problem, it is important to recognize
that the PS rules will automatically generate such forms as
*John looked up it since an NP can consist of just a pronoun.
The solution will involve stating the rule of Particle Movement
in such a way that such sentences are never generated as the
final output of any derivation.

(E5.3) A number of linguists have proposed that there is a
transformation in English called Dative Movement, which re-
lates pairs of sentences such as the following:

(i)   Santa Claus may bring a sack of toys to the children.
       Santa Claus may bring the children a sack of toys.
(ii)   Mr. Ponsonby sent a parcel to his son.
       Mr. Ponsonby sent his son a parcel.
(iii) You have bought three books for Mary.
       You have bought Mary three books.
(iv)   They will sing a song for the little child.
       They will sing the little child a song.

Now consider the following questions:

A. Assume that the base form for the Dative Movement Transformation is the first sentence of each pair and that the output
of the rule is the second sentence:

(a) Mr. Ponsonby sent a parcel to his son.
      ↓
(b) Mr. Ponsonby sent his son a parcel.

State the Dative Movement Transformation in words, and then formalize the transformation. (Note: The Dative Movement Transformation deletes the preposition <u>to</u> or <u>for</u> as part of its operation. In order to show this deletion formally, use the computer symbol for zero, $\emptyset$, in the place of the SC corresponding to the preposition in the SD.)

<u>B</u>. Now make the opposite assumption, namely, that the base form of the Dative Movement Transformation is the second sentence of each pair and that the output of the rule is the first sentence:

(b) Mr. Ponsonby sent his son a parcel.

(a) Mr. Ponsonby sent a parcel to his son.

State this "Reverse" Dative Movement Transformation in words, and then formalize the rule. (Note: In this case, the transformation will need to add, rather than delete, the prepositions. To see how added material can be represented formally, look at the Passive Rule (5.28) again, where <u>be en</u> and <u>by</u> are added.)

(E5.4) Once you have completed questions (A) and (B) of (E5.3), consider the following sentences and compare them carefully with sentences (i)-(iv) of (E5.3) above:

(i)   a. Santa Claus may bring it to the children.
      b. *Santa Claus may bring the children it.
(ii) a. Mr. Ponsonby sent it to his son.
      b. *Mr. Ponsonby sent his son it.
(iii) a. You have brought it for Mary.
      b. *You have brought Mary it.
(iv) a. They will sing it for the little child.
      b. *They will sing the little child it.

These sentences indicate that a condition of some sort must be placed on the Dative Movement Rule in order to prevent the (b) sentences from being generated. Consider the following questions:

<u>A</u>. State in words why the (b) sentences above are ungrammatical—what do they have in common that makes them so?

<u>B</u>. What specific condition must be placed on the Dative Movement Rule <u>as formulated in question (A) of (E5.3)</u> in order to prevent the ungrammatical sentences?

<u>C</u>. On the other hand, what condition must be placed on the Dative Movement Rule <u>as formulated in question (B) of (E5.3)</u> in order to prevent the ungrammatical sentences? It should become evident that the condition on the Dative Movement Rule needs to be stated quite differently depending on which formulation is chosen.

<u>D</u>. <u>For Further Thinking</u>: In what way are the facts given in (i)-(iv) above reminiscent of the facts about Particle Movement given in (i)-(iv) of question (E5.2)? In what way is the condition on Particle Movement similar to the condition(s) on Dative Movement (in either formulation)? Can a <u>unified</u> statement of these facts be built into our theory as it now stands?

(E5.5) The Question Rule is stated as follows in the text:

(i)

$$\text{SD: NP} \quad - \quad \text{Tense} \quad (\left\{ \begin{array}{l} \text{Modal} \\ \text{have} \\ \text{be} \end{array} \right\})$$

$$\qquad 1 \qquad\qquad\qquad 2$$

SC: 2   1

(See example (5.31).

It was pointed out in the text that the specification of three distinct elements, <u>Modal</u>, <u>have</u>, and <u>be</u>, as alternatives in the second term of the SD might seem clumsy, but that this formulation was in fact justified by the fact that even the main verb <u>be</u> is fronted in questions, as in <u>Is Jill a teacher</u>? Consider, however, an imaginary rule such as (ii):

(ii)

$$\text{SD: NP} \quad - \quad \text{Tense} \quad (\left\{ \begin{array}{l} \text{obviously} \\ \text{never} \end{array} \right\})$$

$$\qquad\qquad\qquad\qquad\qquad\qquad V$$

$$\qquad 1 \qquad\qquad\qquad 2$$

SC: 2   1

This rule would have the effect of converting <u>John saw Mary</u> into <u>Saw John Mary</u>, <u>John never saw Mary</u> into <u>Never John</u>

saw Mary, John obviously saw Mary into Obviously John saw
Mary. (Or at least it would have an effect very much like this.)
    Formally, this imaginary rule is just as simple as the Ques-
tion Rule. Yet although the English Question Rule seems perfectly natural, we would never expect to find a language that
included a rule like (ii) in its grammar. Think about the implications of this situation. Does it expose weaknesses in the
theory developed so far? If so, try to state those weaknesses
explicitly, and explain why they should be avoided if possible.
See if you can suggest any generally applicable or specific
ways of improving the current model so as to exclude rules
like (ii). If possible, suggest ways of reformulating rule (i)
so that it is able to represent the fact that Modal, have, and
be are members of the same word class. (Note: This problem
is open-ended. It is not likely that the reader will find any
fully satisfactory solution.)

CHAPTER 5: SUGGESTED READINGS
The student who is interested in pursuing the question of formalizing transformations (and the formal properties of transformations) is likely to find very little in the transformational
literature that he or she will be able to grasp easily at this
point. Much of the work on the formal properties of transformations is highly technical in nature, for example, Chomsky
and Miller (1963) and Chomsky (1963). A somewhat less technical treatment of the formal properties of transformations
can be found in several recent textbooks on mathematical linguistics, in particular, Wall (1972), Kimball (1973), and Gross
(1972). A nontechnical discussion of how to formalize transformations can be found in Bach (1964). For students who wish
to gain practice in formalizing rules and doing derivations, we
can cite Burt (1971). Although that work is not without errors
and although Burt often makes quite different assumptions from
those that we make, the student should nevertheless be able to
profit from working through some of the examples found there.
    Additional discussion of the behavior of auxiliary have and
be contrasted with that of the main verbs have and be can be
found in Chomsky (1957, section 7.1). Readers interested in
pursuing the rule of There Insertion will find a useful bibliography and an interesting alternative to our account in Jenkins
(1972). The problem of the derived structure of There Insertion is treated in Akmajian and Wasow (forthcoming), in which

it is argued that if Affix Hopping is split into two separate rules and if certain instances of <u>be</u> are shifted from VP into Aux, then <u>There</u> Insertion can produce well-motivated derived structures.

For an account of the Dative Movement Rule, see Jackendoff and Culicover (1971); they propose that the rule should actually be merged with several other similar rules. Although the final section of that paper may be difficult to understand at this point, the earlier sections will provide a good introduction to additional important data relating to Dative Movement.

Chapter 6

ORDERING SIMPLE TRANSFORMATIONAL RULES

6.1. ORDERING THE TRANSFORMATIONS

In this chapter, we will present arguments for ordering a number of transformations, formalizing those rules that were not
formulated explicitly in chapter 5. This will prepare the way
for a discussion of several transformational analyses of tag
questions. Our discussion of tags is important, not because the
tag construction itself has great significance, but because the
discussion will raise the important question of how the rules
of our grammar should interact to produce the simplest overall grammatical system. We will generally take the transformations in the order in which they seem to apply, showing what
justification there is for this order. The reader will be provided with relevant data before the argument is presented and
should always attempt to construct the argument before reading further.

6.1.1. Dative Movement/Passive

The first rule we will consider is Dative Movement, which we
alluded to in exercise (E5.3). It has the effect of transforming
the structure underlying sentences such as (6.1a) into the structure underlying sentences such as (6.1b):

(6.1) a. Mary gave a book to the man.
      b. Mary gave the man a book.

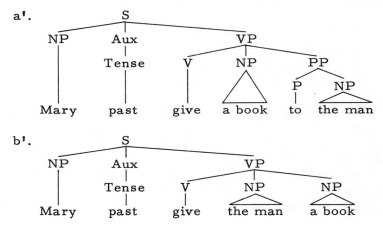

We will assume that Dative Movement transforms the (a)-type
structure into the (b)-type structure, rather than vice versa;
in most cases, this decision will have little effect on our argumentation, and it is at least as well motivated as the reverse option.

Notice that the rule of Dative Movement has the effect of
moving the indirect object (i.e., the NP within the prepositional phrase in (6.1a)) to the position immediately following
the verb (and deleting the preposition to), thus making that NP
the new direct object. We can state the rule as follows:

(6.2) Dative Movement (Optional)

$$\text{SD: V} - \text{NP} - \begin{Bmatrix} \text{to} \\ \text{for} \end{Bmatrix} - \text{NP}$$

$$\begin{array}{cccc} 1 & 2 & 3 & 4 \end{array}$$

$$\text{SC: } 1+4 \quad 2 \quad \emptyset \quad \emptyset$$

The data given in exercise (E5.3) show that Dative Movement
can operate when the indirect object contains for (note the sentences They bought a book for the child and They bought the
child a book), and thus we have included for in the SD along
with to.

It should be pointed out that Dative Movement is a governed
rule; that is to say, the possibility of its application depends
on the specific main verb of the sentence. Thus, verbs such
as give, send, lend, and throw allow Dative Movement, while
verbs that are very similar in meaning, such as transmit,
broadcast, and relay do not:

(6.3) a.   I sent the message to him.
           I sent him the message.
      b.   I transmitted the message to him.
           *I transmitted him the message.

One way to express the fact that main verbs govern the Dative
Movement Rule is to assume that among the syntactic features
associated with verbs there are rule features that mark a verb
as either undergoing or failing to undergo a rule. Hence, verbs
such as send might be marked [+ Dative Movement], while those
such as transmit would be marked [- Dative Movement]. Term 1
of the SD might then be represented more properly as [+ Dative

Movement]. Although this sort of device would mark verbs appropriately, it in no way explains why certain verbs undergo Dative Movement and others do not, a fact we have not yet properly accounted for.

The Dative Movement Rule has the effect of creating a new direct object, by moving in the NP from the indirect object position. This suggests that Dative Movement may interact with Passive, since the Passive Rule, among other things, moves the direct object of the verb to the front of the sentence. The two rules partially "overlap" in the syntactic context in which they apply, and thus it is quite likely that they apply in a fixed order. In order to determine this, we will have to re-examine sentences (6.1a) and (6.1b), along with several others. Use the following sentences to construct for yourself an ordering argument for Dative Movement and Passive:

(6.1') a. Mary gave a book to the man.
       b. Mary gave the man a book.
       c. A book was given to the man by Mary.
       d. The man was given a book by Mary.

Try to give a complete derivation for each of these sentences.

It turns out that the Dative Movement Rule must precede the Passive Rule if the sentences of (6.1') are to be generated simply. We can prove this to be so by assuming the contrary; that is, let us assume that the rules apply in the opposite order, namely, (1) Passive and (2) Dative Movement. Since both rules are optional, there are at most four possibilities for applying them; and if the four acceptable sentences of (6.1a)-(6.1d) are to be derived by applying these rules, then each must be generated by one of the following orderings:

	(i)	(ii)	(iii)	(iv)
Passive:	Applies	Applies	Not	Not
Dative Movement:	Applies	Not	Applies	Not

Does this work out correctly?

It is clear that (iv) yields (6.1'a); the most basic sentence

results if neither optional rule applies. Option (iii), where only
Dative Movement applies, yields (6.1'b); while option (ii), with
only the Passive applying, must yield (6.1'c). Example (6.1'd)
is left for us to derive—and we have only option (i) open to us,
where both the rules apply. Does that option yield (6.1'd)?

When we try to apply both rules in the order Passive/Dative
Movement, the following derivation will result:

(6.4)   Mary   past   give   a book   to the man
         Passive: a book   past be en give   to the man   by Mary
         Dative: does not apply
         (= (6.1'b) A book was given to the man by Mary.

Since the Dative Rule applies only when an NP comes between
the V and to, it will never apply after Passive has applied, removing the necessary NP between V and to. Thus, no ungrammatical sentence results, but the target sentence, (6.1'd), cannot be generated.
   If the rules apply in the order (1) Dative/(2) Passive, then
all the sentences of (6.1') are generated, as can easily be veri-
fied; we will give only the derivation of (6.1'd):

(6.5)   Mary   past   give   a book   to the man
         Dative: Mary   past   give   the man   a book
         Passive: the man   past be en   give   a book   by Mary
         (= (6.1'd)) The man was given a book by Mary.

The correct order is therefore:
1. Dative
2. Passive

6.1.2. Passive/Negative Insertion/Contraction

The Negative Insertion Transformation was introduced informally in chapter 3 (see (3.66)), and in exercise (E4.4) the reader
was asked to modify that rule in any way necessary to ensure
that it would be consistent with the analysis of the auxiliary
system introduced in that chapter. As the reader may have discovered, we must state the rule of Negative Insertion as follows:

(6.6) <u>Negative Insertion</u> (Optional)

SD: NP — Tense ($\left\{\begin{array}{l}\text{Modal}\\\text{have}\\\text{be}\end{array}\right\}$)

    1   2

SC: 1   2 + <u>not</u>

This rule resembles the Question Transformation in its reference to <u>Tense</u> followed optionally by <u>Modal</u>, <u>have</u>, or <u>be</u>. Since the rule places <u>not</u> immediately after <u>have</u> or <u>be</u>, it will have the effect of inserting <u>not</u> between <u>have</u> and <u>en</u> or between <u>be</u> and <u>ing</u>. This is necessary in order to ensure that the inserted <u>not</u> does not interfere with the operation of Affix Hopping in derivations such as (6.7a):

(6.7) a.   John present have en go
    Negative Insertion: John present have not en go
    Affix Hopping: John have present not go en
                    <u>John has not gone.</u>

However, when Tense is the only member of Aux in a tree, the insertion of a negative will correctly block Affix Hopping (just as the Question Rule blocks it in, e.g., <u>Did Bill see John?</u>), resulting in the application of <u>Do</u> Support:

(6.7) b.   Bill past see John
    Negative Insertion: Bill past not see John
    Affix Hopping: [Cannot apply; <u>not</u> intervenes
                  between <u>past</u> and <u>see</u>]
    <u>Do</u> Support: Bill do past not see John
                  <u>Bill did not see John.</u>

Given the formulation of Negative Insertion (6.6) and taking into account the way in which the rule operates, shown in (6.7), try to order Passive and Negative Insertion. With the proper ordering, you should be able to derive the sentence <u>John was not seen by Bill</u> from the underlying structure <u>Bill past see John</u>.

The correct order of application of these rules is (1) Passive/(2) Negative Insertion, as the following derivation shows:

(6.8) a.   Bill past see John
          Passive: John past be en see by Bill
          Negative Insertion: John past be not en see by Bill
                                <u>John was not seen by Bill</u>.

The passive <u>be</u> must be introduced into a sentence before the negative <u>not</u> can be placed after it. The opposite ordering leads to bad consequences:

(6.8) b.   Bill past see John
          Negative Insertion: Bill past not see John
          Passive: John past not be en see by Bill
          <u>Do</u> Support: John do past not be en see by Bill
                                *<u>John did not be seen by Bill</u>.

If the rules apply in this order, the negative will be inserted after Tense; this will cause <u>Do</u> Support to apply, wrongly, generating ungrammatical sentences and making it impossible to generate, e.g., <u>John was not seen by Bill</u>. Hence, we can conclude that the order so far is:
1. Dative
2. Passive
3. Negative Insertion
Let us now examine a further rule to be ordered, namely, <u>Contraction</u>. The effect of this rule can be seen in the following pairs of sentences:

(6.9) a. 1. The President <u>is not</u> willing to speak.
         2. The President <u>isn't</u> willing to speak.
      b. 1. Hoover <u>did not</u> destroy the files.
         2. Hoover <u>didn't</u> destroy the files.
      c. 1. The old men <u>had not</u> seen the sleek ship.
         2. The old men <u>hadn't</u> seen the sleek ship.
      d. 1. One <u>can not</u> consort with gorillas.
         2. One <u>can't</u> consort with gorillas.
      e. 1. Marx's theories <u>will not</u> account for the dollar
            shortage.
         2. Marx's theories <u>won't</u> account for the dollar short-
            age.

In each case we see that the rule of Contraction has the effect of reducing the word <u>not</u> to the word that we spell as <u>n't</u>. We may regard this reduced form as being attached directly to the auxiliary verb immediately to the left of the negative. In other words, in the uncontracted form, the auxiliary verb and negative <u>not</u> constitute two separate words; the effect of Contraction <u>is</u> to reduce the two words to one word. (Note, incidentally, that a few auxiliaries change pronunciation when contracted; thus, <u>will + not</u> = <u>won't</u> and <u>shall + not</u> = <u>shan't</u>.)

We will leave until the next section the problem of how to represent the contraction process by means of a transformation. Regardless of how we formulate the Contraction Rule, it should be obvious how it is ordered: since Contraction has the effect of adjoining the negative word <u>not</u> to an auxiliary verb, it follows that the rule cannot apply until <u>not</u> has been inserted within the auxiliary. Hence, Contraction must apply after the rule of Negative Insertion. Whenever two rules are related in this particular way—i.e., whenever one rule cannot apply until another rule has operated to supply the former with material necessary for its operation—we say that they are <u>intrinsically ordered</u> (otherwise, when rules could logically be ordered in any way, but must nevertheless be ordered in some fixed way to derive the correct output, we say that they are <u>extrinsically ordered</u>).

The ordering so far is therefore:
1. Dative
2. Passive
3. Negative Insertion
4. Contraction

6.1.3. Negative Insertion and Contraction/Question

Arguments for the crucial ordering of two rules must be based on sentences in which (a) both rules apply and (b) the rules "overlap" in the context in which they operate. For example, we know that both the Dative Movement Rule and the Negative Insertion Rule can operate on the same sentence. However, we cannot speak of any direct ordering between these two rules, simply because the Dative Movement Rule operates exclusively within the VP and the Negative Rule exclusively within the Aux. Hence, a situation could never arise in which the operation of one rule had any effect on the operation of the other rule, and they could quite easily operate in either order. (In fact, we

know that these two rules must be <u>indirectly</u> ordered, by a
principle that has been referred to as <u>transitivity of rule or-
dering</u>: we have shown that the Dative Rule must be followed
by the Passive Rule, and that the Passive Rule, in turn, must
be followed by the Negative Insertion Rule; therefore, since
Negative Insertion must be ordered after a rule that must be
ordered after Dative Movement, it follows that Negative Insertion itself also follows the Dative Rule.)

Before we examine reasons for the ordering of the Question
Rule with respect to Negative Insertion and Contraction, it
would be valuable for the reader to attempt to construct a set
of data that is crucial for this argument. The task is to find
a set of sentences in which (a) some combination of these rules
has applied and (b) the rules have interacted with each other in
crucial ways. Sentences satisfying part (a) should be easy to
find; the important part of the exercise is to know when (b) has
been satisfied as well.

The data that are crucial for establishing an ordering among
Negative Insertion, Contraction, and the Question Transformation have to do with the fact that negative questions may appear
in two different forms:

(6.10) a. <u>Has</u> he <u>not</u> followed the correct procedures?
      b. <u>Hasn't</u> he followed the correct procedures?

The negative element <u>not</u> may either be uncontracted and left
behind in the sentence (as in (6.10a)), which we will regard as
grammatical even though it is overly formal, or it may be contracted with the first auxiliary verb, in which case it is fronted
with that verb in the question (as in (6.10b)). Further, if the
negative element has been fronted, it <u>must</u> be contracted with
the auxiliary; if it is not, an ungrammatical sentence results:

(6.10) c. *<u>Has not</u> he followed the correct procedures?

Thus, our rules must be formulated and ordered in such a way
that the two variants of the negative question shown in (6.10a-b)
will be generated, while (6.10c) will not. What ordering will
generate the desired sentences, while excluding (6.10c)?

If we order Negative Insertion and Contraction before the

Question Rule, we can generate negative questions in a simple
fashion. Sentence (6.10a) would have the following derivation:

(6.11)   he pres have en follow . . .
    Negative Insertion: he pres have not en follow . . .
    Question: pres have he not en follow . . .
    Output (after Affix (= (6.10a)) <u>Has he not followed the</u>
    Hopping):   <u>correct procedures?</u>

In this derivation we have applied the rule of Negative Insertion but have chosen not to apply the optional rule of Contraction. When the Question Rule applies, it fronts <u>pres</u> and <u>have</u>,
and we derive (6.10a).

   In the derivation for (6.10b), we have chosen to apply Contraction:

(6.12)   he pres have en follow . . .
    Negative Insertion: he pres have not en follow . . .
    Contraction: he pres haven't en follow . . .
    Question: pres haven't he en follow . . .
    Output (after Affix (= (6.10b)) <u>Hasn't he followed the</u>
    Hopping):   <u>correct procedures?</u>

After Negative Insertion we have applied the Contraction Rule,
and it is natural to assume that contraction has the effect of
"joining" <u>n't</u> to <u>have</u>, making them a unit. When the Question
Rule applies, it again fronts <u>pres</u> and <u>have</u>. Since a contracted
negative is now attached to <u>have</u>, it also moves to the front of
the sentence, and we can thus derive (6.10b). (We will show in
a moment how we can formalize the notion that the Question
Rule fronts a contracted element along with the auxiliary.)

   We have succeeded in deriving the two well-formed examples
of (6.10), and our system gives us no way to derive the ungrammatical (6.10c). To produce that particular sentence, we would
need to have an uncontracted negative element with a fronted
auxiliary; but, given our rules, there is no way that can happen.
Hence, the statement and ordering of our rules leads to the
correct results.

   Now consider what would happen if the Question Rule <u>pre-</u>
<u>ceded</u> Negative Insertion and Contraction:

(6.13)   he pres have en follow . . .
         Question: pres have he en follow . . .
         Negative Insertion: does not apply

If the Question Rule operates first, the Negative Insertion Rule,
as we have stated it in (6.6) above, will not apply. That rule requires the tense (and auxiliary, if any) to follow the subject NP;
but if the Question Rule has applied first, the Tense (plus any
auxiliary) will precede the subject, as above in (6.13). Hence,
the SD of Negative Insertion is not met if the Question Rule applies first, unless the Negative Rule is changed so that it will
apply to structures produced by the Question Rule. If we did
that, it would be necessary to state Negative Insertion so that
it could insert not in either of two places: (a) immediately after
the fronted auxiliary (to generate sentences such as (6.10b)) or
(b) after an auxiliary verb that follows the subject NP (to generate (6.10a)). Furthermore, the normally optional rule of Contraction would have to be made obligatory in case not had been
placed after a fronted auxiliary, in order to avoid sentences
such as (6.10c). In short, if the Question Rule were ordered
before Negative Insertion and Contraction, then our overall account of the facts illustrated in (6.10) would be greatly complicated. Thus, the first ordering discussed above permits us to
capture significant generalizations about English and is to be
preferred.
    At this point, it is worth considering how we might formalize
the rule of Contraction in such a way as to ensure that the not
is incorporated (in some sense) into the preceding auxiliary
element. We want to guarantee that the Question Rule will always front a contracted negative along with the first part of Aux
but will never front an uncontracted negative. One possibility
for representing the process of contraction would be to use the
operation of Chomsky adjunction for this purpose (cf. section
5.2). We can illustrate this in the following example, wherein
not is Chomsky-adjoined to Modal by making a copy of the node
Modal immediately above the original node and using the newly
copied node to dominate not:

(6.14) a.

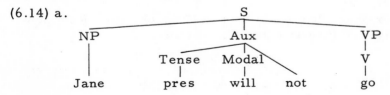

b.

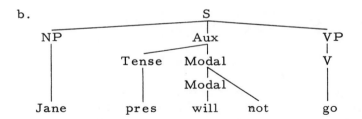

The new configuration, the relevant portion of which we show in (6.14c), has just the properties we need to represent the process of contraction.

(6.14) c. Modal

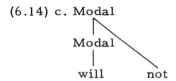

Since will and not are now dominated by the same node, both will be fronted by the Question Rule.

Strictly speaking, we need to make a number of other minor changes in order to use Chomsky adjunction in this way in the Contraction Rule. Chomsky adjunction always involves adjoining constitutents to nodes, not to lexical items. Hence, when we Chomsky-adjoin not to will, we adjoin not to the node Modal that dominates will. Now recall that we want Contraction to operate not only with Modals but with have and be as well (cf. (6.10a) and (6.10b) above). However, we have not explicitly provided either of these verbs with a category node—they simply attach under the node Aux.

(6.15)

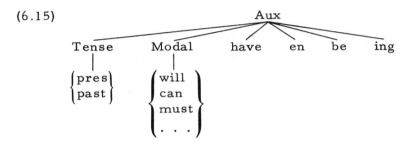

If we are to use Chomsky adjunction to represent contraction in cases involving have and be, we must provide these elements with dominating nodes that can be used for the adjunction. This might be achieved by a simple change in our PS rules for Aux:

(6.16) Aux → Tense (Modal) (V en) (V ing)

We would then have to assume that <u>have</u> and <u>be</u> are entered in the lexicon with the feature [+ V] and, further, that <u>have</u> has the subcategorization feature +[___ en] and that <u>be</u> has the feature +[___ ing] and + [___ en]. Then <u>have</u> will <u>be</u> inserted into the Aux before <u>en</u>, and <u>be</u> will be inserted before <u>ing</u>:

(6.17)

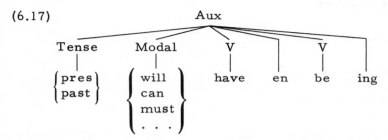

The resulting structure is one in which both <u>have</u> and <u>be</u> have their own dominating nodes, and <u>not</u> could be Chomsky-adjoined to either of them as follows:

(6.18) a.

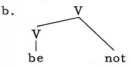

   b.

```
        V
      /   \
     V
     |
     be        not
```

We can then state the rule of Contraction thus:

(6.19) <u>Contraction</u> (Optional)

SD: Tense ({ Modal / V }) - not
                1   2
SC: 1 # nt   ∅

(We have used the symbol # to represent Chomsky adjunction, as in chapter 5, and n't will henceforth appear in rules as nt.) The rule has the effect of deleting the element not and inserting the element nt, Chomsky-adjoining it to the right of term 1. We will assume this version of contraction from now on but will not represent have and be as dominated by V except when they are main verbs.

Having at least sketched what a contraction rule might look like, we arrive at the following ordered list:
1. Dative
2. Passive
3. Negative Insertion
4. Contraction
5. Question

6.1.4. Passive/There Insertion/Negative Insertion/Question
For the first time, we must now go back and insert a rule at an earlier point in the order. This is necessary because there are strong arguments that There Insertion must precede Question, and there is even some reason to order it before Negative Insertion. It certainly must follow Passive. The reader should attempt to discover relevant data for this ordering argument.

That There Insertion follows Passive is shown by sentence pairs such as (6.20a) and (6.20b).

(6.20) a. There was a man arrested in the park by the police.
       b. *There arrested the police a man in the park.

The passive be and the indefinite subject a man, which both result from the application of the Passive Rule, are crucial for the proper application of There Insertion in (6.20a). As (6.20b) shows, the corresponding active is an ungrammatical sentence. (See the discussion of There Insertion in chapter 5.)

The argument that There Insertion precedes Question is similarly clear:

(6.21) Was there a woodpecker in the elm tree?

Example (6.21) is derived from something like (6.22) (ignoring affixes), by the application of the Question Rule.

(6.22) There was a woodpecker in the elm tree.

The Question Rule inverts the first auxiliary and the subject NP. If it applied first, it would destroy the environment for There Insertion, which includes as part of its SD the sequence NP - Tense - (Modal) - (have en) - be. If Question had applied, part of the Auxiliary would precede the subject NP; hence, There Insertion must precede the Question Rule.

Thus There Insertion must come somewhere between Passive and Question. Can we narrow down the possibilities still further? The relevant rules are Negative Insertion and Contraction:

(6.23) Passive
$\begin{bmatrix} \text{Negative Insertion} \\ \text{Contraction} \end{bmatrix}$
        Question

Recall that in There Insertion the original subject is moved to a position immediately to the right of be:

(6.24) a. A man was in the park.

   b. There was a man in the park.

But when a negative and be are both present, the negative intervenes:

(6.25) a. ? A bear was not in the park.

   b.   There was not a bear in the park.

If not has been introduced by the time There Insertion applies, then the latter rule will explicitly have to permit not to occur, as in the following version:

(6.26) There Insertion (Complicated Version)

       SD: NP - Tense - (Modal) - (have en) - be (not)
            [- Def]
              1   2   3   4   5
       SC: there   2 3 4 5 +1

But if There Insertion precedes Negative Insertion, then the
optional not will never need to be specified in the SD of the
rule. (It will be inserted later.) We conclude that the simplest
overall ordering is therefore as follows:
1. Dative
2. Passive
3. There Insertion
4. Negative Insertion
5. Contraction
6. Question

6.1.5. Passive/Number Agreement/There Insertion

So far we have paid little attention to the process whereby a
tensed verb is conjugated to agree with the subject of its sentence in person and number, a process that has nearly disappeared in modern English. For regular verbs, the form of the
verb is invariant except for the third person singular in the
present tense:

(6.28) a. Present Tense

I bake	we bake
you bake	you bake
he, she, it bakes	they bake

b. Past Tense

I baked	we baked
you baked	you baked
he, she, it baked	they baked

   Given that the overwhelming majority of English verbs are
not at all modified for subject agreement, except in the third
person singular present tense, there would appear to be no
need for a general verb agreement rule (of the sort that would
be required, say, in Latin). We need only to guarantee that
verbs will end up with the suffix -s in the present tense when
the subject is third person singular. We could achieve this in
our theory in various ways. For example, at the simplest
level we could simply assume that there is a transformation
of Third Person Marking that replaces the present tense marker, pres, by the symbol s, just in case the subject is third
person singular. Thus, in the present tense, most verb forms
would have pres attached to them, while a subset would have

pres replaced by s. This would serve to distinguish the third
person singular verbs from all the others, and that is all we
require of our theory.

However, there are two classes of verbs that form exceptions to what we have just said about verb agreement. The
first is the class of modal verbs (will, would, can, could, may,
might, etc.), which display no verb agreement at all, not even
when the subject is third person singular and the verb is present tense. The second class of exceptions consists of a single
verb, namely, the verb be, which displays more variation for
subject agreement than any other verb in the language.

(6.29) a. Be, Present Tense

I am	we are
you are	you are
he, she, it is	they are

b. Be, Past Tense

I was	we were
you were	you were
he, she, it was	they were

We must assume, then, that the agreement of be is regulated
by a special transformation that has the effect of attaching
person and number markings to the Tense element of sentences
containing the verb be (we would, of course, combine third
person marking with this number agreement rule).

If we assume that all nouns contain syntactic features marking their number and person (recall the discussion of Reflexivization in chapter 5), then we can formalize a general rule of
Number Agreement as follows:

(6.30) Number Agreement (Obligatory)

$$
\text{SD:} \qquad \text{NP} \; - \; \begin{Bmatrix} \text{pres} \\ \text{past} \end{Bmatrix}
$$
$$
\begin{bmatrix} \alpha \text{ person} \\ \beta \text{ plural} \end{bmatrix}
$$
$$
\qquad\qquad\qquad 1 \qquad\qquad 2
$$
$$
\text{SC:} \; 1 \qquad 2
$$
$$
\begin{bmatrix} \alpha \text{ person} \\ \beta \text{ plural} \end{bmatrix}
$$

In stating this rule, we have used the variables α and β to stand
for feature values. Thus, nouns can either be [1 person], [2
person], or [3 person] (i.e., first, second, or third person),
and the notation [α person] is used to denote any of these three.
Further, nouns will either be [+plural] (plural nouns) or [-plural]
(singular nouns), and the notation [β plural] stands for either one
of these. The Number Agreement Rule copies the person and
plural features of the head noun of the subject NP, whatever they
are, onto the tense markers pres or past. (In the SC of the rule,
term 2, which refers to either pres or past, is shown with the
features copied from term 1, the subject NP. We assume that
these features will have been "spread" onto the whole subject
NP from the head N.)

To illustrate the operation of the rule, consider the following
input tree:

(6.31) a.

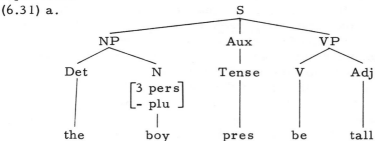

The subject NP in this case contains a third person singular
head noun, boy. Number Agreement will apply to this tree
(since the subject NP immediately precedes pres) and will
copy the noun features onto pres:

(6.31) b.

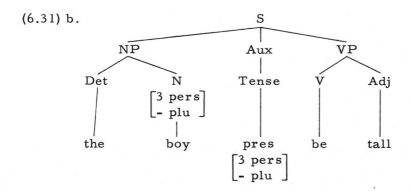

The later rule of Affix Hopping will attach the tense element to the verb be:

(6.31) c.

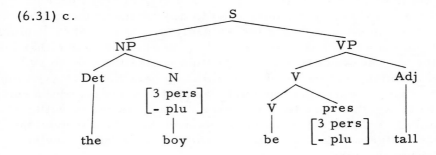

(We have Chomsky-adjoined the tense to the verb as part of Affix Hopping—see the appendix to this chapter.) The verb be is now associated with a tense marker, which contains, in addition, the markings for person and plural originally marked on the subject. The Spell-Out Rules will now interpret this complex of information as the third person singular form of be, namely, is. In this way we can derive the proper verb form for any tensed verb of the language. For example, if the verb in example (6.31) had been the main verb bake (with a suitable object, etc.), Number Agreement, and later Affix Hopping, would have had the result of placing a third person singular tense on the verb. This complex would have been interpreted as the third person form bakes; all non-third person cases would result in the simple form bake (in the present tense, of course). In this way, we can use the Number Agreement Rule, required for the verb be, for all verbs of the language.

Having stated the rule of Number Agreement, let us turn to the question of how it is to be ordered with respect to Passive and There Insertion. We can easily illustrate the operation and ordering of the rule with the following examples:

(6.32) a. Mary is training two monkeys.
    b. Two monkeys are being trained by Mary.
    c. Two men are training the monkey.

Obviously the rule of Number Agreement must follow Passive, for it is the plural derived subject (two monkeys, resulting from the Passive Rule) that induces plural agreement in (6.32b).

In that sentence the tensed verb takes the form <u>are</u>, just as it does in the active sentence (6.32c), which starts out with a plural subject.

Consider now the sentences in (6.33)-(6.35).

(6.33) a. A salmon <u>is</u> in the bathtub.
      b. Several salmon <u>are</u> in the bathtub.

(6.34) a. There <u>is</u> a salmon in the bathtub.
      b. There <u>are</u> several salmon in the bathtub.

(6.35) a. There <u>was</u> a man arrested in the park.
      b. There <u>were</u> some men arrested in the park.

We have already seen that the verb <u>be</u> agrees with the subject of a sentence (as in (6.32) and now (6.33)), and this raises an interesting question about verb agreement in sentences such as those of (6.34) and (6.35). In these sentences the verb does not seem to agree with the subject, <u>there</u>, but rather with the NP that <u>follows</u> the verb <u>be</u>. However, with the proper ordering of the rules of <u>There</u> Insertion and Number Agreement, the agreement patterns in (6.34) and (6.35) will be perfectly regular. We will not present the ordering argument any further but will simply pose the following question: Given the data in (6.33)-(6.35), how should <u>There</u> Insertion and Number Agreement be ordered?

The reader should at this stage review all the ordering arguments, placing in the correct order all the rules dealt with so far (including Number Agreement). The ordering that so far seems correct will be given in the next section.

6.1.6. Affix Hopping/Do Support

These two rules were shown to have to apply in the order (1) Affix Hopping/(2) <u>Do</u> Support, when <u>Do</u> Support was first introduced in the discussion of Passive and Question in chapter 4. There it was also pointed out that Affix Hopping must follow Question. Both arguments, which we will not repeat here, depend on pairs like the following:

(6.36) a. Jemima <u>went</u> to the pond.
      b. <u>Did</u> Jemima <u>go</u> to the pond?

The reader can easily reconstruct the argument by carefully
working through these examples. (See the appendix to this
chapter for a formal statement of these rules.)

We have now established the ordering given in (6.37).

(6.37)   1. Dative
               2. Passive
               3. Number Agreement
               4. <u>There</u> Insertion
               5. Negative Insertion
               6. Contraction
               7. Question
               8. Affix Hopping
               9. <u>Do</u> Support

A curved line connecting two rules indicates that they are crucially ordered with respect to one another, i.e., that an argument exists for ordering them in that particular way.

6.2. THE TAG RULE

We turn now to an interesting but problematic case that we discussed informally in chapter 1: the Tag Rule. Although frequently mentioned by transformational linguists, this rule has
not been given much attention and is relatively poorly understood. Our discussion of the formulation and ordering of the
Tag Rule in this section must be viewed in that light; it is primarily intended to show how the attempt to discover a maxi-
mally simple grammar leads us to set up a rather abstract
analysis of tag questions and other apparently unrelated phenomena. The reader should remain skeptical of the details of
our analysis, while noting the form of the argument.

    First of all, notice that it appears to be necessary to prevent
a situation in which both the Question Rule and the Tag Rule apply to a single sentence. If we start with the basic sentence
(6.38a), then we can either apply the Question Rule to yield
(6.38b) or the Tag Rule to produce (6.38c). If we try to apply
both, then the output will be (6.38d), an impossible sentence.

(6.38) a.   The flowers bloom in the spring.
   b.   Do the flowers bloom in the spring?
   c.   The flowers bloom in the spring, don't they?
   d. *Do the flowers bloom in the spring, don't they?

How can we guarantee that the Tag Rule will not apply if the
Question Rule does and vice versa? In forming a tag for a declarative sentence, we must (a) copy the tensed auxiliary at
the end of the sentence, (b) make it negative in the tag if it is
positive in the main sentence (and vice versa), and (c) copy the
subject of the sentence (in pronoun form) into the tag right
after the auxiliary element:

(6.39) a. Herbert has not grasped the main point, <u>has he</u>?
   b. Mary can sing Christian hymns, <u>can't she</u>?

Of course, we would now analyze sentences such as those in
(6.39) as follows:

(6.40) a. Herbert - pres - have - not - en - grasp the main
    point, pres - have - he
   b. Mary - pres - can - sing Christian hymns, pres -
    can#nt she

It would thus appear that the following rule expresses what
happens when a tag question is formed (though, as we shall
see, it is far from being a satisfactory formulation of the rule):

(6.41) <u>Tag Formation</u> (Optional) (First Version)

$$\text{SD: NP} - \text{Tense} \quad (\left\{ \begin{array}{l} \text{Modal} \\ \text{have} \\ \text{be} \end{array} \right\}) \quad - \quad \text{(not)} \quad - \quad \text{X}$$

   1   2   3   4

SC: 1   2   3   4   2 # <u>nt</u> 1

<u>Conditions</u>: (a) <u>nt</u> must not be added if <u>not</u> is present as
        term 3 of the SD;
     (b) The second occurrence of 1 in the SC
       must be the pronoun corresponding to 1
       of the SD.

As we can see, this version of the Tag Formation Rule is rath-

er complicated, but it will nevertheless generate appropriate
tags. To see how it operates, let us take sentence (6.40b),
which we analyze as follows:

(6.40) b.

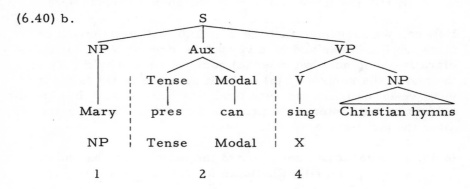

This tree clearly meets the SD of our Tag Formation Rule
(term 3, not, is not present in this tree, an option allowed by
our rule), and the rule would have the following effect:

(6.40) b'.

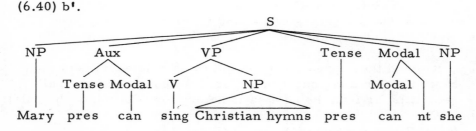

Tense and Modal have been copied at the end of the sentence
(with nt Chomsky-adjoined to Modal), and the subject NP has
been copied in pronoun form. Although we will modify this rule
significantly in a short while, let us assume for the moment
that (6.41) is adequate for our purposes.

Now that we have managed to formalize our rule, we have,
in fact, built into it a way of preventing it from applying to any
sentence to which Question has applied: given the way we have
stated the Tag Formation Rule, it will never apply to questions
as long as we order it after the Question Rule, and sentences
such as (6.38d) will never be generated. Why?

The reason that the Tag Rule in (6.41) will never apply to structures generated by the Question Rule is that the following terms appear in the SD of the Tag Rule:

(6.42)
$$\text{NP} \; - \; \text{Tense} \; \left(\left\{ \begin{array}{l} \text{Modal} \\ \text{have} \\ \text{be} \end{array} \right\} \right)$$

$$\underline{\qquad\qquad\qquad\qquad}$$

    1   2

If the Question Rule has operated, the Tense (etc.) will already have been moved to the <u>left</u> of the subject NP, and hence the Tag Rule cannot apply. Assuming that the Tag Rule is ordered <u>after</u> Question, its SD would be met only if the Question Rule had not applied. The order must be as follows:

(6.43) 1. Dative
       2. Passive
       3. Number Agreement
       4. <u>There</u> Insertion
       5. Negative Insertion
       6. Contraction
       7. Question

       | 8. Tag Formation |

       9. Affix Hopping
      10. <u>Do</u> Support

While this could conceivably be a correct solution, it raises a number of important issues that cannot be overlooked. In particular, the account just sketched fails to capture a number of interesting relationships between tag questions and regular yes/no questions:

(a) Tags are never formed on questions. At present this is represented as purely accidental—the result of ordering the Tag Rule after the Question Rule.

(b) The copy of the subject NP and the first auxiliary in the tag are in precisely the same order they would normally take in questions:

He has arrived, <u>hasn't he</u>?
<u>Hasn't he</u> arrived?

So far, this fact is simply an accident in our theory.

(c) The negative in the tag must be contracted, if it precedes the copy of the subject, just as it is when fronted in questions:

*John has arrived, has <u>not</u> he?   John has arrived, has<u>n't</u> he?
*Has <u>not</u> John arrived?   Has<u>n't</u> John arrived?

(d) There is another somewhat formal version of negative tags in which the full negative appears to the right of the copied subject NP. Again, this is parallel to ordinary questions:

John has arrived, <u>has</u> he <u>not</u>?
<u>Has</u> John <u>not</u> arrived?

Rule (6.41) would need to be modified to generate this form of tag but would not, of course, be able to provide any explanation of the structural parallel with questions.

In addition, notice that according to our account <u>not</u> is inserted by the Tag Rule <u>as well as</u> by Negative Insertion—and the two rules independently happen to insert <u>not</u> in such a way that it appears in tags in precisely those positions it would occupy as a result of the combined effects of three rules operating together: Negative Insertion, Contraction, and Question (see points (c) and (d) above). Consequently the Tag Rule (6.41) <u>duplicates</u> the effect of those three rules and thus misses an important set of generalizations. Obviously it would be preferable to try to replace our account of tags with one in which these generalizations were represented as significant rather than as purely accidental.

What we really want, then, is some way of permitting independently needed rules (other than the Tag Rule) to generate certain aspects of the structure of tags. For example:

(a) We want Negative Insertion to position <u>not</u> in tags as well as in regular questions. This would account for the similar positioning of <u>not</u> in both cases.

(b) If Contraction applied in tags, as it does in questions, we could account for the similar contraction facts in both cases.

(c) We would like the Question Rule to <u>invert</u> the copied subject and first auxiliary of tags, taking along the contracted negative if there is one, just as it does in questions. This would account for the fact that tag questions, like yes/no questions, permit only contracted negatives to appear before the subject NP.

On the basis of these general hints of what is required in principle to relate tags and questions, the reader should try to construct a new Tag Rule, ordered differently in the grammar, which is formulated so as to allow Negative Insertion, Contraction, and Question to operate in the derivation of tags.

If certain properties of tags are to result, not from the Tag Formation Rule itself, but rather from Negative Insertion, Contraction, and Question, then the tag structure must be formed before these rules apply. Therefore Tag Formation will have to operate at least before Negative Insertion. At the same time, we can be sure that the Tag Rule must follow Passive, for the latter rule is responsible for forming derived subjects that are copied into tags. Compare the following two sentences:

(6.44) a. John saw the children, didn't he?
　　　 b. The children were seen by John, weren't they?

Therefore the new Tag Rule presumably occurs between Passive and Negative Insertion—i.e., at one of the points marked below:

Passive
───────▶
Number Agreement
───────▶
There Insertion
───────▶
Negative Insertion

Since there can appear in tags, as in (6.45a and b),

(6.45) a. There are elephants in the attic, aren't there?
　　　 b. Elephants are in the attic, aren't they?

we may assume that Tag Formation follows There Insertion—there cannot be copied into a tag unless it has already been inserted into the main sentence. The order will therefore have to be as in (6.46):

(6.46)   1. Dative
         2. Passive
         3. Number Agreement
         4. <u>There</u> Insertion

         ┌─────────────────────────┐
         │ 5. Tag Formation   │
         └─────────────────────────┘

         6. Negative Insertion
         7. Contraction
         8. Question
         9. Affix Hopping
         10. <u>Do</u> Support

Now we need a rule to suit this ordering.

If Negative Insertion is to insert <u>not</u> and Contraction is to contract it where necessary, and if Question is to invert the subject and first auxiliary, then all the Tag Rule need do is copy the subject (as a pronoun), followed by the first auxiliary:

(6.47) <u>Tag Formation</u> (Second Version)

$$
\begin{array}{l}
\text{SD: NP} \quad - \quad \text{Tense} \quad (\left\{ \begin{array}{l} \text{Modal} \\ \text{have} \\ \text{be} \end{array} \right\}) \quad - \quad \text{X} \\
\qquad 1 \qquad\qquad\qquad\quad 2 \qquad\qquad\quad 3 \\
\text{SC: 1 2 3} \quad 1 \quad 2 \\
\qquad\qquad\quad [+\text{Pro}]
\end{array}
$$

(In the SC of (6.47) we simply write [+ Pro] beneath the copied term 1, in order to represent the fact that the copy is in pronoun form. See the discussion of features in chapters 2 and 5.) Applied to a form like (6.48a), this rule will derive (6.48b):

(6.48) a. John - pres will - go
       b. John - pres will - go - he - pres will

Concentrating only on the tag of (6.48b), we find that Negative Insertion, Contraction, and Question could yield the desired output:

(6.49)   John pres will go he pres will
       Negative Insertion: John pres will go he pres will <u>not</u>
       Contraction: John pres will go he pres <u>will#nt</u>

[handwritten note: Why not pres will John go]

[handwritten note in left margin: try apply to just one aux + tense II]

← Question: John pres will go <u>pres will#nt</u> he
Affix Hopping
(and other rules):   <u>John will go, won't he?</u>

And since Contraction is optional, it need not be applied:

(6.50)   John pres will go he pres will
Negative Insertion: John pres will go he pres will <u>not</u>
Question: John pres will go <u>pres will</u> he not
Affix Hopping
(and other rules):   <u>John will go, will he not?</u>

Unfortunately, this derivation of tag questions has very serious problems. These are related to the fact that Negative Insertion and Question (a) apply optionally and (b) can apply to the main clause as well as the tag. The reader should examine derivations (6.49) and (6.50) carefully in the light of these comments, trying to discover precisely how those derivations could go wrong.

Under our present analysis we have no way of preventing the following derivations:

(6.51) a.   John pres will go he pres will
Negative Insertion: John pres will <u>not</u> go he pres will <u>not</u>
Contraction: John pres <u>will#nt</u> go he pres <u>will#nt</u>
Question: John pres will#nt go <u>pres will#nt</u> he
Affix Hopping
(and other rules):   *<u>John won't go, won't he?</u>

b.   John pres will go he pres will
Negative Insertion: John pres will go he pres will <u>not</u>
Contraction: John pres will go he pres <u>will#nt</u>
Affix Hopping
(and other rules):   *<u>John will go, he won't?</u>

c.   John pres will go he pres will
Negative Insertion: John pres will go he pres will <u>not</u>
Contraction: John pres will go he pres <u>will#nt</u>
Question: <u>pres will</u> John go <u>pres will#nt</u> he
Affix Hopping
(and other rules):   *<u>Will John go, won't he?</u>

In (6.51a) Negative Insertion has applied to both the main clause and the tag; in (6.51b) the Question Rule—which is optional—has not applied at all; and in (6.51c) it has applied to both main clause and tag. Nothing in our grammar will prevent any of these possibilities. Obviously our analysis is seriously wrong.

Now we come to a very important general point—much more significant, in fact, than the particular analysis of tags that is under discussion. All the problems mentioned in the preceding paragraph derive from the optional nature of Negative Insertion and Question. Within our present framework these rules must obviously be optional: if they were obligatory, then they would apply in the derivation of every sentence generated by the grammar, and thus only negative questions would be generated. But there is another way of building optionality into the grammar. Instead of making Negative Insertion optional, for example, we could optionally generate not at a certain point in the tree by PS rules; then we could have the Negative Insertion Transformation obligatorily move this element, if it is present, into the required position after the first auxiliary. Some specific rules and examples will help to make this clear.

Let us assume that the first rule of the PS grammar includes an optional not (we will assume that this occurs at the beginning of the S, but there are other possible positions):

(6.52) S → (not) NP Aux VP

The other PS rules are just as before, but the Negative Insertion Transformation, which we reformulate as an obligatory rule, is now stated (and renamed) as in (6.53):

(6.53) Negative Placement (Obligatory)

$$
\text{SD: not} \; - \; \text{NP} \; - \; \text{Tense} \; \left(\begin{Bmatrix} \text{Modal} \\ \text{have} \\ \text{be} \end{Bmatrix} \right)
$$

$$
\begin{array}{cccc}
 & 1 & 2 & 3 \\
\text{SC:} & 2 & 3+1 &
\end{array}
$$

A derivation might now begin along the following lines:

(6.54)   not John pres will go
        Negative Placement: John pres will not go
        etc.

Of course, since rule (6.53) requires the presence of <u>not</u> in order to operate, it will never apply to a positive sentence. So the new transformation of Negative Placement never <u>inserts</u> <u>not</u> into a sentence but only operates on a sentence in which the <u>PS</u> rule (6.52) has generated a <u>not</u>. The new rule places this <u>not</u> into its correct position after the first auxiliary, moving it from initial position in the string.

It may seem that we are ignoring our earlier discussion (chapter 3) intended to show that negative sentences could not be appropriately generated by PS rules. But recall that the point of that discussion was to show that PS rules could not properly <u>position</u> the <u>not</u> after the first auxiliary. Just as we proposed that affixes are generated by PS rules but placed in proper position by a transformation, so we are now proposing that <u>not</u> is generated by PS rules and moved to the correct place in the Aux by a transformation.

It has been shown so far only that the version of Negative Placement that uses the PS rule (6.52) and the transformation (6.53) will work; we have not proved that it provides a simpler overall grammar. We will not try to provide a general justification for the alternative treatment but will simply demonstrate how it can be used to overcome some of the problems with the original analysis of tags indicated by derivations (6.51a-c).

Consider derivation (6.51a), repeated below:

(6.51) a.   John pres will go he pres will
       Negative Insertion: John pres will <u>not</u> go he pres will <u>not</u>
       Contraction: John pres will#nt go he pres will#nt
       Question: John pres will#nt go pres will#nt he
       Affix Hopping
       (and other rules):   *John won't go, won't he?

The problem with this derivation is that there are two negatives inserted in the sentence instead of just one (either in the main clause or in the tag):

(6.55) a. John will go, won't he?
       b. John won't go, will he?

But in the new analysis, a negative sentence is generated with <u>not</u> in initial position. There will be no way for Negative Placement to create an extra, unwanted <u>not</u> in the tag; the output of

(6.51a) will obviously be avoided. The following is one possible alternative to derivation (6.51a) in the new theory:

(6.56)   not John pres will go he pres will
   Negative Placement: John pres will <u>not</u> go he pres will
   Contraction: John pres <u>will#nt</u> go he pres will
   Question: John pres will#nt go <u>pres</u> <u>will</u> he
   Affix Hopping
   (and other rules):   <u>John won't go, will he?</u>

However, we still have to derive (6.55a), where <u>not</u> is in the tag and not in the main clause. The Negative Placement Rule needs to insert <u>not</u> either in the main clause or in the tag question. But as that rule ((6.53), repeated below) is stated now, it will place <u>not</u> only in the main clause:

(6.53) <u>Negative Placement</u> (Obligatory)

$$\text{SD: not} - \text{NP} - \text{Tense} \quad (\left\{ \begin{matrix} \text{Modal} \\ \text{have} \\ \text{be} \end{matrix} \right\})$$

$$\begin{matrix} \quad 1 \qquad 2 \qquad\qquad\qquad 3 \\ \text{SC:} \quad 2 \quad 3+1 \end{matrix}$$

As can be seen from the statement of this rule, exactly one NP may intervene between <u>not</u> and term 3 of the SD. Hence, <u>not</u> will always be placed immediately after the <u>first</u> occurrence of term 3; and it will never be placed after some <u>later</u> occurrence of this term:

(6.57) not John pres will go he pres will

Obviously, it would be desirable to modify the formal statement of Negative Placement so that it would be able to insert the negative <u>either</u> in the main clause <u>or</u> the tag. How could this be done?

At the moment, the simplest way is to restate the rule with a variable, <u>X</u>, between <u>not</u> and the following NP:

(6.58) <u>Negative Placement</u> (Obligatory) (Revised)

$$\text{SD: not } - \text{ X } - \text{ NP } - \text{ Tense } \left(\begin{cases} \text{Modal} \\ \text{have} \\ \text{be} \end{cases} \right)$$

$$\begin{array}{cccc} 1 & 2 & 3 & 4 \\ \text{SC: } 2 & 3 & 4+1 \end{array}$$

Since rule variables can be <u>null</u>—i.e., rules can operate even if there is no portion of the input tree that corresponds to the variables—Negative Placement will now be able to place <u>not</u> either in the main clause or in the tag. Forms such as (6.57) can be analyzed in two different ways with respect to the new rule:

(6.59) a. not   John   pres will   go he pres will

not (X) NP Tense Modal
 1   (2)   3   4

(In this case we have chosen to interpret the variable <u>X</u> as null.)

b. not John pres will go he   pres will

not   X   NP Tense Modal
 1   2   3   4

(In this case we allow <u>X</u> to stand for all the material between <u>not</u> and <u>he</u>.)

Given the new Negative Placement Rule, sentences such as (6.55a) can be derived as follows (again, the derivation begins after Tag Formation has operated):

(6.60)   not John pres will go he pres will
Negative Placement: John pres will go he pres will <u>not</u>
Contraction: John pres will go he pres <u>will#nt</u>
Question: John pres will go <u>pres will#nt</u> he
Affix Hopping
(and other rules):   <u>John will go, won't he?</u>

Our analysis of negation involving the PS rule (6.52) and the revised Negative Placement Rule (6.58) provides a satisfactory

account of the facts of negation in tagged sentences. First of
all, PS rule (6.52) allows only one not per sentence; hence, it
is now impossible to generate sentences in which not appears
both in the main clause and in the tag. Second, the revised
Negative Placement Rule (6.58) is able to place not in a tag as
well as in a main clause; and because we actually utilize the
general Negative Placement Rule in tag questions, we can account for the fact that the negative appears in just the same
syntactic environment (i.e., immediately after Tense and any
of Modal, have, or be) in both main clauses and tags.

Notice incidentally that the PS rule (6.52) generates not as
an optional constituent of S, so that sentences can be generated
without not. Given the way we have stated the revised Tag Formation Rule in (6.47), there is nothing to prevent it from operating on sentences that lack negation. Consequently, it will now
generate sentences like John went home, did he? with no negatives at all. Unlike tagged sentences with two negatives, such
as the output to (6.51a) (which our analysis properly excludes),
these positive forms are fully grammatical, though they carry
a rather different meaning from those that incorporate a negative; they have sometimes been called "challenge" tags. We
can simply permit our rule to generate them along with the two
forms of (6.55).

So far we have not tried to capture the relationship between
tags and regular questions set out earlier; our attention has
been directed solely to the problem of negatives. Thus, we
have no way of preventing the Question Rule from operating in
both the main clause and the tag, producing such ungrammatical outputs as that of (6.51c).

Now we must ensure that the new Tag Rule (6.47) and the
Question Rule do not permit us to generate *Will John go won't
he?, *Will John go he won't?, or *John will go he won't? Originally we prevented tagged questions, such as the first two examples, by ordering Tag after Question and making the Tag
Rule apply only to sentences with elements in the order NP –
Tense ($\left\{ \begin{array}{l} \text{Modal} \\ \text{have} \\ \text{be} \end{array} \right\}$). (See the discussion of example (6.42) above.)
We can no longer use that method, because the new Tag Rule
comes before Question—it must come before Question if we are
to use the Question Rule to produce the inverted word order
found in tags. However, the new rules for negation introduced

above suggest an analogous treatment of questions that avoids these problems. Instead of regarding questions as being derived by an optional inversion transformation operating on the same structure as that of declarative statements, let us suppose that the PS rules optionally introduce an element that, if present, obligatorily triggers the application of the Question Rule. If we call this element Question, or Q for short, then the first PS rule could be further modfied:

(6.61) S → (Q) (not) NP Aux VP

Then the Question Transformation could be restated as an obligatory rule, as follows:

(6.62) Question (Obligatory) (Revised)

$$
\text{SD: Q - NP - Tense } \left(\left\{ \begin{array}{l} \text{Modal} \\ \text{have} \\ \text{be} \end{array} \right\} \right)
$$

$$
\begin{array}{cccc} & 1 & 2 & & 3 \\ \text{SC:} & 1 & 3 & 2 \end{array}
$$

(The not optionally generated between Q and the subject NP by the PS rules will, of course, have been moved away by Negative Placement by the time the Question Rule operates, so it does not appear in rule (6.62) at all.)

The Tag Rule can now be reformulated so as to prevent the generation of *Will John go won't he?, etc. This new Tag Rule (like the new Question Rule) works only on sentences having an initial Q, and if it moves this Q to the end of the main clause (i.e., immediately preceding the tag itself), then only the tag itself will be operated on by the Question Rule. If Q has been moved in this fashion, there cannot then be a Q at the beginning of the main clause, and the main clause will not be subject to the Question Rule. Hence this formulation of the Question and Tag Rules will automatically prevent tagged questions such as *Will John go won't he? The Tag Formation Rule will have to look roughly like (6.63).

This new Tag Formation Rule still carries out the essential operations of copying the subject of the main clause into the tag and of copying the Tense plus first auxiliary element (thus, the SC of the rule shows terms 3 and 4 copied at the end of the

(6.63) <u>Tag Formation</u> (Optional) (Second Revision)

$$\text{SD: Q - (not) - NP - Tense } (\left\{\begin{matrix} \text{Modal} \\ \text{have} \\ \text{be} \end{matrix}\right\}) - X$$

$$
\begin{array}{ccccccc}
 & 1 & 2 & 3 & & 4 & & 5 \\
\text{SC:} & 2\ 3 & 4 & 5 & 1 & 3 & 4 & \\
 & & & & & [+\text{Pro}] & &
\end{array}
$$

sentence). However, it operates only on structures that contain Q, which will in turn trigger the operation of the Question
Transformation. Term 1 of the SD, which is the symbol Q, is
moved to the end of the sentence and placed at the beginning of
the tag. This guarantees that the Question Rule will always apply in tags and never in main clauses preceding tags; as we
have reformulated the Question Rule, it is obligatory and must
operate when Q is present. The following derivations should
serve to illustrate how our revised rules work:

(6.64)   Q not John pres will go
       Tag Formation: not John pres will go Q <u>he</u> <u>pres</u> <u>will</u>
       Negative Placement: John pres will go Q he pres will <u>not</u>
       Contraction: John pres will go Q he pres <u>will#nt</u>
       Question: John pres will go Q <u>pres</u> <u>will#nt</u> he
       Affix Hopping
       (and other rules):   <u>John will go, won't he?</u> (= (6.55a))

(Sentence (6.55b) differs only in that <u>not</u> is placed in the main
clause.) Note that the symbol Q, used to trigger the Question
Rule, does not actually show up in surface structures the way
<u>not</u> does. To account for this, we could assume for the moment
that Q is somehow deleted by the end of the derivation. In chapter 10 we shall examine another function of Q and show that
there may be contexts in which it is actually realized in surface structure. Until then, nothing crucial hinges on how Q is
deleted.

(6.65)   Q not John pres will go
       Negative Placement: Q John pres will <u>not</u> go
       Contraction: Q John pres <u>will#nt</u> go
       Question: Q <u>pres</u> <u>will#nt</u> John go
       Affix Hopping
       (and other rules):   <u>Won't John go?</u>

Our new account of tags derives them from structures containing Q; by moving the Q from the beginning of the main clause,
it prevents tagged questions such as that in (6.51c) and at the
same time automatically forces inversion in the tag itself, preventing forms like (6.51b), *John will go, he won't?

Let us sum up. By reformulating Negative Placement and
Question as obligatory rules that are triggered by elements
optionally generated by the PS rules, and by having the Tag
Rule work only on sentences with initial Q, moving the Q to
the end of the sentence, we have accounted for the following
facts:

(a) If a sentence has a tag, then the main clause of that sentence may not have the inverted word order of a question
(cf. *Will John leave, will he?).

(b) The word order in a tag must be inverted, exactly as it is
in a regular question; tags may not have simple declarative
order (cf. *John won't leave, he will?).

(c) If a negative is generated in a tagged sentence, it must appear either in the main sentence or in the tag but may not
appear in both places (cf. *John didn't leave, didn't he?).

(d) The syntactic environment for the negative element not is
identical in both main clauses and tags (i.e., in both cases
not appears immediately after Tense plus the first auxiliary
element).

(e) The negative in tags may be contracted or uncontracted;
whichever pattern holds, however, it must be identical with
the contracted and uncontracted patterns in regular questions (cf. Shouldn't John leave?, Should John not leave?,
*Should not John leave?; John should leave, shouldn't he?,
John should leave, should he not?, *John should leave should
not he?).

The analysis of tags that we have presented in this section is
essentially intended to express what we take to be a significant
syntactic generalization: namely, that the syntactic form of tags
is systematically similar to the syntactic form of regular questions and negative sentences, and that the derivation of tags
should therefore involve the very same rules that operate in the
derivation of ordinary questions and negative sentences. The argumentation we have used to establish our analysis has crucially involved the assumption that in many cases transformational
rules must be ordered in a fixed linear fashion. Thus, by order-

ing the Tag Formation Rule before the Negative Placement and Question Rules (and, in addition, by appropriately reformulating the latter rules), we are able to generate tags in such a way that they will be appropriate inputs for later rules such as Negative Placement, Contraction, and Question.

Finally, let us notice that in our attempt to account for the syntactic problems posed by tags, we have been led to an increasingly <u>abstract</u> underlying representation of sentences. For example, negative sentences and questions no longer have the same underlying form as simple declarative sentences: negative sentences now must contain an initial <u>not</u> in their underlying form, questions must contain the symbol Q, negative questions contain both of these elements, and positive statements contain neither of them. Recall that in our earlier theory all four of the following sentences were derived from exactly the same underlying form:

(6.66) a. Ed has been sweating.
       b. Ed has not been sweating.
       c. Has Ed been sweating?
       d. Hasn't Ed been sweating?

All four sentences would have been derived from the underlying form (6.67a), and the differences among them would have arisen as a result of the application of different transformations:

(6.67) a.

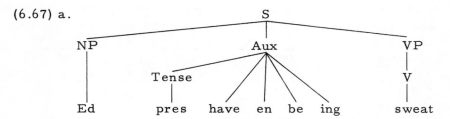

Using the earlier formulation of our rules, provide a derivation for each of these sentences as it would have been done within that previous framework.

Given the reformulation of our grammar that we have carried out in this section, we now know that each of the sentences of (6.66) derives from a distinct—and more abstract—underlying

form. Sentence (6.66a) derives from tree (6.67a), as before.
However, sentences (6.66b)-(6.66d) now derive from underlying
trees (6.67b)-(6.67d), respectively:

(6.67) b.

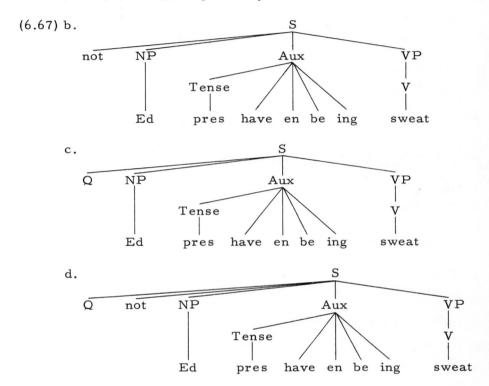

Using the rules we have formulated in this chapter and the trees
given in (6.67), and taking care to use the reformulated Negative Placement and Question Rules of this section, provide a
derivation for each of the sentences of (6.66).

CHAPTER 6: APPENDIX

ORDERED LIST OF TRANSFORMATIONS
What follows is a properly ordered list of the important transformations that we have discussed so far, for which ordering
arguments were either presented in the text or alluded to in
exercises. (This list is not intended to exhaust the transformations that operate on simple sentences.)

(A6.1) <u>Dative Movement Transformation</u> (Optional)

SD: V – NP – $\begin{Bmatrix} \text{to} \\ \text{for} \end{Bmatrix}$ – NP

     1   2   3   4

SC: 1 + 4 2   ∅   ∅

(A6.2) <u>Passive Transformation</u> (Optional)

SD: NP – Aux – V – NP

     1   2   3   4

SC: 4   2 > be + en 3 + by # 1

(A6.3) <u>Reflexivization</u> (Obligatory)

SD: NP – Aux – V – X – NP

     1   2   3   4   5

SC: 1 2 3 4   5

                        [+ REFLEXIVE]

Condition: 1 = 5

(Note: We have ordered Reflexivization after Passive in order to prevent derivations with the opposite order, as follows:

John – past – hurt – John

          ↓ <u>Reflexivization</u>

John – past – hurt – John

                      [+ REFL]

          ↓ <u>Passive</u>

John – past – be + en – hurt by John

[+ REFL]

*<u>Himself was hurt by John.</u>

Although our ordering prevents ungrammatical sentences such as the one just given, it nevertheless will allow derivations such as the following one:

John – past – hurt – John

          ↓ <u>Passive</u>

John – past be + en – hurt by John

↓ <u>Reflexivization</u>

John – past be + en – hurt by John
[+ REFL]

<u>?John was hurt by himself.</u>

For many speakers of English, sentences such as <u>John was</u>
<u>hurt by himself</u> are grammatical only in a contrastive sense,
i.e., only if the sentence is understood in a context such as
<u>John wasn't hurt by Mary, he was hurt by himself.</u> If there are
circumstances under which such sentences are not grammatical,
then we should presumably prevent their generation. Since ordering of these rules will not do so, some independent principle
must be found for excluding them.)

(A6.4) <u>Number Agreement</u> (Obligatory)

SD: NP
$\begin{bmatrix} \alpha \, \text{person} \\ \beta \, \text{plural} \end{bmatrix}$ – $\begin{Bmatrix} \text{pres} \\ \text{past} \end{Bmatrix}$
        1   2
SC: 1   2
$\begin{bmatrix} \alpha \, \text{person} \\ \beta \, \text{plural} \end{bmatrix}$

(A6.5) <u>There Insertion</u> (Optional)

SD: NP – Tense – (Modal) – (have en) – be
    [- Def]
     1   2   3   4   5
SC: <u>there</u>   2   3   4   5 + 1

(A6.6) <u>Tag Formation</u> (Optional)

SD: Q – (not) – NP – Tense ($\begin{Bmatrix} \text{Modal} \\ \text{have} \\ \text{be} \end{Bmatrix}$) – X

     1   2   3   4   4   5
SC: 2 3 4 5 1   3   4
            [+ PRO]

(Note: The Tag Formation Rule adds the feature [+ PRO]
to the copied subject, i.e., term 3 in the SC, to indicate

that the copied subject must appear in its corresponding pronoun form.)

(A6.7) <u>Negative Placement</u> (Obligatory)

$$\text{SD: not} \quad - \quad X \quad - \quad NP \quad - \quad \text{Tense} \quad (\begin{Bmatrix} \text{Modal} \\ \text{have} \\ \text{be} \end{Bmatrix})$$

$$\qquad\quad 1 \qquad\quad 2 \qquad 3 \qquad\qquad\qquad 4$$

SC: 2 3 4 + 1

(A6.8) <u>Contraction</u> (Optional)

$$\text{SD: Tense} \quad (\begin{Bmatrix} \text{Modal} \\ \text{V} \end{Bmatrix}) \quad - \quad \text{not}$$

$$\qquad\qquad\qquad 1 \qquad\qquad\qquad 2$$

SC: 1 # <u>nt</u> Ø

(A6.9) <u>Question</u> (Obligatory)

$$\text{SD: Q} \quad - \quad NP \quad - \quad \text{Tense} \quad (\begin{Bmatrix} \text{Modal} \\ \text{have} \\ \text{be} \end{Bmatrix})$$

$$\qquad 1 \qquad\quad 2 \qquad\qquad\qquad 3$$

SC: 1 3 2

(A6.10) <u>Affix Hopping</u> (Obligatory)

SD: Affix - V
       1   2
SC: 2 # 1

(Note: This rule, as written above, is not properly formalized. Our trees have no nodes in them labeled <u>Affix</u>, and Modals are not dominated by V; we have written the rule this way as a shorthand device. If the rule were formulated more accurately, it would be stated roughly as follows:

$$\text{SD:} \begin{Bmatrix} \text{pres} \\ \text{past} \\ \text{ing} \\ \text{en} \end{Bmatrix} - \begin{Bmatrix} \text{Modal} \\ \\ \text{V} \end{Bmatrix}$$

$$\qquad\quad 1 \qquad\qquad 2$$

SC: 2 # 1

There is a much simpler statement of the rule involving syntactic features, but we shall not present that
version here.)

(A6.11) <u>Do</u> Support (Obligatory)

> SD: X - Tense
>   1   2
> SC: 1 <u>do</u> # 2

Condition: X ≠ Modal or V

(Note: The condition on <u>Do</u> Support given immediately
above guarantees that the rule will operate just in case
Tense is not adjoined to a verb. Thus, its SD will be
satisfied only if Negative Placement, Question, etc.,
have operated on the input structure.)

CHAPTER 6: EXERCISES

(E6.1) Provide a complete derivation for each of the following
sentences, taking care to apply rules in their correct order.
Make sure that you know why the rules must apply in the order
you have used in each derivation:

(i)   There weren't many students applying for jobs, were
      there?
(ii) Couldn't John have given himself a birthday present?
(iii) My uncle's house in the woods wasn't found by the police.

(A derivation will consist of an underlying tree structure followed by a series of trees, each showing the effect of applying
a transformation to the one before. For examples of derivations, see text.)

(E6.2) Construct as many derivations as possible that begin
with each of the following underlying structures and that involve at least three rules in each derivation:

(i)

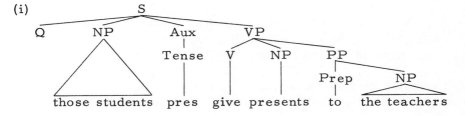

(ii)

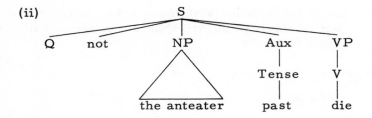

(E6.3) In the exercises to chapter 1 we referred to imperative sentences such as the following:

(i)   Drink your milk!
(ii) Leave the room!
(iii) Close the door!

Let us assume that such sentences are actually derived from fuller underlying forms such as the following:

(iv) You will drink your milk!
(v) You will leave the room!
(vi) You will close the door!

The Imperative Transformation will have the effect of deleting the subject you and the modal will from imperative sentences:

You will drink your milk. ⟹ Drink your milk.

Disregarding how we might state such a rule formally, answer the following questions:

A. In what order must the rules of Imperative and Reflexive apply to produce sentences such as Wash yourself!, Help yourself!, etc.?

B. Why? What ungrammatical sentences result if the rules are applied in the wrong order?

(E6.4) A number of linguists have proposed that there is a rule of English called Quantifier Floating, which has the effect of transforming the (a) sentence of (i) into the (b) sentence.

(i) a. All the men have found their way home.
    b. The men have all found their way home.

Thus, the quantifier <u>all</u> (as well as <u>each</u>) is optionally moved by Quantifier Floating to the position after the first auxiliary verb:

(ii) a.

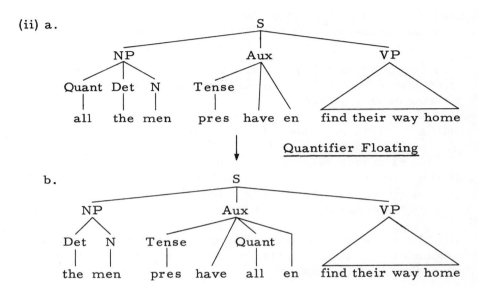

It is apparently the case that Quantifier Floating can apply only to noun phrases in <u>subject</u> position. Hence, a sentence such as (iiia) cannot be transformed into (iiib).

(iii) a. I have executed <u>all</u> the rebels.
    b. *I have <u>all</u> executed the rebels.

<u>A</u>. Give a rough formal statement of Quantifier Floating.

<u>B</u>. How must Quantifier Floating be ordered with respect to Passive? The following data should be taken into account:

(iv) a. They executed all the rebels.
    b. All the rebels were executed by them.
    c. The rebels were all executed by them.

(v) a. All the kids have seen the flea.
    b. The kids have all seen the flea.

    c.   The flea has been seen by all the kids.
    d. *The flea has all been seen by the kids.

(Note: In working on this problem, you should also take into account the pair of examples given in (iii) above.)

C. How must Quantifier Floating be ordered with respect to the Question Rule? The following sentences provide evidence bearing on this question:

(vi) a.   All the men have been running.
      b.   The men have all been running.
      c. *The men have been all running.
(vii) a.   Have all the men been running?
      b.   Have the men all been running?
      c. *Have the men been all running?

(E6.5) For many speakers of English (but not all), emphatic sentences may contain instances of the emphatic particle, so, as in the following examples:

(i)   a. I will so complete the course!
     b. He did so walk out on us!
     c. They have so been stealing the money!
     d. The FBI could so have been spying on us!

The particle so may never appear in questions:

(ii) a. *Will you so complete the course?
     b. *Did he so walk out on us?

Nor does so appear overtly in negative sentences:

(iii) a. *He didn't so walk out on us.
      b. *They haven't so been stealing money.

Negative emphatic sentences instead show heavy stress on the negative not:

(iv) a. He did not walk out on us!
     b. They have not been stealing money!

Consider the following proposed explanation for these facts.
Along with the other presentence elements Q and not, there is
also an emphatic marker, Emp, generated somewhere in presentence position:

(v) S → ... Emp ... NP Aux VP

A transformation must be formulated to place Emp in the correct position inside Aux. When Emp is generated in positive
sentences, it is eventually spelled out as so; when it appears
in negative sentences, it is not overtly realized but is "spelled
out" as heavy stress on not.

A. How can PS rule (v) be formulated so as to guarantee that
Emp optionally occurs in positive or negative sentences but
never in questions?

B. Given the fact that so never occurs in questions, what additional evidence does this provide for postulating the abstract
elements Q and Emp? How would we have to account for this
fact in a grammar with no such presentence elements?

C. How must the rule of Emp Placement be formally stated so
as to ensure that Emp is positioned correctly within the Aux?
How must the rule be ordered? Is the formulation of this rule
similar to that of any of the other rules we have studied? If so,
can Emp Placement be collapsed with any other rule(s) into a
single rule?

D. We have stated that when Emp occurs in negative sentences,
it is spelled out as heavy stress on not. However, one might
instead propose that Emp is eventually spelled out as either in
negative sentences, based on pairs such as the following:

(vi)   a. He did so steal the money!
       b. He didn't either steal the money!
(vii) a. They have so given us a hard time!
       b. They haven't either given us a hard time!

How should Emp be spelled out in negative sentences: should
it be realized as stress on not or spelled out as the word either
as in the above examples? What evidence, if any, can you find

that would have a bearing on this issue? In thinking about this question, it would be valuable to consider sentences with the particle too, as in the following examples:

(viii) a.   He did too steal the money!
       b.   They have too given us a hard time!
       c. *They haven't too given us a hard time!

How do these examples fit into the rest of the data we have examined?

Keep in mind that a problem of this sort has no one "correct" answer. Rather, its purpose is to aid in exploring the grammar of emphatic sentences; the way to "answer" the exercise is to propose a hypothesis about so, etc., that you think is promising, to provide as much evidence for it as you can, and in additon to give counterexamples to the hypothesis, if you think of any.

CHAPTER 6: SUGGESTED READINGS

The issues we have raised in this chapter concerning the ordering of rules are discussed in detail in much of the transformational literature. At this stage it would be very useful for readers to review the article by Postal (1964b) mentioned in the suggested readings for chapter 1, which deals with the Reflexive and Imperative Rules and their ordering. Burt (1971) provides detailed derivations using many of the orderings that we have discussed, and it would be useful to look at that work, too. Readers who wish to pursue some of the specific orderings, after they have built up further background, might be interested in reading Fillmore (1965), which deals with dative verbs and indirect object constructions. This involves the ordering between Dative Movement and Passive. Fillmore's work is written in an earlier grammatical framework, which will be difficult for beginners to follow without guidance at this stage. (Kuroda's (1968) review of Fillmore provides an interesting critique of that work.) In a more recent paper, one that should not be difficult to follow, Jackendoff and Culicover (1971) discuss the relationship between Dative Movment and other rules. They propose a novel view of the problems discussed by Fillmore and Kuroda.

For those interested in pursuing the general problem of rule ordering at greater depth, we can cite a number of recent papers that call in question some of the arguments that have been used in classical transformational theory to establish rule ordering. In particular, the papers by Koutsoudas (1972), Lehmann (1972), and Ringen (1972) should provide a useful start. These references assume considerable familiarity with linguistic theory.

DELETION, RECOVERABILITY, AND MEANING

7.1. SUMMARY OF TRANSFORMATIONAL OPERATIONS

We have so far examined a number of individual transformations, but we have not yet asked what operations, in general,
transformations may carry out. Let us classify the individual
transformational rules proposed so far according to the operations they perform on input trees to produce corresponding output trees. It turns out that all of these rules can be regarded
as consisting of one or more of the following four elementary
operations:

a. Movement (or Reordering)
b. Copying
c. Insertion
d. Deletion

We will summarize each of these informally. (For more technical details the reader is referred to the readings listed at
the end of chapter 5.) Before proceeding, attempt to list the
transformations that reorder elements, those that copy or insert elements, and those that delete. Some rules will fall into
more than one class.

7.1.1. Movement

Perhaps the majority of the well-known transformations of
English have the effect of moving constituents from one part
of a tree to another. For example, the Passive Transformation has the effect of moving the subject and object NPs from
their original positions and adjoining them in new positions on
the tree; the Question Transformation moves Tense plus the
first auxiliary (if any) to the left of the subject NP; the Dative
Movement Transformation moves the indirect object NP to a
position immediately after the verb, making it the new direct
object; our revised Negative Placement Transformation has
the effect of moving the sentence-initial not to a position within
the auxiliary; Affix Hopping involves a very limited kind of
movement, by which affixes are positioned after relevant verbs
and attached to them. In general, it seems to be the case that

only single constituents (i.e., no more and no less than one
constituent) may be reordered by a transformation. (Note that
the Question Rule as we have formulated it is an exception, in
that it may move up to two constituents at a single time.) If it
is true that movement rules may generally operate only on
single constituents, then these rules provide us with fairly
good tests for constituent structure (as was implicit in our discussion in chapter 2).

7.1.2. Copying
We refer here to rules that have the effect of adding a copy of
an existing constituent in a new part of the tree. For example,
the Tag Formation Rule copies the subject and relevant portion
of the auxiliary at the end of the main sentence, leaving the
original constituents in their place. In all cases, copying rules
that apply to NPs have the effect of converting either the copied
NP or "original" NP into a pronoun. (The Tag Formation Rule
has the former effect.) Other copying rules move an NP from
its position within a sentence and leave a pronoun copy of the
NP in that position. For example, there appears to be a rule
(referred to as Dislocation) that has the effect of moving an NP
from its position in a main clause, either to the right of the
main sentence (as in (7.1b) and (7.2b)) or to the left of the main
sentence (as in (7.3a, b)):

(7.1) a. My father is a brilliant man.
     b. He is a brilliant man, my father.

(7.2) a. I donated that old book that I like to the library
        yesterday.
     b. I donated it to the library yesterday, that old book
        that I like.

(7.3) a. My father, he's a brilliant man.
     b. That old book that I like, I donated it to the library
        yesterday.

In either case, the rule has the effect of leaving a pronoun copy
of the moved NP in the position originally occupied by the NP.
Thus, a copying rule involves movement—but there is always
the original NP or a pronoun "trace" left behind to show where
the NP has been moved from. (Notice, incidentally, that Tag

Formation is actually a combination of "pure" movement and copying: the subject and relevant portion of the auxiliary are copied at the end of the sentence, but the symbol Q is moved into the tag, with no trace of its existence left behind in the main clause.)

7.1.3. Insertion
We have examined a number of rules that have the effect of adding or inserting material into trees. The Passive Transformation inserts be en and by (hence, Passive is actually made up of two kinds of operations: movement and insertion); Do Support has the effect of inserting do whenever a Tense marker has been "stranded"; and the rule of There Insertion inserts the word there in appropriate contexts in sentences with the verb be. (We are no longer counting Negative Placement as an insertion rule; given our reformulation of it in chapter 6, it must now be classed as a movement rule.) Notice that these rules have in common one important property: each inserts words that have no independent meaning (i. e., ones that do not contribute to the meaning of the sentence) but are merely grammatical function words of various sorts. Thus, neither be en nor by in the passive construction can be said to have any independent meaning, nor do these add any new meaning to passive sentences; the do of Do Support functions to carry tense but carries no special meaning; the word there inserted by There Insertion is similarly devoid of meaning and merely serves to fill the subject position of the sentence. The fact that the insertion rules we have studied have the effect of adding semantically empty words into trees suggests that we can perhaps limit all insertion rules in this way. This property will take on added significance in the final section of this chapter (section 7.6).

Recall that we have also specified another way in which insertion should probably be limited. In our discussion of the placement of by by the Passive Rule, we pointed out that we wanted to prevent that rule from building new structure (see chapter 5 for discussion). We argued that transformations probably should not be allowed to build structure (except perhaps by Chomsky adjunction) but only to modify structure that is already present. We will assume that the operation of insertion should be constrained so that, in general, structure building is prevented.

7.1.4. Deletion

So far we have scarcely examined any rules that have the effect of deleting material from trees. In our formulation of the Dative Movement Rule, the preposition <u>to</u> (or <u>for</u>) is deleted when the indirect object is moved, but this trivial case is the only example of deletion we have formalized. However, a number of interesting issues arise when we consider deletion. We will begin to examine these with the help of a construction that we have already mentioned in exercises: the imperative.

7.2. THE IMPERATIVE TRANSFORMATION

A number of linguists have proposed that the imperative sentences of (7.4) derive from the fuller underlying sentences listed in (7.5):

(7.4) a. Leave the room!
      b. Drink your milk!
      c. Take out the cat!

(7.5) a. You will leave the room!
      b. You will drink your milk!
      c. You will take out the cat!

Imperative sentences, of themselves, seem to consist of nothing but a <u>verb phrase</u>:

(7.6)

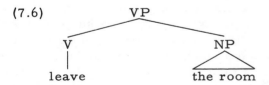

On the surface, they never occur with subjects or with auxiliary verbs. Given this, our PS rules will currently not generate them, since the rule for expanding S makes the subject NP and Aux obligatory constituents. We could very easily modify the PS rules so that they would generate a VP alone for imperatives and <u>NP - Aux - VP</u> for all other sentences. This would represent a trivial modification to the grammar. (How could the rule for expanding S be formulated in order to provide for these alternatives?) However, there is independent evidence for deriving imperatives from fuller underlying structures (such as those basic to (7.5a-c)) by means of a deletion transformation. In working through the exercises and readings to chapter 1, especially the article by Postal (1964b), the nature of this evidence should have become clear to the reader. Try to reconstruct the arguments and if necessary reread Postal's article before proceeding.

We will quickly summarize three of the main arguments for deriving imperatives from underlying sentences containing you as the subject and will as the modal auxiliary. The following two sentences are relevant:

(7.7) a. Wash yourself!
     b. Leave the room, won't you?

The first argument concerns the derivation of reflexives. In (7.7a) the reflexive pronoun yourself occurs. Recall that in our statement of Reflexivization in chapter 5, we required that the reflexive NP be identical with the subject of the sentence.

(7.8) a. I like me $\Rightarrow$ I like myself.
     b. You struck you $\Rightarrow$ You struck yourself.
     c. He shaved him $\Rightarrow$ He shaved himself.

If imperative sentences are regarded as having no subject, then our account of reflexivization will be complicated. If (7.7a), Wash yourself!, were generated without a subject, then what would be the source for the reflexive form yourself? We would presumably need to add a special rider to Reflexivization that would introduce yourself (and not, e.g., himself) into sentences lacking subjects. But then we would completely miss the generalization illustrated by the facts of (7.8).

On the other hand, if we regard imperatives as deriving from sentences with you as the subject, then we can generate the reflexive pronoun in a perfectly regular way. Following the analysis of the reflexive given in chapter 5 and the analysis of the imperative suggested above, a sentence such as (7.7a) would derive from a sentence such as (7.9):

(7.9) You will wash you.

The Reflexivization Transformation will then mark the second occurrence of you with the feature [+Reflexive]. We assume that after Reflexivization has operated in its normal fashion, the Imperative Transformation operates on (7.9) to delete the subject you and the modal will. (Why is the opposite order— i.e., Imperative first, followed by Reflexivization—not correct?)

The second piece of evidence for the suggested analysis of the imperative is represented by sentence (7.7b), which we repeat here:

(7.7) b. Leave the room, won't you?

The argument that has been used in this case runs as follows: we know that the Tag Rule must be stated in such a way that it copies the subject and first auxiliary into the tag; if imperative sentences are generated without these constituents, then the normal Tag Rule will have nothing to operate on to produce (7.7b). In order to maintain the simplest formulation of the Tag Rule, we should generate imperatives from sentences that contain you as the subject and will as the auxiliary verb.

Another bit of evidence that has been offered to demonstrate that will (or at least some modal) is in the auxiliary in imperative sentences has to do with the fact that the verb in imperative sentences is tenseless. This is not so easy to see in the cases we have examined so far, in which each of the verbs is appropriate for a second person subject, but if we examine cases in which the imperative contains be as a main verb we see that it must be tenseless:

(7.10) a. Be quiet!
       b. *Are quiet!

If the verb of the imperative were a tensed verb (and therefore subject to Number Agreement—see the appendix to chapter 6), then we would expect imperatives such as (7.10b) to be well formed. However, only (7.10a) is acceptable. We can explain this if we assume that it derives from (7.11):

(7.11) You will be quiet!   (cf. *You will are quiet!)

The effect of the underlying modal is to prevent Tense from being attached to be by Affix Hopping and thus to guarantee that be is tenseless.

The observations we have made so far can be brought together by adding the following transformation to our grammar:

(7.12) Imperative Transformation (Optional)

    SD: you - Tense   will - VP
         1   2   3
    SC: ∅ ∅ 3

As long as this rule follows the Reflexivization and Tag Rules, we can provide a reasonably satisfactory account of how sentences such as those in (7.7) are generated. This analysis of the imperative is not without problems, however. For example, one minor difficulty arises because the Tag Rule, as we stated it in chapter 6, will not apply to an underlying structure of the form (7.13):

(7.13) you – Tense will – leave the room

This is because we stated the Tag Rule so as to apply only to structures containing an initial Q, the symbol used to trigger the operation of the Question Transformation. Therefore, if we wanted to have the Tag Rule apply to imperative sentences, we would need to modify the statement of the rule in some manner so that it would apply to forms such as (7.13). The question of how to generate tags in imperative sentences is an extremely interesting one, but to discuss it here would take us too far afield. (See the exercises at the end of this chapter, which contain sufficient data to illustrate the relevant problems.)

7.3. THE KATZ-POSTAL HYPOTHESIS

Although we have only sketched a rough statement of the Imperative Transformation (and there is no doubt that the rule as we have stated it is in need of further refinement), the important point to notice is that there is fairly good evidence for supposing the existence of some transformation that deletes you and a modal verb such as will. Given the need for a transformation of this sort, we can point out some of the interesting general properties of such a process of deletion. First, notice that the rule deletes specific elements that carry meaning: you

and will. It is no accident that the meaning of an imperative
seems to include the meaning of those elements in some way,
despite the fact that they have been deleted. For example, a
command such as Jump in the water! is understood as being
addressed to a second person you and as involving an action
to be carried out in the future (suggested by the modal will).
Notice that we did not try to argue for the presence of you and
will in the underlying structure of imperatives on the basis of
meaning. We gave purely formal arguments. The syntactic
rules for forming tags and reflexives and for producing number agreement would have had to be complicated if such elements as you and will were not present at some level in imperatives. Consequently, the fact that imperatives embody the
meaning of you and will is a significant additional fact about
them, which was not automatically built into our account. This
is worth emphasizing because it is often hard to see, at first,
that in providing arguments for syntactic structures we are
never directly concerned with meaning.
    Yet, there is obviously a very close relationship between the
syntactic pattern of a sentence and aspects of its meaning, and
we are generally far more aware of the general meaning of sentences than we are of details of their syntax. Despite this very
close relationship and despite the fact that we often have difficulty in dissociating the purely syntactic form of a sentence
from its meaning, we have up to now been concerned solely
with syntactic structure, and our arguments have not been
based upon hypotheses about what sentences mean. However,
we must mention at least one particular hypothesis about certain systematic relationships holding between syntactic structure and meaning that has become important in the development of syntactic theory. Originally formulated by Katz and
Postal (1964) (and hence known as the Katz-Postal Hypothesis),
this has been put forward in a number of different versions; we
can state it as follows:

(7.14) Katz-Postal Hypothesis
        Transformations are meaning-preserving, in the fol-
        lowing sense: if two surface structures derive from
        exactly the same underlying structure and if their deri-
        vations differ only in that an optional transformation has
        applied in one but not the other, then they must have the
        same meaning.

Before looking again at the Imperative Transformation in the
light of this hypothesis, we can illustrate it by means of a number of transformations introduced in previous chapters. Take
an active-passive pair such as (7.15a, b):

(7.15) a. David killed Goliath.
       b. Goliath was killed by David.

These two sentences derive from the same underlying form and
differ only in that the optional rule of Passive has applied in the
derivation of (7.15b). In one sense these may differ in meaning,
for the first is "about" David and the second "about" Goliath,
and thus they may differ in emphasis, etc. But in most important respects they have the same meaning. In particular,
they have precisely the same truth conditions—i.e., there is
no state of affairs that could make one true and the other false—
and thus we may say they are cognitively synonymous (or have
the same cognitive meaning). If we concentrate only on cognitive meaning, as defined loosely above in terms of truth conditions, then as far as examples (7.15a) and (7.15b) are concerned, the Passive Rule is consistent with the form of the
Katz-Postal Hypothesis given in (7.14). The application of the
Passive Rule to derive (7.15b) has made no change in meaning.

    A wide range of active-passive pairs would provide similar
evidence, and the synonymy (in the relevant sense) of all of the
following examples suggests that the same holds for Dative
Movement:

(7.16) a. Jonathan gave the harp to David.
       b. Jonathan gave David the harp.
       c. David was given the harp by Jonathan.
       d. The harp was given to David by Jonathan.

Again, let us emphasize that we did not make any reference to
meaning in justifying these rules in the first place. If the Katz-
Postal Hypothesis holds for both Dative Movement and Passive,
this is an additional, interesting fact about how transformations
work. Does Reflexivization obey the Katz-Postal Hypothesis in
this form? What about the Question and Negative Insertion Rules
(a) as originally formulated and (b) as restated in chapter 6 (as
Question and Negative Placement)?

The Reflexivization Rule appears to be consistent with hypothesis (7.14); that is, transforming a structure such as I hurt
me into the sentence I hurt myself changes the shape of the
original input but surely not its meaning. On the other hand,
in their original form, neither the Question Rule nor Negative
Insertion support the hypothesis. Recall that both (7.17a) and
(7.17b) were originally derived from a single underlying tree,
(7.18):

(7.17) a. Samson liked honey.
       b. Samson did not like honey.

(7.18)

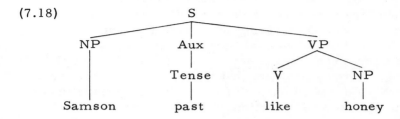

Under that formulation, (7.17a) and (7.17b) differ only in that
the latter has undergone the optional rule of Negative Insertion.
Yet they obviously differ in meaning (indeed, any conditions
that will make the first true will make the second false, and
vice versa). Hence, the old Negative Insertion Transformation
was altogether inconsistent with this version of the Katz-Postal
Hypothesis.

However, a grammar that includes an optional not in the
phrase structure rule expanding S (S → (not) NP Aux VP) and
a transformation of Negative Placement (see chapter 6) is consistent with the proposal. Under the revised analysis, (7.17a)
and (7.17b) differ crucially in underlying form—before any
transformation has been applied to them—in that only the latter includes not:

(7.19) a.

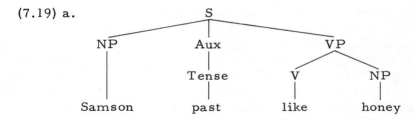

(7.19) b.

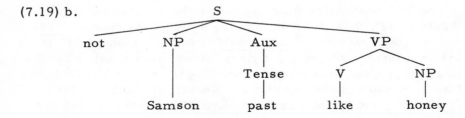

Trees (7.19a) and (7.19b) are identical except for the presence of <u>not</u> in (7.19b), and we can obviously ascribe the difference in meaning between <u>Samson liked honey</u> and <u>Samson didn't like honey</u> to this difference in underlying structure.

Similarly, the earlier version of the Question Rule seems incompatible with the "meaning-preserving" hypothesis. Although it is hard to define exactly <u>how</u> a statement-question pair such as <u>Samson liked honey</u>/<u>Did Samson like honey?</u> differ in meaning, there is no doubt that they do differ. Once again, the account proposed in chapter 6 (in which Q appears in the underlying structure of questions) is consistent with the Katz-Postal Hypothesis as stated above, since we can ascribe the difference in meaning between questions and statements to the presence of Q in the underlying structure of the former. It is interesting that this should be the case, especially since our reformulation of the rules for negatives and questions was motivated solely by the syntactic structure of tags.

However, not all of the rules we discussed in chapter 6 are completely consistent with the Katz-Postal Hypothesis. In fact, the Tag Rule itself seems to be an interesting counterexample. To see why, consider the fact that, as our rules now stand, the two sentences of (7.20) will derive from the same underlying structure, namely, (7.21):

(7.20) a. John didn't leave the room, did he?
       b. John left the room, didn't he?

(7.21) Q – not – John – past – leave the room

The two sentences of (7.20) differ only in that the rule of Negative Placement has placed <u>not</u> in the main clause of (7.20a) but in the tag of (7.20b). Despite this difference, the two sentences have undergone just the same rules (i.e., Tag Formation, Negative Placement, Contraction, Question, etc.). Yet the two sentences of (7.20) do not seem to have the same meaning. For example, sentence (7.20a) can be used in a situation in which the speaker supposes that John has not left the room and the response to (7.20a) is expected to be negative (i.e., No, John didn't leave the room). On the other hand, (7.20b) is used in just the opposite situation: here the speaker supposes that John has indeed left the room, and the answer to (7.20b) is expected to be positive (i.e., Yes, John did leave the room). It seems, then, that we must either modify the Katz-Postal Hypothesis to allow certain transformations to modify meaning in specific ways, or we must reanalyze the process of tag formation in such a way that it will be consistent with the hypothesis. Which alternative is correct can only be determined by further empirical research.

Another class of apparent counterexamples to the Katz-Postal Hypothesis can be constructed with rules such as the Passive. Although the rule is meaning-preserving in many contexts, there are instances in which its application seems to change meaning. For example, there are many speakers of English who do not interpret the following active-passive pairs as synonymous:

(7.22) a. Many arrows have not hit the target (but, then again, many arrows have hit it).
b. The target has not been hit by many arrows (*but, then again, many arrows have hit it).

(7.23) a. Few people have read three of Hemingway's novels.
b. Three of Hemingway's novels have been read by few people.

The obvious way of deriving (7.22b) and (7.23b) is by applying the Passive Rule to the structures that underlie (7.22a) and (7.23a). If that is correct, then it would seem that the Katz-Postal Hypothesis will have to be weakened so that only certain specific aspects of meaning are never changed by the operation of any transformational rule. In a fully worked out version of this weaker form of the hypothesis, it would be necessary to specify exactly which aspects of meaning remain unchanged by transformations.

Let us now return to imperatives. It was proposed that an optional transformation, Imperative (7.12), should derive the first member of each of the following pairs from the second:

(7.24) a. Drop that swarm of bees!
      b. You will drop that swarm of bees!

(7.25) a. Find the queen!
      b. You will find the queen!

We observed earlier that the imperatives seemed to express in
some way the meaning of the deleted you and will and that this
was interesting in view of the fact that our arguments for the
underlying presence of these elements had been purely syntactic. Now we can be rather more precise about why this fact
was interesting: it shows that in this respect the Imperative
Transformation is consistent with the Katz-Postal Hypothesis,
for the meaning of the deleted elements is not lost as a result
of the operation of the Imperative Rule, even though the words
you and will are deleted.

    Notice what the hypothesis means for deletion rules in gen-
eral. If transformations are to preserve meaning, then whenever a rule deletes an element from a tree it must be possible
to determine from the statement of the rule that has applied,
along with the output tree, what elements have been deleted
(otherwise there would be a change in meaning). As long as the
Imperative Transformation mentions the specific elements you
and will in its SD (see (7.12)), then we know exactly what has
been deleted from any tree to which the rule applies: i.e., we
can always recover the deleted items. Given the Katz-Postal
Hypothesis, all deletions must be recoverable in this sense.
(We will discuss below ways of making deletion recoverable
other than by deleting only specified elements.) As we shall see,
the well-motivated deletion transformations do seem to involve
only recoverable deletion and hence appear to be consistent
with the Katz-Postal Hypothesis.

    We should point out at least one further issue connected with
our analysis of imperatives before going on to other deletion
transformations. Consider the meaning of the paired examples
given above as (7.24) and repeated here:

(7.24) a. Drop that swarm of bees!
      b. You will drop that swarm of bees!

Although a sentence like (7.24b) can be used to give an order, it also has another use, namely, to make a statement about the future, as in (7.26):

(7.26) You will drop that swarm of bees if you aren't careful.

An imperative such as (7.24a) cannot be used in this way. Thus (7.27) is anomalous:

(7.27) *Drop that swarm of bees if you aren't careful!

What seems to be going on here is that sentence (7.24b) is ambiguous: it can either be a command or a statement about the future. If our analysis of the imperative is to be consistent with the Katz-Postal Hypothesis, then we must find some way to ensure that (7.24b) is allowed to undergo the Imperative Transformation only in its command sense. In this regard, it has been proposed that imperative sentences contain, in deep structure, an abstract marker Imperative (Imp), which distinguishes them from statements (just as, for example, Q distinguishes questions from statements in deep structure). Following this suggestion, (7.24b) would actually derive from two distinct underlying forms:

(7.28) a. Imp – you – pres – will – drop that swarm of bees
b. you – pres – will – drop that swarm of bees

The ambiguity of the sentence can now be ascribed to the fact that it derives from two underlying forms, and we can state the Imperative Transformation in such a way that it requires the symbol Imp in its SD (just as the Question Rule, for example, requires Q in its statement). This would guarantee that the Imperative Transformation would be meaning preserving.

However, notice that we have introduced the symbol Imp strictly for the purpose of making the Imperative Rule consistent with the Katz-Postal Hypothesis, and we have not provided any independent syntactic evidence that Imp is necessary. Contrast this with the postulation of the symbol Q: we introduced Q for reasons that had nothing to do with meaning, but rather because it allowed us to state certain generalizations concerning the syntactic relation between tags and the clauses with which they are associated. If we are to use the symbol Imp to distinguish imperatives from statements, then here too we must find independent syntactic evidence showing that Imp would allow the overall set of syntactic rules to be simplified. In the absence of such independent evidence, we must leave it as an open question whether imperative sentences contain Imp in their underlying form; hence, no decision has been taken as to whether the Imperative Transformation is completely consistent with the Katz-Postal Hypothesis. However, whether or not the Imperative Rule changes meaning, there still remains one crucial way in which the rule is surely consistent with the hypothesis; namely, the deletion of <u>you</u> and <u>will</u> is always recoverable (in the sense described above), and the meaning of the imperative incorporates the meanings of those missing lexical items.

7.4. AGENT DELETION

Another deletion rule that has been frequently proposed would derive the sentences of (7.29) from the corresponding sentences of (7.30):

(7.29) a. Sam was fired yesterday.
      b. These files will be examined.
      c. The rock was moved.

(7.30) a. Sam was fired <u>by someone</u> yesterday.
      b. These files will be examined <u>by someone</u>.
      c. The rock was moved <u>by someone</u> (or <u>something</u>).

It may not seem obvious that the sentences of (7.29) should be regarded as reduced passive sentences. For example, one might want to claim that a sentence such as (7.29a) simply derives from a structure such as the following:

(7.31)

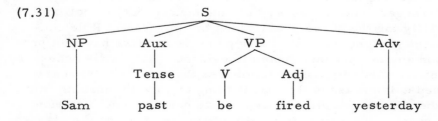

On this analysis, all the sentences of (7.29) are generated directly by PS rules. Is there any evidence that a sentence such as Sam was fired should be regarded as a reduced form of Sam was fired by someone and, hence, as ultimately deriving from the active source someone - past - fire - Sam? Although a clear answer may not be easy to construct, try to formulate such evidence before reading further.

Some evidence for deriving the examples of (7.29) from passive sentences comes from the fact that the so-called adjectives in structures such as (7.31) would include a subset that corresponds exactly to the set of transitive verbs in past participle form (i.e., in the form they assume in passive sentences). If we regarded fired as an adjective in sentence (7.29a), we would have to suppose that the lexicon contained an adjective corresponding in form to the past participle of every such verb (e.g., dried, stopped, broken, etc.) but none such as disappeared corresponding to the past participles of intransitive verbs.

Moreover, there are certain irregularities in the meaning and even acceptability of certain passives, which we have not mentioned before. For example, the verb fit can undergo Passive only when it is used with a human subject in underlying structure:

(7.32) a. John's new suit fits him.
       b. *John is fitted by his new suit.

(7.33) a. The tailor fitted John (for his new suit).
       b. John was fitted (for his new suit) by the tailor.

There are agentless forms containing fit, and they correspond only to sentences such as (7.33b), as in the following example:

(7.34) John was fitted (for his new suit) today.

Consider next the verb want, which has even stranger restrictions in the passive. Whereas we find sentences such as John is wanted by his mother, we do not generally find forms like *That cake is wanted by Mary corresponding to Mary wants that cake. As we might expect, an "agentless" form such as John is wanted (at 2 o'clock) is perfectly acceptable, but normally *That cake is wanted is not.

It is not impossible that such facts could be accounted for in the adjective analysis—but there is no obvious way of dealing with them. In any case, there is evidence of a different kind that makes the adjective analysis seem very unlikely. This argument involves the prepositions in sentences such as (7.35a, b):

(7.35) a. John was <u>laughed at</u> (when he proposed that idea).
       b. John can be <u>relied on</u>.

It is not clear how these sentences can be generated if we assume that they are produced directly by PS rules in structures such as (7.31). For one thing, our PS rule for prepositional phrases (i.e., <u>PP → P NP</u>) always generates an NP following a preposition. Yet no NP follows the prepositions of (7.35). On the other hand, it would be easy to derive sentences such as (7.35) on the hypothesis that they are reduced passive sentences.
     Example (7.35a) would have the following underlying form:

(7.36)

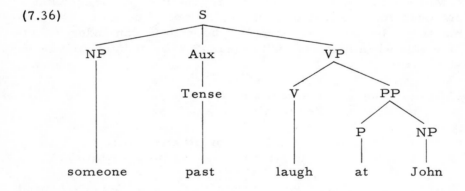

<u>John</u> in sentence (7.35a) derives from an underlying form in which it is the object of the preposition <u>at</u>. The Passive Rule as we have formulated it requires an input structure of the form NP - Aux - V - NP; hence, it will not apply to this tree, since we can isolate only the sequences NP - Aux - V - PP or NP - Aux - V - P - NP. Thus, we must relax the requirements of the Passive Rule, allowing an <u>optional</u> preposition to appear in its SD (NP - Aux - V - (P) - NP), so that it will produce the following output:

(7.37)

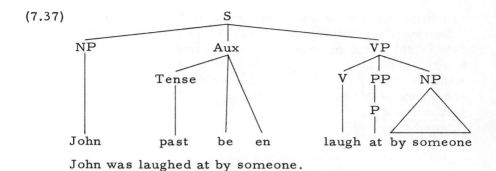

John was laughed at by someone.

At this point in our derivation, let us suppose that a transformation of <u>Agent Deletion</u> applies. We might formulate the rule as follows:

(7.38) <u>Agent Deletion</u> (Optional)

$$\text{SD: NP} - \text{X} - \text{be en} - \text{V} - \text{Y} - \begin{Bmatrix} \text{by someone} \\ \text{by something} \end{Bmatrix}$$

$$\begin{array}{ccccccc} & 1 & 2 & 3 & 4 & 5 & 6 \\ \text{SC:} & 1 & 2 & 3 & 4 & 5 & \emptyset \end{array}$$

This rule has the effect of deleting the <u>agent phrase</u>, <u>by someone</u> (or <u>by something</u>), in a passive sentence; it would produce the following output from tree (7.37):

(7.39)

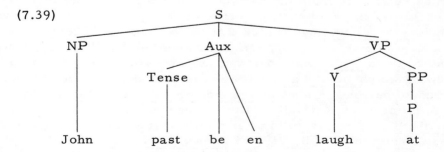

After the operation of Affix Hopping, we have derived the desired sentence, <u>John was laughed at</u>. By a similar process, we could derive all the examples of (7.29) from those of (7.30). The analysis we have just proposed provides a natural explanation for the presence of the "stranded" preposition <u>at</u>, and it does not seem likely that the adjective analysis could provide as natural an account for a sentence such as (7.35a).

But we must now ask the reader: Why have we formulated rule (7.38) in the particular way we have? Why should the deleted phrase be just <u>by someone</u> or <u>by something</u>? Why is a sentence such as <u>John was fired</u> not derived from any of the sentences below by a rule deleting <u>by NP</u> instead of <u>by</u> $\left\{ \begin{array}{l} \underline{someone} \\ \underline{something} \end{array} \right\}$?

(7.40) a. John was fired <u>by the boss</u>.
      b. John was fired <u>by the person</u> who <u>hired him</u>.
      c. John was fired <u>by Bill</u>.

There is actually no independent evidence for deriving <u>John was fired</u> from <u>John was fired by someone</u> rather than from an infinite number of different sources such as <u>John was fired by Bill</u>, . . . <u>by Joe</u>, . . . <u>by the woman in the red hat</u>, and so on. But if the transformation of Agent Deletion is to be subject to the condition that deleted elements must be recoverable and the condition that rules must not change meaning, then this seems to be the most natural way of stating the transformation. Since there is evidence that there must be a transformational source for agentless passives, and since the condition on recoverability requires that we not delete any element unless it can be recovered from the derivation, we postulate that the deleted NP is one of a specific, limited set of particular elements: <u>someone</u> or <u>something</u>. Notice that if we stated the Agent Deletion Rule in a general way, i.e., if we stated the SD so that the general term <u>by NP</u> were deleted, then we would have no way of knowing which <u>particular</u> NP may have been deleted; the deleted NP could be <u>John</u>, <u>the woman in the red hat</u>, <u>the boss</u>, or any of an infinite set of possible NPs. However, the sentence <u>John was fired</u> does not seem to be infinitely ambiguous; it does not mean <u>John was fired by Bill</u>, or <u>John was fired by the boss</u>, or any other of an infinite set of sentences of this sort. By stating the rule of Agent Deletion so that it specifically mentions the NPs <u>someone</u> or <u>something</u>, we know that the rule has deleted exactly one of these two NPs, and no others.

Whether pairs of sentences like <u>John was fired</u> and <u>John was fired by someone</u> are really synonymous is not clear. When they interact with pronouns, as in the following examples, they certainly do not seem to have exactly the same meaning:

(7.41) a. Mary was fired by <u>someone</u> and she wants to punch
           <u>him</u> on the nose.
       b. *Mary was fired and she wants to punch him on the
           nose.

In (7.41a), <u>him</u> can refer to the person who fired Mary, but
(7.41b) has only a rather strange reading in which <u>him</u> refers
back to someone mentioned earlier in the discourse. Furthermore, there are sentences that resemble agentless passives
that appear to have no source at all:

(7.42) a. The house was surrounded.
       b. *The house was surrounded $\begin{Bmatrix} \text{by someone} \\ \text{by something} \end{Bmatrix}$.

If we were to derive (7.42a) by Agent Deletion, in the manner
discussed above, then its only source would be the ungrammatical (7.42b). To what extent such facts are evidence against
deriving <u>John was fired</u> in the way suggested is a question we
must leave open. We will go on now to a very different kind of
deletion rule.

7.5. DELETION UNDER IDENTITY
There is another way in which recoverable deletion can be carried out. For example, consider the following sentences:

(7.43) a. Ellsberg was arrested by the FBI and <u>Fonda was too</u>.
       b. I can't see you tomorrow, but <u>Sam may</u>.

These sentences seem to consist of a complete sentence, followed by the conjunction <u>and</u>, followed by what we can call <u>el-</u>
<u>liptical sentences</u> (i. e. , those incomplete sentences such as
<u>Fonda was too</u> and <u>Sam may</u>). Taken out of context, these are
meaningless and could not stand alone. Yet, when conjoined
with full sentences as above, they are not only meaningful but
also quite commonly used in ordinary speech.
    The meaning of each of the elliptical sentences is dependent
on the meaning of the sentence that precedes it. Thus, <u>Fonda</u>
<u>was too</u> is taken to mean that Fonda was arrested by the FBI
too; <u>Sam may</u> is taken to mean that Sam may see you tomorrow.

In each case we have reconstructed the meaning of the incomplete sentence on the basis of the meaning of the preceding sentence.

Although these observations may seem rather obvious at first
glance, we should note that sentences such as those in (7.43)
present our theory with several nontrivial problems. First of
all, we have no way of generating elliptical sentences such as
those just cited. Our PS rule for sentences, i.e., $\underline{S \to NP \ Aux}$
$\underline{VP}$, always generates structures that are "complete," and there
is no way we can generate a "partial" structure such as $\underline{Fonda}$
$\underline{was}$. Second, we have seen that the elliptical sentences following $\underline{and}$ in (7.43) bear a special relationship to the sentences
preceding $\underline{and}$: the meaning we assign to the elliptical clauses
seems to coincide with part of the meaning of the main clauses
preceding $\underline{and}$. Thus, however we may choose to generate elliptical clauses, we must ensure that our theory reflects the
fact that they are dependent on the preceding sentences, at least
for their meaning.

Given these facts and the fact that transformational rules have
the power to delete elements, it is natural to seek a derivation
for the sentences of (7.43) from fully expanded pairs of sentences joined by $\underline{and}$:

(7.44) a. [Ellsberg was arrested by the FBI] and [Fonda was
            arrested by the FBI] too
                              ↓
       b. Ellsberg was arrested by the FBI and Fonda was too.

(7.45) a. [I can't see you tomorrow] but [Sam may see you to-
            morrow]
                              ↓
       b. I can't see you tomorrow but Sam may.

For each case, the (a) sentence that provides the putative source
for the (b) sentence is itself fully grammatical. This is the first
time we have dealt with units longer than a single simple sentence, and our rules will have to be modified somewhat merely
to generate the (a) forms. Hence, if those are to provide the
basis for the (b) forms, we must first find a way to generate
the full sentences.

Let us examine some $\underline{conjoined \ sentences}$ of the simplest
sort:

(7.46) a. The dog barked and the cat screamed.
       b. Mt. Fuji was scaled in 1896 and Mt. Everest was
          scaled in 1955.
       c. We gave money to the Friends of Mars and they gave
          money to the Society of Gorillas.

Each of these sentences seems to consist of two complete sentences joined by the word <u>and</u>, and the simplest structure we
could assign to (7.46a) would be (7.47):

(7.47)

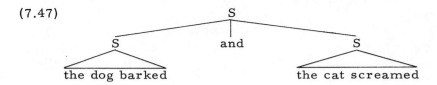

Structure (7.47) embodies the claim that (7.46a) is a sentence
consisting of two complete sentences joined by <u>and</u>, a structure
that seems reasonable at this stage. How would we need to
modify our PS rules to generate conjoined structures such as
(7.47)?

An obvious rule to begin with would be the following:

(7.48) S → S and S

This rule would in fact generate (7.47) and works fine as long
as we restrict ourselves to cases in which only two sentences
have been conjoined. However, when we examine cases in which
there are more than two conjuncts, we find that the rule is problematic in that it does not permit us to add further conjoined
sentences in a simple coordinate structure. Consider how a
sentence such as the following would be generated:

(7.49) The dog barked and the cat screamed and I fell out of
       my bed and the toilet ran over.

How many different structures would be assigned to this sentence by rule (7.48)? Follow the rule strictly!

In order to generate sentence (7.49), the rule must generate four sentences (i.e., S nodes) joined by <u>and</u>. The following structures represent only a sample of the total number of structures that rule (7.48) would assign to this sentence:

(7.50) a.

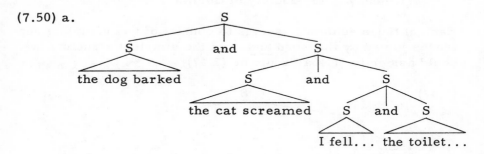

b.

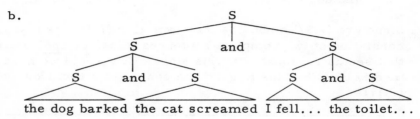

Rule (7.48) can only conjoin <u>pairs</u> of sentences; thus, in order to generate more than just two conjoined sentences, it must always generate these longer sentences by means of <u>pairs</u>. For this reason, the rule generates only complex structures like (7.50) for a sentence like (7.49).

Yet that sentence may well have the simple structure shown in the following diagram:

(7.51)

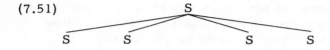

As long as we want to be able to generate structures like (7.51) (as well as those of (7.50), of course), we must introduce a new formalism into our PS rules, shown in the following additional rule expanding S:

(7.52) $S \rightarrow S^{\underline{n}}$, $\underline{n} \geq 2$

The superscript $\underline{n}$ in the symbol $S^{\underline{n}}$ means that any number of

S nodes may be generated under S; and to ensure that at least
two Ss are generated we include the notation $n \geq 2$ ("n is greater
than or equal to 2"). When an S is expanded by this rule, then
that S will dominate two or more instances of S, thus creating
trees such as (7.51). Each S dominated by the top S can in turn
be expanded by the familiar rule S → (Q) (not) NP Aux VP.

We also need to make provision for inserting and between
the coordinate Ss. We might propose to do this by a transformation of Conjunction Insertion that would simply insert and
between each pair of sentences dominated by S—i.e., between
each of the lower S nodes in (7.51). But notice that, in general,
when and occurs, or can occur also:

(7.53) a. John went to town and Bill went to town.
       b. John went to town or Bill went to town.

(7.54) a. Sam cooked the fish and he ate it.
       b. Sam cooked the fish or he ate it.

We would expect or to be inserted by the same rule that inserts and; so the rule of Conjunction Insertion would presumably have to insert either one of these words in coordinate
structures such as (7.51). The putative rule might look like
this:

(7.55) Conjunction Insertion (Obligatory)

SD: $_S[S - S]_S$

      1   2

SC: $1 + \left\{ \begin{array}{l} \text{and} \\ \text{or} \end{array} \right\} + 2$

(The notation $_S[S - S]_S$ indicates that two sentences are dominated by a single S indicated as $_S[\ldots]_S$. We refer to such
bracketing as labeled bracketing.) Now comment on this transformation in the light of the Katz-Postal Hypothesis. Is this a
meaning-preserving rule, or does it change meaning?

Rule (7.55) obviously changes meaning and hence is incompatible with the Katz-Postal Hypothesis. That a change of

meaning is brought about by the rule should be obvious from
the fact that (7.53a) is not synonymous with (7.53b) (and likewise for (7.54)). But under the present proposal the (a) and
(b) sentences would be derived from a single underlying structure—something like (7.51). Depending on whether and or or
was introduced by the rule of Conjunction Insertion, the (a) or
(b) sentence would be produced. Under the Katz-Postal Hypothesis, transformations cannot introduce meaningful elements
such as and or or.

We can modify PS rule (7.52) to introduce and and or, so
that no real violation of the meaning-preserving hypothesis
will result. For example, we could replace rule (7.52) ($S \rightarrow$
$S^{\underline{n}}$, $\underline{n} \geq 2$) by the following:

(7.56) $S \rightarrow S \left(\begin{Bmatrix} and \\ or \end{Bmatrix} S \right)^{\underline{n}}$, $\underline{n} \geq 1$

Here we introduce a new notational device, namely, paren-
theses that are marked by a superscript, $\underline{n}$: $(\ )^{\underline{n}}$. The interpretation of this notation differs in an important way from that
of regular parentheses. While regular parentheses are intended
to represent optional constituents in PS expansions, super-
scripted parentheses indicate that the elements within the parentheses must be chosen and may be repeated in the expansion as many times as $\underline{n}$ specifies. Here, we have specified n
as being greater than or equal to 1 ("$n \geq 1$"); hence, rule (7.56)
is an instruction to rewrite S as S followed by any number of
occurrences of and S (or or S) greater than one. This rule will
thus generate trees such as the following ones among many
others:

(7.57) a.

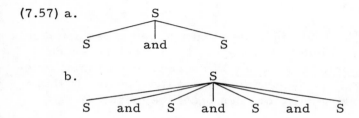

b.

Each S dominated by the highest S may in turn be expanded by
our familiar PS rule for S, namely, $S \rightarrow$ (Q) (not) NP Aux VP
(or it may be reexpanded by rule (7.56) so that further conjoined

structures are generated). Our transformational rules will apply to each conjoined sentence, as they normally do to any single independent sentence. The only change in our grammar is that we have added a new rule for expanding S that allows us to generate conjoined structures.

As long as we include a rule such as (7.56) in our grammar, it will be possible to generate structures such as the following:

(7.58)

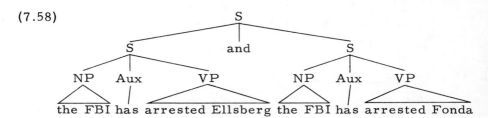

(Here we have shown the conjoined sentences after all relevant transformations have applied to each one. In the examples to follow, we will also assume that each conjoined S has undergone transformations.)

Now that we have provided for the initial derivation of full sentences joined by and (or or), let us return to a consideration of sentence (7.43a):

(7.43) a. Ellsberg was arrested by the FBI and Fonda was too.

Let us assume that this sentence derives from a conjunction of full sentences:

(7.43') a. Ellsberg was arrested by the FBI and Fonda was arrested by the FBI too.

Ignoring too, we can assign sentence (7.43'a) a structure such as (7.43'b):

(7.43') b.

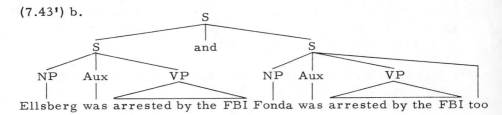

(Keep in mind that the Passive and other rules have operated
in both conjoined sentences.) The verb phrases of the conjoined
sentences are identical, and it would appear that we could generate sentences such as (7.43a) by deleting the verb phrase of
the rightmost sentence of (7.43'b). Let us propose a transformation of VP Deletion:

(7.59) VP Deletion (Optional)

    SD: VP - X - VP
         1   2   3
    SC: 1   2   ∅

    Condition: 1 = 3

This rule has the effect of deleting the constituent VP when it
is identical to another VP in the preceding structure. If we apply this rule to (7.58) we derive the following tree:

(7.60)

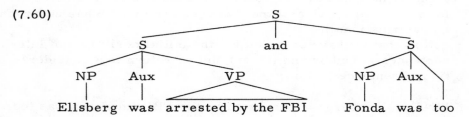

Notice that the rule of VP Deletion shows how it is possible
to permit deletion to remove elements from a structure quite
freely, as long as these elements are matched by an identical
set of elements in the preceding structure that are "left behind"—i.e., that are not deleted. In this way we do not need to
limit deletion to specified elements (as in Imperative and Agent
Deletion) in order to ensure that deletion is recoverable. No
meaning change is brought about by the application of VP Deletion to tree (7.58); the reduced sentence Ellsberg was arrested
by the FBI and Fonda was too has the same meaning as the full
sentence shown in tree (7.58). For example, our account predicts that the sentence cannot mean:

(7.61) *Ellsberg was arrested by the FBI and Fonda was in
      jail too.

The only items that can be "understood" in the second VP are
items precisely identical to those actually occurring in the
first VP. Hence, even though there are an infinite number of
VPs that rule (7.59) could delete, the deleted elements are in
practice identical to elements left behind, so we can always
tell exactly what has been deleted from any particular sentence.

7.6. THE STATUS OF THE CONSTITUENT VP
We have so far stressed the theoretical significance of VP Deletion as an example of deletion under identity, which occurs
in a number of rules (some of which we will discuss in succeed-
ing chapters). However, now that we have introduced the rule,
it would be worthwhile to reconsider questions raised in earlier
chapters concerning the existence of a VP constituent. For example, in section 2.1 we were unable to show decisively that a
simple sentence such as John saw Mary should have a structure
that includes a VP, as follows:

(7.62)

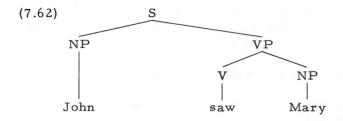

Similarly, in section 5.1 we raised the issue of whether the derived structure of passive sentences, such as The Colts were
beaten by the Jets, should include a VP constituent as in (7.63):

(7.63)

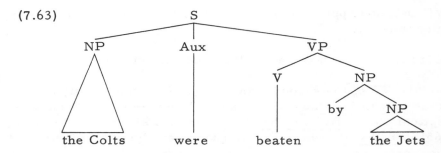

In those earlier chapters we simply made the assumption that

phrases such as saw Mary and beaten by the Jets formed single
syntactic constituents dominated by VP.

But now notice that as a result of that assumption we are able
to state a rule of VP Deletion to account for sentences such as
(7.64a, b):

(7.64) a. John will see Mary, and Bill will ___ too.
       b. The Colts were beaten by the Jets, and the Dolphins
         were ___ too.

However, the reader should be aware that sentences such as
those of (7.64) provide evidence for a VP constituent only if it
is true that a single constituent is deleted in deriving those sentences. We have not explored any alternative account for those
sentences and have not demonstrated that only single constituents should be deleted in their derivation. Although other possibilities exist, it appears that VP Deletion is most simply
stated in terms of single VP constituents.

It should be pointed out, however, that VP Deletion is not the
only rule that must operate in the derivation of elliptical clauses
such as those in (7.64). For example, consider sentences such
as the following:

(7.65) Sam will be teaching a class and Bill will too.

Given our assumptions so far, this sentence would derive from
a form such as (7.66):

(7.66) Sam will be $_{VP}$[teaching a class]$_{VP}$ and Bill will be
      $_{VP}$[teaching a class]$_{VP}$ too

If VP Deletion applies to a structure such as this, the following
sentence results:

(7.67) Sam will be teaching a class and Bill will be too.

Since the VP of the second clause of (7.66) includes only the
phrase teaching a class, only that will be deleted, leaving the
elliptical clause Bill will be. However, the elliptical clause of
(7.65) is Bill will, where the auxiliary verb be has been deleted.
Given facts such as this, we must assume that there is a second
deletion rule, Auxiliary Deletion, which operates after VP De-

letion and optionally deletes auxiliary verbs of the elliptical clause (up to, but not including, the leftmost auxiliary verb) when they are identical with auxiliary verbs in the preceding structure. Thus, the material deleted from the second clause of (7.65) (i.e., be teaching a class) does not form a single constituent (since be is part of Aux), but it is likely that the deletion is carried out by two separate rules.

Much more could be said about the operation of the rule of VP Deletion, but any further discussion would take us far afield from the central concerns of this chapter. (For further exploration of this rule, see the exercises and suggested readings at the end of this chapter.) Whether or not VP Deletion is to be stated exactly as we have stated it above in (7.59), the point remains that as long as the rule involves deletion under identity, then that deletion will always be recoverable. For this reason, VP Deletion (like the rules of Agent Deletion or Imperative, which delete specified elements) will be consistent with the Katz-Postal Hypothesis.

CHAPTER 7: EXERCISES
(E7.1) The rule of Agent Deletion has the effect of deleting by someone or by something from passive sentences. Notice that the rule must not apply to active sentences such as (i):

(i) Mary was standing by someone.

Although this sentence is superficially quite similar to a passive sentence (such as Mary was hit by someone), we must insure that Agent Deletion does not apply to (i) to produce a hypothetical output such as Mary was standing.

A. Show that the rule of Agent Deletion, as we have stated it in this chapter in (7.38), will correctly fail to apply in the derivation of sentences such as (i) and will apply only to passive sentences.

B. What does this show about the ordering of Agent Deletion with respect to other relevant transformations?

(E7.2) The rule of There Insertion is normally a meaning-preserving rule:

(i)   a. Many people were at the party.
      b. There were many people at the party.

Sentences (ia) and (ib) are cognitively synonymous. However, there are circumstances under which the rule of There Insertion is not meaning-preserving:

(ii) a. Many people weren't at the party.
      b. There weren't many people at the party.

This phenomenon is not peculiar to the rule of There Insertion, since, as we have already seen, the Passive Rule is sometimes not meaning-preserving. Thus, while (iiia) and (iiib) may have the same meaning, (iva) and (ivb) differ in meaning very much as (iia) and (iib) do:

(iii) a. Many people attended the party.
      b. The party was attended by many people.

(iv) a. Many people didn't attend the party.
      b. The party wasn't attended by many people.

Now consider the following questions:

A. What is the difference in meaning between sentences (iia) and (iib) and between (iva) and (ivb)? Contrast the situations that could be described by the (a) sentences with the situations that could be described by the (b) sentences.

B. What causes the difference in meaning between the sentences of (ii) and the sentences of (iv)? That is, what is it about these particular examples that distinguishes them from the sentences of (i) and (iii)?

C. Given the hypothesis you have formed in part (B), what other sentence pairs do you predict will show an analogous meaning difference? Stated equivalently, what other rules, beside There Insertion and Passive, do you predict will have non-meaning-preserving applications?

(E7.3) In this chapter, we discussed sentences such as The dog barked and the cat yawned, which consist of two complete sentences joined by <u>and</u>. Of course, conjunction is not limited to conjunction of sentences but may also occur with NPs or VPs:

(i) a. <u>John and Bill</u> left.
     b. John <u>ate the cheese and drank</u>.

There are at least two possible ways to account for such instances of conjunction.

<u>A</u>. One might propose that all conjunction derives from sentence conjunction. This means that (ia) and (ib) would derive from full conjoined sentences, as in (iia) and (iib):

(ii) a.

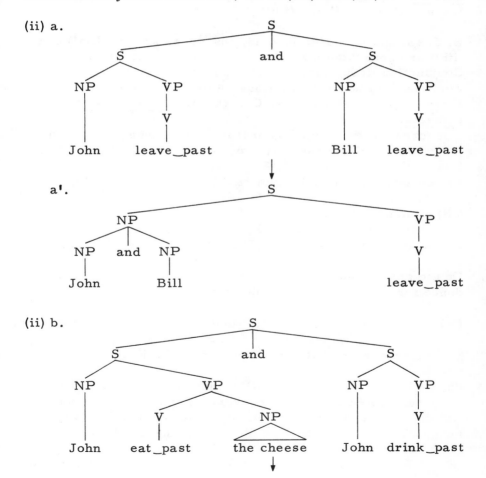

(ii) b'.

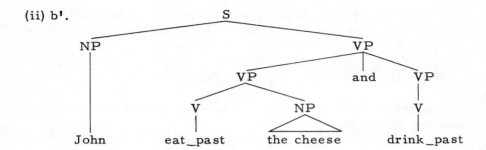

This analysis of conjunction involves a rule of <u>Conjunction Reduction</u>, which transforms trees such as (iia) and (iib) into trees such as (iia') and (iib').

B. One might propose, instead, that trees such as (iia') and (iib') are generated directly by the PS rules and do not involve Conjunction Reduction. The PS rules for expanding NP and VP would have to be modified along the lines of rule (7.56) to generate conjoined structures. Call this the <u>Base Conjunction Hypothesis</u>.

It turns out that both Conjunction Reduction and Base Conjunction may be necessary to account for conjunction in English. On the one hand, sentences such as the following provide evidence for the Base Conjunction Hypothesis:

(iii) a. John and Mary are similar.
     b. The truck and the train collided.
     c. Nixon and Mao met in Peking.

On the other hand, sentences such as those in (iv) provide evidence for the Conjunction Reduction Hypothesis:

(iv) a. Mary was given a medal and promoted to full professor.
     b. The thief stumbled and was caught by the police.
     c. He was seen by the police and by the FBI.

Show why the sentences of (iii) cannot plausibly be derived by Conjunction Reduction and, conversely, why the sentences of (iv) cannot plausibly be derived by Base Conjunction. (It is not necessary to specify how Conjunction Reduction is to be stated.)

(E7.4) We have presented a more or less conventional view of

imperative sentences in this chapter, but consider the following proposal for deriving imperatives. First, assume that the
underlying form of imperative sentences contains you as the
subject and a modal within the Aux. The following is a possible
underlying form:

(i) a. you – Tense – will – leave the room

Now, contrary to the analysis presented in the text of this
chapter, assume that the subject and first auxiliary are inverted, as though the Question Transformation had operated:

(i) b. Tense – will – you leave the room

It is interesting to note at this point that a sentence with the
syntactic form of a question, such as Will you leave the room?,
can in fact be used as an imperative sentence; that is, it can
be used under the right circumstances to request an action or
give a command. Thus, it is not unreasonable to suppose that
the Question Transformation applies in the derivation of imperative sentences (naturally, significant modifications would
have to be made in the statement of the rule, since it operates
only when Q is present). The next step in the derivation of imperatives on this analysis involves a rule known as VP Fronting,
which has the effect of moving the VP to the initial position in
the sentence. Hence, (ib) would be transformed by this rule into (ic):

(i) b. Tense – will – you – leave the room
    c. leave the room – Tense – will – you
       Leave the room, will you.

Finally, will you may optionally be deleted from the end of the
sentence by a reformulated Imperative Rule.
    On this analysis of imperatives—call it the Fronting Analy-
sis—the Tag Rule as we have stated it in chapter 6 plays no
role in forming what looks, on the surface, like a tag (will you).
Thus, an analysis that is radically different from the one presented earlier can lead to identical surface forms. However,
the two theories are by no means identical in the predictions
they make. At this point, construct a set of arguments either
in favor of, or against, the Fronting Analysis of imperatives.

In answering this, consider the data at the end of this paragraph and any other pertinent examples you may have discovered. (We have placed a star (*) next to any form that does
not seem to be a proper imperative.) These sentences are provided only as a starting point for the exercise, and some examples may not be relevant to the arguments you devise. The
point is to formulate a hypothesis about imperatives and provide arguments for one analysis over another where possible;
but you may well find that no single hypothesis accounts for
all facts.

(ii) a. Close the door, can't you?
      b. Read that book, will you?
      c. Run downstairs, why don't you?
      d. *Leave the room, must you?
      e. *Read the book, should you?

(iii) a. *Don't close the door, can you?
      b. Don't leave the room, will you?
      c. Run downstairs, why don't you?
      d. *Don't run downstairs, why don't you?
      e. ?Can you not close the door?
      f. Will you not close the door?
      g. *Not close the door, can you?
      h. *Not close the door, will you?

(iv) a. Don't leave the room!
      b. *Leave the room, don't you!
      c. Don't you leave the room!
      d. *Don't you leave the room, will you?

(v)   a. *Can you close the door, can't you?
      b. *Will you close the door, won't you?

CHAPTER 7: SUGGESTED READINGS
The analysis of imperative sentences has provided a number
of fairly resistant problems for syntacticians, and papers discussing these problems include Bolinger (1967), Hasegawa
(1965), and Thorne (1966), among others. Arguments concerning an underlying imperative morpheme (analogous to Q) can be
found in Katz and Postal (1964). A useful summary of many of
these issues is provided in Stockwell, Schachter, and Partee

(1973), which also includes a bibliography on the subject (see chapter 10).

The Katz-Postal Hypothesis and the general issue of whether transformations change meaning have been the subject of much controversy in recent research, and the reader can make a beginning on this problem by consulting Katz and Postal (1964) as well as Partee (1971). A discussion of meaning changes introduced by the Passive Rule (see our section 7.4) can be found in the latter work.

The rule of VP Deletion and other deletions under identity are discussed in Ross (1969). An interesting, if highly problematic deletion rule known as Gapping is discussed by Ross (1971), Jackendoff (1971), Maling (1972), and Hankamer (1973), among others. These papers should be read after the student completes several more chapters of this book. They contain many useful leads for research topics.

AN INTRODUCTION TO SENTENCE EMBEDDING

8.1. SENTENCE EMBEDDING UNDER NP

The grammar we have built up in the preceding chapters will generate simple sentences such as (8.1) with the underlying structure shown in (8.2):

(8.1) That fact surprises me.

(8.2)

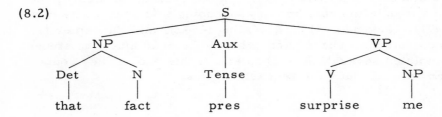

However, there are sentences quite closely resembling sentence (8.1) that our grammar as yet fails to generate:

(8.3) The fact that the earth revolves around the sun surprises me.

This sentence contains elements within it that are virtually identical to parts of sentence (8.1), namely, The fact . . . surprises me. However, (8.3) is unlike (8.1) in that it contains the phrase that the earth revolves around the sun, which in traditional grammar would be referred to as a clause (or a that clause). There are numerous other examples we could cite of sentences containing nouns such as fact, idea, claim, observation, notion, belief, theory, or hypothesis followed by that clauses. For example:

(8.4) a. The idea that the earth could revolve around the sun was quite revolutionary.
   b. He denied the claim that he had been arrested by the police.
   c. The observation that there are two marbles in the box proves nothing.

d. We are not impressed by <u>the notion that every sentence has a deep structure.</u>

e. We can attribute his odd behavior to <u>his belief that he is possessed by a spirit.</u>

What is interesting about <u>that</u> clauses is that if we subtract the word <u>that</u> from the clause we seem to be left with an ordinary sentence of English:

(8.5) a. (that) The earth revolves around the sun.

b. (that) The earth could revolve around the sun.

c. (that) He had been arrested by the police.

d. (that) There are two marbles in the box.

e. (that) Every sentence has a deep structure.

f. (that) He is possessed by a spirit.

Each clause in (8.5) could stand alone as an independent sentence having a subject NP (such as <u>the earth</u> in (8.5a) and <u>he</u> in (8.5c)), an Aux (which would be just <u>present tense</u> in (8.5a) but presumably <u>past – have – en</u> in the underlying structure of (8.5c)), and a VP (such as <u>revolve around the sun</u> in (8.5a)). Thus, <u>that</u> clauses possess the internal structure (i.e., NP – Aux – VP) that we have hitherto associated only with sentences; yet they are in turn <u>embedded</u> within larger sentences.

It would be very natural to account for both of these properties of sentences containing <u>that</u> clauses by representing the clause as an <u>S</u> that is itself <u>dominated</u> by some other <u>S</u>. Thus, for example, we might propose that sentence (8.3) derives from the structure shown in (8.6).

(8.6)

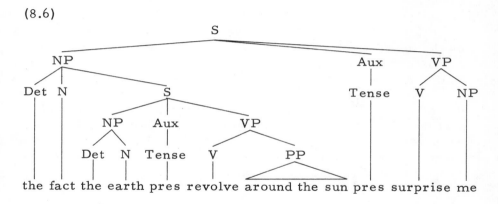

the fact the earth pres revolve around the sun pres surprise me

The structure shown in (8.6) is basically like that shown in
(8.2), except that the subject NP of (8.6) dominates not just
Det and N but in addition the symbol S, which in turn dominates the clause the earth - pres - revolve - around -
the sun. (We have ignored the placement of the word that for
the moment; we return to this question later.)

In claiming that a that clause has essentially the same structure as a sentence (and hence representing the that clause as
being dominated by a second S in tree (8.6)), we are committing
ourselves to a rather strong claim. For example, recall that
the Passive Rule applies to a tree of the form NP - Aux -
V - NP. If that clauses possess the same internal structure
as sentences, then any that clause with the structure NP -
Aux - V - NP should undergo the Passive Rule. In fact,
there is justification for saying that that clauses have the same
structure as sentences only if they behave in many ways as sentences do in relation to the transformations that can apply to
them. After all, the structural components of a sentence are
precisely what determine its ability to undergo transformations.

That being the case, we should be able to find that clauses
that show signs of having undergone transformations. Consider
sentence (8.4b) in the light of this. What would be the most likely
underlying structure for He denied the claim that he had been
arrested by the police?

It seems fairly clear that sentence (8.4b) would derive from
the underlying structure shown in (8.7a). Notice that the that
clause satisfies the SD of the Passive Transformation, as illustrated in (8.7a). If the Passive Transformation now operates
on the lower S, we derive the structure shown in (8.7b). After
rules such as Number Agreement and Affix Hopping have applied
to this structure, we obtain the desired output.

The fact that transformations such as Passive can apply to
embedded that clauses provides confirmation of our analysis
that these clauses are instances of the constituent S. For, as
we have seen, rules such as Passive (as well as Dative Movement, There Insertion, and so on) all apply within S and rear-
range its constituents. The reader should now endeavor to find

(8.7) a.

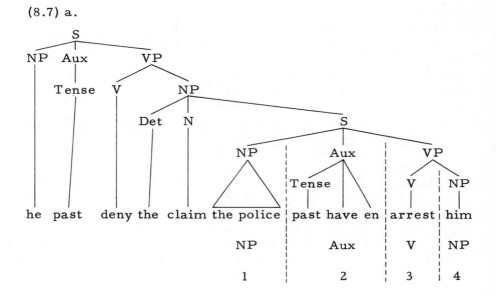

(8.7) b.

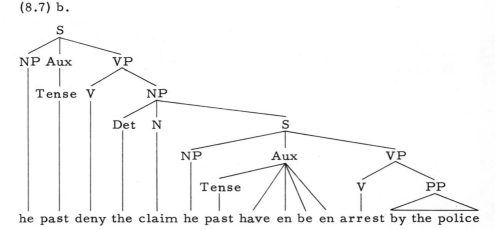

examples where Dative Movement, <u>There</u> Insertion, etc., have
applied to <u>that</u> clauses.

In examples such as (8.4b), where the Passive Rule has applied, we find confirmation of the claim, represented by the
lower S in tree (8.6), that a <u>that</u> clause has the internal struc-

ture of a sentence. Of course, that clauses are not "sentences" in the superficial sense: a clause such as that the earth revolves around the sun could not stand alone as a meaningful sentence in a discourse. Nevertheless, we would clearly be missing an important generalization if we did not assign a single label to that clauses and full "sentences." Hence we represent both by S, and in the same way we will apply the term sentence to both, referring to the higher (or matrix) sentence and lower (or embedded) sentence, for obvious reasons.

So far, then, we have provided some justification for labeling the that clause as an S. We must now consider some of the implications of the way in which the embedded S is attached in trees (8.6) and (8.7): as part of an NP. Tree (8.6) embodies the claim that the subject NP of the higher S is the fact that the earth revolves around the sun, for the embedded S is dominated by the NP that is the subject of the higher S. How can we use the Passive Transformation, this time operating on the higher S, to confirm that this claim is correct?

The passive sentence I am surprised by the fact that the earth revolves around the sun shows that the Passive Rule treats the phrase the fact that the earth revolves around the sun as a single NP constituent. Structure (8.8a) in fact satisfies the SD of the Passive Rule (we have abbreviated the structure of the embedded sentence).

(8.8) a.

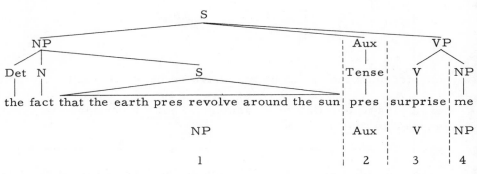

The Passive Rule will apply to this structure as it normally applies to any structure meeting its SD, and thus the subject NP—

including its embedded sentence—will be moved to the position
following the verb (with <u>by</u> added to it), as shown in (8.8b).

(8.8) b.

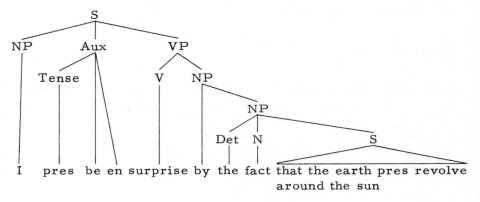

Thus, as long as S is attached under NP, as in (8.8a), the Passive Rule will operate as it normally does to produce (8.8b).

Let us now turn to the question of how our PS rules must be
modified so as to generate the structures we have given in
(8.6), (8.7), and (8.8), taking the subject NP of structure (8.6)
as a representative example:

(8.9)

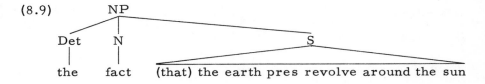

How must we modify our PS rules to generate such NPs? Continue to ignore the placement of the word <u>that</u>.

Recall that in section 2.3 we formulated a PS rule for NP:

(8.10) NP → (Det) N (PP)

In order to generate NPs such as (8.9) above, we simply need
to add another PS rule allowing S to appear after the symbol N:

(8.11) NP → (Det) N (S)

Just as an optional PP may appear in postnominal position, so may an optional S. The two rules given in (8.10) and (8.11) may be collapsed using braces:

(8.12) NP → (Det) N ($\left\{\begin{matrix} PP \\ S \end{matrix}\right\}$)

This rule will allow the NP to be expanded so that either an optional S or an optional PP follows the head noun. No other rules of the grammar need to be modified. Rule (8.12) allows S to appear in the proper position within NP, and the embedded S will in turn be expanded by the rule we have already formulated for S:

(8.13) S → (Q) (not) NP Aux VP

This means that rule (8.13) will have to apply <u>twice</u> in the derivation of the underlying structure of sentences such as (8.6):

Rule	Derivation					
S → (Q) (not) NP Aux VP	NP				Aux	VP
VP → V (NP)	NP				Aux	V
NP → (Det) N ($\left\{\begin{matrix} PP \\ S \end{matrix}\right\}$)	Det N		S		Aux	V
S → (Q) (not) NP Aux VP	Det N	NP	Aux	VP	Aux	V

Tree

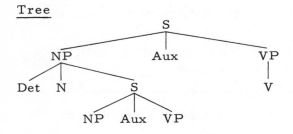

Recall that in chapter 2 we showed that the rule corresponding to (8.10) above was recursive, in that it allowed an NP to contain an embedded PP that could in turn contain another NP, and so on. Rule (8.11) (as well as the abbreviated rule (8.12)) is also recursive, since it allows NP to contain S, which in

turn may contain NPs containing further instances of S, producing sentences of the sort illustrated below:

(8.14) Ted denied the claim that Bill had spread the rumor
       that Mary disliked the fact that Sam had tortured her
       pet anteater.

If we examine the structure that our rules assign to this sen-
tense, we find the configuration of (8.15) at the "highest" (S^1)
level of structure.

(8.15) a.

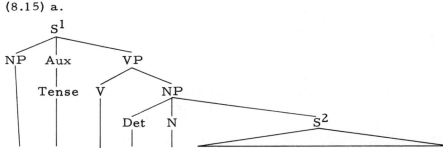

Ted past deny the claim that Bill had spread the rumor that
                           Mary disliked the fact that Sam had
                           tortured her pet anteater

(We have numbered the S nodes for ease of reference only.)
The object of the verb <u>deny</u> consists of the NP <u>the   -   claim   - </u>
<u>S^2</u>, in which S^2 is expanded as illustrated in (8.15b).

(8.15) b.

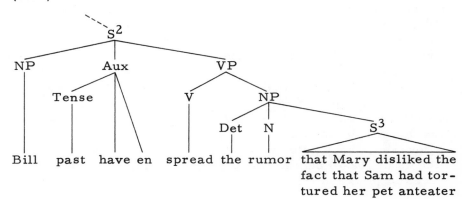

Bill past have en spread the rumor that Mary disliked the
                                       fact that Sam had tor-
                                       tured her pet anteater

This embedded sentence in turn contains yet another embedded
sentence, S^3, which is expanded as shown in (8.15c).

(8.15) c.

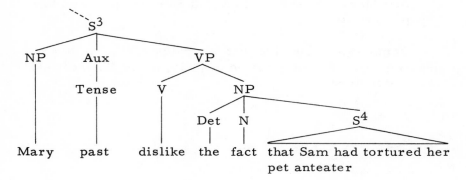

This embedded sentence contains another: <u>Sam - past -
have - en - torture - her pet anteater</u>, S^4.

Thus, the whole sentence, (8.14), has the structure shown
in (8.15'). This tree would be correctly generated by successive applications of the rules for expanding NP and S, i.e.,
(8.12) and (8.13). In other words, now that we have introduced

the rule $NP \rightarrow (Det) \ \ N \ \ (\left\{ \begin{matrix} PP \\ S \end{matrix} \right\})$ into our grammar, we have

allowed for the possibility that sentences can be embedded
within larger sentences to a potentially infinite depth.

We must make explicit another of the implications of our
modified rule for NP (i.e., (8.12)). Since NPs can appear in
both subject and object position in a sentence, we have automatically provided for the possibility that embedded sentences
will occur within NPs in either of these positions. But that is
precisely what we have already discovered. On the one hand,
sentence (8.3), <u>The fact that the earth revolves around the sun
surprises me</u>, has a sentence embedded as part of the subject
of <u>surprise</u>; while on the other hand, sentence (8.4b), <u>He denied the claim that he had been arrested by the police</u>, has a
sentence embedded in the object of <u>deny</u>. Our PS rules predict
that this will be the case.

However, those rules will not at present generate examples
such as (8.16a-d) below, which are quite similar to the sentences of (8.3) and (8.4):

(8.15')

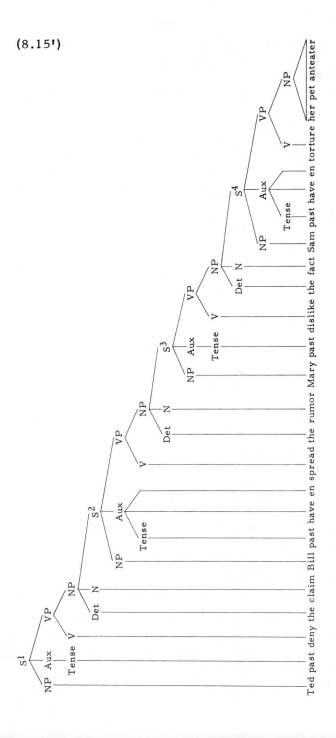

(8.16) a. Many people believe that the earth is round.
     b. He denied that he had been arrested by the police.
     c. That ice melts in warm weather is obvious.
     d. That John refused the money really surprised me.

These examples contain embedded <u>that</u> clauses, but unlike those that we have already dealt with, the clauses are not associated with head nouns such as <u>fact</u>, <u>idea</u>, or <u>theory</u>. We have already seen that <u>that</u> clauses should be analyzed as instances of S in our theory, and, given this, we might assume that the sentences of (8.16) have structures such as the following (taking (8.16a) and (8.16c) as representative examples):

(8.17)

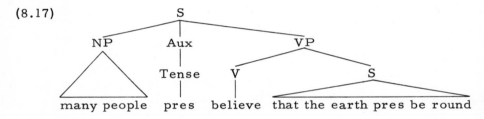

(8.18)

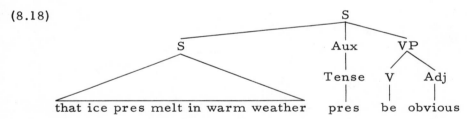

However, there is some evidence that the embedded sentences of (8.16) are dominated by the node NP. How can the following active/passive pair be used to demonstrate this?

(8.19) a. Many people believe <u>that the earth is round</u>.
     b. <u>That the earth is round</u> is believed by many people.

The Passive Transformation has operated on (8.19a) to produce (8.19b) and has had the effect of moving the embedded sentence to initial position in the matrix sentence, just as it would move an ordinary simple NP to that position (as in <u>Many people believe that theory</u> and <u>That theory is believed by many people</u>).

Recall that the SD of the Passive Transformation mentions the node NP:

(8.20) <u>Passive SD</u>
$$\begin{array}{cccc} NP & - & Aux & - & V & - & NP \\ 1 & & 2 & & 3 & & 4 \end{array}$$

Given this statement of the rule, it would not apply to structure (8.17), for in that structure we cannot isolate the sequence <u>NP - Aux - V - NP</u> but only the sequence <u>NP - Aux - V - S</u>. Of course, we could modify the SD of the Passive Rule so that S is an alternative expansion of NP in term 4:

(8.21) <u>Passive SD</u> (Revised)
$$NP - Aux - V - \left\{ \begin{array}{l} NP \\ S \end{array} \right\}$$

The revised Passive Rule could then operate on a structure such as (8.17), since it now can be satisfied by the sequence <u>NP - Aux - V - S</u>.

   However, there is no independent reason for complicating the Passive Rule in this way; moreover, such an analysis would also require that we complicate our PS rules in order to generate trees (8.17) and (8.18) as underlying structures. We would need to reformulate the rules expanding S and VP thus:

(8.22) $S \rightarrow (Q)$ (not) $\left\{ \begin{array}{l} NP \\ S \end{array} \right\}$ Aux VP   (Original rule: <u>$S \rightarrow (Q)$ (not) NP Aux VP</u>)

(8.23) $VP \rightarrow V$ $(\left\{ \begin{array}{l} NP \\ S \end{array} \right\})$ (PP)   (Original rule: <u>$VP \rightarrow V$ (NP) (PP)</u>)

Only if we add S as an alternative to NP in both of these rules, as shown, can we generate embedded Ss in the positions shown in trees (8.17) and (8.18). We would not need to complicate either the PS rules or the Passive Transformation if we were to assume that the embedded sentences of (8.16) were dominated by NP—as were all the other embedded clauses we have referred to so far. We would simply need to permit our rule for NP to expand that node optionally into a plain S, thus:

(8.24)
$$NP \rightarrow \left\{ \begin{matrix} (Det) \ N \ (\left\{ \begin{matrix} PP \\ S \end{matrix} \right\}) \\ S \end{matrix} \right\}$$

Using this rule, we could generate structures like (8.25) for
(8.19a), which would in fact meet the SD of our original Passive Rule.

(8.25)

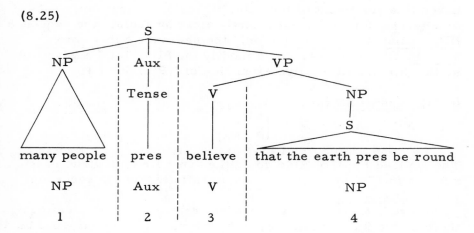

Since the embedded S is dominated by NP, this structure will
now contain the sequence NP – Aux – V – NP and hence
will satisfy the uncomplicated SD of the Passive Rule given in
(8.20). That rule would operate correctly to yield sentence
(8.19b), That the earth is round is believed by many people.
   Since the Passive Rule operates only on transitive sentences,
it cannot be used to show that the subject clause of tree (8.18)
is dominated by NP. But notice that our reformulated rule for
NP, (8.24), will now permit us to generate the following structure:

(8.26)

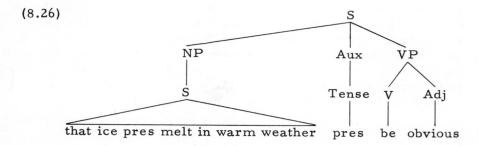

Our PS rule for generating S need not be complicated (as in
$S \rightarrow$ (Q) (not) $\begin{Bmatrix} NP \\ S \end{Bmatrix}$ Aux VP) but can remain in its simplest
form (i.e., $S \rightarrow$ (Q) (not) NP Aux VP), since it already pro-
vides for the node NP in subject position.

We seem to have some initial evidence, then, that the embedded clause in a sentence such as (8.27) is dominated by the
node NP.

(8.27) Many people believe <u>that the world is round</u>.

In this respect, (8.27) is quite similar to (8.28):

(8.28) Many people believe <u>the theory that the world is round</u>.

Let us assume then that embedded <u>that</u> clauses are all dominated by the node NP. This will not only allow us to simplify
our grammar at this stage (as shown above) but will also allow
us to state what seems to be a significant generalization: that
embedded <u>that</u> clauses have the same distribution as simple
NPs. For example, we have already seen cases in which <u>that</u>
clauses, with or without head nouns such as <u>fact</u>, can function
as subjects or objects:

(8.29) a. $\begin{cases} \text{That fact} \\ \text{The fact that ice melts in warm weather} \\ \text{That ice melts in warm weather} \end{cases}$ is obvious.

      b. Many people believe $\begin{cases} \text{this theory} \\ \text{the theory that the earth is round} \\ \text{that the earth is round} \end{cases}$.

We shall continue to assume, then, that embedded <u>that</u> clauses
are dominated by NP.

8.2. EXTRAPOSITION AND IT DELETION

Embedded sentences do not always remain under the NP node,
where (as we have just seen) they are generated by the PS rules.
Consider the following sentences:

(8.30) a. The fact <u>that the rain had ruined the crops</u> was obvious.
      b. The fact was obvious <u>that the rain had ruined the crops</u>.

(8.31) a. The idea <u>that the earth is round</u> had not been formu-
         lated.
       b. The idea had not been formulated <u>that the earth is
          round</u>.

(8.32) a. The theory <u>that the earth is the center of the universe</u>
          was proposed by the ancient Greeks.
       b. The theory was proposed by the ancient Greeks <u>that
          the earth is the center of the universe</u>.

In (8.30a)-(8.32a) the embedded sentence appears "attached to"
its head noun, but in the (b) examples it is placed at the end of
the main sentence. This suggests that there is a rule (which
we call <u>Extraposition</u>) that moves (or extraposes) the embedded
sentence to the end of the main sentence, so that a structure
such as (8.33a) is transformed into a structure such as (8.33b).

(8.33) a.

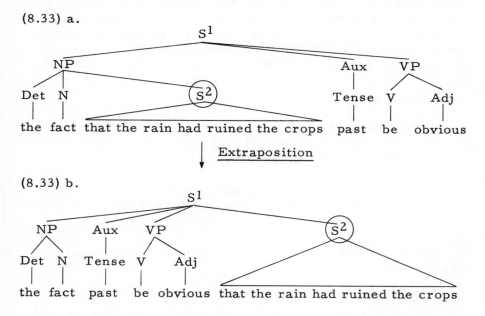

With the rule of Extraposition in mind, let us look at some
further data:

(8.34) a. <u>That the world is round</u> is obvious.
       b. <u>It</u> is obvious <u>that the world is round</u>.

(8.35) a. <u>That Einstein was right</u> is believed by everyone.
     b. <u>It</u> is believed by everyone <u>that Einstein was right</u>.

(8.36) a. <u>That John plays the piano</u> bothers me.
     b. <u>It</u> bothers me <u>that John plays the piano</u>.

Such sentences are reminiscent of those listed in (8.30)-(8.32):
note that in the (a) examples, the <u>that</u> clause is the subject of
the sentence, while in the (b) examples the clause has been
shifted to the end of the main sentence and <u>it</u> appears in subject position. It would thus appear that a process very similar
to Extraposition (cf. (8.33a)-(8.33b)) is going on here: an embedded sentence is shifted to the end of the matrix sentence.
But how can we account for the appearance of <u>it</u> in the (b) examples above?

One obvious possibility is that when the embedded sentence
is moved to the end of the higher one—by Extraposition or some
similar rule—then <u>it</u> is inserted as part of the operation of that
rule. The other possibility is that the PS rules generate <u>it</u> as
the underlying <u>head noun</u> of the NP that dominates the embedded
sentence; then (8.34a) would derive from the following structure:

(8.37)

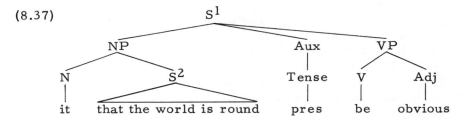

Now, let us suppose that the rule of Extraposition operates here
as in (8.33a)-(8.33b)—that is, it shifts the embedded sentence,
S^2, to the end of the matrix sentence:

(8.38)

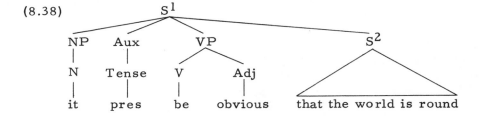

As long as we treat it as an underlying head noun, as in (8.37), then the rule of Extraposition will generate structures such as (8.38) in an automatic way, and we now have a means of accounting for the alternation between sentences such as That the world is round is obvious versus It is obvious that the world is round.

Another consequence of treating it as a head noun is that our rule for expanding NP can be simplified. Recall that the rule we gave in (8.24) (repeated below) allowed NP to be expanded in two alternative ways:

(8.24) $NP \rightarrow \begin{Bmatrix} (Det) \quad N \quad (\begin{Bmatrix} PP \\ S \end{Bmatrix}) \\ S \end{Bmatrix}$

We can now eliminate the bottom half of this rule and return to the original, simpler rule (8.12):

(8.12) $NP \rightarrow (Det) \quad N \quad (\begin{Bmatrix} PP \\ S \end{Bmatrix})$

Among the sequences that this rule generates, there are two that are significant here: Det - N - S and N - S. The first sequence, of course, is the structure for NPs such as the fact that . . . (as in the structures (8.6), (8.7), and (8.8)). The second sequence, i.e., N - S, can be used to generate the sequence it - S required in structures such as (8.37). Given rule (8.13), embedded sentences will either be generated along with "full" head nouns, such as fact, or with the "empty" pronoun it, and our grammar will no longer generate structures such as (8.25), where NP dominates S exclusively.

There is one additional aspect of this analysis that we must make explicit. The rule of Extraposition is obviously optional, since in pairs of sentences such as (8.30)-(8.32) and (8.34)-(8.36), both extraposed and unextraposed variants are possible. However, if Extraposition is optional, our grammar will generate ungrammatical sentences such as (8.39):

(8.39) *It that the world is round is obvious.
　　　　 (cf. The fact that the world is round is obvious.)

If Extraposition is not applied to (8.37), then it will remain in
initial position, next to the embedded S. Consequently we need
to add another transformation to our grammar: It Deletion.
   This rule has the effect of deleting it just in case it immediately precedes S. Consider tree (8.38) again (see p. 281).
In this case, Extraposition has moved S^2 to the end of the matrix sentence; it remains behind in subject position and does
not immediately precede S. Hence, it cannot be deleted. However, if Extraposition does not apply, as in (8.37), it will end
up immediately before S; in this environment It Deletion will
apply, deleting it and yielding That the world is round is obvious.

(8.37)

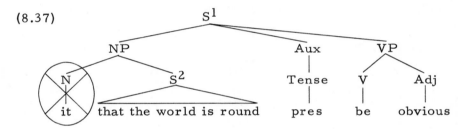

Thus, the rules must be ordered so that Extraposition optionally applies first, then It Deletion. The latter is, of course, obligatory. The two rules can be stated as follows:

(8.40) Extraposition (Optional)

$$\text{SD: X} - {}_{NP}[(\text{Det}) \quad N - S]_{NP} - Y$$
$$\qquad 1 \qquad\quad 2 \qquad\quad 3 \qquad\quad 4$$
$$\text{SC: 1} \qquad 2 \qquad 4 + 3$$

(8.41) It Deletion (Obligatory)

$$\text{SD: X} - {}_{NP}[\text{it} - S]_{NP} - Y$$
$$\qquad 1 \qquad\quad 2 \quad 3 \qquad 4$$
$$\text{SC: 1} \qquad \emptyset \quad 3 \qquad 4$$

   In the Extraposition Rule, the expression ${}_{NP}[(\text{Det}) \quad N - S]_{NP}$
ensures that the rule operates only on an S that is dominated
by the node NP and preceded by (Det) N within that same NP.

Similarly, in our rule of It Deletion we have formulated the expression $_{NP}[\text{it} - \text{S}]_{NP}$ to indicate that the rule operates to delete an it that is dominated by NP and that precedes an S also dominated by that same NP. The reason we have limited the operation of these rules to sequences dominated by the node NP will become clear shortly (see example (8.45)).

We have so far concentrated on examples in which the embedded sentence originates within the subject NP. However, it should be pointed out that Extraposition will also operate on embedded sentences within object NPs. For example, consider a sentence such as (8.42a), with the underlying structure (8.42b).

(8.42) a. I doubt it very much that Mr. X is the murderer.

b.

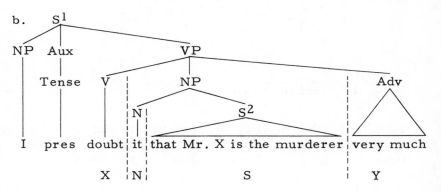

The SD of Extraposition is met in this case, as shown in (8.42c), and the rule shifts S^2 to the end of the main sentence.

(8.42) c.

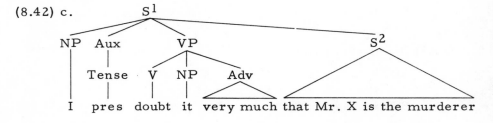

I doubt it very much that Mr. X is the murderer.

Thus, Extraposition may operate on object clauses as well as subject clauses, since both subject and object that clauses will be analyzed as it – S dominated by NP.

   This analysis is not without its problems. Consider (8.43a)
below, which is just like (8.42a) except that it lacks the ad-
verbial very much at the end of the sentence. Presumably it
has the underlying structure shown in (8.43b).

(8.43) a. I doubt that Mr. X is the murderer.

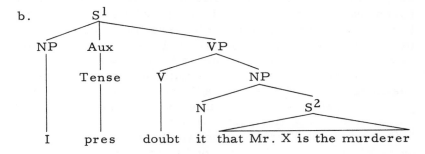

If Extraposition does not apply to (8.43b), then It Deletion will,
to yield (8.43a). However, what happens if we do try to apply
Extraposition to (8.43b)? It is not clear whether Extraposition
can operate on this tree, given that the embedded sentence is
already at the end of the matrix sentence. However, some
speakers accept (8.44) as grammatical:

(8.44) I doubt it that Mr. X is the murderer.

It has been suggested that what may permit it to remain unde-
leted by the otherwise obligatory rule of It Deletion is the fact
that Extraposition has applied to (8.43b). The effect of this
would be to move the embedded S out of the NP in which it was
originally generated, yielding the structure shown in (8.45).

(8.45)

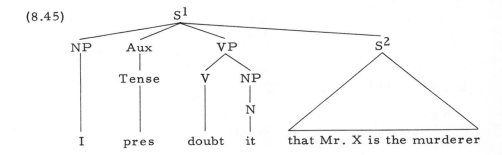

A careful examination of rule (8.41), It Deletion, will show
that it can no longer apply to this sentence, since in (8.45) the
contiguous N and S are not dominated by NP as required by the
SD of the rule.

The application of Extraposition to structures such as (8.43b)
is sometimes referred to as vacuous extraposition, since in
such cases the rule results not in a change of linear word order
but simply a change in constituent structure. It has been proposed that such vacuous applications of a rule should be blocked
(since, for one thing, many speakers find sentences such as
(8.44) unacceptable) by the following restriction: for any rule
in which a given term is sister-adjoined to a variable, the rule
will not apply if the variable is null. In the statement of Extraposition, (8.40), S is sister-adjoined to the variable Y. Since
Y is null in (8.43b) (S being already at the end of the higher sentence), the convention just mentioned will prevent the rule
from applying. Whether or not vacuous Extraposition should
be blocked is best left undecided at this time. We will continue
to assume that it is possible, but we could very easily restrict
the rule so as to prevent vacuous application if this should turn
out to be the correct alternative.

Whether this analysis is correct is an open question. In fact,
this is just one of a number of important issues related to Extraposition that are greatly in need of further investigation.

Before proceeding, the reader should find a variety of examples similar to those given above, in which Extraposition
and It Deletion appear to have applied (or could have applied),
and should practice using these rules in derivations.

8.3. THE COMPLEMENTIZERS THAT, FOR-TO, AND POSS-ING

In this section we will turn our attention to a problem we have
ignored throughout our discussion of that clauses: the word
that itself. What is the function of such a word? Informally
speaking, that seems to serve as the marker of an embedded
sentence (or complement sentence), such as that the world is
round in I believe that the world is round. It is often referred
to as a complementizer.

We can easily see that that is not the only complementizer
in English—i.e., it is not the only marker of an embedded
clause:

(8.46) a. That John plays the piano bothers me.
       b. For John to play the piano bothers me.
       c. John's playing the piano bothers me.

(8.47) a. That you left early was very wise.
       b. For you to leave early was very wise.
       c. Your leaving early was very wise.

(8.48) a. Mom hates it that Dad comes home so late.
       b. Mom hates it for Dad to come home so late.
       c. Mom hates Dad's coming home so late.

(8.49) a. That Samantha danced for us was thrilling.
       b. For Samantha to dance for us was thrilling.
       c. Samantha's dancing for us was thrilling.

(8.50) a. The idea that space is curved is not intuitively
          obvious.
       b. The plan for Mr. X to rob the bank was ill-conceived.
       c. The opposition to the government's censoring the
          news was quite strong.

These sentences show that in addition to the complementizer
that, we have the complementizers for-to, and 's-ing ("pos-
sessive-ing" or "poss-ing"). (There are yet other complementizers for English, but we will not discuss them here.) All
three complementizers appear in a variety of constructions, as
will be clear from a careful examination of these examples.
   While there are many similarities among the three complementizers, there are a number of significant differences, too.
Perhaps the most obvious is the fact that they are adjoined in
quite different ways to the trees in which they are inserted.
Thus, that is a single word that precedes the embedded S, and
we can assume initially that it ends up attached in the following
way (though there are other possibilities):

(8.51)

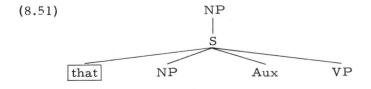

On the other hand, <u>for-to</u> and <u>poss-ing</u> both consist of two elements, and these are attached at different points in the tree.

Let us examine <u>for-to</u> in more detail. In all the (b) examples
of (8.46)-(8.50), <u>for</u> precedes the subject and <u>to</u> precedes the
main verb. But exactly where before the main verb may <u>to</u> appear? Try to answer this by examining data such as the following:

(8.52) a. For John to be playing the piano always bothers me.
       b. For John to have played the piano bothers me.
       c. For John to have been playing the piano bothers me.

(8.53) a. *For John to will play the piano bothers me.
       b. *For John to plays the piano bothers me.

The data in (8.52) and (8.53) clearly suggest that the <u>to</u> of
<u>for-to</u> must appear in a position within the auxiliary. It may
precede auxiliary <u>be</u>, or auxiliary <u>have</u>, or, as in (8.52c),
both <u>have</u> and <u>be</u>. But <u>to</u> cannot occur with any modal verb (cf.
(8.53a)), nor may it occur with a tensed verb (cf. (8.53b)). Thus,
<u>to</u> in some sense "replaces" Tense and Modal within the aux-
iliary system. The <u>for</u> ends up immediately to the left of the
sentence in the same position as <u>that</u>. These considerations
suggest that we should probably assign (8.46b) a derived structure such as (8.54).

(8.54)

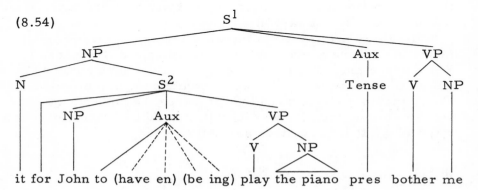

We have not taken a stand yet on how <u>for</u> and <u>to</u> are generated
in the first place—we have merely tried to discover their final
position.

If we turn our attention now to sentences with <u>poss-ing</u>, we see that the possessive marker <u>'s</u> is placed on the subject of the embedded sentence and <u>ing</u> is placed on the verb:

(8.55) John<u>'s</u> play<u>ing</u> the piano bothers me.

At first glance it might appear that the <u>ing</u> of <u>poss-ing</u> is the same <u>ing</u> as that associated with the progressive auxiliary <u>be</u> (note especially the contracted form in (8.56b)):

(8.56) a. John <u>is</u> play<u>ing</u> the piano, isn't he?
       b. John<u>'s</u> play<u>ing</u> the piano, isn't he?

However, it is very easy to show that the <u>ing</u> in (8.55) is not the same as the progressive <u>ing</u> of (8.56). How do the following sentences show us this?

(8.57) a. John's owning a house is unfortunate.
       b. John's having played the piano annoyed me.
       c. John's having been playing the piano annoyed me

In the first place, as (8.57a) shows, the <u>ing</u> of <u>poss-ing</u> can be attached to verbs that normally may not take the progressive:

(8.58) *John is owning a house.

Second, as (8.57b) shows, the <u>ing</u> of <u>poss-ing</u> may attach itself to the auxiliary verb <u>have</u>, and this is decisive evidence that it cannot be the progressive <u>ing</u>. Why? (It should be immediately clear if you have understood Affix Hopping—if it is not, review chapter 4.) Finally, (8.57c) shows that <u>ing</u>, like <u>to</u>, can occur with <u>have</u> when <u>have</u> precedes <u>be</u> in the auxiliary; it should be clear that the <u>ing</u> on <u>having</u> is associated with <u>'s</u>, while the <u>ing</u> on <u>playing</u> is the progressive <u>ing</u> associated with <u>be</u>.
These considerations, along with the fact that <u>ing</u> does not occur with tensed or modal verbs (show this for yourself), suggest that it appears in the auxiliary in a position similar to <u>to</u> at some stage in the derivation, as illustrated in (8.59).

(8.59) (structure for (8.55))

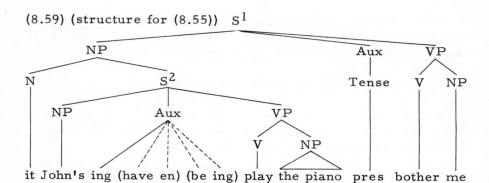

it John's ing (have en) (be ing) play the piano pres bother me

Even though the ing of poss-ing is not the same as progressive ing in its distribution, it is nevertheless an affix, just as progressive ing is; thus, the rule of Affix Hopping operates as it usually does to attach ing to the auxiliary or main verb on its right.

These observations on the three complementizers involve rather superficial aspects of their behavior. The first really interesting comparisons concern differences in the effect of complementizers on the applicability of Extraposition to the embedded sentences with which they appear. Extraposition can move an embedded sentence with for-to just as it can move an embedded sentence with that; the result of its application to (8.60) would be (8.61).

(8.60)

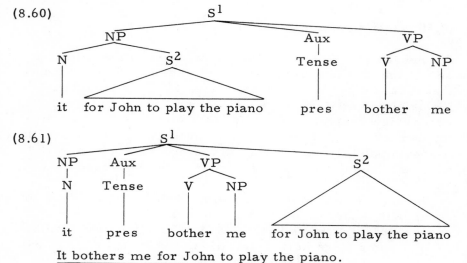

It bothers me for John to play the piano.

We might very well expect Extraposition to operate in the same way on a tree such as (8.62).

(8.62)

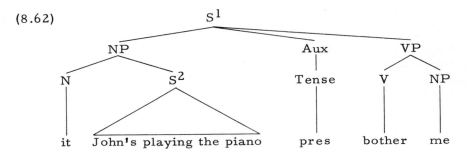

And, in fact, this tree does meet the SD of Extraposition, as the reader can check. However, it seems that Extraposition does <u>not</u> operate when the complementizer of the embedded sentence is <u>poss-ing</u>, as the marginal status of (8.63) shows.

(8.63) *?It bothers me John's playing the piano.

If we compare sentences such as (8.63) with known cases of Extraposition, it certainly seems as though the <u>poss-ing</u> clauses are somehow deviant (unless a strong pause is added):

(8.63') a.   It bothers me that John plays the piano.
       b.   It bothers me for John to play the piano.
       c. *?It bothers me John's playing the piano.
           (cf. It bothers me, John's playing the piano.)

If (8.63'c) is not a result of Extraposition, then that rule will have to have a condition placed on it to prevent it from oper-ating when <u>poss-ing</u> is the complementizer.

Now that we have outlined some of the more superficial syn-tactic properties of the complementizers <u>that</u>, <u>for-to</u>, and <u>poss-ing</u>, let us turn to the question of how they are actually to be generated in trees. We are faced with two alternatives: either (A) complementizers are generated in embedded sen-tences by PS rules, or (B) complementizers are inserted into embedded sentences by transformations. The choice between these two alternatives has not been completely settled in cur-rent research, and, though we will adopt alternative (A), we will not try to argue conclusively for it. Before we describe

this alternative in more detail, it may be useful to outline some
of the restrictions on the distribution of complementizers that
any theory will have to deal with.

First of all, the kind of complementizer that may appear with
a plain embedded sentence (i.e., one without a head noun such
as fact) depends largely on the main verb of the matrix sentence
For example, consider the following patterns:

(8.64) a. I believe that the world is round.
      b. *I believe for the world to be round.
      c. *I believe the world's being round.

(8.65) a. *I insisted on that John would be there on time.
      b. *I insisted on for John to be there on time.
      c. I insisted on John's being there on time.

(8.66) a. *I want that John leave(s).
      b. I want (very much) for John to leave.
      c. *I want John's leaving.

The sentences of (8.64) show that the verb believe can only occur with the complementizer that. In (8.65) we see that the verb
insist (on) takes only poss-ing as its complementizer (in general, embedded sentences following prepositions, such as on,
must have poss-ing). Finally, sentences such as those in (8.66)
show that the verb want allows only for-to. Thus, no matter
how we generate complementizers, we must provide some
mechanism for ensuring that the complementizer on an embedded sentence is appropriate for the main verbs of the higher
sentence.

A similar mechanism must be made available for embedded
sentences that occur with head nouns, such as the following:

(8.67) a. the fact that the earth is round . . .
         *the fact for the earth to be round . . .
         *the fact (of) the earth's being round . . .
      b. the plan for John to steal the money . . .
         *the plan that John steals the money . . .
         *the plan (of) John's stealing the money . . .
      c. the opposition to John's leaving the company . . .
         *the opposition to that John leaves the company . . .
         *the opposition for John to leave the country . . .

Just as some verbs must occur with one specific complementizer but not others, so abstract nouns such as <u>fact</u>, <u>plan</u>, and
<u>opposition</u> restrict the choice of complementizer.

The choice of complementizer does not depend only on the
main verb of the matrix sentence or the head noun of the NP
in which it is embedded. There are other relevant factors.
For example, in some cases the presence or absence of certain modal auxiliaries can affect the choice of complementizer:

(8.68) a.   That you left early was very wise.
            For you to leave early was very wise.
            Your leaving early was very wise.
       b. *That you leave early would be very wise.
            For you to leave early would be very wise.
          ?Your leaving early would be very wise.

Thus, it appears that the adjective <u>wise</u> allows all three complementizers, except when the modal <u>would</u> is present, in
which case only a <u>for-to</u> clause seems fully acceptable. Such
sentences seem to show that the placement of complementizers—
however it is to be done—must be sensitive not only to the main
verb of the matrix sentence but also to other verbs of the sentence, such as the modal in (8.68b).

It may be worth pointing out that although the starred examples above in (8.64)-(8.68) have been regarded as structurally ill-formed, i.e., as ungrammatical, it may be the case that
these examples are structurally well-formed but simply deviant in meaning. In that case, a sentence such as <u>That you leave</u>
<u>early would be very wise</u> might be generated by our grammar
(just as sentences such as <u>John occurred</u> are generated by the
grammar—see chapter 2). If we choose this alternative, complementizers could be generated quite freely with any main
verb, modal verb, or head noun such as <u>fact</u>. The deviance of
the starred examples of (8.64)-(8.68) would then be regarded
as purely a matter of meaning. However, it is generally assumed that the syntactic rules must account at least partially
for the distribution of complementizers.

If, making that assumption, we generate complementizers
directly by the PS rules, then those rules will presumably need
to incorporate some mechanism for appropriately restricting
complementizer distribution. We will outline very briefly how
this might be accomplished for the restrictions on main verbs.

First, we shall assume that embedded sentences differ slightly from independent sentences in that they inherently contain complementizers. We will therefore not expand the noun phrase into (Det) N ($\left\{\begin{matrix}\text{PP}\\\text{S}\end{matrix}\right\}$) but will use the symbol $\bar{\text{S}}$ ("S bar") to represent embedded sentences. Hence, our rule for NP will now be modified as follows:

(8.69) NP → (Det) N ($\left\{\begin{matrix}\text{PP}\\\bar{\text{S}}\end{matrix}\right\}$)

The following new rules will serve to expand $\bar{\text{S}}$:

(8.70) a. $\bar{\text{S}}$ → Comp S

b. Comp → $\left\{\begin{matrix}\text{that}\\\text{for-to}\\\text{poss-ing}\end{matrix}\right\}$

The PS rule for expanding S (S → (Q) (not) NP Aux VP) will now be able to expand the S node dominated by $\bar{\text{S}}$. Thus, the rules of (8.70), along with our other PS rules, will generate structures such as (8.71).

(8.71)

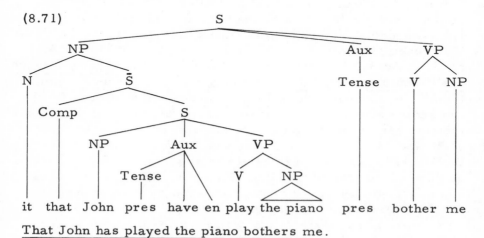

it   that   John   pres   have en   play the piano   pres   bother   me

That John has played the piano bothers me.

This differs from our previous treatment of embedded sentences only in that we have introduced a way of generating complementizers in underlying structure. Notice that this new analysis, like the previous one, captures the important generalization that embedded clauses and independent sentences have the same internal structure, since both are dominated by the symbol S.

The underlying structure for embedded sentences with <u>for-to</u> is quite similar to the structure we have just seen. For example, see (8.72).

(8.72)

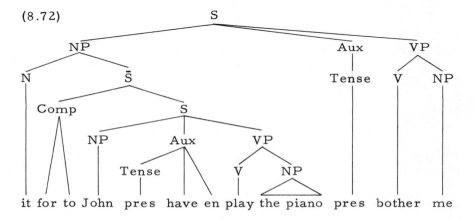

it for to John pres have en play the piano pres bother me

The embedded S̄ of structures such as (8.72) is subject to a further transformational operation that will place <u>to</u> (or <u>ing</u>, if <u>poss-ing</u> had been generated) within the Aux of the embedded sentence, replacing the Tense (and, if present, Modal). We will not attempt to state this transformation but will simply assume that it always applies in structures such as (8.72), resulting in the placement of <u>to</u> (or <u>ing</u>) as shown in (8.72').

(8.72')

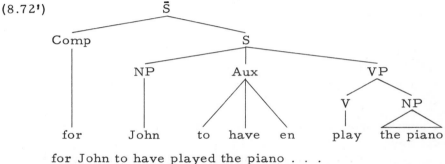

for John to have played the piano . . .

Now that we have a means of generating complementizers in
deep structures, we must provide some mechanism for guaranteeing that complementizers cooccur with the proper verbs
(or head nouns). We could account for at least some of the
facts by extending somewhat the use of subcategorization features, so that verbs could be marked with features that permitted them to be inserted only in trees containing appropriate
complementizers. For example, verbs such as say, think, believe, propose, expect, deny, and forget would be marked with
the syntactic feature +[___ that], indicating that the complement sentence in the object NP may begin with the complementizer that. Verbs such as want, like, or hate would be marked
as +[___ for], indicating that this class of verbs may occur
with for-to. Adjectives such as (be) obvious, (be) odd, and (be)
false and verbs such as bother seem to require the feature
+[that ___], indicating that their subject complements take the
complementizer that (as in That John left early was obvious).
Verbs that take more than one kind of complementizer, such
as hate or bother, would be marked with more than one subcategorization feature indicating the complementizers they may
cooccur with.

The PS rules might then generate a tree such as (8.72'').

(8.72'')

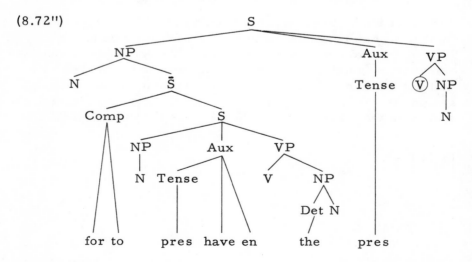

Then the process of lexical insertion, in operating on the cir-
cle node, V, would be able to enter only a verb marked +[for-
to ___], because of the complementizer in the subject NP. (Of

course, the verb would also have to be transitive, because of the NP to its right.) Hence <u>bother</u> could be inserted, to yield (8.72), but <u>think</u> or <u>want</u> (for example) could not.

This very brief account of a possible mechanism for restricting the insertion of verbs is not intended to be more than a sketch. For one thing, although the use of syntactic features begins to account for the distribution of complementizers, we still have no way of explaining the distributional facts related to modals, as in the following sentences:

(8.73) a. That you left early was very wise.
      b. *That you leave early would be very wise.
      c. For you to leave early would be very wise.

As we have already seen, when the modal <u>would</u> occurs in these sentences, the subject complement must have <u>for-to</u> and may not have <u>that</u> as its complementizer. It could be that modals, like main verbs, are associated with syntactic features indicating the complementizers that may occur with them. Similarly, head nouns such as <u>fact</u> might also require subcategorization features, as shown by (8.67). However, we will leave it as an open question exactly how these facts are to be accounted for.

We must point out again the possibility of an entirely different way of generating complementizers. The PS rules could generate embedded sentences without complementizers, as we assumed until this section. Then a transformation would have to insert the appropriate complementizers within embedded sentences. This transformation would have to be made sensitive to the main verb and modal of the higher sentence, the head noun of the noun phrase containing the embedded sentence, and so on, thus limiting complementizers to appropriate environments in a way quite comparable to the one discussed above for PS rules and subcategorization features. We will not consider this alternative at all; at present it seems to have no advantages over the position we have already adopted.

8.4. REDUCED COMPLEMENTS: EQUI NP DELETION

So far we have been concerned only with embedded clauses with the internal structure of full sentences. When the complementizer is <u>that</u>, the complement sentence itself is in the same form it would take if it were an independent sentence standing

alone. Thus, corresponding to the embedded S in (8.74a) is the
independent sentence (8.74b):

(8.74) a. I believe that my telephone is ringing.
　　　 b. My telephone is ringing.

With for-to and poss-ing, if we simply "abstract" the complementizer in this way, we do not leave behind a full, independent
sentence. (For one thing, to and ing in some sense "replace"
Tense, as we saw in the previous section.) Nevertheless, the
embedded sentences with these complementizers seem to have
all the components of a sentence: NP - Aux - VP.
　　However, there are certain complements that do not appear
to have a surface subject. In this chapter we will limit our attention to a small class of such cases. Among these are the
following:

(8.75) a. I would hate to find the house empty.
　　　 b. We would prefer to leave the room now.
　　　 c. Sam wants (very much) to go to college.

The underlined complements in (8.75) have been referred to as
infinitival clauses. Although phrases such as to find the house
empty and to leave the room now have no overt subjects (and
hence may also be called reduced complements), notice that
they are interpreted as if there were a subject associated with
the verb of the complement. For example, the sentences in
(8.75) can be roughly paraphrased by (8.76a-c):

(8.76) a. I would hate it if I found the house empty.
　　　 b. ?We would prefer it if we left the room now.
　　　 c. Sam would (very much) like it if he [i.e., Sam]
　　　　 went to college.

At least in meaning, then, the reduced complement seems to
have a subject, and that subject is coreferential with the subject of the matrix sentence; that is, it refers to the same individual as the subject of the matrix sentence. This is reflected
in (8.76) by the underlining of the coreferential NPs. (We will
assume that Sam and he are interpreted as being coreferential
in (8.76c).)
　　Now note that there are certain sentences with for-to clauses

that are unacceptable, as illustrated below.

(8.77) a. I would hate for John to find the house empty.
       b. *I would hate for <u>me</u> to find the house empty.

(8.78) a. We would prefer for you to leave the room now.
       b. *<u>We</u> would prefer for <u>us</u> to leave the room now.

(8.79) a. Sam wants (very much) for his daughter to go to
          college.

       b. *<u>Sam</u> wants (very much) for $\left\{\frac{\text{him}}{\text{Sam}}\right\}$ to go to college.

(Example (8.79b) is acceptable if <u>Sam</u> or <u>him</u> in the complement is interpreted as being <u>noncoreferential</u> with <u>Sam</u> in the
matrix S.)
In these cases, a <u>for-to</u> complement is unacceptable if its overt
subject is coreferential with the subject of the matrix sentence.
When the complementizer is <u>that</u>, there is no such restriction:

(8.80) a. I believe that <u>I</u> am sick.
       b. <u>We</u> are hoping that <u>we</u> will win.
       c. Only <u>Sam</u> is betting that $\left\{\frac{\text{he}}{\text{Sam}}\right\}$ will win.

Thus, the unacceptability of (8.77b)-(8.79b) appears to be related to the fact that the complementizer in each is <u>for-to</u>.
    Now notice that those examples can be paired with the re-
duced complements of (8.75)—which, as we saw, are interpreted as if they had subject NPs in their complements:

(8.81) a. *<u>I</u> would hate for <u>me</u> to find the house empty.
       b. I would hate to find the house empty.

(8.82) a. *<u>We</u> would prefer for <u>us</u> to leave the room now.
       b. We would prefer to leave the room now.

(8.83) a. *<u>Sam</u> wants for $\left\{\frac{\text{him}}{\text{Sam}}\right\}$ to go to college.
       b. Sam wants to go to college.

The reader now possesses sufficient information to suggest an underlying structure for these reduced complements and a derivation for them that will explain

(A) the unacceptability of a for-to complement with a subject that is coreferential with the matrix subject, and
(B) the interpretation of a reduced complement (of the type discussed here) as if it had a subject that was coreferential with the matrix subject.

One way we can account for these facts is to use a rule, which has been called Equi NP Deletion, which obligatorily deletes the subject of a for-to (or poss-ing) clause just in case it is coreferential with the subject of the matrix clause. Thus, the (a) sentences below would be transformed into the (b) sentences, as shown:

(8.84) a. I would hate for me to find the house empty.

        ↓ Equi NP Deletion

   b. I would hate for ___ to find the house empty.

(8.85) a. We would prefer for us to leave the room now.

         ↓ Equi NP Deletion

   b. We would prefer for ___ to leave the room now.

(8.86) a. Sam wants very much for Sam to go to college.

           ↓ Equi NP Deletion

   b. Sam wants very much for ___ to go to college.

If Equi NP Deletion (or Equi, for short) operates in the manner just shown, note that it will have the effect of leaving for adjacent to to, as in the (b) examples. We need another transformation, applying after Equi, to delete for (obligatorily) when it is directly adjacent to to. This transformation would have the following effect (using only (8.84b) as our example):

(8.84) b. I would hate for ___ to find the house empty.

       ↓

         For Deletion

↓

   c. I would hate ___ ___ to find the house empty.

   I would hate to find the house empty.

Let us now ask how a rule such as Equi can account for the facts we have discussed. First of all, we noted that sentences such as (8.84a) are unacceptable:

(8.84) a. *I would hate for me to find the house empty.

We also noted that sentences such as I would hate to find the house empty must be interpreted in such a way that the missing subject of the complement sentence is coreferential with the subject of the matrix sentence. Both facts are explained at once by a rule of Equi. If (a) Equi deletes the subject of a for-to clause when it is coreferential with the subject of the matrix sentence and (b) if it is an obligatory rule, then every sentence like (8.84a) would undergo the rule. This would explain why no such sentences exist at the surface structure level. Second, Equi produces sentences such as I would hate to find the house empty if and only if the subject of the complement is coreferential with the subject of the matrix—and this accords precisely with the way we interpret the subject of the reduced clause to find the house empty.

There are other predictions made by the analysis that, since they are borne out, provide us with further justification for certain aspects of it. Consider a deep structure such as (8.87).

(8.87)

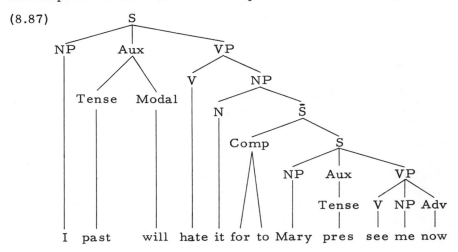

If It Deletion (and Affix Hopping) apply to this structure, we
have the sentence (8.88).

(8.88) I would hate for Mary to see me now.

However, notice that in this instance the complement sentence
Mary pres see me now meets the SD of Passive. As we saw
earlier, that rule can apply within embedded sentences, and
we would expect it to be able to apply to (8.87). What happens
if it is applied? Try to work out an acceptable derivation using
the Passive Rule on the lower S of (8.87).

First of all, Passive has the effect shown in (8.89).

(8.89)

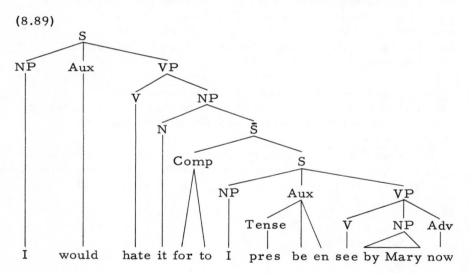

Once the to of the complementizer replaces Tense (as discussed
earlier in the chapter), this structure becomes (8.90).

(8.90) *I would hate for me to be seen by Mary now.

(We assume that It Deletion has applied.)
The effect of the Passive Rule has been to modify the complement sentence in such a way that its subject becomes the NP I,
which is coreferential with the matrix subject. An unacceptable sentence appears to result. However, (8.90) now meets

the SD of the obligatory rule of Equi, and the derivation must therefore continue:

(8.91) a. I would hate for me to be seen by Mary now.

Equi

b. I would hate for ___ to be seen by Mary now.

For Deletion

c. I would hate ___ to be seen by Mary now.

The final output, I would hate to be seen by Mary now, is fully acceptable.

It is important to notice how this derivation using the rules of Equi and Passive operating on an embedded S explains the presence of the passive be en and by - NP in a reduced complement such as (8.91c). If reduced complements did not start out as full sentences in underlying structure (i.e., if we were to generate a special class of subjectless infinitival clauses), it would be hard to account for the presence of these passive elements without duplicating the effect of the Passive Rule.

CHAPTER 8: EXERCISES

(E8.1) Provide a derivation for each of the following sentences. In each case, give the deep structure tree and illustrate the operation of each transformation by giving the tree that results from applying that rule.

(i)   It is believed by everyone that drugs are dangerous.
(ii) That the defendant was spotted by the police was not acknowledged by the court.
(iii) I believe that John knows that Mary intends to claim that it is obvious that her anteater has fleas.

(E8.2) List four different sentences of English that can be derived from the accompanying structure. In each case indicate what rules have applied in the derivation, showing briefly how those rules have operated.

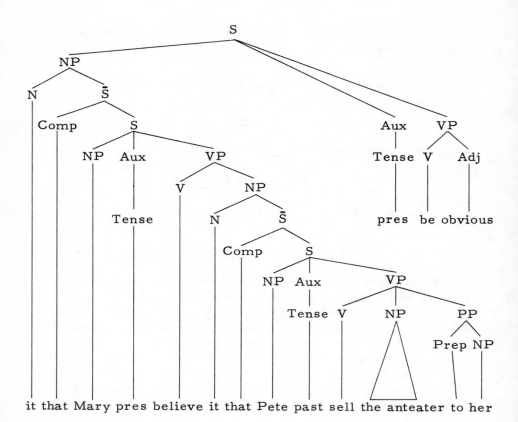

it that Mary pres believe it that Pete past sell the anteater to her

(E8.3) In chapter 5 we discussed the rule of Reflexivization, which has the effect of converting an NP into a reflexive pronoun (by adding to it the feature [+REFL]) when it is identical with an NP to its left—in our formulation, when it is identical with the subject of the sentence:

(i) a. <u>John</u> shaved <u>John</u>.

↓ <u>Reflexivization</u>

  b. <u>John</u> shaved <u>himself</u>.

In order to get this rule to operate properly on complex structures of the sort that we have been discussing, we must place a restriction on it, as shown by the examples (ii) and (iii):

(ii) a. <u>John</u> wants Mary to like <u>him</u>.

  b. *John wants Mary to like himself.
     (cf. John wants Mary to like herself.)

(iii) a. I know that Mary cut me.
      b. *I know that Mary cut myself.
          (cf. I know that Mary cut herself.)

It is clear that the (b) examples are ungrammatical, but there
is nothing to prevent the Reflexivization Rule from deriving
them from the (a) examples. Recall how the rule was stated:

(iv) Reflexivization (Obligatory)

       SD: NP - Aux - V - X - NP
            1   2   3   4   5
       SC: 1   2   3   4   5
                                    [+REFL]
       Condition: Term 5 = term 1

Given this statement, the underlying structure for a sentence
such as (iiia) would meet the SD of the rule, which would apply,
eventually yielding such sentences as (iiib).

A. Show precisely how the underlying structure for (iiia) meets
the SD of rule (iv) and hence why it is that this formulation of
Reflexivization allows the ungrammatical (iiib), and similar
forms, to be derived.

B. Formulate a further condition to be placed on the Reflexivization Rule so as to block the generation of such forms as (iib)
and (iiib), while allowing the grammatical counterparts of those
sentences to be produced. In formulating this condition, make
use of the following examples and any additional data you may
find:

(v)   a. John wants to wash himself.
      b. *John wants Mary to wash himself.
      c. John wants Mary to wash herself.

(vi) a. I hope that Mary will wash herself.
      b. I hope that Mary will wash me.
      c. *I hope that Mary will wash myself.

(vii) a. We would prefer for <u>Herb</u> to help <u>himself</u>.
     b. <u>We</u> would prefer for <u>Herb</u> to help <u>us</u>.
     c. *<u>We</u> would prefer for Herb to help <u>ourselves</u>.

<u>C</u>. Show how sentences (va-c) can be used to establish an ordering between Equi and Reflexivization. (Recall the argument for ordering Reflexivization and the Imperative Rule.)

(E8.4) In the text, we argued that the derivation of sentences such as <u>We would prefer to leave</u> involves the rule of Equi. Keeping this in mind, consider the following data:

(i)   I tried to run out of the room.
(ii) Sam started to sing "La Cucaracha."
(iii) Balthazar tends to like young girls.

Whereas verbs such as <u>want</u>, <u>prefer</u>, and <u>hate</u> allow complement subjects to be noncoreferential with their own subjects (as in <u>John wants (for) Mary to leave</u>), verbs such as those cited above do not allow this possibility:

(iv) *I tried for Bill to run out of the room.
(v) *Sam started for Betty to sing "La Cucaracha."
(vi) *Balthazar tends for Justine to like young girls.

Therefore, since the complements of these verbs never contain overt subjects, we might suspect that these complements— unlike the complements of verbs such as <u>want</u>— do not derive from full underlying sentences.
    Provide evidence that the complements of (i)-(iii) actually do come from full underlying sentences. Discuss your evidence in detail, showing why it is relevant. (Hint: Certain transformations that apply to full sentences will operate within these complements. Review section 8.4.)

(E8.5) In this chapter we discussed the rule of Extraposition, which has the effect of moving embedded sentences to the end of the matrix sentence. In light of that rule, consider sentences such as the following:

(i) a. A review <u>of the new bestseller</u> will appear soon.
     b. A review will appear soon <u>of the new bestseller</u>.

(ii) a. I bought a photo <u>of Washington's birthplace</u> today.
     b. I bought a photo <u>today of Washington's birthplace</u>.
(iii) a. An argument <u>against the proposal</u> was raised last night.
     b. An argument was raised last night <u>against the proposal</u>.

<u>A</u>. Try to account for the relationship between the (a) and the (b) sentences given above by formalizing a rule to relate the pairs.

<u>B</u>. In what way(s) is your rule similar to the rule of Extraposition discussed in this chapter? Can the two rules be collapsed into a single rule? If so, show how, and if not, show why.

CHAPTER 8: SUGGESTED READINGS

A great deal has been written about complementation, but before trying to become acquainted with the literature, the reader would be well advised to work through the next chapter. There is little published material that could be tackled now without considerable difficulty by the otherwise unprepared reader, since there are still many aspects of this very complex area that we have not yet introduced.

However, there are two readings that may be useful at this stage. Burt (1971, part III) provides a series of derivations using the rules we have discussed, and although her assumptions are not always the same as ours, it would be instructive to compare her account with ours in detail. Whereas Burt provides little explanatory text, Rosenbaum (1969) gives a good summary of the issues dealt with in this chapter.

Rosenbaum (1967), which forms the basis of all recent work on the subject, will need to be read at some stage by anyone with a serious interest in the theory of complementation. However, many aspects of Rosenbaum's analyses have been shown to be wrong, while a number of points that he believed he had settled now appear much more undecided than he thought. In any case, Rosenbaum's book is extremely difficult to read, partly because related material is widely scattered through the work. We suggest that the reader attempt no more than a first reading of pages 33-58 and 79-80 of chapter 4, <u>Noun Phrase Complementation</u>—after working through the earlier references.

Those who are interested in pursuing the transformational treatment of complementizer insertion, mentioned in the present chapter but not discussed here, may want to read chapter 3

of Rosenbaum (1967) as well, since that chapter constitutes his
original presentation of that theory. The alternative phrase
structure treatment, which we adopted here but did not justify,
has been defended by Bresnan (1970).

Some readers may find it interesting to read Postal (1970)
as well as Rosenbaum (1970) for a discussion of aspects of what
has come to be known as the Control Problem for the rule of
Equi. Rosenbaum's solution is no longer generally accepted;
in fact, there is no generally accepted solution at the present
time. Although we will not discuss this problem in the text, it
is one that might well be pursued as a research topic at a later
stage. It will then be necessary to read Grinder (1970), Kimball
(1971), and Grinder (1971) and to follow up references given
there. (See also the suggested readings for chapter 9.)

In this chapter we have stated the rule of Extraposition as a
single, unified transformation. However, it has been argued
by Ross (1967) that there are at least two kinds of extraposition
in English and that the rule of Extraposition must therefore be
broken down into two separate transformations. For further
discussion of Ross's argument, with an alternative approach
to the facts, see Koutsoudas (1973).

A radically different approach to the whole analysis of complex sentences is one that uses "generalized transformations"
rather than PS rules to form complex sentences. That framework was assumed in the early transformational literature such
as Chomsky (1957). The most important works dealing specifically with complex sentences from that point of view are Lees
(1960), Fillmore (1963), and Chomsky (1958). In his final chapter, Rosenbaum discusses these works briefly, together with
Poutsma (1904) and Jespersen (1956) (the latter two are not by
transformational grammarians). All of these works (early
transformational and nontransformational alike) were written
under assumptions that now appear to be wrong (see Chomsky
1965, 128-138, concerning generalized transformations). Although not very likely to have immediate relevance to theoretical points discussed in this book, they can all be read with
profit.

Chapter 9

EQUI, RAISING, AND VERB CLASSES

9.1. THE PROBLEM OF THE VERB FORCE

We have just investigated the source of sentences like the following:

(9.1) John would prefer to leave early.

(9.2) John would prefer (for) you to leave early.

In both cases, the underlying tree, shown in (9.3), contains a
sentence dominated by the object NP (a <u>sentential object</u>, as it
is often called).

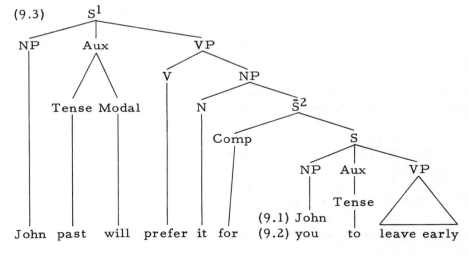

In the derivation of (9.1) Equi applies, deleting the subject of
$\bar{\bar{S}}^2$, i.e., <u>John</u>, since it is coreferential with the subject of S^1;
however, no important changes occur between the deep and
surface structure of (9.2).

At first blush, sentence (9.4) might seem parallel to (9.2):

(9.2) John would prefer you to leave early.

(9.4) John will force you to leave early.

We might suppose that the underlying structure of (9.4) contains a sentential object exactly like that of (9.2), as shown in
(9.5).

(9.5)

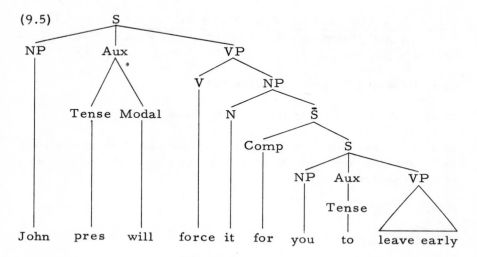

However, there are a number of reasons for thinking that the
underlying structure of (9.4) is more complex than this (and,
in fact, that Equi is one of the rules that must apply in its derivation).

Recall that one of the strongest arguments for (9.3), in particular for the NP that dominates the embedded S, is the form
of the passives corresponding to (9.1) and (9.2). Thus, the sentences of (9.6) (which are parallel to (9.1) and (9.2)) have the
passive counterparts given in (9.7):

(9.6) a. Most of the students would prefer to leave early.
      b. Most of the students would prefer for you to leave early.

(9.7) a. To leave early would be preferred by most of the
         students.
      b. For you to leave early would be preferred by most of
         the students.

As long as we suppose that the complement sentence occurring
as the object of prefer is dominated by NP—as in structure
(9.3)—then the Passive Transformation will be able to operate
on that sentential object as a whole, and we have a natural

means of generating the sentences of (9.7). (Incidentally, some speakers of English find that sentences such as those in (9.7) sound more natural if Extraposition has been applied after the Passive Rule, e.g., It would be preferred by most of the students for you to leave early. Moreover, many speakers find that if an NP such as John replaces most of the students in these examples, they become very much less acceptable, e.g., ?To leave early would be preferred by John. We do not have any explanation for this fact, but it does not reduce the force of the argument that the Passive Rule must apply in the derivation of (9.7).)

Now contrast this with force:

(9.8) *For you to leave early will be forced by most of your friends.

By analogy with prefer, (9.8) should be the result of applying the Passive Rule to tree (9.5), as can be seen in (9.9).

(9.9) a.

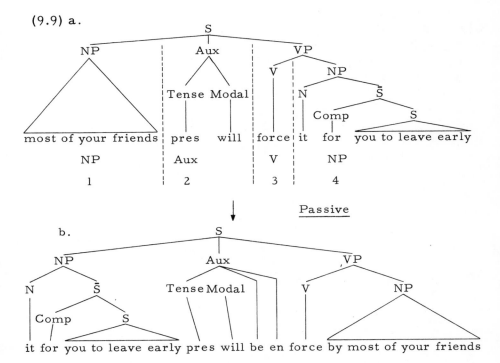

But the passive sentence (9.8) is totally unacceptable, and thus derivation (9.9) cannot be correct. Yet there is a passive for (9.4). What is it? And how might we modify the Passive Rule, or the underlying structures for force, in order to generate it without also deriving (9.8)?

The passive counterpart of sentence (9.4) is (9.10):

(9.10) You will be forced to leave early by John.

When the Passive is applied to prefer, the whole complement sentence is fronted, while the same rule applied to a sentence containing force as the main verb fronts only the apparent subject of the complement sentence and cannot move the entire complement. We might try to account for these facts by allowing the Passive Rule to operate in the following way on sentences containing force, as illustrated in (9.11).

(9.11) a.

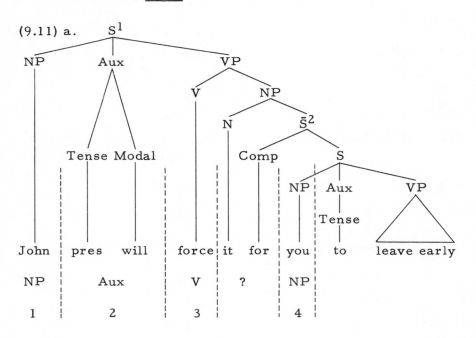

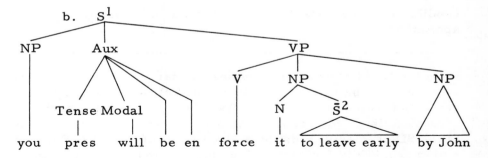

What we have done here is to permit the Passive Rule to "look down" into the complement sentence for its fourth term (i.e., NP), thus moving the subject of that lower sentence instead of the higher NP, the one that dominates $\bar{S}^2$. It may seem unnecessary to allow rules to satisfy their SDs partly within a matrix sentence and partly within an embedded sentence, but there is nothing in our theory at present to prevent this from happening. In fact, Equi is such a rule: it must delete the subject of an <u>embedded</u> sentence on the basis of its identity with the subject of the <u>matrix</u> sentence, in order to yield surface forms like (9.1).

It might appear to be the case, therefore, that the Passive Rule as modified would automatically generate the correct passive forms for <u>force</u>. But now we have a problem. We need to prevent the rule from operating in this new fashion when <u>prefer</u> is the main verb, since sentences like (9.12) are ungrammatical:

(9.12) *You would be $\left\{ \begin{array}{l} \text{preferred} \\ \text{hated} \end{array} \right\}$ to leave early by most of the

      people.

Thus we have to prevent Passive from generating such forms with <u>prefer</u> while permitting them with <u>force</u>; and at the same time we must ensure that sentences such as (9.8) (*For you to leave early will be forced by most of your friends) are blocked while parallel sentences such as (9.7b) (For you to leave early would be preferred by most of the students) are permitted. The Passive Rule will therefore have to move the <u>whole object NP</u> for <u>prefer</u> but apparently <u>only the embedded subject</u> for <u>force</u>. We might try to state these facts directly by placing special conditions on the Passive Rule. What would be wrong with this approach?

On the basis of what we have seen so far, the conditions that would have to be placed on Passive to exclude the undesirable derivations would be complex. We might phrase them somewhat as follows: for verbs of the <u>prefer</u> class, the fourth term of the SD of Passive must be a constituent of the same S as the main verb, while for verbs of the <u>force</u> class, it must be in the embedded S. However, such a "solution" would be totally unexplanatory; it would merely state the facts without relating them to anything else. Before accepting an ad hoc analysis of this sort, we must search for a more explanatory account. We are faced with two superficially similar sentences, <u>John would prefer you to leave early</u> and <u>John will force you to leave early</u> (and many other similar pairs), which behave differently with respect to the operation of a given transformation. Rather than ascribe this difference to chance or treat it as an isolated fact (as we would be doing if we simply placed special conditions on the Passive Rule), we want to see if there are other differences between the sentences—more specifically, between the verbs <u>prefer</u> and <u>force</u>, in this instance—that can be systematically related to the observed difference.

We already have a clue that could point us in the right direction. Recall that we looked at the passive sentences of (9.7) in the first place because they provided evidence for the original analysis of <u>prefer</u>. That is, the fact that we could produce acceptable passives such as <u>For you to leave early would probably be preferred by everyone</u> suggested that the verb <u>prefer</u> was followed by the embedded S (For) you to leave early, which in turn was dominated by NP. The fact that <u>force</u> does not permit these particular passives indicates that there is as yet no evidence for analyzing <u>force</u> as a verb followed by an NP dominating S, as in (9.5) (repeated here in somewhat simplified form):

(9.5)

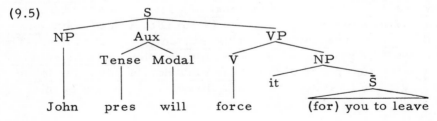

If the underlying structure of John will force you to leave contained no NP object dominating S, then we would have no reason
to expect a passive of the form *For you to leave will be forced
by John; in this event, the differences between force and prefer
might fall into a pattern predictable from a single basic difference in the underlying structures in which they occur.

   We might therefore suppose that, instead of (9.5), the underlying structure for a force sentence is (9.5'):

(9.5')

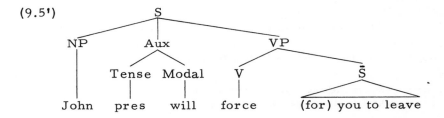

With this analysis we could account for the two different passive constructions of force and prefer by placing the following
condition on the Passive Rule: that the fourth term of its SD be
satisfied by the highest NP immediately following the verb mentioned in the SD. The highest NP immediately following prefer
is the NP that dominates the whole complement S, and thus
Passive may move the whole complement. On the other hand,
in a structure with force, such as (9.5'), the highest NP in this
position turns out to be the subject of the complement (i.e.,
you). Hence, Passive may front this NP, and we seem to have
a means of accounting for the different behavior of these verbs
with respect to the Passive Rule.

   Let us see to what extent this reanalysis of force will predict other aspects of its behavior. When we were discussing
believe in chapter 8, we pointed out that this verb could occur
either with sentential objects or with ordinary NP objects.

(9.13) a. Mabel believes that her poodle is a good pianist.
       b. Mabel believes that story.

In the same way prefer can occur with either type of object:

(9.14) a. John would prefer (for) you to leave now.
       b. John would prefer the bigger cake.

The lexical entries for believe and prefer thus include the feature +[___ NP]. This would automatically permit either verb to occur in the underlying structures of the (a) sentences as well as the (b) sentences, provided we analyzed the former as having sentential objects in the way that we have proposed.

In contrast, however, force does not occur freely with ordinary NP objects. There are some very special idiomatic uses, as in (9.15a, b):

(9.15) a. Jane forced the issue.
       b. Jill forced the door.

However, we do not find (9.16a) or (9.16b):

(9.16) a. *Marmaduke forced the event.
       b. *Millicent forced that fact.

Hence, there is no strong evidence from this quarter for analyzing force as having a sentential object, and the ungrammaticality of (9.16) would be predicted by analyzing force as being subcategorized by the feature +[___ S̄] and hence as occurring only in trees such as (9.5').

There is one further piece of evidence that an NP dominates the embedded sentences that occur with believe and prefer. (We did not discuss this in chapter 8, but it is often cited as being relevant.) This evidence is based on a construction in English that has come to be called the Pseudocleft. An example such as (9.17a) has the pseudoclefted forms (9.17b) and (9.17c):

(9.17) a. The mouse ate the soy grits.
       b. What the mouse ate was the soy grits.
       c. What ate the soy grits was the mouse.

Corresponding to the ordinary declarative sentence The mouse ate the soy grits are two different pseudoclefts; one, (9.17b), in which the object NP, the soy grits, follows the verb was, and the other, (9.17c), in which the subject NP, the mouse, follows it. The rest of the original sentence, preceded by what, is to the left of was. Precisely how pseudoclefts are formed need not concern us (it is, in any case, still open to a great deal of debate). What is relevant is that in all the cases examined above— and in fact in most pseudoclefts—the constituent following be is an NP.

With this brief background, consider the sentences of (9.18):

(9.18) a.   What Mabel believes is <u>that her poodle has developed laryngitis</u>.
       b.   What I would prefer is <u>for you to get out of here</u>.
       c.   *What John will force is <u>(for) you to leave at once</u>.
       d.   *What John will force you is <u>to leave at once</u>.

We see that the verbs <u>believe</u> and <u>prefer</u> may occur in a pseudo-cleft construction in which the verb complement appears to the right of <u>be</u>, but (9.18c) and (9.18d) show that this is not possible with the verb <u>force</u>. Once again, we have evidence that <u>force</u> patterns quite differently from <u>prefer</u>. In light of the fact that the constituent after <u>be</u> is generally an NP, the difference between <u>force</u> and <u>prefer</u> might be explained as follows: if the complement of <u>prefer</u> is dominated by NP, we would expect to find pseudocleft sentences such as (9.18b), but if the complement of <u>force</u> is not dominated by NP, then we have no reason to expect sentences such as (9.18c) or (9.18d).

Thus far we have established the following differences between <u>prefer</u> and <u>force</u>:

(i)   <u>Force</u> does not undergo Passive in the same way as <u>prefer</u>.
(ii) <u>Force</u> does not occur freely with ordinary NP objects.
(iii) <u>Force</u> does not occur in pseudocleft constructions in which the embedded S̄ occurs after <u>be</u>.

All these observations point toward an analysis in which there is no sentential object of the sort shown in tree (9.5); rather, they are consistent with the analysis suggested in (9.5').

Now let us look at another difference between the two verbs <u>prefer</u> and <u>force</u>—one that cannot be explained by our current hypothesis:

(9.19) a.   John would prefer there to be more than three people at the party.
       b.   *John will force there to be more than three people at the party.

To evaluate the significance of the ungrammaticality of the second example, we must establish a derivation for the first. How would (9.19a) be derived?

There is only one natural way to derive that example. The PS rules and lexicon will produce (9.20).

(9.20)

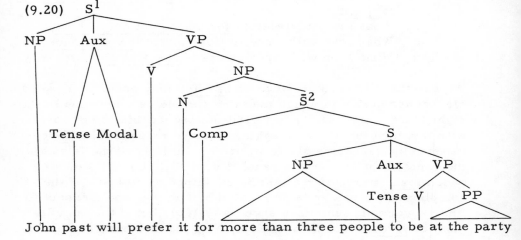

There Insertion will apply in $\bar{\bar{S}}^2$, as shown in (9.21).

(9.21)

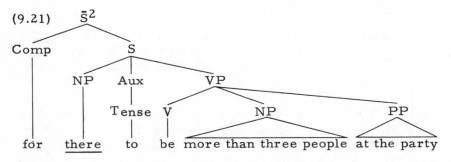

After the usual rules of It Deletion and Affix Hopping have applied, the result will be sentence (9.19a). There is no difficulty in deriving this sentence, and there is every reason to expect to hear sentences like (9.19a).

But if, as we have been supposing, force could occur in trees such as (9.5'), which is essentially the same as (9.20) (except for the fact that no NP dominates the embedded S̄), then there would be no way to prevent (9.19b) from being generated in precisely the same way as (9.19a). Notice that if There Insertion had not applied in $\bar{\bar{S}}^2$, then instead of (9.19a) and (9.19b) we would have (9.21a) and (9.21b):

(9.21) a. John would prefer more than three people to be at
           the party.
       b. John will force more than three people to be at the
           party.

And these are both perfectly acceptable sentences. The ungrammaticality of (9.19b), then, seems to be directly related
to the fact that There Insertion has applied in the complement
sentence of force. So to block (9.19b) directly, we would somehow need to prevent There Insertion from applying on S^2, just
in case force were the main verb of S^1.

Of course, this is a particularly unattractive way of viewing
the data. Some other explanation of (9.19b) must be forthcoming.
What we want is an underlying structure for force sentences
that differs from that of prefer sentences in just the right way
to account for all these observations at once. Let us summarize
again:

(9.22) a. Force does not act as if it had a sentential object:
           i.   There are no passives of the form *For you to
           leave early will be forced by John.
           ii. There are no pseudocleft sentences such as
           *What John forced was for you to go.
           iii. The verb force does not occur freely with ordinary
           NP objects.
       b. Yet, force does have passives of the form Bill was
           forced to leave by John, while prefer does not.
       c. Force does not occur in sentences in which There
           Insertion has applied to the embedded complement,
           such as *John forced there to be three men at the
           party.

As is so often the case when one is trying to develop a scien-
tific explanation for a set of data, there is no automatic route
to the correct solution. In this instance it is far from obvious
how to analyze force in order to account naturally for these apparently unconnected facts. Faced with such a situation, the
linguist has to guess—or use intuition. If he is lucky, he stumbles
upon a solution that allows all the seemingly disparate facts to
fall into place. If that happens, then he is able to demonstrate
that his guess was right (or at least better than any other).

We suggest that the reader, who is now in possession of all

the relevant facts, spend some time trying to discover an appropriate underlying structure for force. Two hints are all we will provide. First, recall that in all previous cases we have discussed, the Passive Transformation moves the direct object of a verb into subject position. (We raised the possibility that it might be moving the subject of an embedded sentence in order to yield forms such as Bill was forced to leave by John; but as we saw, that analysis causes difficulties with prefer. Let us instead return to our earlier assumptions.) The second hint is this: The solution will involve an extension of the rule of Equi, introduced in section 8.4.

9.2. AN ANALYSIS OF FORCE

Although a solution may not have been obvious, it should be easy to see the justification for our analysis once it is presented. In outline, it is as follows. The underlying structure for a sentence with force, such as (9.4), is roughly as shown in (9.23).

(9.23)

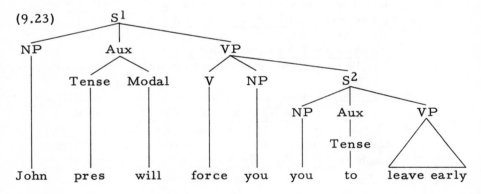

Compare this with the underlying structure for the superficially similar prefer sentence (9.2), which is illustrated in (9.24). Whereas prefer has a sentential object, force has an ordinary NP object (you in this instance); this NP is identical to the subject of the complement sentence, which comes to the right of the object (and is not part of it). At some point in the derivation of (9.23), Equi applies, deleting the lower subject on the basis of its identity with the object of the matrix S, as shown in (9.25).

(9.24)

(9.25) a.

b.

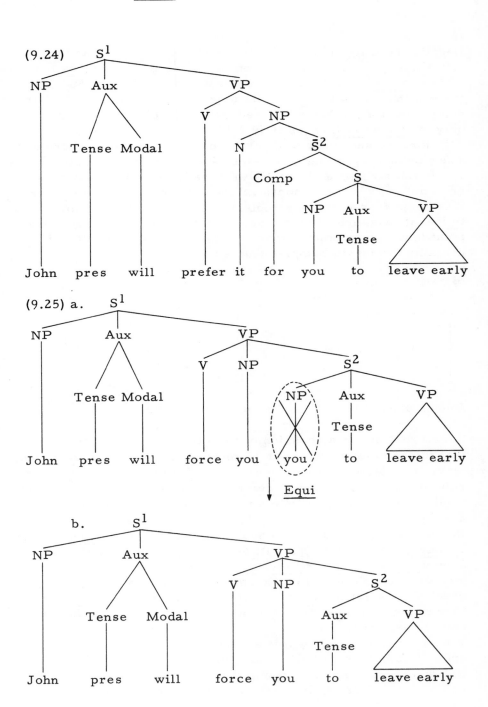

Despite their superficial similarity, sentences (9.2) and (9.4) differ quite significantly even on the surface, for the you that follows prefer is actually the subject of an embedded S̄, while the you that follows force is its original object; in addition, the complement after force is a reduced complement consisting only of to leave early (as in (9.25b)).

Before we show how well justified this analysis is, there are a few points regarding complementizers that must be cleared up. In the structures of (9.25) we have ignored the placement of Comp in the complement sentence of force. However, note that to appears in those complements, as in John will force you to leave; thus, the simplest assumption we could make at this point (and one commonly made) is that the complement of force contains the for-to complementizer:

(9.25')

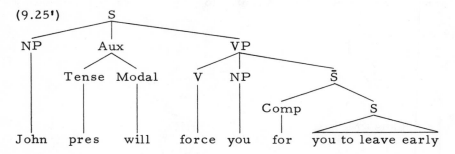

Recall that in our discussion of the rule of Equi, we proposed that for be deleted whenever it immediately precedes to; hence, from an underlying form such as I prefer for me to leave, the rule of Equi would yield I prefer for to leave. At that point, we needed the rule of For Deletion in order to eliminate for and arrive at the form I prefer to leave. In a similar fashion, if we have an underlying form such as John will force you for you to leave, the rule of Equi will delete you, producing the form John will force you for to leave. As long as we already have a rule of For Deletion in our grammar, it will operate here as usual, thus allowing us to derive John will force you to leave. Hence, we will make the assumption that force takes the for-to complementizer.

Now we can show how this analysis explains the facts listed under (9.22). First of all, since force does not take a sentential object, it is not surprising that it does not behave as if it had one (cf. (9.22a)). In particular, the complement is not fronted by the Passive Rule because it is not dominated by an NP immediately after the V. Instead, the Passive Rule will analyze and transform a force sentence as shown in (9.26), as-suming that it operates after Equi.

(9.26) a.

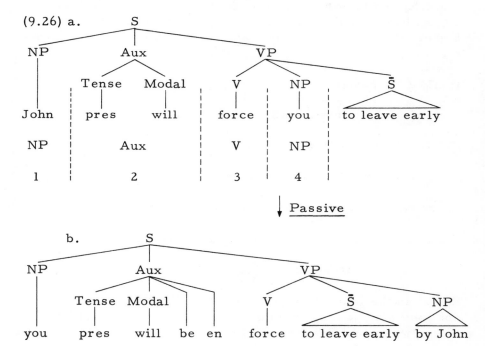

This output is precisely what we need, as noted in (9.22b). Notice that this analysis permits us to say that Passive al-ways operates within one sentence at a time. Since we have abandoned structures such as (9.5') for force, we no longer need to complicate the Passive Rule by imposing the ad hoc condition mentioned above that allowed the rule to front the subject of the complement of force, while allowing it to front the whole complement of prefer. Now Passive operates in a uniform way for both verbs: the rule fronts the direct object of the verb, whether it is sentential (as with prefer) or just a simple NP (as with force).

9.3. OBLIGATORY EQUI WITH FORCE

The most interesting consequence of our analysis is the way in which it explains the facts about There Insertion (9.22c).

To show how this works, we need to clarify some aspects of the operation of Equi that we have been glossing over. We have not provided an explicit formalization of Equi but have informally stated it as a rule that deletes the subject of an embedded sentence having the complementizer for-to (or poss-ing) under identity with some NP in the matrix S. With want or prefer, that higher NP (called the controller) is the subject NP of the matrix S:

(9.27) a. John wants [for John to go]

     b. John wants to go.

(9.28) John wants [for Bill to go]

     (Here the NPs are not identical, so Equi does not apply.)

In the case of force, the controller is the object of the matrix S:

(9.29) a. John forced Bill [for Bill to leave early]

     b. John forced Bill to leave early.

Since, in the interpretation of sentence (9.29b), it is Bill and not John who leaves, we must assume that the "missing" subject of the complement is identical with the matrix object. Precisely what it is that determines which of the higher NPs is to be the controller is still not fully understood—see the suggested readings for this chapter—but it is clear that want (or prefer) differs from force in this respect: the controller for want is the higher subject, while force's controller is the higher object.

   There is a more important difference between these two verbs, however. The structure represented in (9.28) does not meet the SD of Equi, and the rule does not apply; yet a fully acceptable sentence nevertheless results: John wants (for) Bill to go. In this way, want can appear either with full complements (as in (9.28)) or with reduced ones (as in (9.27)). But what if the SD of Equi is not met by a sentence containing force?

   The following structure represents such a case:

(9.30) John forced Bill [for Alex to leave early]

There is obviously no acceptable surface sentence corresponding to this form. Yet our PS rules and lexicon will generate
such examples freely. One way of dealing with this problem is
to state that for verbs such as _force_ (but not for _want_) the SD
of Equi must be met. Notice that this is different from saying
that the rule is obligatory. Even for _want_ or _prefer_ the rule is
obligatory: if its SD is met, then it must apply, deleting the
subject of the lower sentence. If that were not so, the grammar
would generate sentences such as *I want for me to go, as well
as I want to go.
    But what we are now suggesting is that whenever _force_ ap-
pears in a tree, the rule of Equi must be able to apply to that
tree—in particular, the relevant NPs _must_ be identical at the
time that Equi applies. As long as we can guarantee that the
SD is always met, Equi will always apply since, as we have
seen for _want_, it is obligatory. Precisely how we should go
about building this requirement into the grammar for verbs of
the _force_ class remains very unclear. We will simply assume
that there is a formal mechanism available in the model that
will require that the SD of Equi be met for _force_, rejecting (or
filtering out) any tree that does not satisfy the rule, and we will
explore some of the consequences of this view.
    A crucial point to notice is that the application of _other_ trans-
formations to an underlying structure can sometimes determine
whether a particular underlying form will undergo Equi and ultimately result in a grammatical output. For example, consider
the underlying structure roughly represented by (9.31):

(9.31) John persuaded Bill [for the doctor to examine Bill]

If this structure were to undergo no significant rules prior to
the point in the derivation where Equi should apply, the SD of
that rule would not be met and the derivation would be blocked
by the requirement that Equi apply to all sentences with _force_,
persuade, etc. However, what would happen if the Passive Rule
were applied to the embedded S? (If necessary refer to the discussion of reduced complements in section 8.4.)

The immediate result of that application would be (9.32):

(9.32) John persuaded Bill [for Bill to be examined by the doctor]

The SD of Equi would now be met, that rule would obligatorily apply, and the final output would be (9.33):

(9.33) John persuaded Bill [to be examined by the doctor]

But how would we derive (9.34)?

(9.34) John persuaded the doctor to examine Bill.

The underlying structure in this instance would be (9.35):

(9.35) John persuaded the doctor [for the doctor to examine Bill]

If no significant transformations applied, Equi would then operate, deleting the lower subject, to produce (9.34). (If Passive applied in the lower S, then the result would be blocked, since Equi could not apply.)

It is worth observing that this account of the derivation of pairs such as (9.33) and (9.34) leads to an interesting result that in part confirms our analysis of force, persuade, and similar verbs. Notice that the two sentences in question are not synonymous. The first, (9.33), is true if Bill was reluctant to be examined but if, as a result of John's talking to him, he agreed to undergo the examination. The second claims that it was the doctor who, as a result of John's efforts, became willing to do the examining. These are by no means the same state of affairs. Now if we had analyzed persuade like want, (9.33) and (9.34) (which mean quite different things) would be derived from a single deep structure, differing only in that the Passive Rule had applied to the embedded S in the former sentence. The fact that our analysis has led us automatically to set up distinct underlying structures for these sentences that are distinct in meaning provides some confirmation for our hypotheses.

We are now in a position to assess the relevance of the fact that there are no sentences of the form (9.36), although (9.37) is acceptable.

(9.36) *John $\begin{Bmatrix} \text{forced} \\ \text{persuaded} \end{Bmatrix}$ there to be three of his friends at the party.

(9.37) John $\begin{Bmatrix} \text{forced} \\ \text{persuaded} \end{Bmatrix}$ three of his friends to be at the party.

What underlying structure would be required if we were to generate (9.36)?

_____

The required structure would be roughly (9.38).

(9.38)

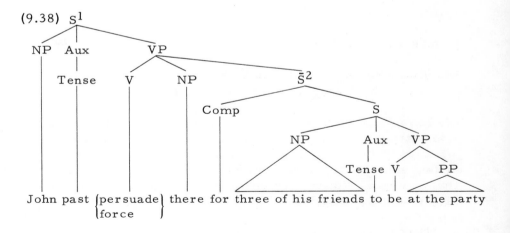

The rule of <u>There</u> Insertion would apply on $\bar{\bar{S}}^2$, yielding <u>For there to be three of his friends at the party</u>. The existential <u>there</u> would presumably then be available for deletion by Equi, and (9.36) would be the final output.

Why would this derivation never occur?

The answer is that, as we showed in chapter 5, the existential there is not introduced by PS rules at all but rather by the transformation of There Insertion; and that rule places there only in the subject position of sentences containing be. Hence, there is no way in which there could be inserted into the object position of verbs such as force or persuade. Given our account of these verbs, our rules already predict that (9.36) would be ungrammatical, for they do not even generate the requisite underlying structure (i.e., (9.38)). Thus, our final analysis of force, as represented by deep structure (9.23) with obligatory Equi, accounts for all of the facts we summarized in (9.22). Since this analysis accounts for the There Insertion facts—which the other analyses do not—it is superior to them.

9.4. RAISING TO OBJECT (BELIEVE)

There is another superficially similar sentence that must be added to those already discussed:

(9.39) John believes Bill to be a criminal.

Comparable examples containing prefer and force are (9.40a, b):

(9.40) a. John prefers Bill to be a criminal.
b. John forced Bill to be a criminal.

We have found evidence for positing specific, different underlying structures for sentences such as (9.40a) and (9.40b). What about (9.39)? Using data of the type discussed in the preceding section, try to determine the underlying structure of that sentence. Notice, incidentally, that there is a very similar sentence containing believe:

(9.41) John believes that Bill is a criminal.

This does not necessarily come from the same underlying structure as the believe sentence containing an infinitive clause (i.e., to be a criminal in (9.39)), but in your investigation you should obviously take into account the existence of such a sentence as (9.41). The following is a summary of the tests that proved useful in the previous section; these, too, must be taken into consideration:

(9.42) a. <u>Prefer</u> acts as if it had a sentential object, but <u>force</u> does not:
i. There are passives such as <u>For you to leave early would be preferred by everyone</u> but not *<u>For you to leave early will be forced by everyone</u>.
ii. There are pseudocleft sentences such as <u>What John would prefer is for you to go</u> but not *<u>What John forced was for you to go</u>.
iii. The verb <u>prefer</u> occurs freely with ordinary NP objects, alone, as in <u>John prefers the cake</u>, but the verb <u>force</u> does not: *<u>John forced the cake</u>.
b. There is evidence that the NP that precedes the infinitival phrase after <u>force</u> is the real object of that verb, whereas the superficially similar NP after <u>prefer</u> appears to be just the subject of its complement sentence. Thus, this NP can be acted upon by Passive with <u>force</u>, yielding <u>Bill was forced by his doctor to eat cookies</u> but not *<u>Bill was preferred by his doctor to eat cookies</u>.
c. If <u>force</u> has an ordinary NP as its direct object and must undergo Equi, while <u>prefer</u> is simply followed by a sentential object, this will explain why <u>There</u> Insertion is impossible in the complement of <u>force</u>: *<u>John forced there to be more exams taken in his class than in any other</u>. At the same time, it is perfectly acceptable with <u>prefer</u>: <u>John prefers there to be more exams taken in his class than in any other</u>.
d. The proposed analyses of <u>force</u> and <u>prefer</u> (along with the consideration that transformations do not generally change meaning—see chapter 7) would explain the fact that there is a radical difference in meaning between <u>John forced Bill to kiss Mary</u> and <u>John forced Mary to be kissed by Bill</u>. At the same time, the sentences in the corresponding pair with <u>prefer</u> differ only in emphasis, if at all: <u>John prefers Bill to kiss Mary</u>; <u>John prefers Mary to be kissed by Bill</u>.

Now find out how believe behaves when followed by an infinitive clause. That should be easy. Try, at the same time, to discover a way of deriving sentences such as (9.39) (John believes Bill to be a criminal) that will explain all the data. That will be more difficult!

As we explore the structure of sentences such as (9.39), we will discuss the evidence in the order in which it is set out in our summary (9.42). Starting with (9.42a), i.e., evidence for a sentential object dominated by NP, it turns out that the behavior of believe is different, depending on what sort of complement it appears with. For example, there are no passive sentences of the form (9.43):

(9.43) *For Bill to be a criminal is believed by John.

This suggests that believe, in (9.39), does not have a sentential object. Similarly, there are no pseudocleft sentences of the form (9.44):

(9.44) *What John believes is (for) Bill to be a criminal.

Thus, believe acts like force in these ways. On the other hand, believe occurs freely with appropriate plain NPs as objects:

(9.45) John believes that story.

In fact we used this verb in the previous chapter to demonstrate the existence of sentential objects, for when believe occurs with that complements, both passive and pseudocleft constructions are found:

(9.46) a. That Bill is careful is believed by few of his friends.
       b. What Martha believes is that Bill is careful.

Thus, there is clear evidence that the verb believe must be marked in the lexicon to permit it to occur in trees of the following form:

(9.47)

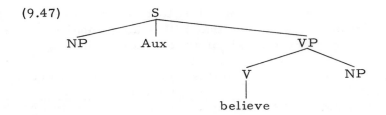

The object can be either a plain NP, as in (9.45), or a sentence, as in the underlying forms related to (9.46). Thus, believe acts like the verb prefer in these respects.

In addition, if the ungrammaticality of the passive and pseudo-cleft versions of believe + infinitive sentences such as (9.43) and (9.44) is taken to indicate that believe occurs in structures like those for force, then we will have to permit believe to occur in structures such as (9.48)—but only when the complement is a for-to clause:

(9.48)

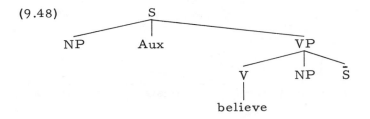

So far then, believe seems to occur either in prefer-type structures or force-type structures, depending on the complement type that occurs with the verb.

Let us assess the rest of the evidence in the light of this observation. Continuing through the data in the order set out in (9.42), we find that the next point, (9.42b), strongly favors underlying structures such as (9.48) for believe + infinitive sentences. For believe sentences of this sort again behave just like force sentences—and not like examples containing believe that-S or prefer:

(9.49) a. Some of us believe Bill to be a criminal.
            Bill is believed by some of us to be a criminal.
        b. One of us forced Bill to be a criminal
            Bill was forced by one of us to be a criminal.

(9.50) a. *Bill is believed by some of us that is a criminal.
       (cf. Some of us believe that Bill is a criminal.)
       b. *Bill is preferred by all of us to be a criminal.

Thus, the NP following <u>believe</u> in (9.49a) acts like its direct
object, so that in this instance <u>believe</u> behaves like <u>force</u>.
    On the other hand, (9.42c) strongly favors an analysis of <u>be-</u>
<u>lieve</u> that is <u>different</u> from that of <u>force</u>. If the underlying
structure of (9.39), <u>John believes Bill to be a criminal</u>, contained <u>Bill</u> as a separate direct object, there would be no way
of generating sentences such as (9.51):

(9.51) Algy believes <u>there</u> to be a monster in the pool.

If <u>believe</u> were analyzed like <u>force</u>, the underlying structure
of (9.51) would have to be (9.52):

(9.52)

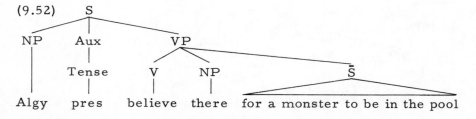

The ungrammaticality of comparable sentences with <u>force</u> (e.g.,
<u>*Algy will force there to be a monster in the pool at nine o'clock</u>)
was explained by the fact that <u>there</u> is never generated in object
position. But, by the same reasoning, (9.52) is not a possible
underlying tree, and hence the existence of sentence (9.51) provides very strong evidence against an analysis for <u>believe</u> that
requires (9.52) as the underlying structure for (9.51).
    Although it would be too strong to claim that the fourth kind
of evidence, summarized in (9.42d), argues in the same way
against analyzing <u>believe + infinitive</u> like <u>force</u>, it certainly
provides no support for such an analysis. Recall that two sentences like the following can be true under very different circumstances:

(9.53) a. John forced Bill to kiss Mary.
       b. John forced Mary to be kissed by Bill.

This is not true of the following sentences, which are virtually synonymous:

(9.54) a. John believes Bill to have kissed Mary.
       b. John believes Mary to have been kissed by Bill.

Hence, there is no advantage whatever to be gained by deriving (9.54a) and (9.54b) from different structures, as in the <u>force</u> analysis.

We now seem to have reached a somewhat paradoxical situation. There is some evidence suggesting that <u>believe</u> should occur in underlying structures like those for <u>prefer</u>:

(i)   With <u>that</u> complements, <u>believe</u> allows passive and pseudo-cleft forms;
(ii) <u>Believe</u> occurs with simple NP objects;
(iii) <u>There</u> Insertion may occur within the complement of <u>believe</u>; and
(iv) Sentences (9.54a) and (9.54b) are virtually synonymous.

On the other hand, there is some evidence suggesting that <u>believe</u> occurs in underlying structures like those for <u>force</u>:

(i) When <u>believe</u> takes an infinitive complement, passives such as (9.43) and pseudocleft constructions such as (9.44) are impossible; and
(ii) The NP following <u>believe</u> acts as its direct object and hence may be fronted by the Passive Rule, as in (9.49a).

How can our grammar reflect the fact that <u>believe</u> acts both like <u>prefer</u> and like <u>force</u>?

Faced with what seems to be a dilemma, it is easy to conclude that English is just unsystematic—at least in this respect. However, it turns out that there is really no contradiction between the two kinds of evidence summarized above. In fact, a more careful examination of both sets of evidence provides a number of clues to the correct analysis. It turns out that we can explain the facts about <u>believe</u> if we assume that <u>believe</u> originates in deep structures like those for <u>prefer</u> but that <u>believe</u> sentences also undergo a transformation that, at some later stage in the derivation, transforms that structure into a <u>force</u>-type structure. Thus, let us suppose that <u>believe</u> always

occurs in underlying structures like those for <u>prefer</u>. Then
sentence (9.39), with an infinitive following <u>believe</u>, would
have an underlying structure in which the embedded sentence
is in the NP object:

(9.55)

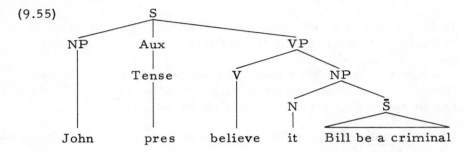

(We will discuss in a moment the question of what complementizer appears in these cases.) Such an underlying structure would account for the occurrence of sentences such as
(9.51) derived by <u>There</u> Insertion. Underlying this would be
(9.56):

(9.56)

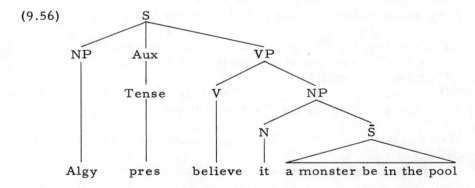

<u>There</u> Insertion could apply in the embedded S, and it would be
unnecessary to generate <u>there</u> as the object of the matrix S.
    The arguments <u>against</u> a structure such as (9.55) all hold
for <u>the stage in the derivation after There Insertion</u>; they involve a demonstration that certain transformational rules apply
to <u>believe</u> sentences later in the derivation in a way that suggests a structure similar to <u>force</u>:

(9.57)

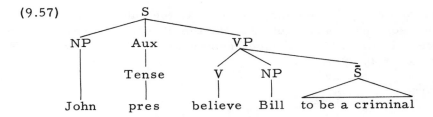

If, at the stage when Passive applies, this is the structure for sentence (9.39), it explains why (9.58a) is a grammatical sentence and (9.58b) is not:

(9.58) a.   Bill is believed by John to be a criminal.
       b.   *(For) Bill to be a criminal is believed by John.

In other words, if <u>believe</u> originates in <u>prefer</u>-type structures but ends up in <u>force</u>-type structures, then we can account for its apparently contradictory properties.

     In order to accomplish the transformation of structures like (9.55) into structures like (9.57), a new rule will have to be added to the grammar in order to <u>raise</u> the subject of the complement of <u>believe</u> into the matrix sentence, so that it becomes the object of <u>believe</u>. At the same time, the remainder of the complement sentence will have to be detached from the object NP and moved to a position directly under VP. To illustrate this process, let us assume that the complementizer present in the deep structure of <u>believe + infinitive</u> constructions is <u>for-to</u>. This means that the sentence <u>John believes Bill to be a criminal</u> would derive from the structure shown in (9.59a).

(9.59) a.

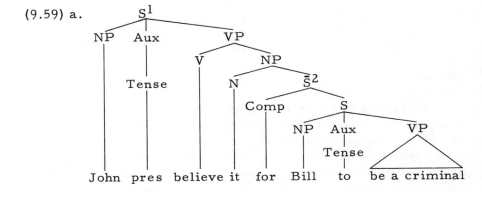

The new rule proposed above will raise the subject of the embedded sentence, substituting it for the pronoun it, while movin the remainder of the embedded sentence out from under the NP node, as in (9.59b).

(9.59) b.

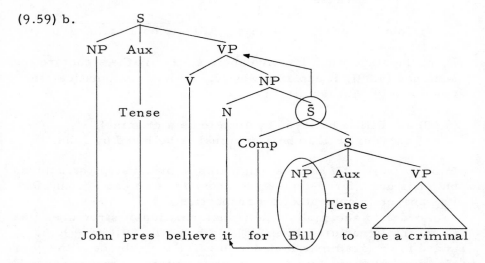

The output of such a rule operating on (9.59a) would be (9.59c).

(9.59) c.

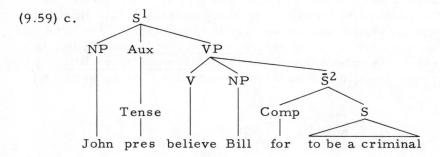

(We will assume that the embedded S̄ ends up under VP rather than S.)

At this stage the former subject of the complement sentence has become the direct object of the verb in the higher sentence. In the remaining complement sentence, now under the main VP node, the complementizer for is directly adjacent to to, and, as we have already seen in cases of Equi, under these circumstances for deletes. We will assume that whenever a complementizer is deleted, the node S̄ is also automatically deleted, and we arrive at (9.59d):

(9.59) d.

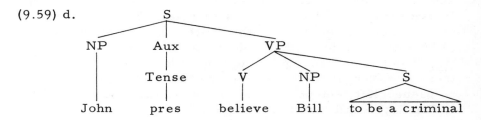

The embedded S and its subject do not change linear order relative to any other constituent: they are simply regrouped into a new constituent structure.

The rule transforming (9.59a) into (9.59c) can be referred to as Raising to Object (indicating, in part, the effect of the rule), and it is often simply called Raising (see section 9.5 for discussion of another rule quite similar to Raising to Object). The statement of this rule has been the subject of controversy in the literature. Some linguists have proposed that structures such as (9.59a) must first undergo Extraposition, to remove S̄2 from the domination of NP, and then a rule of It Replacement, which raises the complement subject and substitutes it for it in the preceding structure. However, other linguists have argued that structures such as (9.59a) are transformed in one step into structures such as (9.59c) and claim that Extraposition plays no role in the derivation of (9.59c). We will assume the latter view here but will leave the formalization of Raising to Object as an open question at this point. The reader can investigate the various formulations of the rule cited in the literature given in the suggested readings for this chapter.

Now let us summarize how our analysis of the verb believe accounts for the facts we have examined in this section. First of all, believe is a verb that may occur either with that or for-to complements, and it occurs in deep structures like those for prefer, e.g., (9.59a). If believe occurs with a that clause, rules such as Passive may apply to the complement as a whole (see chapter 8). On the other hand, if believe occurs with a for-to complement, then the rule of Raising to Object must apply, i.e., a structure such as (9.59a) is obligatorily transformed into a structure like (9.59c). Notice that if Raising to Object were not obligatory, then ungrammatical sentences would result, such as *John believes for Bill to be careless. We assume that Raising to Object precedes both the Passive Rule and the process of pseudocleft formation. Given this ordering, Passive may apply to structures such as (9.59c), fronting the direct object of believe. Furthermore, by the time structure (9.59c) has been formed, the deep structure NP object of believe has been broken up by the rule of Raising to Object, and there is no longer an NP dominating the complement S. Hence, no pseudocleft sentence can be formed in the manner of (9.44).

Finally, recall that There Insertion may apply within the complement sentence of believe (cf. (9.56)). Since believe originates in a structure like that for prefer, we have every reason to suppose that There Insertion may apply within the complement; after that rule has applied, the rule of Raising to Object can operate. Hence, sentences such as (9.51) can be derived.

Notice that Raising to Object, like Dative Movement, appears to be a governed rule. That is, it must only apply to a special class of verbs, such as believe, acknowledge, or understand, and not to prefer, want, hate, etc., which are analyzed as having the same deep structure. It is the fact that Raising to Object applies only to the former class that accounts for the differential behavior of these two classes of verbs with respect to the Passive Transformation, among others. If we could avoid having to make Raising to Object a governed rule but could predict whether it would apply to a verb on the basis of other facts about that verb, this would add considerably to the explanatory value of our account, but at present we are unable to motivate any deeper explanation of these differences.

The rule of Raising to Object, whether governed or not, together with underlying structures such as (9.59a) for believe, will account for all the relevant data in a very natural way. The goal set out at the beginning of this section has been achieved: we have provided satisfactory analyses for sentences like (9.39), as well as those like (9.40a) and (9.40b) (repeated here):

(9.39) John believes Bill to be a criminal.

(9.40) a. John prefers Bill to be a criminal.
       b. John forced Bill to be a criminal.

According to our analysis, (9.39) and (9.40a) are alike in underlying form (and are unlike (9.40b) at that level). Raising to

Object then applies to (9.39). As a result, the tree for that example resembles the structure of (9.40b) by the time Passive applies. The fact that believe acts like prefer on the one hand and like force on the other is now accounted for by generating believe in prefer-type structures and then transforming those trees (by Raising to Object) into force-type structures. The rule of Raising to Object is therefore well-motivated to the extent that it provides the only satisfactory way of generating the observed patterns of grammaticality for sentences containing believe with an infinitive.

9.5. MORE VERB CLASSES

It has emerged from our discussion so far that the verbs prefer, believe, and force appear in surface structures that are virtually identical; yet they are generated in underlying structures that are radically different. The surface similarities, we have argued, can be attributed to the operation of rules such as Equi and Raising to Object, which have the effect of removing complement subjects either by deletion (Equi) or by movement into the matrix sentence (Raising to Object). The differentiation of verb classes along the lines we have discussed is one of the most interesting results of transformational syntax, since nowhere else is the distinction between surface and underlying form more striking.

In this section we will examine some other classes of verbs, showing once again that similar surface forms actually derive from quite disparate underlying forms. We will concentrate on the following kinds of sentences:

(9.60) a. John prefers to be at the party.
b. John condescended to be at the party.
c. John seems to be at the party.

As we shall see, the evidence for differentiating among the verbs prefer, condescend, and seem is quite similar to the evidence we have already discussed for prefer, force, and believe, and we will therefore only sketch the arguments.

In many respects, in sentences such as (9.60b, c) condescend and seem appear to be very similar in behavior—and quite different from prefer. For one thing, neither of these two new verbs can appear with an additional (for) NP between the verb and to:

(9.61)
$*$John $\begin{Bmatrix} \text{seemed} \\ \text{condescended} \end{Bmatrix}$ (for) Bill to swim underwater.

(9.62) John preferred (for) Bill to swim underwater.

Second, neither can appear in passive or pseudocleft constructions or with plain NPs in the way that <u>prefer</u> can:

(9.63) a.
To swim underwater would be $\begin{Bmatrix} *\text{seemed} \\ *\text{condescended} \\ \text{preferred} \end{Bmatrix}$ by few of us.

b.
What John $\begin{Bmatrix} *\text{seemed} \\ *\text{condescended} \\ \text{preferred} \end{Bmatrix}$ was to swim underwater.

c.
John $\begin{Bmatrix} *\text{seemed} \\ *\text{condescended} \\ \text{preferred} \end{Bmatrix}$ the oysters.

These facts might be explained in a number of ways. One method would be to postulate underlying structures for both <u>seem</u> and <u>condescend</u> that were very similar to those for <u>prefer</u> (i.e., structures in which an embedded S followed immediately after the verb). We would have to permit Equi to apply, just as it does for <u>prefer</u> (i.e., with the subject of the higher S as the controller), but with two crucial changes:

(i) Both <u>seem</u> and <u>condescend</u> would be like <u>force</u> in that any tree containing them would <u>necessarily</u> meet the SD of Equi and hence have to undergo that rule, and

(ii) with both <u>seem</u> and <u>condescend</u>, again as with <u>force</u>, the embedded S would be dominated directly by VP and not by an NP.

The underlying tree for (9.60b, c), for example, would then be roughly as shown in (9.64). How would the two stipulations listed as (i) and (ii) above help to provide an account of the data in (9.61)-(9.63)?

(9.64)

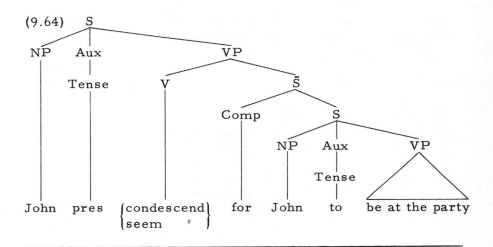

If seem and condescend obligatorily met the SD of Equi, then sentences like (9.61) would never occur (they would be directly excluded by that requirement). In fact, they would be excluded in precisely the same way as examples like *John forced Bill (for) Mary to be at the party. The second requirement, that the S be directly dominated by VP, would obviously prevent the Passive and Pseudocleft Rules from applying (since they apply to NPs). Since seem and condescend would be marked +[___ S̄] and not +[___ NP] in the lexicon, to permit them to be entered in tree (9.64), we would not expect them to occur with ordinary NP objects. (Recall that we analyzed force as having an S̄ directly dominated by VP, following its ordinary NP direct object; thus, if our accounts are correct, there appears to be at least some sort of correlation between the obligatory application of Equi and the appearance of an S̄ directly dominated by the VP.)

The analysis just sketched seems in fact to be more or less justified for condescend, but it will not work for seem. In fact, we need only one example to show this:

(9.65) There seem to be several alligators waiting for John.

How does this sentence show that the analysis for condescend will not work for seem?

Under an analysis similar to that proposed for condescend,
(9.65) would have a deep structure that could be represented
roughly as (9.66):

(9.66)

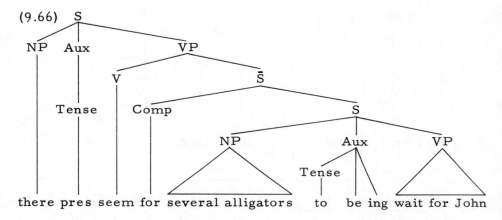

there pres seem for several alligators   to   be ing wait for John

However, since there appears only as a result of the application of There Insertion, the PS rules will not generate tree
(9.66). In particular, they would not insert there as the underlying subject of seem. Hence, this grammar wrongly predicts
that (9.65) is not a possible sentence. It is easy to show that
this is in fact the right result for condescend. Find an example that supports our analysis of condescend in this respect.

Any example in which existential there is the subject of condescend will demonstrate the point, for example:

(9.67) *There condescended to be several of the committee
        at the door.

Our rules would never generate a tree such as (9.66), and we
would need one like it in the relevant aspects in order to derive (9.67). Our analysis of condescend (as a verb undergoing
Equi controlled by its subject) therefore predicts the ungrammaticality of (9.67) and is, to that extent, confirmed. At the
same time, of course, (9.65) demonstrates that that analysis
cannot possibly be right for seem.
    Now recall how we were led to analyze believe in order to
derive such sentences as John believes there to be several

tomatoes in his cereal. After we apply There Insertion in the embedded S, Several tomatoes are in his cereal, the derived subject of be becomes the object of believe by Raising to Object. Can a similar "raising" solution work for a sentence with seem, such as (9.65)?

In thinking about this question, it is obviously necessary to consider how a sentential complement for seem would be generated in the first place. For some time now, we have been looking at cases in which the embedded S is generated within VP, to the right of the main verb of the matrix sentence; there are indeed sentences containing seem in which a whole embedded sentence occurs to its right:

(9.68) It seems that John was at the party.

However, in such cases notice that the surface subject has to be it:

(9.69) *Bill seems that John was at the party.

In light of this fact, a possible analysis of the underlying structure of (9.68) is (9.70):

(9.70) a.

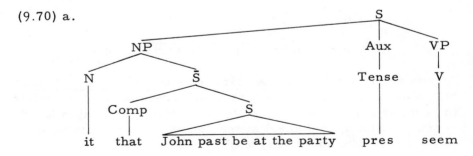

Rather surprisingly, according to this analysis seem is an underlying intransitive verb that takes a complement sentence as its subject. If no transformations apply to this tree (except for It Deletion), an ungrammatical sentence results:

(9.71) *That John was at the party seems.

Therefore we would have to claim that the verb <u>seem</u>, in a
structure such as (9.70a), <u>requires</u> the application of the rule
of Extraposition, to produce (9.70b):

(9.70) b.

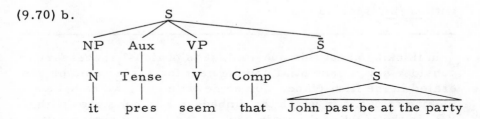

After the application of rules such as Affix Hopping, we are
left with sentence (9.68).

Now how could we derive sentences such as (9.60c), <u>John
seems to be at the party</u>? The sentential subject in a structure
such as (9.70a) could contain the complementizer <u>for-to</u> instead of <u>that</u>:

(9.72) a.

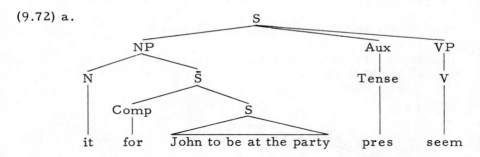

At this point we will assume that a rule of <u>Raising to Subject</u>
obligatorily applies, a rule that would have the effect of raising
the complement subject (substituting it for <u>it</u>) and adjoining the
remnant of the complement at the end of the VP. Raising to
Subject operating on (9.72a) would produce (9.72b):

(9.72) b.

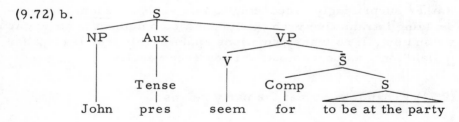

We must assume that Raising to Subject is obligatory, like
Raising to Object; otherwise, structures such as (9.72a) would
result in ungrammatical sentences:

(9.73) *For John to be at the party seems.

Although the operation of Raising to Subject is fairly clear,
we will nevertheless leave the formalization of the rule as an
open question, as we did with Raising to Object. A number of
linguists have supposed that Raising to Subject and Raising to
Object are in fact the same transformation, while others have
maintained that the two rules are distinct and should be kept
separate. Naturally, the formalization of Raising to Subject
will vary quite radically depending on whether or not it is collapsed with Raising to Object, and there is little point in formalizing the rule until the deeper issues concerning Raising
are better understood. (We will assume that Raising to Subject
is distinct from Raising to Object, but once again we refer the
reader to the suggested readings for literature dealing with the
Raising controversy.)

Like Raising to Object, Raising to Subject is a governed rule;
that is, it will apply only to a special class of verbs including
seem. Other verbs in this class are happen and appear, so that
the analysis of sentences such as John happened to be at the
party or John appeared to be at the party will be analogous to
that of sentences with seem.

Now notice that this analysis of seem, which we have presented in a rather arbitrary fashion, permits us to account for
sentence (9.65), There seem to be several alligators waiting
for John, in the same way that the rule of Raising to Object
permitted us to account for John believes there to be alligators
in the pool, for example. Since the surface subject of seem in
(9.65) is raised into that position by the rule of Raising to Subject, this sentence will automatically be generated by a grammar containing that rule. We will not demonstrate this in detail. Nor will we show in detail how our present analysis accounts for the similarities between condescend and seem exemplified in (9.61) and (9.63). We leave it as an exercise for
the reader to confirm that it does indeed account for these
similarities—and hence that entirely different analyses of
seem and condescend can account both for the basic difference

between these verbs exhibited by examples (9.65) and (9.67) and for the similarity in their behavior shown by (9.61) and (9.63).

CHAPTER 9: APPENDIX
A REVIEW OF THE EVIDENCE

In this chapter we have been distinguishing verbs into different classes. We have seen numerous cases in which verbs occur on the surface with reduced, i.e., infinitival, complements:

(A9.1) a. I would prefer to leave. (Equi)
   b. I wouldn't condescend to leave. (Equi)
   c. John seems to have left. (Raising to Subject)
   d. I believe Mary to be brilliant. (Raising to Object)
   e. I forced John to be careful. (Equi)

Each of these complements lacks a subject; in some cases Equi has deleted the subject, but in other cases the Raising Rules have moved the subject into the matrix sentence. On the other hand, in a sentence such as (A9.1f) none of these rules has applied, and the embedded sentence is intact.

(A9.1) f. I would prefer (for) John to leave.

The underlying structures we have arrived at can be summarized as follows:

(A9.2) prefer (want, hate, like, hope, desire, love)

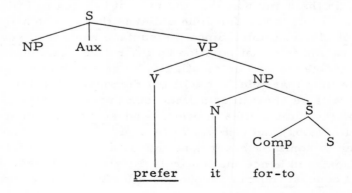

The rules of Equi (controlled by the higher subject) and <u>For</u> Deletion operate to produce surface forms such as <u>We want to leave</u> and <u>They hate to sing</u>. Surface forms such as <u>I want John to leave</u> and <u>I would prefer (for) Mary to go</u> are derived from essentially the same underlying structure, but since the subject of the higher S and that of the lower S are not coreferential, Equi does not apply and (in some cases) the deletion of <u>for</u> is optional.

(A9.3) <u>force</u> (<u>persuade</u>, <u>allow</u>, <u>coax</u>, <u>help</u>, <u>order</u>, <u>permit</u>, <u>make</u>, <u>cause</u>)

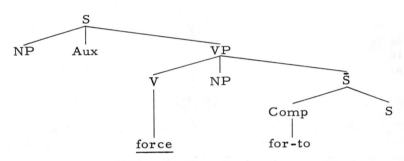

The rules of Equi (controlled by the higher object) and <u>For</u> Deletion operate to produce surface forms for this class such as <u>We forced them to sing</u> and <u>Bill coaxed Sam to eat bagels</u>. For this class, the SD of Equi <u>must</u> be met.

(A9.4) <u>believe</u> (<u>assume</u>, <u>know</u>, <u>perceive</u>, <u>find</u>, <u>prove</u>, <u>understand</u>, <u>imagine</u>)

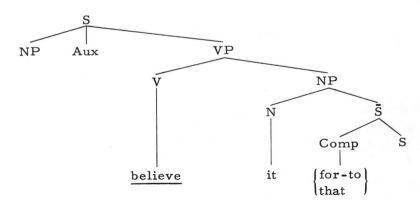

When <u>that</u> is the complementizer, sentences such as <u>We be-lieve that the world is round</u> are generated. When <u>for-to</u> is the complementizer, Raising to Object and <u>For</u> Deletion ob-ligatorily operate to produce sentences such as <u>We believe him to be a fool</u> and <u>The court proved him to be an addict.</u>

(A9.5) <u>condescend</u> (<u>dare</u>, <u>endeavor</u>, <u>fail</u>, <u>manage</u>, <u>proceed</u>, <u>refuse</u>)

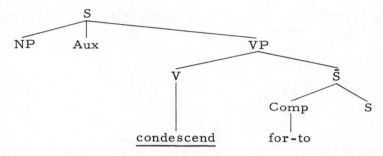

Equi (controlled by the higher subject) and <u>For</u> Deletion ob-ligatorily apply to such structures to produce sentences such as <u>He condescended to sing</u> and <u>He failed to do his work.</u>

(A9.6) <u>seem</u> (<u>appear</u>, <u>happen</u>, <u>be likely</u>, <u>be certain</u>, <u>turn out</u>)

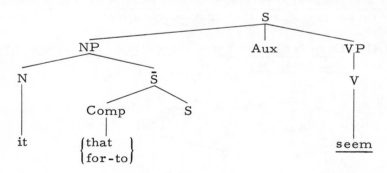

When <u>that</u> is the complementizer, Extraposition applies (ob-ligatorily for this class of verbs) to produce sentences such as <u>It seems that I am sick.</u> When <u>for-to</u> is the complementizer, then Raising to Subject must apply, to produce sentences such as <u>I seem to be sick.</u>

The analyses we have discussed here were arrived at by examining the following kinds of evidence:

A. The Passive Transformation: For some verbs, like prefer, the entire complement may be fronted by Passive, while for others, such as force, this is not possible. On the other hand, verbs such as force allow their direct objects to undergo Passive. Believe patterns with force in this regard, in contrast to prefer, but only because the embedded subject has been raised into the object position of the matrix sentence.

The Passive Transformation gives us an indication as to the NP status of a complement only at the point in the derivation at which the Passive Rule applies. For example, the complement of believe + infinitive constructions will not undergo Passive: *For John to be a fool is believed by us. Nevertheless, we still analyze believe as taking an underlying NP-dominated complement (see (9.55)). The rule of Raising to Object operates to break up the NP complement by the time Passive applies; this explains why no passives such as *For John to be a fool is believed by us can be formed. Thus, if a verb does allow its complement to undergo Passive, we have a good indication that the complement is dominated by NP. If the verb does not allow Passive to operate on the complement, however, we know only that the complement is not dominated by NP at the point where Passive applies; we do not necessarily know that the complement was not dominated by NP in underlying structure. Further evidence would be needed at that point to decide the issue.

B. The Pseudocleft Construction: If the complement of a verb can appear after be in a pseudocleft construction, then it is generally assumed that the complement must be dominated by NP. Again, that the complement cannot appear after be does not necessarily show that the complement was not dominated by NP in underlying structure. Believe does not appear in pseudocleft sentences such as *What I believe is John to be a fool. Nevertheless, in underlying structure it occurs with an NP that dominates its complement sentence. Here again, the rule of Raising to Object has operated to break up the complement structure, so that no pseudocleft construction can be formed. Thus, we can use the test positively but not neces-

sarily negatively: if a verb occurs in a pseudocleft construction and its complement appears after be, then the complement
is dominated by NP; however, the fact that the verb does not
allow this possibility only shows that at some point in the derivation the complement is not dominated by NP; it does not
necessarily show us anything about the underlying structure
of the complement.

C. Occurrence with Simple NPs: Almost all verbs that have
complements dominated by NP can also occur with simple NPs
in that position: I believe that John left vs. I believe the story.
One exception is the verb seem: although we analyze it as
taking an underlying NP subject, there are no sentences such
as *The story seems.

D. There Insertion: If existential there occurs as the object of
a verb (I believe there to be a lot of problems with this) or as
the subject of a verb other than be (There seem to have been
many people here), then we have a good indication that the
Raising Rules have operated. This is simply because good
arguments exist that there should only be introduced by the
rule of There Insertion, which will place it in subject position
only when the verb be is present. Hence, there cannot be generated as an object or as the subject of verbs other than be.
(Of course, there does occur with prefer, as in I would prefer
there to be less noise. Sentences such as this one do not show
that Raising has taken place; rather, for has been optionally
deleted and there is simply the subject of the embedded S.)

E. Change in Meaning Caused by Passive Operating on the
Complement: Sentences such as John forced the doctor to examine Bill and John forced Bill to be examined by the doctor
are different in meaning. We account for this difference by
assigning these sentences different underlying structures, as
long as we analyze force as in (A9.3) above. The sentences I
believe the doctor to have examined John and I believe John to
have been examined by the doctor are synonymous. We can account for this, since both sentences derive from a single underlying structure, namely, (A9.4). When Passive changes
meaning in this way, it is usually a good indication that the
verb class in question takes Equi in its derivation.

We have by no means exhausted the set of verb classes or
the possibilities for assigning underlying structures to them,
nor have we utilized the full range of evidence that has been
used in recent research on complementation. We invite the
reader to use the sort of evidence listed above to discover
further verb classes in the exercises that follow. We will not
deal further with such questions, for the reader is now in possession of the principal analytical tools needed to explore the
structure of complex sentences in greater detail.

CHAPTER 9: EXERCISES
(E9.1) For each of the following sentences, provide an underlying structure and show in a step by step fashion, using tree
diagrams, what transformations apply in the derivation:

(i)   The board found him to be hated by all his colleagues.
(ii) It seems that John is expected by the committee to resign.
(iii) I would hate to be expected to be there on time.
(iv) There happens to be a frog in the tank.
(v)   Bill seems to have forced Mary to leave.
(vi) The world is believed by most scientists to be round.

(E9.2) Consider the verb <u>try</u> in sentences such as the following:

(i) a. Herb tried to eat the banana.
    b. Some people try to be arrested by the police.

<u>A</u>. What underlying structure should be assigned to these sen-
tences, and what rules operate in their derivation?

<u>B</u>. Provide specific evidence for the hypothesis you have formed
in (A). In doing so, compare your analysis of <u>try</u> with the analyses of <u>prefer</u>, <u>seem</u>, and <u>condescend</u> presented in the text. In
what way(s) is <u>try</u> similar to each of these verbs, and in what
way(s) does it differ? To answer this, refer to specific tests
we have formulated in this chapter. The following data (along
with data of your own) should also be considered in your answer:

(ii) a. *John tried for Bill to leave.
      b. John tried to leave.

(iii) *There tried to be an explosion yesterday.
(iv) ?What he tried was to read the book in two hours.
(v)   We will certainly try this plan.

(E9.3) Consider the verb <u>tend</u> in sentences such as the following:

(i)   Doctors <u>tend</u> to recommend aspirin more often.

Provide an underlying structure for sentence (i), and show
what rules operate in its derivation. Justify your analysis as
you did in exercise (E9.2). The following data, and any other
data you find, should be considered in your answer:

(ii) a.   Gentlemen tend to prefer blondes.
      b. *To prefer blondes is tended by gentlemen.
      c. *What gentlemen tend is to prefer blondes.
(iii) a.   An increase in salaries tends to cause inflation.
      b.   Inflation tends to be caused by an increase in
           salaries.
(iv)   There tend to be fewer smokers these days.

If your analysis of <u>tend</u> is correct, then you should be able to
explain the difference between the following two sentences:

(v)   a. *It tends that gentlemen prefer blondes.
      b.   It tends to be true that gentlemen prefer blondes.

Why is (vb) possible, but not (va)?

(E9.4) Consider the class of verbs of "temporal aspect,"
which includes <u>begin</u>, <u>start</u>, <u>commence</u>, <u>continue</u>, <u>resume</u>,
<u>keep</u>, <u>stop</u>, <u>finish</u>, etc., in sentences such as the following:

(i)   John began to read Dante's <u>Inferno</u>.
(ii) They started running down the road.
(iii) Herb kept singing the final act of <u>The Magic Flute</u>.
(iv) He finally stopped making a nuisance of himself.
(v)   There began to be a pain in his right leg.

In terms of the kinds of evidence discussed in this chapter,
how should the above verbs be analyzed? That is, what under-

lying structure would be plausible for the above sentences (and others like them), and why? What transformations should operate in the derivation of these sentences? In what way are these verbs similar to—or different from—the verbs prefer, seem, and condescend? (Answer this exercise as you did exercises (E9.2) and (E9.3).)

(E9.5) So far in our work on complementation, we have discussed clear cases in which verbs are either of the sort that undergoes Equi or of the type that undergoes Raising. However, some verbs might be analyzed in both ways, i.e., as deriving from two distinct sources, one operated on by Equi and the other by Raising to Object. Use the following data (and any other data you may find) concerning the verb expect to show why it has to be analyzed in two distinct ways: i.e., that it must be analyzed both like prefer and like believe.

(i)   a. None of us expected John to resign suddenly.
      b. For John to resign suddenly was expected by none of us.
      c. What none of us expected was for John to resign
         suddenly.
      d. None of us expected this situation.
(ii) a. We expect Nixon to resign immediately.
      b. We expect to resign immediately.
      c. We expect Nixon to be investigated thoroughly.
      d. We expect to be investigated thoroughly.
(iii) a. They expected Bill to leave the country.
      b. Bill was expected by them to leave the country.
      c. Someone expected there to be a full house.
      d. There was expected to be a full house.

In answering this question, specify carefully in what ways expect is similar to prefer on the one hand and believe on the other hand.

(E9.6) Classify the following verbs according to their complementizers (for-to, poss-ing, or that) and deep structures; state also whether they take Equi or Raising.

allow	order
happen	warn
decide	dismay

recommend	distress
tempt	decide
seem	tell
advise	continue
manage	incite
begin	remind

CHAPTER 9: SUGGESTED READINGS

The analysis of verbs such as prefer, force, believe, condescend, and seem into distinct syntactic classes is among the most interesting arguments in the syntax of complementation. The first comprehensive treatment of this area within the transformational literature is Rosenbaum (1967), which deals with the sorts of evidence we have examined in this chapter (and which is, in many ways, still the most detailed treatment of this area of complementation). In addition, it may be valuable for the reader to begin working through Burt (1971), parts III and IV. Although those sections cover material we have not yet discussed, they should provide some review of what we have done here and will aid in anticipating work that we cover in the next chapter. The assumptions and analyses in Burt (1971) are not always those we have adopted here, and a good exercise would be to specify precisely how our treatment of complementation so far differs from that of Burt and how the two treatments in turn compare with Rosenbaum (1967). Perlmutter (1970) is also quite relevant to the concerns of this chapter, in that it examines the various syntactic contexts in which the verb begin can be found. A criticism of Rosenbaum's (1967) theory of complementation can be found in Lakoff (1966).

In regard to the controversy concerning the rule(s) of Raising, Rosenbaum (1967) first proposed that Raising be stated as a single rule but that Extraposition should apply in the derivation of all sentences with Raising. (Rosenbaum refers to the rule of Raising as Pronoun Substitution.) Lakoff (1966) criticizes this view and argues that Raising does not involve Extraposition at any stage of the derivation. In the same paper, Lakoff notes the problems of stating Raising (which he refers to as It Replacement) as a single rule. Further modifications of the rule of Raising can be found in Kiparsky and Kiparsky (1971). McCawley (1970) argues that the rule of Raising provides evidence relating to underlying word order in English and assumes a unified statement of the rule. Chomsky (1973) questions the existence of the rule of Raising to Object, and Postal (1974) attempts to provide arguments in favor of the rule. The latter reference is a particularly valuable source of relevant data and interesting hypotheses about Raising. Arguments that Raising to Subject and Raising to Object are distinct rules are provided in Szamosi (1973), with some discussion of the issue in Berman (1974).

The rule of Equi was proposed and discussed by Rosenbaum (1967), and that work, along with Rosenbaum (1970), discusses the so-called "control problem," i. e., the problem of determining which matrix NP deletes the complement subject. Rosenbaum proposes what he terms the <u>Minimal Distance Principle</u>, but this is criticized by Postal (1970, 437-448). The article by Postal not only provides a good deal of data concerning the control problem but also discusses the general arguments in favor of a rule of Equi.

An alternative to the rule of Equi is discussed by Jackendoff (1972), who argues that complements with missing subjects are not derived by a deletion rule such as Equi but are essentially generated with "empty" subjects.

As the reader progresses and masters the basic readings on complementation, it would be worthwhile to examine Bresnan (1970) and Emonds (1970). Both works provide detailed criticisms of previous research on complementation and propose important new ideas on the subject. The theory of complementation applied to languages other than English can be found in R. Lakoff (1968), which discusses Latin, and Kayne (to appear), which discusses French.

COMPLEX ORDERING OF RULES

10.1. THE CYCLE

In the last section of chapter 9 we saw how the rules of Equi
and Raising to Subject could account for the difference in behavior between condescend and seem. We must now consider
whether both rules can operate within a single derivation and,
if so, how they are ordered. That both can operate in one derivation is shown by examples (10.1) and (10.2).

(10.1) John appears to want to know physics.

(10.2) John wants to appear to know physics.

The structure underlying (10.1) would be roughly as shown in
(10.3).

(10.3)

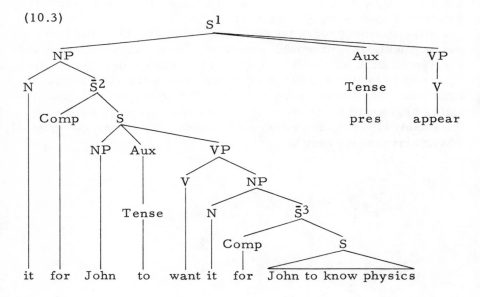

(See the discussion of seem in chapter 9.) Let us assume that
the rule of Equi precedes Raising to Subject. It will delete the
occurrence of John in the complement of want in (10.4a) and
(10.4b).

(10.4) a. it - [for John to want it [for <u>John</u> to know physics]] -
          pres - appear

                                    $\downarrow$ <u>Equi</u>

(10.4) b. it - [for John to want it [for _____ to know physics]] -
          pres - appear

The higher occurrence of <u>John</u>, which is the subject of <u>want</u>,
can now be raised into the subject position of the highest sentence by the rule of Raising to Subject, while the remainder
of the complement is placed at the end of VP:

(10.4) c.
John - pres - appear [for _____ to want [for _____ to know physics]]

          Raising to Subject

<u>For</u> Deletion will apply, yielding the desired output, (10.1)
<u>John appears to want to know physics</u>; thus, it seems to be
possible to give the rules the order (1) Equi (2) Raising to
Subject.
     However, in order to establish that the rules are strictly
ordered, we must show that the opposite ordering has unacceptable consequences. Let us now try to apply the rules in
the opposite order to the same underlying structure, (10.3).
The derivation starts as shown in (10.5):

(10.5) a. it - [for John to want it [for John to know physics]] -
          pres - appear

                    $\downarrow$ Raising to Subject

     b. John - pres - appear [for _____ to want it [for John to
        know physics]]

Now we must try to apply Equi, but a problem has arisen.
Raising to Subject has had the effect of moving the NP <u>John</u>
into the highest structure, so that it is no longer the subject
of <u>want</u>:

(10.6)

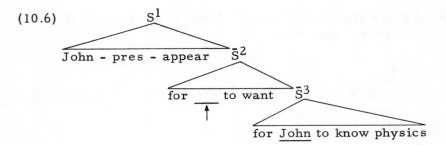

Can Equi now apply to delete the occurrence of <u>John</u> in $\bar{S}^3$?

Given the way we have discussed Equi so far, the rule should
not be able to operate on tree (10.6). In structures containing
main verbs such as <u>want</u>, the controller of Equi must be the
<u>subject</u> of the main verb. However, in (10.6) the verb <u>want</u> has
no subject—it has been raised into the higher sentence, S^1.
Therefore, Equi could not apply here and an unacceptable sentence would result: *<u>John appears to want John to know physics</u>.
What if we were to modify our assumptions about Equi at this
point, in order to allow it to operate on a structure such as
(10.6)? If we allowed <u>John</u> in $\bar{S}^3$ to delete under identity with
<u>John</u> in S^1, the desired output could be generated.

However, we do not in general want to permit the controller
NP to be the subject of a sentence higher than <u>want</u>. To see
why, consider what would happen if our grammar had generated
the (highly schematized) structure shown in (10.7).

(10.7)

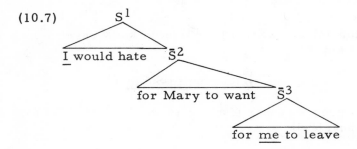

<u>I would hate it for Mary to want me to leave</u>.

This is a perfectly well formed sentence. Notice, however,
that the subject of $\bar{S}^3$ is identical with the subject of S^1 (since

we count I and me as identical for purposes of coreference).
What if we allowed Equi to operate in this case, in such a way
that me in $\bar{S}^3$ were deleted under identity with I in the sentence
higher than want? What sentence would be derived? What prob-
lem(s) can you see with this derivation?

It should be clear that Equi would produce the following output:

(10.8) I would hate [for Mary to want [for ___ to leave]]

Although (10.8) represents a completely grammatical sentence—
I would hate for Mary to want to leave—it has entirely the wrong
meaning for the deep structure from which we have just derived
it. In sentence (10.8) only Mary can be understood as the subject of leave—i.e., it can mean only that Mary would do the
leaving (and can never mean that I would do the leaving). Yet,
if (10.8) were derived from structure (10.7), and if Equi operated as shown, then we would predict that it should have the
same meaning as (10.7)—assuming that transformations do not
change meaning. And there is no justification at all for thinking
that they change meaning in the radical way that would be required to derive (10.8) from (10.7). However, if we continue
to restrict the rule of Equi so that the controller of the deletion must always be exactly one sentence up, then the rule
would never apply to (10.7), and that structure could result
only in I would hate (for) Mary to want me to leave, never I
would hate (for) Mary to want to leave.
   If Equi is restricted, the rule will be unable to operate on
(10.6). Since we are currently ordering Raising to Subject before Equi, the underlying subject of want (which should control
Equi) has already been raised into a position two sentences
higher than the NP to be deleted. The restriction that was
needed to block Equi from applying to the subject of hate and
the subject of the lowest S in (10.7) will automatically prevent
Equi from operating in (10.6). This would prevent us from
deriving (10.1), John appears to want to know physics. The
first ordering, in which Equi applied first, had no bad consequences. Our attempt to apply the rules in the opposite order
prevents us from deriving the desired output. Therefore, on
the basis of example (10.1) we must conclude that the rules

are strictly ordered as (1) Equi and (2) Raising to Subject.
  Let us now turn our attention to example (10.2), the underlying structure for which must be (10.9).

(10.9)

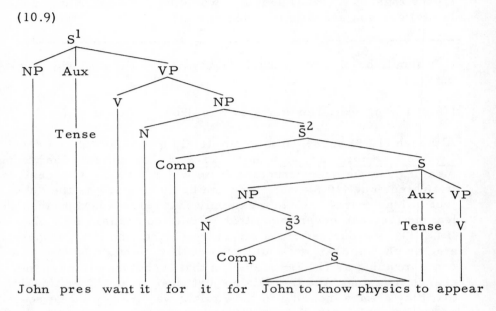

John pres want it   for it   for John to know physics to appear

We have just established that Equi must apply before Raising to
Subject. But it cannot apply to (10.9), since the only NP that
could be deleted is the lower occurrence of John in $\bar{\bar{S}}^3$, which
is more than one sentence down from the potential controller
in S^1. Therefore, the SD of Equi is not met, the rule does not
apply, and we proceed to Raising to Subject. This has the ef-
fect of moving the lowest occurrence of John (in $\bar{\bar{S}}^3$) into the next
higher sentence, $\bar{\bar{S}}^2$, making it the derived subject of appear as
shown in (10.10).

(10.10) John - pres - want - it [for John to appear [for ___ to
        know physics]]

Since we are following the order (1) Equi/(2) Raising to Subject,
we cannot now apply the former rule, and we are left with *John
wants (for) John to appear to know physics—which is unacceptable on the intended reading, where the two instances of John
are coreferential.

However, if we <u>reverse</u> the order of the rules, then our derivation works out without any complications:

(10.11) a. John - pres - want - it [for it [for John to know
          physics] to appear]

          ↓ <u>Raising to Subject</u>

       b. John - pres - want - it [for John to appear [for ___
          to know physics]]

          ↓ <u>Equi</u>

       c. John - pres - want - it [for ___ to appear [for ___
          to know physics]]

After <u>For</u> Deletion and other relevant rules have applied, we
derive <u>John wants to appear to know physics</u>. In this derivation,
Raising to Subject (operating on (10.11a) has had the effect of
moving the NP <u>John</u> from the lowest sentence into the next higher
one, putting it in a position from which it can then be deleted by
Equi.
     But now we have reached an ordering paradox. In order to
derive sentence (10.1), we found that we needed to apply Equi
first, followed by Raising to Subject, and that the opposite ordering would not work. Yet, in order to derive sentence (10.2),
we need to apply Raising to Subject first, followed by Equi. It
is time to examine more carefully some of our assumptions
about rule ordering.
     When we discussed rule ordering in chapter 6, recall that we
had not dealt with any complex sentences. Here our ordering
paradox has arisen with two rules that "cross" sentence bound-
aries. Equi deletes the subject of a lower sentence on the basis
of some NP in the next higher sentence, while Raising to Subject
raises an NP from a lower sentence into the next higher sentence. This suggests that the problem of ordering these rules
results from the way we have assumed rules apply to complex
sentences. For we have been assuming, in demonstrating the
existence of an ordering paradox, that transformations apply
at once to <u>all</u> the relevant places in a tree where their SDs are
met—i.e., that rules may scan the entire tree structure at
once.
     Instead, we might apply the rules in a <u>cyclic</u> fashion, first
to the most deeply embedded S in a tree, then to the next higher

sentence, and so on, working our way "from the bottom up." Then, given the following sort of tree, all the rules that could be applied would first apply to $\bar{S}^3$, in their proper order, then to $\bar{S}^2$, and finally to S^1, as illustrated in (10.12).

(10.12)

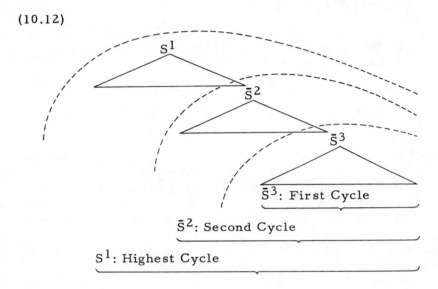

$\bar{S}^3$: First Cycle

$\bar{S}^2$: Second Cycle

S^1: Highest Cycle

In each <u>cycle</u>, the rules apply only to the sentence that forms that cycle; some rules, e.g., Equi, will apply to certain material in lower sentences as well. However, on a given cycle the rules may not utilize any material from higher sentences.

If we assume that rules apply cyclically, then we can apply the rules of Equi and Raising to Subject in one fixed order and thus entirely avoid the rule ordering paradox. Consider again the underlying structure for <u>John appears to want to know physics</u> (given schematically):

(10.13)

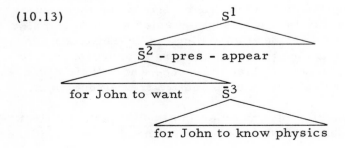

We begin with $\bar{S}^3$. No rules of relevance apply on that cycle.
Notice, in particular, that the SD of Equi cannot be met on
the $\bar{S}^3$ cycle. Since Equi is a rule that deletes the subject of
a lower sentence on the basis of some NP in the next higher
sentence, it will never be the case that it could apply on the
first cycle, since that cycle includes only the most deeply embedded sentence. Therefore, nothing relevant to our derivation
happens on $\bar{S}^3$, and we can move up to $\bar{S}^2$. On that cycle, Equi
applies to delete the subject of $\bar{S}^3$, as shown in (10.14).

(10.14)

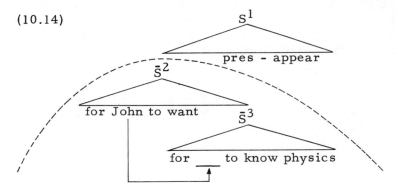

No further rules of relevance will apply to $\bar{S}^2$. Finally, we
move up to S^1, and on that highest cycle Raising to Subject can
apply, as shown in (10.15).

(10.15)

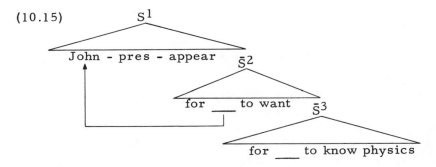

Raising to Subject could not be applied on any cycle except the
very highest one, since only when the top sentence has been
reached is the SD of the rule met. Why?

The SD of Raising to Subject is not met until the S^1 cycle because <u>appear</u>, which triggers the operation of that rule, is a constituent of S^1. Since rules can never "look up" to higher sentences when applying in lower cycles, the rule of Raising to Subject will apply only on the S^1 cycle. Meanwhile, since the SD of Equi was met on the $\bar{S}^2$ cycle, it will have already operated. Thus we can see that no matter how the rules of Equi and Raising to Subject turn out to be ordered <u>within</u> a single cycle, they will, in examples such as this, automatically apply in the right order in the derivation (i.e., (1) Equi/(2) Raising to Subject), provided they are applied cyclically. Equi will automatically precede Raising to Subject in such derivations, because the SD of Equi is met on a cycle lower than that of Raising to Subject.

Provided Equi and Raising to Subject are applied cyclically, they will also produce the desired result for <u>John wants to appear to know physics</u>, no matter how they are ordered within a single cycle. We begin again with the underlying structure (10.16) for that example.

(10.16)

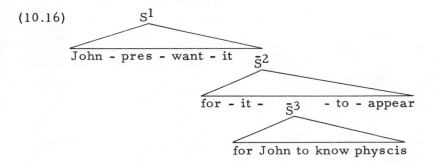

No relevant rules apply on $\bar{S}^3$. On $\bar{S}^2$ Equi cannot apply because the SD is not met. In $\bar{S}^2$ there is neither an Equi verb such as <u>want</u> nor a controller NP. Raising to Subject can apply, however; it raises the subject of $\bar{S}^3$, making it the derived subject of $\bar{S}^2$, as illustrated in (10.17). This is the only relevant rule to apply on $\bar{S}^2$. On the S^1 cycle, we find that Equi can operate, deleting the subject of $\bar{S}^2$, as shown in (10.18). Now we see that if rules apply cyclically, the SD of Equi will not be met until the <u>highest</u> cycle in this case, whereas the SD of Raising to Subject will be met on the lower cycle of $\bar{S}^2$. This is just the reverse of what happened in the derivation of the first sentence,

(10.17)

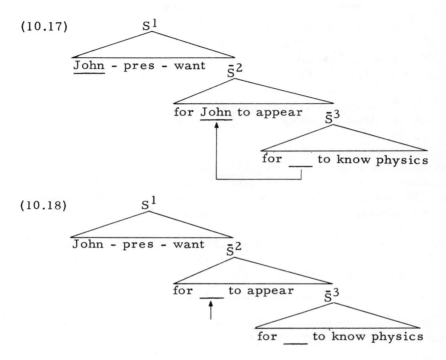

(10.18)

John appears to want to know physics. Given a cyclic method
of application, this result is guaranteed, because the verbs
appear and want reverse their positions in the trees: appear
(which takes Raising to Subject) is in the higher sentence in
one case, while want (which takes Equi) is higher in the other.
Hence, either Equi or Raising to Subject will apply first, depending on which of the two verbs (appear or want) is reached
first in the cycle. (Incidentally, it is difficult to determine
whether the rules of Equi and Raising to Subject—or, for that
matter, Raising to Object—ever have to be applied in a specific
order within a single cycle, and we will not try to deal with that
question here.)

Let us now try to clarify further the relation between cyclic
ordering and linear ordering (i.e., the ordering within each
cycle). Recall that, in chapter 6, we established the following
ordering for simple transformations:

(10.19)   1. Dative Movement
          2. Passive
          3. Reflexivization

4. Number Agreement
5. There Insertion
6. Tag Formation
7. Negative Placement
8. Contraction
9. Question Transformation
10. Affix Hopping
11. Do Support

The rules will apply in this linear order on every cycle in the derivation of a complex sentence. In order to ensure that this point is clear, try to provide a derivation for the following sentence, showing carefully how the rules apply on each cycle:

(10.20) Mary is believed by the police to have been forced by
        John to tell her father that she was not given the
        money by Herb.

The example sentence would derive from an underlying structure such as the (schematic) tree shown in (10.21).

(10.21)

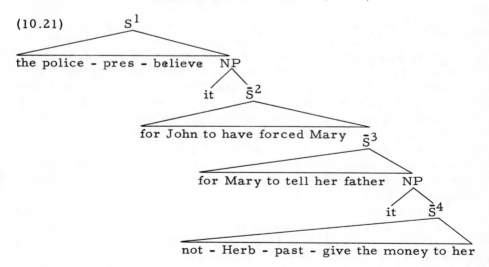

We apply the rules beginning with the lowest cycle, $\bar{S}^4$. The first rule in our linear order is the rule of Dative Movement, and we can apply that to $\bar{S}^4$, as indicated in (10.22).

(10.22) a. [not - Herb - past - give the money <u>to her</u>]

        ↓ <u>Dative Movement</u>

    b. [not - Herb - past - give <u>her</u> the money]

The next rule, Passive, applies to the output of Dative Movement to produce (10.22c):

(10.22) c. [not - she - past - be en - give the money by Herb]

The next three rules—Reflexivization, <u>There</u> Insertion, and Tag Formation—do not apply in this derivation. However, Negative Placement must apply, as usual:

(10.22) d. [she - past - be - not - en - give the money by Herb]

And finally, Affix Hopping must apply:

(10.22) e. [she - be past - not - give_en the money by Herb]

It should be clear, then, that on the first cycle, $\bar{S}^4$, we have applied all the relevant rules in the linear order specified in (10.19).

    Now that we have run through the entire list of rules on the first cycle, we may move up to the second cycle of tree (10.21), $\bar{S}^3$, and reapply the rules from the beginning of the list. However, it turns out that on that cycle none of the rules in the list is relevant to this derivation; that is, our desired output requires no important transformational operations on the $\bar{S}^3$ cycle (we ignore the placement of <u>to</u>, and affixes, if any):

(10.23) [for Mary to tell her father [that she was not given the money by Herb]]

We can then move up to the third cycle, i.e., $\bar{S}^2$.

    At this point, we have under consideration the following portion of the underlying structure:

(10.24) a. [for John to have forced <u>Mary</u> [for <u>Mary</u> to tell her father [that she was not <u>given</u> the money by Herb]]]

On this cycle the SD of Equi must be met; the subject of the complement of <u>force</u> must be deleted by that rule. In addition, as we can see from the form of example (10.20), we will have to apply Passive on this cycle in order to yield <u>for Mary to have been forced by John</u> . . . . Thus we need to determine how Equi is ordered with respect to the <u>simplex</u> transformations in list (10.19), i. e. , those rules that apply within a single sentence. In particular, does it apply before or after Passive? If we apply Passive first, the output will be roughly (10.24'):

(10.24') [for <u>Mary</u> to have been forced by John [for <u>Mary</u> . . .]]

If we now try to apply Equi, a problem arises. What it is may not be very obvious at first, but try to see where the difficulty lies before reading further.

The difficulty in trying to apply Equi to (10.24') arises from the way in which the rule operates. As we have seen, the verbs that take Equi fall into at least two classes (and possibly more): those like <u>want</u>, whose subject is the controller for Equi, and those like <u>force</u>, whose object is the controller. In this instance, since it is the <u>object</u> of <u>force</u> that controls Equi, there would be no difficulty if Equi preceded Passive. It would apply not to (10.24') but to (10.24a), which we repeat here:

(10.24) a. [for John to have forced <u>Mary</u> [for <u>Mary</u> to tell her
          father [that she was not given the money by Herb]]]

The conditions for Equi are met, and the rule applies to produce the following output:

(10.24) b. [for John to have forced Mary [for ___ to tell her
          father [that she was not given the money by Herb]]]

Passive will now apply, yielding (10.24c):

(10.24) c. [for Mary to have been forced by John [for ___ to
          tell her father [that she was not given the money by
          Herb]]]

If we had applied the Passive Rule first, the result would have been (10.24'), in which <u>Mary</u> is the derived subject and

not the object. (In fact force has no direct object in (10.24').)
Hence, the conditions for the operation of Equi with force would
not be met, and the output of such a derivation applied to $\tilde{S}^2$
would be (10.24"):

(10.24") [for Mary to have been forced by John [for Mary to
              tell her father [that she was not given the money by
              Herb]]]

This is unacceptable with the desired coreferential reading and,
in any case, will not lead to the target sentence (10.20). Thus,
we can conclude that in order to maintain the generalization that
it is the object of force that controls Equi, the latter rule must
precede Passive in the linear ordering given in (10.19). (We can
assume that Equi follows Dative Movement, though there is no
strong evidence for this.)
      Applying these rules in the correct order, we derive (10.24c)
and then move up to the highest cycle. There, the rules of Raising to Object and then Passive must apply in order to derive
Mary is believed by the police . . . . We will not show any
further details of this derivation because the broader point has
already been made: on each particular cycle, the rules are applied in a fixed linear order; they are then reapplied in the same
order on each successive cycle until the derivation ends. (See
the appendix to this chapter for a list of ordered rules, including
new rules such as Extraposition, Equi, and the Raising Rules.
Further rule ordering arguments can be explored in the exercises to this chapter.)

10.2. LAST-CYCLIC RULES

We will assume from here on that rules apply cyclically. However, there is one aspect of our account of the cycle that must
be modified. We have stated that rules apply in linear order on
each cycle, and we have thus at least implied that any of the
transformations in our list may apply on any cycle. However,
this is not strictly true. Certain transformations must not be
allowed to apply to embedded sentences but may only apply on
the highest cycle.
      For example, consider a rule such as the Tag Formation
Transformation discussed in chapter 6. The rule may apply to
a main clause (i.e., a nonembedded sentence) but in general
must not be allowed to apply to any subordinate clause (i.e.,
embedded sentence):

(10.25) a. Mary left the room.
       b. Mary left the room, didn't she?

(10.26) a. John asked whether Mary left the room.
       b. *John asked whether Mary left the room, didn't she?

The ungrammaticality of (10.26b) indicates that even if the SD
of Tag Formation should be met in an embedded clause, the
rule must not apply. To account for such facts, then, it seems
that rules must be divided into at least two classes: <u>cyclic rules</u>,
which may apply on any cycle as long as their SDs are met and
hence may apply both to main clauses and to any subordinate
clause; and <u>last-cyclic rules</u>, which may only apply on the
highest cycle, i.e., to the main clause. The Tag Formation
rule must be listed as a last-cyclic rule, and we will assume
that, by convention, any such rule is prevented from applying
until the highest cycle is reached.

Consider next the Question Transformation. This, too, must
be listed as last-cyclic, in order to prevent the ungrammatical
sentence in the following example:

(10.27) a. I asked whether <u>Mary could have read the book.</u>
       b. *I asked whether <u>could Mary have read the book.</u>

It might be objected at this point that there is no need to list
the Tag Formation and Question Rules as last-cyclic, since
they never apply unless the symbol Q is present and we have
not shown that Q is present in the underlying structure of
embedded sentences such as <u>whether Mary could have read the
book</u>. However, we will demonstrate in the next section of this
chapter that there is some evidence for supposing that the symbol Q is present in complements of verbs such as <u>ask</u>; if this is
the case, then the SD of the Tag Formation and Question Rules
would be met in the embedded sentences of (10.26a) and (10.27a).
Since we must prevent their application in such circumstances,
we must list the rules as last-cyclic.

Another last-cyclic rule we could cite is the rule of <u>VP Pre-
posing</u>, which has the effect shown in the following example:

(10.28) a. They say that John can't pass the test, but <u>he will
           pass the test</u>!
       b. They say that John can't pass the test, but <u>pass the
           test he will</u>!

Under certain special circumstances, this rule may move the VP to initial position within a sentence. However, if the input to VP Preposing is in an embedded sentence, then an ungrammatical output results:

(10.29) a.   They say that John can't pass the test, but I believe
             that he will pass the test.
        b. *They say that John can't pass the test, but I believe
             that pass the test he will.

Thus, VP Preposing must be listed as a last-cyclic rule in order to prevent its application to embedded sentences, as in (10.29b).

It is often noted that last-cyclic rules seem to differ from ordinary cyclic rules in certain respects. For one thing, last-cyclic rules tend to break up or reorder structures in a radical way. For example, the Question Rule inverts the subject and first auxiliary, and VP Preposing inverts the original order of the subject and VP. In each case, the output is a structure that could not possibly have been derived by PS rules.

In contrast, the Passive Rule changes the position of NPs and even inserts material into the tree, yet it yields a derived structure that is parallel to others directly generated by the base component. This can be seen by comparing (10.30) with (10.31):

(10.30)

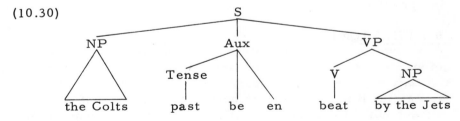

The Colts were beaten by the Jets.

(10.31)

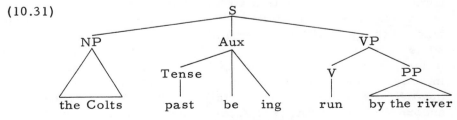

The Colts were running by the river.

Structures (10.30) and (10.31) correspond to completely different, unrelated sentences: the former is generated by the Passive Transformation, and the latter is generated directly by PS rules. Yet they are parallel.

It is possible that only last-cyclic rules can produce derived structures that differ significantly from trees generated by the base rules and, in contrast, that the operation of cyclic rules is in some sense structure preserving. While this is an interesting possibility well worth exploring (because of what it may be able to tell us about the structure of human language in general), we cannot go into greater detail here. (See the suggested readings at the end of this chapter.)

Notice how the cyclic principle itself, to the extent that it applies in all languages, makes significant progress toward a general specification of what human language can be like. It makes an important empirical prediction about rule ordering: it embodies the claim that transformations never need to apply to matrix sentences before they apply to embedded sentences. Earlier we examined cases involving Equi and Raising to Subject in which one of the two rules must apply on a lower cycle before the other rule applies on a higher cycle. But there are no known cases in which one rule must apply on a higher cycle before another rule (or the same rule) applies on a lower cycle, and this may very well be one possibility that is never realized in human language. If so, then the cyclic principle makes a correct prediction about how rules must apply in all languages.

10.3. WH FRONTING

So far we have examined only transformations that either operate within a single sentence (such as Passive, There Insertion, and Dative Movement) or operate across two sentences (Equi and the Raising Rules). A very important class of transformations that we have not yet discussed are those that are unbounded in their application, i.e., ones that may operate across an indefinite number of sentences within a tree. These are generally rules that move constituents leftward to the initial position in a sentence, from a position that can be indefinitely "far down" in some lower sentence. We will see how a rule of this sort can in fact be cyclic—and yet not apply until the very highest cycle in some cases. In order to make sense of this, however, we must first examine in some detail the operation of at least one unbounded rule of English. After determining how such a rule

is to be stated, we can return to the question of its position
within the cycle.

In addition to yes/no questions of the sort we have already
discussed, a grammar of English must account for questions
of the following sort:

(10.32) a. Which student will Dr. No flunk?
     b. What car would you like to drive?
     c. Which spot did he pick for the picnic?

These questions are characterized by having a question word
in initial position (i.e., a so-called WH word, such as which
or what) and have come to be called WH Questions. In order
to see how such sentences are derived, we might well begin by
asking how WH words are generated.

Recall that our PS rule for NP specifies a Det constituent,
which includes, among other things, the articles the and a, as
well as demonstratives such as this and that:

(10.33)

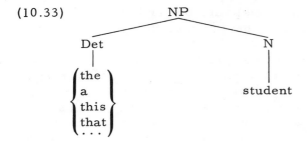

If we were to allow our PS rule for Det to include the WH words
which and what, then we would have a fairly natural way to introduce these items into NPs:

(10.34)

$$\text{Det} \rightarrow \left\{ \begin{array}{l} \text{the} \\ \text{a} \\ \ldots \\ \text{which} \\ \text{what} \end{array} \right\}$$

(10.35)

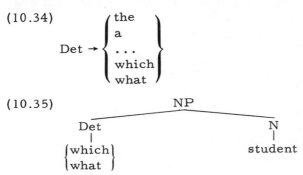

This analysis is not merely a handy means of introducing WH words into trees but also makes correct predictions about the distribution of which and what within NPs. For example, rule (10.34) embodies the claim that which or what will not be able to cooccur with any of the other determiner elements (just as, say, articles may not cooccur with demonstratives):

(10.36) a. *the which boy
          *which the boy
          *the that boy

It seems likely that some such analysis is correct, and it will certainly suffice for our purposes.

Along with WH questions such as those in (10.32), we also find questions such as (10.37a-f):

(10.37) a. Who does he like?
        b. What would you like to read?
        c. Where has the aardvark gone now?
        d. When was U. S. Grant president?
        e. Why should the tree pollen bother him now?
        f. How can two frogs beat up a turtle?

Whereas the earlier examples contain question words that are part of larger noun phrases—i.e., which and what function as determiners within NPs such as which student—the questions of (10.37) all contain question words such as who, which constitute NPs themselves, like proper names (though the WH word what functions both as a determiner, as in What car did you like?, and as a full NP, as in What did you like?). We will not discuss in any detail how question words such as those in (10.37) are derived. The simplest assumption we can make, which is adequate for our purposes, is that who and what are simply expansions of the node NP:

(10.38)

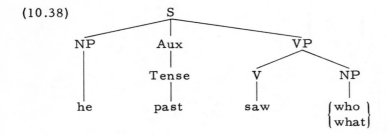

Furthermore, we can assume that <u>where</u>, <u>when</u>, <u>why</u>, and <u>how</u>
are expansions of the node Adv (<u>adverb</u>) in sentence final position, as shown in (10.39).

(10.39)

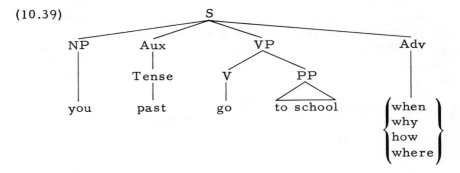

This last class of WH words, then, would be treated as being
parallel to adverbs such as <u>yesterday</u>, <u>for no reason</u>, <u>by car</u>,
and <u>in Cambridge</u>, which provide the "answers" to the question
words. To provide a detailed justification for this analysis would
be largely irrelevant to our concerns here and would take us too
far afield. (See the suggested readings at the end of the chapter.)

Without more ado, let us proceed to further details of the generation of WH questions, in particular of (10.32a). If <u>which</u> is
an alternative expansion of Det, then it should be able to occur
with any NP generated by the grammar; hence, trees such as
the following can be generated:

(10.40)

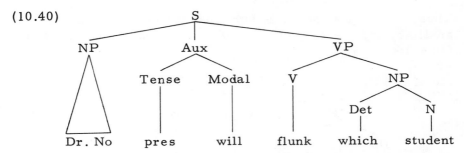

This structure is presumably the underlying form for question
(10.32a). Why? Consider how the PS rules for English would
need to be altered in order to generate (10.32a) directly. (You
can assume the existence of the Question Rule formulated in
earlier chapters.)

We will not discuss the PS analysis in detail, but it should
be clear that PS rules would have to generate an "extra" NP,
to the left of the subject, containing a WH word; at the same
time, they would have to generate one NP fewer in the VP. As
we can see, this analysis is obviously incorrect. Given that
our PS rules generate trees such as (10.40), we must assume
that the WH phrase in such structures is fronted by a transformation—WH Fronting—that will transform tree (10.40) into
(10.41):

(10.41)

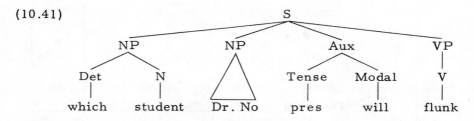

At this stage the WH NP has been fronted into its proper position, but the derivation of the question is still not finished.

In the question Which student will Dr. No flunk?, the auxiliary
verb will has been inverted with the subject of the sentence,
Dr. No, in a fashion parallel to the inverted word order of
regular yes/no questions:

(10.42) Will Dr. No flunk the student?

Thus, we must somehow ensure that the inversion of the first
auxiliary and the subject takes place, so that we can generate
(10.43):

(10.43)

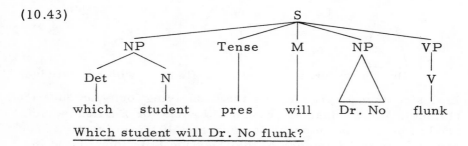

Which student will Dr. No flunk?

What existing rule(s), along with WH Fronting, may we use to
derive (10.43)? In what order should the rules apply? Do we need

to posit any new rules to derive this structure? Use the data
we have already given, along with any other examples you may
wish to use, to answer these questions.

First of all, we might suppose that the underlying structure
of WH questions, like that of yes/no questions, contains the
symbol Q. Certainly on semantic grounds we would expect
questions in general to share this feature. Moreover, if Q
were present in WH questions, then we would have an automatic way of accounting for the inversion of the subject and
auxiliary in examples such as (10.43). To see why, let us assume that Q is present in (10.40):

(10.44) a.

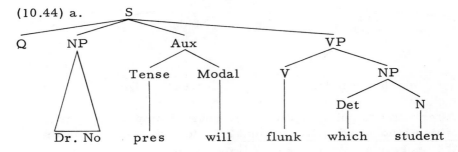

Notice that this structure will meet the SD of what we have
termed the "Question Transformation" in previous chapters,
i.e., the rule that inverts the tensed auxiliary with the subject of the sentence. Since we now have another rule that applies in the derivation of questions, namely WH Fronting, it
would be wise to rename the "Question Transformation" as the
Subject-Auxiliary Inversion Rule, which we repeat here for
convenience:

Subject-Auxiliary Inversion (Subject-Aux Inversion) (Obligatory)

$$\text{SD: Q - NP - Tense } \left(\left\{ \begin{array}{l} \text{Modal} \\ \text{have} \\ \text{be} \end{array} \right\} \right)$$

$$\begin{array}{llll} & 1 & 2 & & 3 \\ \text{SC:} & 1 & 3 & 2 \end{array}$$

Since tree (10.44a) meets the SD of Subject-Aux Inversion,
that rule will produce the following output:

(10.44) b.

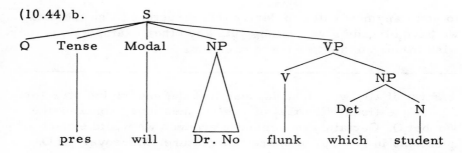

Next, we assume that WH Fronting applies to convert this tree into the following one:

(10.44) c.

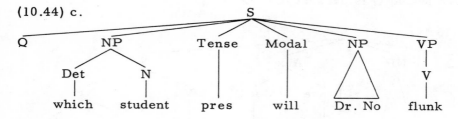

After Affix Hopping applies, our desired output is generated: Which student will Dr. No flunk? As long as we assume that the underlying structure of WH questions contains Q, and if Subject-Aux Inversion applies before WH Fronting, we can automatically account for the inverted order of the subject and the first part of the Aux in WH questions without modifying any of our previous rules. (Note that this ordering of the rules is not the only one that has been proposed: in some analyses WH Fronting precedes Subject-Aux Inversion, and in fact this may even be desirable in our system. See the suggested readings for this chapter, as well as exercise (E10.4).

10.4. THE POSITION OF WH FRONTING IN THE CYCLE

We are now in a position to formulate the rule of WH Fronting and to consider how it applies in relation to the cycle. In section 10.3 we examined in detail the derivation of a sentence in which the WH NP was fronted from object position: (10.32a) Which student will Dr. No flunk? The examples in (10.37) showed that a WH word generated in other positions in a simplex sentence could also be fronted, and we can assume that the rule will have to be formulated so that it will move any WH word (and its associated NP, if any) to the initial position in a simplex S. But now consider these examples:

(10.45) a. Who will Samuel marry?
b. Who did Sheila say that Samuel would marry?
c. Who did Max think Sheila said Samuel would marry?
d. Who did Charley claim that Max thought Sheila said Samuel would marry?

Using the above examples, as well as the others cited earlier, try to formulate a rule of WH Fronting. How must the rule be stated? And how will it apply in terms of the cyclic ordering of rules?

The sentences of (10.45) show that the rule of WH Fronting is <u>unbounded</u>: it may front a WH word that is located indefinitely far from the sentence where it ends up. As an illustration, consider the operation of WH Fronting on sentence (10.45d) (which we greatly abbreviate here), shown in (10.46).

(10.46)

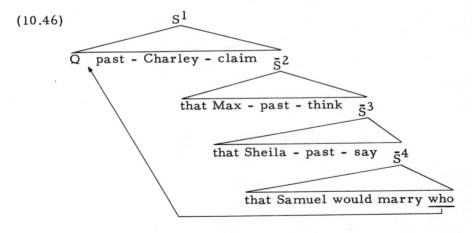

(Note that the last-cyclic rule of Subject-Auxiliary Inversion has already applied on the top cycle.) In the derivation of sentence (10.45d), the WH word <u>who</u> will be fronted from a position that is three sentences "down" from the initial position of the highest sentence. Examples such as (10.45d) can easily be expanded further, and there is, in principle, no upper bound to the number of embedded sentences that may intervene between the original position of the WH word and the sentence to which it is moved.

Now, given our classification of rules into cyclic and last-cyclic, there are at least two logically possible ways in which WH Fronting might apply to complex structures. On the one hand, it might be a cyclic rule that applies on each cycle, fronting the WH word to the initial position of each successive embedded sentence until the highest sentence is reached (sometimes referred to as a successive cyclic application of the rule). On the other hand, WH Fronting might be a last-cyclic rule, which simply fronts the WH word in one step on the highest cycle of the tree. These possibilities are illustrated below:

(10.47) a. Successive Cyclic Application of WH Fronting

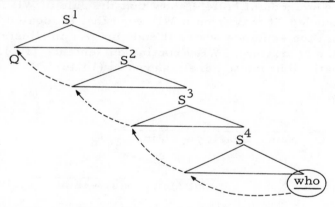

b. Last-Cyclic Application of WH Fronting

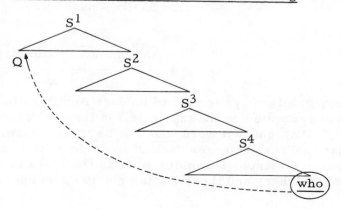

There is no way of choosing between these modes of application on an a priori basis, and it is necessary to look for evidence favoring one or the other. At present it seems likely that WH Fronting is not a successive cyclic rule but rather applies as shown in (10.47b). We will cite just one argument favoring that conclusion—one that has come to be known as the "Preposition Orphan" argument.

This argument is based on the observation that WH Fronting may optionally front a preposition in sentences such as the following:

(10.48) a. Q - you gave the book to who(m)
        b. Who(m) did you give the book to?
        c. To whom did you give the book?

The preposition to may either be left behind, as in (10.48b), or it may be optionally fronted, as in (10.48c). The same fact holds true when WH Fronting applies to a complex structure, as in the following example:

(10.49) a. Q - you believed that Mary gave the book to who(m)
        b. Who(m) did you believe that Mary gave the book to?
        c. To whom did you believe that Mary gave the book?

As in the previous example, to may either be left behind or fronted along with the WH word. Exactly how this fact should be built into our account of WH Fronting is not crucial—the important point is that the preposition may optionally be left behind or fronted.

The import of this fact will become clear if we look again at the two modes of application of WH Fronting illustrated in (10.47). Assume that the following schematic representation is the underlying form for (10.49a):

(10.50) a. Q - you-past-believe [that Mary-past-give the book to who]

If WH Fronting applies in a successive cyclic fashion, then it will apply on the first cycle to move the WH word to the beginning of the complement of believe. Since the rule may optionally front the preposition to, the following output could result:

(10.50) b. Q - you-past-believe [to who-that Mary-past-give
                  the book]

On the next cycle, the WH word would be fronted again, this
time to the initial position of the main clause. Since the preposition can also be moved to initial position by WH Fronting,
the following output could be derived:

(10.50) c. Q - to who-you-past-believe [that Mary-past-give
                  the book]
                  To who(m) did you believe that Mary gave the book?

So far, no problems arise.
   However, recall that WH Fronting optionally fronts the preposition to. Given this, there is nothing to prevent the rule from
operating in the following way on (10.50b):

(10.50) b. Q - you-past-believe [to who - that Mary-past-give
                  the book]
          d. Q - who-you-past-believe [to - that Mary-past-give
                  the book]

In this case, the preposition to in (10.50b) has been stranded
(i.e., "orphaned") in a position where it may not appear in
surface structure:

(10.51) *Who did you believe to that Mary gave the book?

Hence, it has been argued that a successive cyclic application
of WH Fronting can lead to ungrammatical sentences such as
(10.51), since the rule may optionally leave the preposition behind at the beginning of any embedded sentence in its journey
up a complex structure such as (10.47a).
   It should be fairly clear that the problem of the preposition
orphan is avoided completely if WH Fronting is a last-cyclic
rule. Consider again an input such as (10.50a):

(10.50) a. Q - you-past-believe [that-Mary-past-give the book
                  to who]

If WH Fronting is last-cyclic, it will not be allowed to apply
until the highest cycle is reached. At that point, the rule will

move the WH word in one step to initial position in the sentence and will have the option of either leaving the preposition behind or fronting it:

(10.52) a. Q - who-you-past-believe [that-Mary-past-give the book to]
   Who did you believe that Mary gave the book to?
b. Q - to who(m)-you-past-believe [that-Mary-past-give the book]
   To who(m) did you believe that Mary gave the book?

Given this mode of application, there is no way that WH Fronting can leave a preposition behind in any medial position in the sentence, in the manner of the ungrammatical sentence (10.51). (It should be pointed out there may be other ways of blocking (10.51), and consequently the argument which we have just given is by no means conclusive.)

Let us assume, for the moment, that the argument is satisfactory. Then it appears that we must conclude that WH Fronting is last-cyclic. However, this conclusion would be premature, since it overlooks a third logical possibility for the application of WH Fronting: the rule might be a cyclic rule, but its formal statement might be such that the SD of the rule was only satisfied on the highest cycle. For example, this would be the case if we were to state the rule of WH Fronting so that it would operate only when the symbol Q were present:

(10.53) WH Fronting (Obligatory)

SD: Q - X - [+ WH]
    1   2   3
SC: 1 + 3 2 $\emptyset$

We have used the symbol [+ WH] to represent the WH words generated by our rules. The variable, $\underline{X}$, is a crucial part of the statement of the rule and represents all the material that may intervene between a WH word and the initial position of the tree. Recall that since WH words may be fronted from indefinitely far down in a structure, there is no way we could specify exactly all the material that could intervene between the WH word and the initial position; hence, the rule of WH Fronting must use a variable in the fashion shown in (10.53).

(Rules of this sort are sometimes called variable movement
rules.) Since the rule fronts the WH NP to the position immediately to the right of Q, the SD of the rule will not be satisfied unless the symbol Q is present.

Consequently, a successive cyclic application of the rule to
the tree schematized in (10.47a) is impossible simply because
the symbol Q does not appear in any cycle except the very
highest; the SD of (10.53) will not be met until the highest cycle.
Even if WH Fronting is listed as a cyclic rule, its application
in a case such as (10.46) will always appear to be last-cyclic.
This situation seems at first to be a mere artifact of our theory:
is there any way we could distinguish a last-cyclic rule of WH
Fronting from a cyclic version of the rule as stated in (10.53)?
Otherwise, it is pointless to claim that the rule is cyclic but
that its SD is not met until the highest cycle. We need to find
independent evidence (1) that WH Fronting should be stated so
that its SD contains Q, and (2) that it applies on lower cycles
and not just on the very highest. It turns out that there is some
evidence bearing on both of these questions.

10.5. CYCLIC WH FRONTING: EMBEDDED QUESTIONS
To see what sort of evidence would show that WH Fronting applies cyclically when Q is present, let us examine a class of
constructions known as embedded questions: that is, complements of certain verbs within which WH Fronting has taken
place. The following examples contain typical instances of embedded questions (underlined):

(10.54) a. I wonder who Mary loves.
        b. They don't know what broke the window.
        c. It isn't clear where he goes to school.
        d. They then asked why John had left.
        e. I know that Mary told Bill how to bury the money.
        f. The prosecutors want the witness to tell who Nixon
           met with.

In the sentences of (10.54), the WH words have been moved, not
to the beginning of the entire sentence, but only to the beginning
of the complements of verbs such as wonder, ask, know, and
say, and adjective phrases such as be clear. So, if we view a
sentence such as (10.54a) as deriving from a source roughly
representable as (10.55a), then WH Fronting apparently must

be allowed to move the WH word just to the beginning of the complement:

(10.55) a. I-pres-wonder [Mary-pres-love <u>who</u>]

$\downarrow$ <u>WH Fronting</u>

     b. I-pres-wonder [who-Mary-pres-love]

The fact that WH Fronting applies within an embedded sentence in these cases strongly suggests that it is, in fact, a cyclic rule. If it were a last-cyclic rule, then its application to a structure such as (10.55a) should not be possible. This is because the rule would not be able to apply until the highest cycle had been reached; but then, in order to front the WH word in the proper way (i.e., only to the beginning of the complement), WH Fronting would have to apply only within the embedded sentence. That is, WH Fronting would have to "go back" to a cycle that has already been passed, operating only on that previous cycle and ignoring the current one. In general it is possible to avoid this sort of rule application and to restrict rules in such a way that their SDs must be satisfied (at least partially) within the highest sentence on any particular cycle. This seems to be a natural part of the notion of cyclic application and is sometimes referred to as <u>strict cyclicity</u>: rules may not apply exhaustively within a lower cycle that has already been passed in the application of rules to a structure. This may not appear to be a very strong argument for claiming that WH Fronting is cyclic, but if (as may very well be the case) there are no other rules that ever have to violate the principle of strict cyclicity, it would obviously be wrong to violate that principle just in order to make WH Fronting a last-cyclic rule. Therefore, we may conclude tentatively that WH Fronting is cyclic. (For further discussion of these issues, see the suggested readings for this chapter.)

Let us now see to what extent we can justify including Q in the SD of the rule. It is obviously appropriate to include it for ordinary WH questions, since there is independent justification for an initial Q in those, in order to trigger Subject-Aux Inversion (see section 10.3). Thus the initial Q provides an excellent definition of the point to which the WH word is fronted in non-embedded questions, though there are other ways of guaranteeing that fronting is always to the initial position.

If there is a conclusive argument for including Q, it will apparently have to come from embedded questions. Given that WH Fronting can move a WH word to the beginning of an embedded complement, as in (10.55b), we might ask whether the rule can move a WH word to the beginning of <u>any</u> successively higher structure. For example, consider a structure such as (10.56):

(10.56) a. the prosecutors-pres-want [for the witness to tell
          [Nixon-past-met-with <u>who</u>]]

There are two embedded sentences "below" the verb <u>want</u>, but WH Fronting can move <u>who</u> only to the beginning of the complement of <u>tell</u>, and no higher:

(10.56) b. the prosecutors-pres-want [for the witness to tell
          [<u>who</u>-Nixon-past-met with]]
       c. *the prosecutors-pres-want [<u>who</u> for the witness to
          tell [Nixon-past-met with]]

How, then, can we guarantee that in embedded questions such as (10.56a) the rule of WH Fronting will move the WH word to the beginning of the embedded question, but no further? In considering this problem, it would be good to review the formulation of WH Fronting and to ask whether it will apply at all in its present formulation to a structure such as (10.56a).

If WH Fronting is stated as in (10.53), then it crucially mentions Q in its SD, and it will not apply at all to (10.56a). This suggests an interesting way of preventing the derivation of (10.56c). We have already seen that most, if not all, embedded sentences are preceded by a complementizer. We might say that every embedded question contains the symbol Q as its complementizer and, hence, that verbs such as <u>wonder</u>, <u>ask</u>, and <u>know</u> are subcategorized to occur with Q (just as verbs may be subcategorized for <u>that</u>, <u>for-to</u>, and so on). On this analysis, a sentence such as (10.54a) would have the structure shown in (10.57). (We will leave it as an open question whether the complement of <u>wonder</u> is in fact dominated by NP. What evidence would bear on this?) Given underlying structures such as (10.57), the WH Fronting rule as stated in (10.53) will automatically apply correctly to produce (10.58).

(10.57)

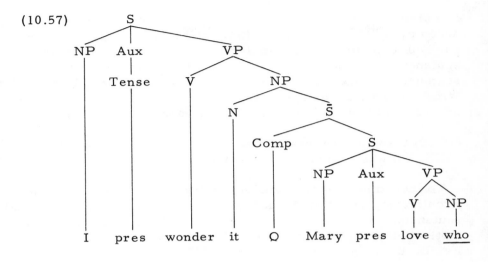

(10.58)

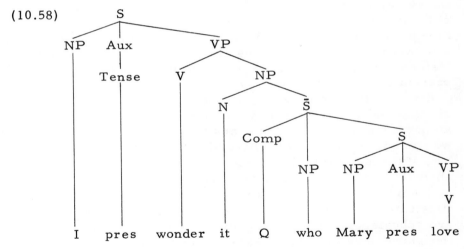

With this derivation in mind, let us return to the derivation
of the sentence The prosecutors want the witness to tell who
Nixon met with, given in (10.56a). In light of the modifications
we have just made, the underlying structure for that sentence
is now (10.59):

(10.59) the prosecutors-pres-want [for the witness to tell
        [Q - Nixon-past-meet-with who]]

Since tell is a verb that can take an embedded question as a

complement, it must be permitted to take complements preceded by Q. On the other hand, the verb want is not subcategorized to occur with Q complements; thus, while there are
sentences such as John told where he had gone, there are no
sentences such as *John wanted where he had gone. Since the
WH Fronting Rule as stated in (10.53) operates only when Q is
present, there is only one way it can operate on (10.59):

(10.60) the prosecutors-pres-want [for the witness to tell
        [Q who - Nixon-past-meet with]]

To the extent that the symbol Q allows us to predict how WH
Fronting applies in embedded questions (and how ungrammatical
sentences such as (10.56c) can be blocked), it seems to be well
motivated; and if so, the rule of WH Fronting will include Q in
its SD. It should be clear now how WH Fronting applies within
the cycle. Even though WH Fronting must be considered a cyclic rule, it will not apply on every cycle of a complex structure but will apply only on those cycles in which Q is present.
For this reason, WH Fronting gives the appearance of being a
last-cyclic rule in some cases—those in which the symbol Q is
present only on the highest cycle.
It seems that we have fairly good motivation, then, for positing the abstract element Q in embedded questions (as well
as in main clause questions), and there is further evidence that
we can add to the proof we have already discussed. In particular, it turns out that the symbol Q may be more than just an
abstract symbol present in underlying structures; it may in fact
be realized in the surface structure of certain sentences. To
illustrate this, consider again verbs such as ask or tell that
are subcategorized to occur with the complementizer Q. Although we have examined cases in which the complements to
such verbs contain WH words, there are also cases in which
such embedded questions contain no WH words at all:

(10.61) a. we-past-ask [Q - Mary-past-leave the room]

Notice that the embedded question here contains Q, followed
by the sequence Mary-past-leave the room, with no WH words
such as who or what. If we assume that Q is not deleted in such
examples but is rather realized as the word whether in surface
structure, then an underlying form such as (10.61a) can serve
as the source for a sentence such as the following:

(10.61) b. We asked <u>whether</u> Mary left the room.

Just as WH questions have embedded question counterparts
(i.e., embedded questions with WH words), yes/no questions
also have embedded counterparts in <u>whether</u> clauses. Thus,
we will assume that Q deletes when immediately followed by
a WH word (hence eliminating it from surface structures in
which it does not overtly appear), but that it remains and is
realized as <u>whether</u> in all other cases. We have provided
further justification for Q to the extent that it provides us with
an account of <u>whether</u> clauses. (Incidentally, it should be borne
in mind that Subject-Aux Inversion is a last-cyclic rule and will
not apply in embedded questions; hence, ungrammatical sentences such as <u>*We asked whether did Mary leave</u> will not be
generated.)
 As always, the analysis is not without difficulties, and if the
postulation of a symbol Q in embedded questions seems to solve
certain problems, it also raises new ones. For example, if Q
is a complementizer in embedded questions, is it also a complementizer when it occurs in main clauses? And hence, do
main clauses, as well as embedded clauses, have complementizers? A more pressing problem is raised by the fact that the
symbol Q may be generated both on a main clause and on some
embedded clause of a given structure. For example, if Q is a
complementizer, the PS rules will generate (10.62a):

(10.62) a. Q - the prosecutors-pres-want [for the witness to
     tell [Q - Nixon past-meet with <u>who</u>]]

If WH Fronting applies on the lowest cycle and Subject-Aux Inversion on the highest cycle, then the following question will
be generated:

(10.62) b. Do the prosecutors want the witness to tell who
     Nixon met with?

However, what is to prevent WH Fronting from applying twice
to this structure? Since the symbol Q is present on the highest
cycle as well as the lowest, nothing in our theory prevents WH
Fronting from moving <u>who</u> on the highest cycle, producing the
ungrammatical (10.62c):

(10.62) c. *Who do the prosecutors want the witness to tell
     Nixon met with?

It is clear that problems of this sort will have to be solved before we can be entirely certain that a complementizer Q is
well justified.

10.6. A NOTE ON RELATIVE CLAUSES

We have noted that WH Fronting is a cyclic rule that does not
apply unless Q is present; hence, the rule often does not apply
until a cycle <u>higher</u> than the one containing the WH word itself.
A similar situation holds in the formation of relative clauses
in English. To see what this means, consider first relative
clauses such as those underlined below:

(10.63) a. The man <u>who we fired</u> walked in.
       b. The book <u>which you lent to John</u> is stupid.
       c. The place <u>where he wants to meet us</u> hasn't been
          chosen.
       d. The time <u>when one could do that</u> has long since
          passed.
       e. The man <u>who John was talking to</u> gave him the book.
       f. The man <u>to whom John was talking</u> gave him the book.

These examples show that in one method of forming English
relative clauses, a WH word appears at the left of the clause,
while the clause itself lacks the NP corresponding to the WH
word. In (10.63a), for example, the WH word <u>who</u> appears at
the left of the embedded clause, which has an $\overline{NP}$ missing: the
object of the verb <u>fire</u>.
    These relative clauses are very similar to the embedded
questions discussed earlier in section 10.5, and many of the
arguments for deriving WH questions by means of a rule of
WH Fronting apply to these relative clauses. (For example,
notice the stranded preposition <u>to</u> in (10.63e).) If such a rule
is involved, then (10.63a) will be derived somewhat as follows:

(10.64) The man <u>we fired who</u> is stupid.

Similarly, (10.63b-e) will be derived as a result of a left-
movement rule that in each case moves the WH word to the
beginning of the relative clause.
    Precisely how relative clauses are formed is best left as an
open question, since there is currently some uncertainty over
the precise nature of their deep structure, as well as over the

movement and/or deletion rules responsible for the final surface forms. What is important for present purposes is that the
rule (whatever it is) linking the WH word that appears at the
left of the clause with the "missing" NP within that clause has
to operate over an unbounded amount of intervening material,
applying cyclically, but often on a cycle higher than the one
containing the WH word itself.

Consider the following sentence:

(10.65) The man who John believed Mary had been talking to
        had already left.

If we assume that some process of fronting is involved in the
derivation of this example, then the WH word will have been
moved as shown in (10.66).

(10.66)

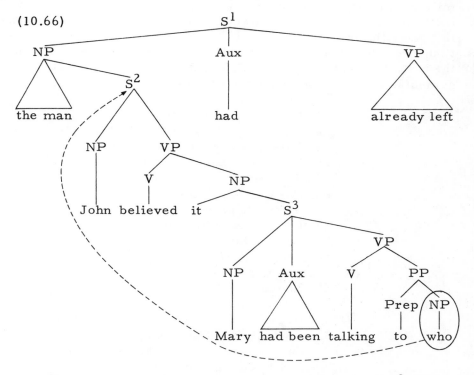

Under this analysis, the WH word that originates in S^3 cannot
be moved to the front of S^2 until the S^3 cycle is completed. In
all relevant respects, therefore, the rule(s) responsible for

the formation of relative clauses are like WH Fronting (see
(10.46), for example). Since we will not discuss the formation
of relative clauses in more detail, the reader is referred to
the suggested readings for a partial listing of the very exten-
sive literature that is relevant to this topic.

CHAPTER 10: APPENDIX
LIST OF ORDERED RULES

The accompanying list of ordered rules includes most of the
transformations we have discussed up to this point. Two rules
connected by a curved line are crucially ordered, in that it is
possible to construct an explicit argument for ordering them
as indicated. Rules unconnected by curved lines are simply un-
ordered with respect to each other (or, at least, no arguments
have been advanced for ordering the rules). The reader is familiar with most of the ordering arguments and should review
them in studying the list. However, some rules have been listed
in a specific order (e.g., Equi, the Raising Rules, Extraposition) even though all the arguments may not have been given in
the text. Exercises (E10.1)-(E10.3) deal with new ordering arguments, and the reader should be able to construct others.

1. Dative Movement (Optional)
2. Equi NP Deletion (Equi) (Obligatory)
3. Raising to Object (Obligatory)
4. Raising to Subject (Obligatory)
5. For Deletion (Obligatory)
6. Passive (Optional)
7. Agent Deletion (Optional)
8. Reflexivization (Obligatory)
9. Extraposition (Optional)
10. It Deletion (Obligatory)
11. Number Agreement (Obligatory)
12. There Insertion (Optional)
13. Tag Formation (Optional) (LC)
14. Negative Placement (Obligatory)
15. Contraction (Optional)
16. Subject-Auxiliary Inversion (Obligatory) (LC)
17. WH Fronting (Obligatory)
18. Affix Hopping (Obligatory)
19. Do Support (Obligatory)

All rules are cyclic rules, unless marked <u>LC</u> ("last cyclic"). Almost all of the rules have been stated formally in the text. The rule of Equi, as we have discussed it, can be stated as follows:

<u>Equi NP Deletion</u> (Obligatory)

$$\text{SD: X - NP - Y-}_{\bar{S}} \, [\left\{ \begin{matrix} \text{Poss} \\ \text{For} \end{matrix} \right\} \text{ - NP - W]}_{\bar{S}} \text{ - Z}$$

$$\qquad\; 1 \quad\; 2 \quad\; 3 \qquad\quad 4 \qquad 5 \quad\; 6 \qquad\; 7$$

SC: 1 2 3 4 $\emptyset$ 6 7

Conditions: (a) 2 = 5

(b) With main verbs such as <u>want</u>, term 2 must be the subject of the verb; with verbs such as <u>force</u>, term 2 must be the object of the verb.

The conditions on the rule of Equi are necessary to ensure that the controller NP is properly specified.

The rule we list here as <u>For Deletion</u> is the rule that applies after Equi and the Raising Rules to delete any occurrence of <u>for</u> that is adjacent to <u>to</u>:

<u>For Deletion</u> (Obligatory)

SD: X - for - to - Y

$\quad\;\; 1 \quad\; 2 \quad\; 3 \quad\; 4$

SC: 1 $\emptyset$ 3 4

CHAPTER 10: EXERCISES

(E10.1) In the list of rules given in the appendix to this chapter, we have listed Raising to Object before Passive. Give a complete derivation for the following sentence, and explain why the rules must be so ordered:

(i) Mary was believed by her doctor to have been cheated by the hospital.

(E10.2) Why do the following sentences show that Raising to Subject must precede Number Agreement and Tag Formation?

(i) a. John seems to be playing the piano.

b. *John and Bill seems to be playing the piano.

  c. John and Bill seem to be playing the piano.
  d. It seems to be true that Bill played the piano.
  e. It seems that Bill played the piano.
(ii) a. It appears that Bill left, doesn't it?
  b. Bill appears to have left, doesn't he?
  c. There seems to be a frog in the box, doesn't there?

(E10.3) How must the rule of WH Fronting be ordered with respect to the rules of Passive and There Insertion? Although
this chapter has already provided the answer to that question—
since we ordered WH Fronting after Subject-Aux Inversion,
which follows both Passive and There Insertion— simply ignore
that particular ordering argument and provide specific arguments for ordering WH Fronting with respect to both Passive
and There Insertion. Consider the following data in formulating
your answer (as well as any other examples you may discover):

(i) Ordering WH Fronting and Passive:
  a. Who hit Mary?
  b. *Mary was hit by who?
  c. Who was Mary hit by?
  d. *Mary hit who?
  e. Who was hit by Mary?

(ii) Ordering WH Fronting and There Insertion:
  a. Who was standing on the dock?
  b. *There was who standing on the dock?
  c. Who was there standing on the dock?
  d. Who was arrested by the police?
  e. *There was who arrested by the police?
  f. Who was there arrested by the police?

Your ordering arguments must show how the ungrammatical
sentences in these examples will be blocked.

(E10.4) In this chapter we assumed that Subject-Auxiliary Inversion preceded WH Fronting. However, that is not the only
conceivable ordering of these rules, and in some analyses WH
Fronting is first. If it does come first, then we must make
some modification in our rules.

A. What changes need to be made, and to which rules? To answer this, construct a number of underlying forms that contain

the symbol Q as well as a WH phrase. Then see what consequences result from applying WH Fronting before Inversion:
will Subject-Aux Inversion have to be modified, and if so,
how?

B̲. There are two assumptions one can make about the operation of WH Fronting: (a) the WH word is fronted to a position
immediately to the right of the symbol Q (and Q is presumably
deleted at a later stage), or (b) the WH word is fronted to the
position of the symbol Q, replacing that symbol. In answering
the question, show how Subject-Aux Inversion must be modified if the second assumption is made.

C̲. Finally, can you think of any evidence we might use in
choosing between the two rule orderings? List this evidence
only if you think of some—do not feel compelled to answer this
part.

(E10.5) We have examined numerous WH questions in which the
WH word originates as the underlying object of the sentence,
but obviously there is an equal number of cases in which the
WH word is the subject (deep or derived) of the sentence:

(i)   a.   Who ate the cheese?
      b.   Which car rolled down the hill?
      c.   What will be cooked by Sam?
      d.   Which boys read the book?

We know that the rule of Subject-Auxiliary Inversion must apply in the derivation of sentences containing Q, as these sentences do, yet on the surface we see no evidence that the rule
has applied. That is, the word order of the sentences of (i)
shows no inversion on the surface:

(ii) a. *Did who eat the cheese?
      b. *Who did eat the cheese?
(iii) a. *Did which car roll down the hill?
      b. *Which car did roll down the hill?

In fact, there is a very simple explanation of why no sentences
such as (ii) and (iii) exist. What is that explanation? You should
be able to answer this simply by providing derivations for the

sentences of (i) and by applying the rules in the form and order set out in this chapter or in the version developed in exercise (E10.4).

(E10.6) In exercise (E8.3) we presented data indicating that a special condition must be placed on the rule of Reflexivization, illustrated by examples such as (ia, b):

(i) a. I know that Mary likes me.
     b. *I know that Mary likes myself.

The supposed underlying form for an ungrammatical sentence such as (ib) would be as follows:

(ii)

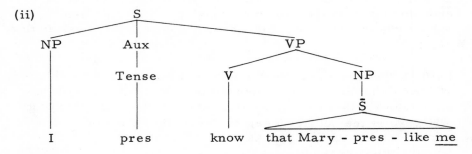

The impossiblility of applying Reflexivization in a structure such as this is apparently due to the fact that one NP, me, is dominated by a sentence that does not dominate the antecedent, I. Reviewing the data of exercise (E8.3), the reader should see clearly that Reflexivization can apply just in case the two relevant coreferential NPs are clause mates, i.e., just in case each NP is dominated by the first S node that dominates the other. Hence, while sentences such as *I know that Mary likes myself are ungrammatical, sentences such as I know that Mary likes herself are perfectly well formed.

Now examine the following two sentences, in which the rules of Reflexivization and Raising to Object have applied:

(iii) a. John believes himself to be an Arab sheik.
      b. I believe Mary to have hurt herself.

Using the derivation of these two sentences, construct an argument that transformations must apply cyclically. To do this, you will need to show that a rule ordering paradox results if transformations do not apply in a cyclic fashion. Therefore, assume that rules are not cyclically ordered. First show in what order Reflexivization and Raising to Object must apply in order to derive (iiia). Then show in what order the rules must apply to derive (iiib). You should have found that a rule ordering paradox results. Finally, show how the paradox can be resolved if rules apply in a cyclic fashion.

CHAPTER 10: SUGGESTED READINGS

The idea that rules apply in a cyclic fashion was proposed in an early paper by Fillmore (1963) and is discussed by Chomsky (1965). Proofs for cyclic application of rules are presented in G. Lakoff (1966) (involving the rules of Raising to Object and Passive), Postal (1970) (involving the rules of Equi and Passive), and McCawley (1970) (involving the rules of Equi and Passive, which we have used in the beginning of this chapter). Jacobs and Rosenbaum (1968) present a simple proof for the cycle involving Reflexivization and Raising to Object, the data from which forms the basis for exercise (E10.6).

The idea that cyclic rules may be structure preserving, while last-cyclic rules tend to alter structure in more radical ways, has been discussed by a number of linguists. The most important research on this question is to be found in Emonds (1970), in which the author discusses a wide range of grammatical phenomena relating to this question.

The grammar of WH words and the rule of WH Fronting have been fairly extensively investigated within the transformational literature. A summary of earlier work on the subject can be found in Stockwell, Schachter, and Partee (1973). The internal structure of WH words is discussed in Chomsky (1958). The Q marker in the structure of questions is discussed by Baker (1970), who provides a number of important arguments. Bresnan (1970) elaborates and expands Baker's notions, proposing that Q be classed as a complementizer. Related to both of these papers is that by Bach (1971), who, like Bresnan, is concerned with universal aspects of question structures. The question of whether WH Fronting applies in a successive cyclic or cyclic manner is discussed by Postal (1972).

A good deal has been written on the structure and formation of relative clauses in English and many other languages. Stockwell, Schachter, and Partee (1973) contains a very useful summary of a number of basic papers, as well as a bibliography of works on relative clauses. Ross (1967) discusses the question of whether WH Fronting in questions and relative clauses can be regarded as the same rule. Schachter (1973) proposes a theory of relative clauses in which the head noun (i.e., the noun modified by the clause) is not present in deep structure but is actually raised from the relative clause itself. Finally, for a wide range of interesting papers on relative clauses in a number of diverse languages, see the volume edited by Peranteau, Levi, and Phares (1972).

BIBLIOGRAPHY

Adams, D., et al., eds. (1971) Papers from the Seventh Regional Meeting of the Chicago Linguistic Society, Department of Linguistics, University of Chicago, Chicago, Ill.

Akmajian, A. and T. Wasow (forthcoming) "The Constituent Structure of VP and AUX, and the Position of the Verb BE," Linguistic Analysis, Spring, 1975.

Anderson, S. A., and R. P. Kiparsky, eds. (1973) A Festschrift for Morris Halle, Holt, Rinehart and Winston, New York.

Bach, E. (1964) An Introduction to Transformational Grammars, Holt, Rinehart and Winston, New York.

Bach, E. (1971) "Questions," Linguistic Inquiry 2:153-166.

Baker, C. L. (1970) "Notes on the Description of English Questions: The Role of an Abstract Question Morpheme," Foundations of Language 6:197-219.

Bar-Adon, A., and W. F. Leopold, eds. (1971) Child Language: A Book of Readings, Prentice-Hall, Englewood Cliffs, N. J.

Berman, A. (1974) "On the VSO Hypothesis," Linguistic Inquiry 5:1-37.

Bierwisch, M., and K. Heidolph, eds. (1971) Progress in Linguistics, Mouton, The Hague.

Binnick, R. I., A. Davison, G. Green, and J. Morgan, eds. (1969) Papers from the Fifth Regional Meeting of the Chicago Linguistic Society, Department of Linguistics, University of Chicago, Chicago, Ill.

Bolinger, D. L. (1967) "The Imperative in English," in To Honor Roman Jakobson, Mouton, The Hague.

Bresnan, J. (1970) "On Complementizers: Toward a Syntactic Theory of Complement Types," Foundations of Language 6:297-321.

Burt, M. K. (1971) <u>From Deep to Surface Structure</u>, Harper and Row, New York.

Campbell, M., et al., eds. (1970) <u>Papers from the Sixth Regional Meeting of the Chicago Linguistic Society</u>, Department of Linguistics, University of Chicago, Chicago, Ill.

Cattell, R. N. (1969) <u>The New English Grammar</u>, MIT Press, Cambridge, Mass.

Chomsky, N. (1957) <u>Syntactic Structures</u>, Mouton, The Hague.

Chomsky, N. (1958) "A Transformational Approach to Syntax," in J. A. Fodor and J. J. Katz, eds. (1964).

Chomsky, N. (1963) "Formal Properties of Grammars," in R. D. Luce, R. R. Bush, and E. Galanter, eds. (1963).

Chomsky, N. (1964) "On the Notion 'Rule of Grammar'," in J. A. Fodor and J. J. Katz, eds. (1964).

Chomsky, N. (1965) <u>Aspects of the Theory of Syntax</u>, MIT Press, Cambridge, Mass.

Chomsky, N. (1966a) "The Current Scene in Linguistics: Present Directions," <u>College English</u>, 27:587-595. [Reprinted in D. A. Reibel and S. A. Schane, eds. (1969)].

Chomsky, N. (1966b) <u>Cartesian Linguistics</u>, MIT Press, Cambridge, Mass.

Chomsky, N. (1967) <u>Language and Mind</u>, Harcourt Brace Jovanovich, New York.

Chomsky, N. (1969) "Linguistics and Philosophy," in S. Hook, ed. (1969).

Chomsky, N. (1973) "Conditions on Transformations," in S. A. Anderson and R. P. Kiparsky, eds. (1973).

Chomsky, N., and G. Miller (1963) "Introduction to the Formal Analysis of Natural Languages," in R. D. Luce, R. R. Bush, and E. Galanter, eds (1963).

Corum, C., T. Smith-Stark, and A. Weiser, eds. (1973)
Papers from the Ninth Regional Meeting of the Chicago
Linguistic Society, Department of Linguistics, University of
Chicago, Chicago, Ill.

Emonds, J. (1970) Root and Structure Preserving Transforma-
tions, unpublished Doctoral dissertation, MIT, Cambridge,
Mass. [Available in mimeographed form from the Indiana
University Linguistics Club, Indiana University, Bloomington,
Indiana.]

Fillmore, C. J. (1963) "The Position of Embedding Transformations in a Grammar," Word 19:208-231.

Fillmore, C. J. (1965) Indirect Object Constructions in English and the Ordering of Transformations, Mouton, The Hague.

Fillmore, C. J., and D. T. Langendoen, eds. (1971) Studies
in Linguistic Semantics, Holt, Rinehart and Winston, New
York.

Fodor, J. A., and J. J. Katz, eds. (1964) The Structure of
Language, Prentice-Hall, Englewood Cliffs, N. J.

Gleason, H. A., Jr. (1955) An Introduction to Descriptive
Linguistics, Holt, Rinehart and Winston, New York.

Grinder, J. (1970) "Super Equi-NP Deletion," in M. Campbell
et al., eds. (1970).

Grinder, J. (1971) "A Reply to 'Super Equi-NP as Dative Deletion'," in D. Adams et al., eds. (1971).

Gross, M. (1972) Mathematical Models in Lingustics, Prentice-
Hall, Englewood Cliffs, N. J.

Halle, M. (1970) "Frontiers of Linguistic Theory," in Linguistics in the 1970's, Center for Applied Linguistics,
Washington, D.C.

Hankamer, J. (1973) "Unacceptable Ambiguity," Linguistic
Inquiry 4:17-68.

Hasegawa, K. (1965) "English Imperatives," in Festschrift for Professor Nakajima, Kenkyusha, Tokyo.

Hasegawa, K. (1968) "The Passive Construction in English," Language 44:230-244.

Hill, A. A. (1958) Introduction to Linguistic Structures, Harcourt, Brace, and World, New York.

Hockett, C. P. (1958) A Course in Modern Linguistics, MacMillan, New York.

Hook, S., ed. (1969) Language and Philosophy, New York University Press, New York.

Jacobs, R. A., and P. S. Rosenbaum (1968) English Transformational Grammar, Ginn, Waltham, Mass.

Jacobs, R. A., and P. S. Rosenbaum, eds. (1970) Readings in English Transformational Grammar, Ginn, Waltham, Mass.

Jackendoff, R. S. (1971) "Gapping and Related Rules," Linguistic Inquiry 2:21-35.

Jackendoff, R. S. (1972) Semantic Interpretation in Generative Grammar, MIT Press, Cambridge, Mass.

Jackendoff, R. S. (1973) "The Base Rules for Prepositional Phrases," in S. A. Anderson and R. P. Kiparsky, eds. (1973).

Jackendoff, R. S., and P. W. Culicover (1971) "A Reconsideration of Dative Movement," Foundations of Language 7:397-412.

Jenkins, L. (1972) Modality in English Syntax, unpublished Doctoral dissertation, MIT, Cambridge, Mass. [Available in mimeographed form from the Indiana University Linguistics Club, Indiana University, Bloomington, Indiana.]

Jespersen, O. (1956) A Modern English Grammar on Historical Principles, Barnes and Noble, New York.

Jespersen, O. (1965) The Philosophy of Grammar, W. W. Norton, New York.

Jespersen, O. (1969) Analytic Syntax, Holt, Rinehart and Winston, New York.

Katz, J. J., and P. M. Postal (1964) An Integrated Theory of Linguistic Descriptions, MIT Press, Cambridge, Mass.

Kayne, R. (to appear) French Syntax: The Transformational Cycle, MIT Press, Cambridge, Mass.

Kimball, J. P. (1971) "Super Equi-NP Deletion as Dative Deletion," in D. Adams et al., eds. (1971).

Kimball, J. P. (1973) The Formal Theory of Grammar, Prentice-Hall, Englewood Cliffs, N. J.

Kiparsky, R. P., and C. Kiparsky (1971) "Fact," in M. Bierwisch and K. Heidolph, eds. (1971).

Klima, E. S., and U. Bellugi (1966) "Syntactic Regularities in the Speech of Children," in D. A. Reibel and S. A. Schane, eds. (1969).

Koutsoudas, A. (1972) "The Strict Order Fallacy," Language 48:88-96.

Koutsoudas, A. (1973) "Extrinsic Order and the Complex NP Constraint," Linguistic Inquiry 4:69-81.

Kuroda, S. Y. (1968) Review of Fillmore (1965), Language 44:374-378.

Lakoff, G (1966) Deep and Surface Grammar, mimeographed. [Available from the Indiana University Linguistics Club, Indiana University, Bloomington, Indiana.]

Lakoff, R. (1968) Abstract Syntax and Latin Complementation, MIT Press, Cambridge, Mass.

Lakoff, R. (1971) "Passive Resistance," in D. Adams et al., eds. (1971).

Langendoen, D. T. (1970) Essentials of English Grammar, Holt, Rinehart and Winston, New York.

Lees, R. B. (1960) The Grammar of English Nominalizations, Mouton, The Hague.

Lehmann, T. (1972) "Some Arguments Against Ordered Rules,' Language 48:541-550.

Luce, R. D., R. R. Bush, and E. Galanter, eds. (1963) Handbook of Mathematical Psychology, Volume II, Wiley and Sons, New York.

McCawley, J. (1970) "English as a VSO Language," Language 46:286-299.

McNeill, D. (1970) The Acquisition of Language, Harper and Row, New York.

Maling, J. M. (1972) "On 'Gapping and the Order of Constituents'," Linguistic Inquiry 3:101-108.

Nida, E. (1966) A Synopsis of English Syntax, Mouton, The Hague.

O'Neill, W. (1969) Introduction to R. N. Cattell, The New English Grammar, MIT Press, Cambridge, Mass.

Partee, B. H. (1971) "On the Requirement that Transformations Preserve Meaning," in C. J. Fillmore and D. T. Langendoen, eds. (1971).

Peranteau, P. M., J. N. Levi, and G. C. Phares, eds. (1972) The Chicago Which Hunt: Papers from the Relative Clause Festival, Department of Linguistics, University of Chicago, Chicago, Ill.

Perlmutter, D. M. (1970) "The Two Verbs Begin," in R. A. Jacobs and P. S. Rosenbaum, eds. (1970).

Postal, P. M. (1964a) "Limitations of Phrase Structure Grammars," in J. A. Fodor and J. J. Katz, eds. (1964).

Postal, P. M. (1964b) "Underlying and Superficial Linguistic Structure," Harvard Educational Review 34:246-266. [Reprinted in D. A. Reibel and S. A. Schane, eds. (1969).]

Postal, P. M. (1970) "On Coreferential Complement Subject Deletion," Linguistic Inquiry 1:439-500.

Postal, P. M. (1972) "On Some Rules That Are Not Successive Cyclic," Linguistic Inquiry 3:211-222.

Postal, P. M. (1974) On Raising, MIT Press, Cambridge, Mass.

Poutsma, H. (1904) A Grammar of Late Modern English, P. Noordhoff, Groningen.

Reibel, D. A., and S. A. Schane, eds. (1969) Modern Studies in English, Prentice-Hall, Englewood Cliffs, N. J.

Ringen, C. (1972) "On Arguments for Rule Ordering," Foundations of Language 8:266-273.

Rosenbaum, P. S. (1967) The Grammar of English Predicate Complement Constructions, MIT Press, Cambridge, Mass.

Rosenbaum, P. S. (1969) "Phrase Structure Principles of English Complex Sentence Formation," in D. A. Reibel and S. A. Schane, eds. (1969).

Rosenbaum, P. S. (1970) "A Principle Governing Deletion in English Sentential Complementation," in R. A. Jacobs and P. S. Rosenbaum, eds. (1970).

Ross, J. R. (1967) Constraints on Variables in Syntax, unpublished Doctoral dissertation, MIT, Cambridge, Mass. [Available in mimeographed form from the Indiana University Linguistics Club, Indiana University, Bloomington, Indiana.]

Ross, J. R. (1969) "Guess Who?" in R. I. Binnick et al., eds. (1969).

Ross, J. R. (1971) "Gapping and the Order of Constituents," in M. Bierwisch and K. Heidolph, eds. (1971).

Schachter, P. (1973) "Focus and Relativization," Language 49:19-46.

Smith, F., and G. A. Miller, eds. (1966) The Genesis of
Language, MIT Press, Cambridge, Mass.

Stockwell, R. P., P. Schachter, and B. H. Partee (1973)
The Major Syntactic Structures of English, Holt, Rinehart
and Winston, New York.

Szamosi, M. (1973) "On the Unity of Subject Raising," in
C. Corum, T. Smith-Stark, and A. Weiser, eds. (1973).

Thorne, J. P. (1966) "English Imperative Sentences," Journal
of Linguistics 2:69-78.

Wall, R. (1972) Introduction to Mathematical Linguistics,
Prentice-Hall, Englewood Cliffs, N. J.

INDEX OF SYMBOLS

$\rightarrow$, 33

(   ) in PS rules, 35

{   } in PS rules, 40

(   ) in transformations, 155

{   } in transformations, 155

+, 147

#, 149

> <, 152

α, β, 198

S^n, 252

$\geqq$, 252-253

$_x[\quad]_x$, 253

$(\quad)^n$, 254

$\bar{S}$, 294